THE

RELIGIONS OF INDIA

THE RELIGIONS OF INDIA.

BY

A. BARTH

AUTHORISED TRANSLATION

BY

REV. J. WOOD,

EDIN.

GYAN

Published by

GYAN

Gyan Publishing House
5, Ansari Road
Daryaganj, New Delhi-110002
Phone: 011-47034999, 9811692060
E-mail: books@gyanbooks.com

Distribution Network
gyanbooks.com
India, USA, Canada, UK, Australia, France

ISBN: 978-81-212-7933-8 (PB)
First Published, 1879

2nd Impression 2023

Printed at: Gyan Press, Delhi.

THE RELIGIONS OF INDIA
Author: A. BARTH, Translator: J. WOOD

TRÜBNER'S

ORIENTAL SERIES.

THE

RELIGIONS OF INDIA.

BY

A. BARTH,

MEMBER OF THE SOCIÉTÉ ASIATIQUE OF PARIS.

AUTHORISED TRANSLATION

BY

REV. J. WOOD,

EDIN.

LONDON:
TRÜBNER & CO., LUDGATE HILL.
1882.

TO

DR. JOHN MUIR,

THIS SKETCH

OF

THE RELIGIONS OF INDIA

IS RESPECTFULLY INSCRIBED

BY

THE AUTHOR

IN GRATEFUL ACKNOWLEDGMENT OF HIS
UNWEARIED SERVICES AS A STUDENT AND INTERPRETER
OF THE FAITHS AND WISDOM OF INDIA,
AND OF HIS GENEROUS PATRONAGE
OF INDIAN RESEARCH.

CONTENTS.

PREFACE.

THE following sketch of the Religions of India appeared originally in 1879 as an article in the *Encyclopédie des Sciences Religieuses*, which is published in Paris under the editorship of Professor Lichtenberger. My aim in composing it was to present, to that class of readers who take interest in questions of historical theology, but who happen to have no special acquaintance with Indianist studies, a *résumé*, which should be as faithful and realistic as possible, of the latest results of inquiry in all provinces of this vast domain. At first I thought I might comprise all I had to say in some fifty pages; but I soon saw that within a space so limited, the work I had undertaken, and which I intended should assume the form of a statement of facts rather than of a series of speculative deductions, would prove absolutely superficial and be sure to give rise to manifold misapprehensions. This first difficulty was easily got over through the friendly liberality of the Editor of the *Encyclopédie*, for, as soon as aware of it, he handsomely offered to concede to me whatever space I might need. Other difficulties remained, however, besides those connected with the subject in itself—which is one of boundless extent and intricacy, and which no special work, so far as I knew, had as yet treated at once as a whole and in detailed particularity—those, viz., which arose out of the general plan of the work in which my sketch was to appear as an article. The *Encyclopédie* admitted only of a small number of divisions into chapters, and no notes.

I had not, therefore, the resource of being able to relegate my *impedimenta* to the foot of the pages, a resource which in such a case was almost indispensable, since I had to address a reader who was not a specialist, and I was myself averse to be obliged to limit myself to a colourless and inexact statement. All I had to say and explain must either be said and explained in the text, or suppressed altogether. The result was that I loaded my text to the utmost possible extent, often, I must say, at the expense of fluency of diction, and I also suppressed a good deal. I left out, with no small reluctance, more than one remark, which, though of secondary, was yet of serviceable importance, because it would have interrupted the continuity of what I sought mainly to develop. I sacrificed especially a considerable number of those particularities, such as not unfrequently defy all attempts at circumlocution, yet impart to matters the exact shade of meaning that belongs to them, but which would have required observations in explanation such as I could have introduced only at the expense of interlarding my pages with an array of incongruous parentheses. In these circumstances I did all I could to retain at least as much as possible of the substance; and those Indianists who may be pleased to look into my work will see, I think, that under the enforced generalities of my exposition there lies concealed a certain amount of minuteness of investigation.

These shortcomings I was able to remedy in a measure in the impressions which I was solicited to issue in a separate form shortly after, and to which I was free to add annotations. By this means it was possible to append the bibliography, as well as a goodly number of detached remarks and technical details. As to the text itself, even if I had had the necessary time, it would have been difficult to have modified it in any important particular. The redaction of a scientific treatise written without divisions into chapters and intended to remain without notes, must assume a form more or less of an abnormal character. If the book is to be of value, this defect of external resources would have to be compensated for by its internal structure. In all its sections it would require to present a more explicitly reasoned sequence of ideas, and to possess to some extent more compactness of structure, into which the introduction of new matter would be attended with difficulty. The article was therefore reproduced in the French edition without alterations. For this very reason also the present edition is in these respects pretty much the same as the French original. Certain inaccuracies in detail have been corrected; in some passages the text has been relieved to the expansion of the notes; in others, though more rarely, material intended at first to appear in the footnotes has been admitted into the body of the work; the transcription of Hindu terms in particular has been rendered throughout more rigorous and complete; but in other respects, the text is unaltered, and the additions, as at first, have been committed to the notes.

These last have not merely been brought up to date, so as to give the latest results,[1] but rendered in general more complete than they were in the French edition, in which they had been thrown together in a somewhat hurried fashion. In my regard, they are not calculated to change the character of the work, which has no pretence in its present form, any more than its original, to teach anything to adepts in Indianist studies. They must needs impart an authoritative weight to my statements, which, except where the original authorities were inaccessible to

[1] The redaction of these notes belongs to the spring of 1880; some few were added in December of the same year. I avail myself of this opportunity to mention the following works which I first became aware of only after the correction of the proofs:—A. Ludwig, Commentar zur Rigveda-Ubersetzung, 1ster Theil, Prag, 1881. A. Kaegi, Der Rigveda, die älteste Literatur der Inder, 2te Auflage, Leipzig, 1881. Sacred Books of the East, Oxford, 1881: vol. x. The Dhammapada, transl. by F. Max Müller; the Sutta-Nipâta transl. from Pâli by V. Fausböll; vol. xi. Buddhist Suttas, transl. from Pâli by T. W. Rhys Davids. H. Kern, Geschiedenis van het Buddhisme in Indië, Haarlem, 1881 (in course of publication). E. Trumpp, Die Religion der Sikhs, nach den Quellen dargestellt, Leipzig, 1881.

me, have not been made on the basis of documents at second hand. They are fitted anyhow to give to those who have only a slight acquaintance with the details of our studies, some idea at least of the immense amount of labour which has within the century been expended on the subject of India. With the view of making this evident I have been careful to supply a rather extensive bibliography, in which the reader will perhaps remark a greater array of references than was necessary to justify my statements. I have, however, prescribed here certain limits to myself. I have not, for instance, except when absolutely necessary, mentioned any books which I did not happen to have by me (in which category I include a host of native publications, with the titles of which I could have easily amplified my references); neither have I referred to works, which, though doubtless not without their value at the time when they appeared, are now out of date, and in which the true and the false are to such an extent intermingled that the citation of them, without considerable correction in an elementary treatise such as this, would have only served to confuse and mislead the uninitiated reader. But except in these cases, and such as I may have omitted from want of recollection, I have endeavoured as much as possible to point out the place of each, especially that of those who led the van in this interesting series of investigations. In fine, as I have already explained, a good many of the notes are simple additions, and ought to be accepted as a sort of appendix in continuation of the text.

Having said this much of the general conditions under which this work was undertaken and drawn up, I have still, with the reader's indulgence, some explanations to make in regard to a matter or two belonging to the contents, in regard to questions which I have thought I ought to waive as being in my opinion not yet ripe for solution, and also as regards the restriction I have imposed on myself in not introducing into my exposition any pronounced peculiarities of private opinion.

The reader who peruses with intelligence what I have written, and is *au courant* with Indianist studies, will not fail to remark that my views on the Veda are not precisely the same as those which are most generally accepted. For in it I recognise a literature that is pre-eminently sacerdotal, and in no sense a popular one; and from this conclusion I do not, as is ordinarily done, except even the Hymns, the most ancient of the documents. Neither in the language nor in the thought of the Ṛig-Veda have I been able to discover that quality of primitive natural simplicity which so many are fain to see in it. The poetry it contains appears to me, on the contrary, to be of a singularly refined character and artificially elaborated, full of allusions and reticences, of pretensions to mysticism and theosophic insight; and the manner of its expression is such as reminds one more frequently of the phraseology in use among certain small groups of initiated than the poetic language of a large community. And these features I am constrained to remark as characteristic of the whole collection; not that they assert themselves with equal emphasis in all the Hymns—the most abstruse imaginings being not without their moments of simplicity of conception; but there are very few of these Hymns which do not show some trace of them, and it is always difficult to find in the book and to extract a clearly defined portion of perfectly natural and simple conception. In all these respects the spirit of the Ṛig-Veda appears to me to be more allied than is usually supposed to that which prevails in the other Vedic collections, and in the Brâhmaṇas. This conviction, which I had already expressed emphatically enough more than once in the *Revue Critique*, I have not felt called upon to urge here, in a work such as this from which all discussion should be excluded as much as possible. I have, nevertheless, given it such expression even here that a careful reader, if he looks, will not fail to recognise it;

anyhow it has not escaped the notice of such an expert in the affairs of India as Professor Thiele of Leyden, with whom I am happy to find myself in harmony of view on the subject of the Veda. That critic has, in consequence, not without reason, challenged[1] me to say why I have not insisted on it more, and if, after this first avowal, I was warranted to draw such a sharp distinction as I have done between the epoch of the Hymns and that of the Brâhmaṇas.

Whether I was right or wrong in doing so, it is not for me to decide. I have pointed out the differences which, as it appears to me, we must admit to exist between the two epochs referred to, differences which I do not think can be accounted for simply by the diverse nature of the documents. In the Brâhmaṇas we have a sacred literature and a new liturgy; the priesthood that inspired the Hymns has become a caste; and there is a theory which is given forth as a law for this caste, as well as the others—one which, whether true or imaginary, is nevertheless in itself a fact. Were it only for these reasons, I should consider myself bound to maintain the generally accepted distinction; but, not to adduce more, I confess that I had another reason—the fear, viz., of being drawn into the subject further than was desirable in a work such as this.

The Hymns, as I have already remarked, do not appear to me to show the least trace of popular derivation. I rather imagine that they emanate from a narrow circle of priests, and that they reflect a somewhat singular view of things. Not only can I not accept the generally received opinion that Vedic and Aryan are synonymous terms, I am even not at all sure to what extent we are right in speaking of a Vedic people. Not that communities did not then worship the gods of the Veda, but I doubt very much if they regarded them as they are represented in the Hymns, any more than that they afterwards sacrificed to them in community after the rites prescribed in the Brâh-

[1] In the *Theologische Tijdschrift* of July 1880.

maṇas. If there is any justice in these views, it is evident that a literature such as this will only embrace what is within the scope of a limited horizon, and will have authoritative weight only in regard to things in a more or less special reference, and that the negative conclusions especially which may be deduced from such documents must be received with not a little reservation. A single instance, to which I limit myself, will suffice for illustration. Suppose that certain hymns of the tenth book of the Ṛig-Veda—a book which the majority of critics look upon with distrust—had not come down to us, what would we learn from the rest of the collection respecting the worship of the *manes* of the departed ? We might know that India paid homage to certain powers called Pitṛis, or Fathers, but we could not infer from that, any more than from the later worship of the Mâtṛis, or Mothers, this worship of ancestors, or spirits of the dead, which, as the comparative study of the beliefs, customs, and institutions of Greece and Rome shows us, was nevertheless from the remotest antiquity one of the principal sources of public and private right, one of the bases of the family and the civic community. I am therefore far from believing that the Veda has taught us everything on the ancient social and religious condition of even Aryan India, or that everything there can be accounted for by reference to it. Outside of it I see room not only for superstitious beliefs, but for real popular religions, more or less distinct from that which we find in it; and on this point, we shall arrive at more than one conclusion from the more profound study of the subsequent period. We shall perhaps find that, in this respect also, the past did not differ so much from the present as might at first appear, that India has always had, alongside of its Veda, something equivalent to its great Çivaite and Vishnuite religions, which we see in the ascendant at a later date, and that these anyhow existed contemporaneously with it for a very much longer period than has till now been generally supposed.

I have in a summary way indicated these views in my work, and that in more passages than one; but it is easy to see how, if I had laid greater stress on them, they might have modified certain parts of my exposition. I did not think that I ought to go against the received opinions on this matter, or that in addressing a public imperfectly qualified to judge, I should attach more weight to my private doubts than the almost unanimous consent of scholars more learned than myself. If it is a wrong that I have done, I confess it, and that as one which I committed wilfully. And, after all, there is so much that is uncertain in this obscure past, and what Whitney says in regard to dates, "in Indian literary history," that they are so many "pins set up to be bowled down again," is so applicable to all hypotheses in this field, that a new opinion would do well to allow itself some considerable time to ripen.

I am accordingly of opinion that the Neo-Brahmanic religions are of very ancient date in India. On the other hand, their positive history is comparatively modern; it commences not much earlier than the time when it becomes dispersed and distracted among that confusion of sects which has prolonged itself to our own time. In order to render an account of these sects, it was my duty to classify them, and I have done so according to the philosophic systems which seem to have at each period prevailed among them. This arrangement I have adopted only in defect of another; for the merely chronological succession, besides being for the earlier epochs highly uncertain, and calculated to involve me in endless repetitions, would have been of slender significance in itself, and would have resolved itself into a bare enumeration, since it is impossible to show, in most cases here, that a succession of the sort involves filiation. I confess, however, that the arrangement adopted is not very satisfactory. The formulæ of metaphysics have penetrated so deeply into the modes of thinking and feeling prevalent in India, that they may in most cases be treated as we do those common quantities which we eliminate in calculation; and it is always hazardous to judge by them of movements of such religious intensity. My sole excuse in this case is the necessity I was under of having some principle of classification, and the difficulty, amounting to impossibility, of discovering another.

I have, before I conclude, to say a few words on two questions which I have purposely evaded, as being hitherto unsusceptible of a satisfactory solution. The first is the question of Caste, its origin and successive developments. I did not entangle myself in this question, in the first place, because of its exceeding obscurity. In fact, we have already a Brahmanical theory of caste, in regard to which we should require to know how far it is true to facts before we venture on explanations, which might very readily prove of no greater validity than a work of romance. I gave this question the go-by, in the second place, because, as respects antiquity, the problem, taken as a whole, is a social rather than a religious one. In sectarian India at present, and since the appearance of foreign proselytising religions, caste is the express badge of Hinduism. The man who is a member of a caste is a Hindu; he who is not, is not a Hindu. And caste is not merely the symbol of Hinduism; but, according to the testimony of all who have studied it on the spot, it is its stronghold. It is this, much more than their creeds, which attaches the masses to these vague religions, and gives them such astonishing vitality. It is, therefore, a religious factor of the first order, and, on this score, I felt bound to indicate the part it now plays and its present condition. But there is no reason to presume that it was the same in the antiquity to which its institution is usually referred, and in which the theory at any rate took its rise that is reputed to regulate it. Still less is it probable that the existing castes, with one exception, that of the Brâhmans, are the heirs in a direct line of the ancient *câturvarṇya.* I have, therefore, felt free to discharge myself from the obligation of inquiring into the origin and more or less probable transformations of the latter, and it was enough to indicate the period onward from which the texts represent the sacerdotal caste as definitely established; that is to say, when we first meet with a precise formula, giving a religious sanction to a state of things which in all probability existed in fact from time immemorial.

The second question of which I have steadily kept clear, is that of the relations which happen to have arisen between the Aryan religions of India and the systems of belief professed either by foreign peoples, or by races ethnographically distinct that had settled in the country. This inquiry thrust itself upon me in relation to Christianity and Islamism; and there is nothing I should have wished more than to do as much in reference to other historical relations of the same kind, if I had thought I could do so with any profit. There is, as regards India, some weak and uncertain indications of a possible exchange of ideas with Babylon, and the legend of the Deluge might not improbably have come from that quarter. But all that can be done in regard to this, is to put the question. For a much stronger reason I have shrunk from following Baron d'Eckstein into the investigation of the far more hypothetical relations with Egypt and Asia Minor. In a very friendly and far too eulogistic criticism of the present work, E. Renan has been pleased to express some regret on this score;[1] and I am very far from maintaining, for my part, that the time will not come when it will be necessary to resume researches in this direction; but to do so now would, in my opinion, be to advance forward in total darkness. The question is different as regards the re-

[1] In the *Journal Asiatique* of June 1880.

ligions of the aboriginal races of India. Here the influences and borrowings from one side, that of the aborigines, are evident, and from the other, the side of the Hindus, are *à priori* extremely probable, an interchange of this kind being always more or less reciprocal. Only it is very difficult to say exactly what the conquering race must have borrowed in this way from the aboriginal races. The religions of these peoples survive in fact under two forms: either in the condition of popular superstitions, which resemble what they are elsewhere; or, as among the tribes which have remained more or less savage, in the condition of national religions to some extent inoculated with Hindu ideas and modes of expression. These religions, in their turn, if we analyse them, are resolvable, on the one hand, into those beliefs and practices of an inferior type, having relation to idol or animal worship, such as we find in all communities that are uncivilised, and, on the other hand, into the worship of the divinities of nature and the elements, such as personifications of the sun, heaven, the earth, the mountains—that is to say, of systems of worship which are not essentially different from those which we meet with at first among the Hindus. In these circumstances, it is obvious that in special studies we might be able to note features of detail which have been borrowed by the more civilised race from that which is less so, but that we could not do much towards determining the effect of these influences and borrowings in their general import, the only question to which it would be possible to give prominency here.

I have only to explain the notation I have adopted in the transcription of the Hindu terms. The circumflex accent, as in *â*, *î*, *û*, indicates that the vowel is long; the vowels *r* and *l* are transcribed by *ṛi* and *ḷi*. It will be observed that *u* and *û* should be pronounced like the French sound *ou*, and that *ai* and *au* are always diphthongs. An aspirated consonant is followed by *h*, and this aspiration ought to be distinctly expressed after the principal articulation, as in *inkhorn*. Of the gutterals, *g* and *gh* are always hard, and the nasal of this order is marked by *ṅ*, to be pronounced as in *song*. The palates *c* and *j* (and consequently their corresponding aspirates) are pronounced as in *challenge, journey*, and the nasal of the same order, *ñ*, like this letter in Spanish. The lingual consonants, which, to our ear, do not differ perceptibly from the dentals, are rendered by *ṭ*, *ṭh*, *ḍ*, *ḍh*, *ṇ*. The sibilants *ç* and *sh* are both pronounced almost as *sh* in English. The anusvâra (the neuter or final nasal) is marked by *ṃ*, and the visarga (the soft and final aspiration) by *ḥ*.

The orthography has been rendered throughout rigorous and scientifically exact; only in a small number of modern names have I kept to the orthography in general use.

A. BARTH.

PARIS, *September* 1881.

INTRODUCTION.

India has not only preserved for us in her Vedas the most ancient and complete documents for the study of the old religious beliefs founded on nature-worship, which, in an extremely remote past, were common to all the branches of the Indo-European family; she is also the only country where these beliefs, in spite of many changes both in form and fortune, continue to subsist up to the present time. Whilst everywhere else they have been either as good as extinguished by monotheistic religions of foreign origin, in some instances without leaving behind them a single direct and authentic trace of their presence, or abruptly cut short in their evolution and forced to survive within the barriers, henceforth immovable, of a petty Church, as in the case of Parseeism,—in India alone they present up to this time, as a rich and varied literature attests, a continuous, self-determined development, in the course of which, instead of contracting, they have continued to enlarge their borders. It is owing in a great measure to this extraordinary longevity that such an interest attaches to the separate and independent study of the Hindu religions, irrespective altogether of the estimate we may form of their dogmatic or practical worth. Nowhere else do we meet with circumstances, on the whole, so favourable for the study of the successive transformations and destiny, so to speak, of a polytheistic idea of the universe. Among all the kindred conceptions that we meet with, there is not another which has shown itself so vigorous, so flexible, so apt as this to assume the most diverse forms, and so dexterous in reconciling all extremes, from the most refined idealism to the grossest idolatry; none has succeeded so well in repairing its losses; no one has possessed in such a high degree the power of producing and reproducing new sects, even great religions, and of resisting, by perpetual regenesis in this way from itself, all the causes which might destroy it, at once those due to internal waste and those due to external opposition. But for this very reason, too, it becomes difficult to conceive in its totality, and in the successive additions made to it, this vast religious structure, the work, according to the most probable computations, of more than thirty centuries of a history that is without chronology, a perfect labyrinth of buildings, involved one in another, within whose windings the first explorers, almost without exception, went astray, so misleading is the official account of them, so many ruins do we meet with of a venerable aspect, and which yet are only of yesterday. Thanks to the discovery of the Vedas,[1] how-

[1] Our first positive acquaintance with the Veda dates from the publication of the celebrated essay of H. T. Colebrooke, "On the Vedas or Sacred Writings of the Hindus," inserted in vol. viii. of the Asiatic Researches, 1805, and reproduced in the "Miscellaneous Essays" of that great Indianist. Next to this fundamental work we must mention the first attempts at an edition of the Ṛig-Veda by the lamented Fr. Rosen, entitled "Rigvedæ Specimen," 1830; "Ṛig-Veda Sanhita, liber primus, Sanscrite et Latine," 1838; and the three memoirs by the founder of the scientific interpretation of the Veda, Prof. R. Roth, "Zur Litteratur und Geschichte des Weda," 1846. Among the more recent publications we take leave to mention, A. Weber, "Akademische Vorlesungen über Indische Literaturgeschichte," 1852, 2d ed. 1876, translated into French by A. Sadons, 1859; into English by J. Mann and Th. Zachariae, 1878; Max Müller, "A History of Ancient Sanscrit Literature as far as it illus-

ever, which has laid bare for us the first foundations of the edifice, it is now easier for us to ascertain where we are in its mazes, although we are very far from saying that the light of day has at length penetrated into all its compartments, and that we are now able to sketch a plan of it that will be free from *lacunæ*.

Anyhow, in undertaking to describe within a limited number of pages this complex whole, it is clear we must resolve at the outset to content ourselves with a summary, and, it may be, disappointingly incomplete sketch. Many significant and characteristic points, the most of the *realia*, and an immense body of myths and legends, and everything which cannot be summarised, we shall have to omit. Of the history of these systems, which have not, however, been the result of mere abstract thinking, but which have grown up in vital relation with the complex and agitated life of every human institution alongside of them, we shall have time to examine only the internal, and, in some degree, ideal side—the development of the doctrines and their affiliation. We shall not be able to study them at once as religions and mythologies. We propose, however, to be more minute in what relates to the Vedas, out of regard to their exceptional importance, since the whole religious thought of India already exists in germ in these old books. Only we shall make no attempt to go farther back, or by

trates the Primitive Religion of the Brahmans," 1859, 2d ed. 1860. The "Indische Studien," which A. Weber edits, and the first volume of which appeared in 1849, are mainly devoted to the investigation of Vedic literature; and the great Sanscrit Dictionary of St. Petersburg, edited between the years 1855 and 1878 by A. Böhtlingk and R. Roth (the Vedic portion being due to Roth), has, more than any other work, contributed to the rapid advancement of these studies. For the information, in part apocryphal, current in Europe at an earlier date on the Veda, see Max Müller, "Lectures on the Science of Language," vol. i. p. 173 *seq.*; and a very curious note by A. C. Burnell, in Ind. Antiq., viii. 98.

the help of the comparative methods to trace up to their origin even the Vedic divinities and forms of thinking. Within these limitations the task we propose to ourselves will, we think, prove vast enough, and we feel only too keenly how imperfect our work will in the end be found to be. We by no means flatter ourselves that we have always succeeded in distinguishing the essential points, in disentangling the principal threads, and preserving to every element in our exposition its just proportion and place. All that we can pledge ourselves to do is, that we shall guard ourselves against introducing into it either a too pronounced peculiarity of view or a factitious lucidity and arrangement.

THE RELIGIONS OF INDIA.

I.

THE VEDIC RELIGIONS.

THE ṚIG-VEDA.

General view of Vedic literature.—Its age and successive formation; priority of the Hymns of the Ṛig-Veda.—Principal divinities of the Hymns: the World and its objects, Heaven and Earth, the Sun, Moon, and Stars.—Agni and Soma.—Indra, the Maruts, Rudra, Vâyu Parjanya.—Bṛihaspati and Vâc.—Varuṇa.—Aditi and the Adityas.—The Solar divinities: Sûrya, Savitṛi, Vishṇu, Pûshan.—Ushas, the Açvins, Tvashtṛi, the Ṛibhus.—Yama, the Pitṛis and the Future Life.—Abstract personifications and mythical figures.—Absence of a hierarchy and a classification of the Gods.—Way in which the Myths have been treated in the Hymns.—Monotheistic conceptions: Prajâpati, Viçvakarman, Svayambhû, &c.—Pantheistic cosmogony: Purusha, the primordial substance, no eschatology.—Piety and morality; co-existence of baser forms of belief and practice, as in part preserved in the Atharva-Veda.—Cultus: speculations regarding sacrifice and prayer: the ṛita and the brahman.—Essentially sacerdotal character of this religion.

THE most ancient documents we possess connected with the religions of India are the collections of writings called the Vedas. These are sometimes reckoned three in number and sometimes four, according as the reference is to the collections themselves or to the nature of their contents; and of these two modes of reckoning, the second is the more ancient.[1] One of the oldest divisions of the *mantras*,

[1] Aitar. Br., v. 32, 1; Taittir. Br., iii. 10, 11, 5; Çatap. Br., v. 5, 5, 10.

or liturgical texts, is, in fact, that which distributes them into *ṛic*, *yajus*, and *sâman*,[1] or, according to a later definition,[2] but one which may be accepted as valid for a period of much greater antiquity,[3] into (*a*) hymns, more strictly verses of invocation and praise, which were chanted with a loud voice: into (*b*) formulæ prescribed with reference to the various acts of sacrifice, which were muttered in a low voice: and into (*c*) chants of a more or less complex structure, and followed by a refrain which was sung in chorus. To possess an accurate knowledge of the ṛics, the yajus, and the sâmans, was to possess the "triple science," the triple Veda. When, on the other hand, there is mention of the four Vedas,[4] the reference is to the four collections as they exist at present, viz., the *Ṛig-Veda*, which includes the body of the hymns; the *Yajur-Veda*, in which all the prescribed formulæ are collected; the *Sâma-Veda*, which contains the chants (the texts of which are, with a very few exceptions, verses of the Ṛig-Veda[5]); and the *Atharva-Veda*, a collection of hymns like the Ṛig-Veda, but of which the texts, when they are not common to the two collections, are in part of later date, and must have been employed in the ritual of a different worship. Besides those collections of mantras, *i.e.*, of liturgical and ritualistic texts, called *Saṃhitâs*, each Veda still contains, as a second part, one or more *Brâhmaṇas*, or treatises on the ceremonial system, in which, with reference to prescriptions in regard to ritual, there are preserved numerous legends, theological speculations, &c., as well as

[1] Atharva-Veda, vii. 54, 2; see Ṛig-Veda, x. 90, 9; Tait. Saṃh., i. 2, 3, 3; Çatap. Br., iv. 6, 7, 1.

[2] The official definition is given in the Mîmâṃsâ-Sûtras, ii. 1, 35–37, pp. 128, 129, of the edition of the Bibliotheca Indica; see also Sâyaṇa's Commentary on the Ṛig-Veda, t. i. p. 23, and Commentary on the Taittirîya Saṃhitâ, t. i. p. 28, edition of the Bibliotheca Indica; Prasthânabheda ap. Ind. Stud., i. p. 14.

[3] Atharva-Veda, xii. 1, 38; Aitar. Br., v. 32, 3, 4; Çatap. Br., ii. 3, 3, 17.

[4] Chândog. Up., vii. 1, 2; Ath.-Veda, x. 7, 20; Brihadâr. Up., ii. 4, 10.

[5] Interesting information on the mode of the formation and the character of these chants will be found in the introduction to A. C. Burnell's edition of the Ârsheyabrâhmaṇa, pp. xi., xli. See also Th. Aufrecht, Die Hymnen des Ṛigveda, 2d ed., Preface, p. xxxviii.

the first attempts at exegesis. In the most ancient redaction of the Yajur-Veda, which is pre-eminently the Veda that bears on ritual, in the Black Yajus, as it is called, these two parts are still mixed up together.[1] Finally, of each Veda there existed several recensions called *Çâkhâs*, or branches, between which there appeared very considerable discrepancies at times.[2] Of these recensions, in so far as

[1] There are for this Veda, as for the others, two collections, the one termed the Saṃhitâ and the other the Brâhmaṇa; but they both contain at once liturgical texts and ritualistic.

[2] 1. Of this literature there have been published, with critical elaborations, *First*, the Ṛig-Veda—

(*a.*) Saṃhitâ: Rig-Veda-Sanhita, together with the commentary of Sayanacharya, edited by Max Müller, 6 vols. in 4to, 1849–74. A reprint without the commentary, The Hymns of the Rig-Veda in Sanhita and Pada Texts, 1873, Die Hymnen des Ṛigveda, herausgegeben von Th. Aufrecht, 2 vols. 8vo, 1861–63, forming vols. vi., vii., of the Indische Studien, and of which a second edition was issued in 1877. These were translated into French by A. Langlois, 1848–51, reprinted in 1872; into English by H. H. Wilson and E. B. Cowell, 1850–63, reprinted in 1868, and by Max Müller in 1869 (first volume only); into German by A. Ludwig, 1876–79, and by H. Grassmann, 1876–77. An edition of the text, with translations into English and Marhatti, The Vedârthayatna by Shankar Pandit, has since 1876 been in the course of publication at Bombay. Of an edition of the text begun by E. Röer in the Bibliotheca Indica (Calcutta, 1848), and accompanied with a commentary and a translation into English, there have appeared only four parts.

(*b.*) Brâhmaṇa: The Aitareya Brahmanam of the Rigveda, edited and translated by M. Haug, 2 vols. 8vo, Bombay, 1863. A more correct edition has just been issued by Th. Aufrecht, Das Aitareya Brâhmaṇa mit Auszügen aus dem Commentare von Sâyaṇâcârya, Bonn, 1879. The Aitareya Araṇyaka, with the commentary of Sâyana Achārya, edited by Râjendralâla Mitra, Calcutta, 1876 (Biblioth. Indica). The Araṇyakas are supplements to the Brâhmaṇas.

2. The Atharva-Veda.

(*a.*) Saṃhitâ: Atharva Veda Sanhita, herausgegeben von R. Roth und W. D. Whitney, 1855–56.

(*b.*) Brâhmaṇa: The Gopatha Brâhmaṇa of the Atharva-Veda, edited by Râjendralâla Mitra and Harachandra Vidyâbhushaṇa, Calcutta, 1872 (Biblioth. Indica).

3. The Sâma-Veda.

(*a.*) Saṃhitâs: Die Hymnen des Sâma-Veda, herausgegeben, übersezt und mit Glossar versehen, von Th. Benfey, 1848. This work has thrown into the shade the prior edition and English translation by J. Stevenson, 1841–43. Sâma Veda Sanhitâ, with the commentary of Sâyaṇa Achārya, edited by Satyavrata Sâmaçramî, Calcutta, 1874 (Biblioth. Indica). This edition, which has reached the fifth volume, comprehends all the liturgical collections of the Sâma-Veda, as well as the Gânas, that is to say, the texts in the form of anthems.

(*b.*) Brâhmaṇas: The Tâṇḍya Mahâbrâhmaṇa, with the commentary of Sâyaṇa Achārya, edited by Anandachandra Vedântavâgîça, 2 vols., Calcutta, 1870–74 (Biblioth. Indica). The final section of the Shaḍviṃçabrâhmaṇa has been published and commented on by A. Weber, Zwei Vedische Texte über Omina und Portenta, in the Memoirs of the Academy of Berlin, 1858. Some short Brâhmaṇas of this

they affect the Saṃhitâs, the fundamental collections, a small number only has come down to us; of the Ṛig-Veda, only one;[1] of the Atharva-Veda, two;[2] of the Sâma-Veda, three;[3] while of the Yajur-Veda there are five, of which three are of the Black Yajus[4] and two of the White Yajus.[5] All this united constitutes the *Çruti*, "the hearing," *i.e.*, the sacred and revealed tradition.

If we except a certain quantity of appended matter, which criticism has no difficulty in discriminating from the

Veda we owe to A. C. Burnell: The Sâmavidhâna-Br., London, 1873. The Vaṃça-Br., Mangalore, 1873. The Devatâdhyâya-Br., ibid., 1873. The Arsheya-Br., ibid., 1876. The same with the text of the Jaiminîya school, ibid., 1878. The Saṃhitopanishad-Br., ibid., 1877. All these texts, with the exception of the last, are accompanied by the commentary of Sâyaṇa. The Vaṃçabrâhmaṇa had been previously published by A. Weber in his Indische Studien, t. iv. We owe, moreover, to Burnell the discovery of the Jaiminîya-Br., of which he published a fragment under the title of "A Legend from the Talavakâra or Jaiminîyabrâhmaṇa of the Sama Veda," Mangalore, 1878.

4. The Yajur-Veda.

(*a.*) The White Yajus: The White Yajur-Veda, edited by A. Weber, 3 vols. 4to, 1849–59, comprehends: (1.) The Saṃhitâ, the Vâjasaneyi-Sanhitâ in the Mâdhyandina, and the Kâṇva-Çâkka, with the commentary of Mahîdhara; (2.) The Çatapatha Brâhmaṇa, with Extracts from the Commentaries; (3.) The Çrautasûtras of Kâtyayana, with Extracts from the Commentaries.

(*b.*) The Black Yajus: Die Taittirîya-Saṃhitâ, herausgegeben von A. Weber, 1871–72, forming vols. xi. and xii. of the Indische Studien. The Sanhitâ of the Black Yajur-Veda, with the commentary of Mâdhava Achârya, Calcutta, 1860. (Biblioth. Indica). The publication, which has reached vol. iv., comprehends nearly half of the text; the editors have been successively E. Röer, E. B. Cowell, Maheçacandra Nyâyaratna. The Taittirîya Brâhmaṇa of the Black Yajur-Veda, with the commentary of Sâyaṇâchârya, edited by Râjendralâla Mitra, 3 vols. 8vo, Calcutta, 1859–70 (Biblioth. Indica). The Taittirîya Araṇyaka of the Black Yajur-Veda, with the commentary of Sâyaṇâchârya, edited by Râjendralâla Mitra, Calcutta, 1872 (Biblioth. Indica). For the Upanishads, which are arranged in this literature in some few cases rightly, in the majority incorrectly, see *infra*.

[1] That of the Çâkalakas.

[2] Besides the vulgate, edited by Roth and Whitney, that of the Paippalâdis, discovered recently at Kashmir, see R. Roth, Der Atharvaveda in Kaschmir, 1875.

[3] Besides the vulgate, which is that of the Kauthumas, those of the Râṇâyanîyas and of the Jaiminîyas. Of a fourth, that of the Naigeyas, we have only fragments. See Burnell, Riktantravyākaraṇa, p. xxvi.

[4] Those of the Taittirîyas (published), of the Kâṭhas (see A. Weber's Indische Studien, iii. 451; Indische Literaturgeschichte, p. 97, 2d edition), of the Maitrâyaṇîyas (see Haug, Brahma und die Brahmanen, 1871, p. 31; A. Weber, Indische Studien, xiii. p. 117; L. Schroeder, Zeitschr. der Deutschen Morgenländ. Gesellsch., xxxiii. p. 177).

[5] Those of the Mâdhyandinas and of the Kâṇvas (published).

genuine stock, we have in these writings, as a whole, an authentic literature, which professes to be what it is, which neither asserts for itself a supernatural origin nor seeks to disguise its age by recourse to the devices of the pastiche. Interpolations and later additions are numerous enough, but these have all been made in good faith. It is nevertheless difficult to fix the age of these books, even in any approximate degree. The most recent portions of the Brâhmaṇas which have come down to us do not appear to go farther back than the fifth century before our era.[1] The rest of the literature of the Veda must be referred to a remoter antiquity, and assigned, in a sequence impossible to determine with any precision, a duration, the first term of which it is absolutely impossible for us to recover. In a general way, it must be conceded that the mantras are, beyond a doubt, older than the regulations which prescribe the use of them; but we must also admit that the entire body of these books is of more or less simultaneous growth, and conceive of each of them, in the form in which it actually exists, as the last term of a long series, the initial epoch of which must have been obviously the same for all of them. An exception, however, will require to be made as regards the great majority of the hymns of the Ṛig-Veda. This Saṃhitâ is, in fact, composed of several distinct collections, which proceeded, in some cases, from rival families, and belonged to tribes often at war with one another. Now, in the liturgy which we meet with in the most ancient portions of the other books, not only are

[1] The two last books of the Aitarêya Araṇyaka, for example, are ascribed by tradition to Çaunaka and his disciple Açvalâyana. Colebrooke, Miscellaneous Essays, t. i. pp. 42 and 333, Cowell's edition. Max Müller's Ancient Sanskrit Literature, pp. 235–239. Yâjñavalkya, who in the Çatapatha Br. belongs already to the past, is not much more ancient. See Westergaard, Ueber den ältesten Zeitraum der Indischen Geschichte, p. 77. In the King Ajâtaçatru of Bṛihadâraṇyaka-Up., ii. 1, and of Kaushîtaki-Up., iv. 1, some think they recognise the prince of that name who was contemporary with Buddha. Burnouf, Lotus de la Bonne Loi, p. 485; see, however, Kern, Over de Jaartelling der zuidelijke Buddhisten, p. 119. Several of the short Brâhmaṇas of the Sâma-Veda, the Adbhutabrâhmaṇa of the Shaḍviṃça, and a great part of the Taittirîya Âraṇyaka are probably much more modern still.

these distinctions in regard to origin obliterated, not only is the general body of the Hymns indiscriminately selected from, but this is done without respect to the integrity of the ancient prayers,[1] a couplet being picked out here, a triplet there, and thus a body of invocations formed of a character altogether new. The liturgy of these books, therefore, is no longer the same as that which we meet with in the Hymns, and the transition from the one to the other would seem to imply a very considerable lapse of time. Speaking generally, we may say these books presuppose not only the existence of the chants of the Ṛig-Veda, but that of a collection of these more or less akin to the collection that has come down to us.

Attempts have been made to estimate the length of time that would be necessary for the gradual formation of this literature, and the eleventh century before the Christian era has been suggested as the age in which the poetry that produced these hymns must have flourished.[2] But taking into account all the circumstances, we are of opinion that this term is too recent, and that the great body of the chants of the Ṛig-Veda must be referred back to a much earlier period. Contrary to an opinion that is often advanced, we consider also a goodly number of the hymns of the Atharva-Veda to be of a date not much more recent;[3] and some of the formulæ prescribed in the Yajur-Veda are in all probability quite as ancient. As to the other liturgical texts, these, when not borrowed from the Hymns or

[1] We do not intend by this to affirm that in the Ṛig-Veda, as we find it, we must consider all the parts which compose it as having preserved their original forms intact. So far from that, there are more or less unmistakable traces in many of them of their having been recast or readjusted. On this subject see the translation by Grassmann, and "Siebenzig Lieder des Rigveda," translated by K. Geldner and A. Kaegi, 1875, a publication executed under the direction of R. Roth. In a general way, the fact in question is indubitable, although in particular cases the problem is often difficult of resolution.

[2] Max Müller, Ancient Sanskrit Literature, p. 572; see A. Weber, Indische Literaturgeschichte, p. 2, 2d edition.

[3] The existence of a collection of the nature of our Atharva-Veda is involved in such formulæ as Taittir. Saṃh., vii. 5, 11, 2, and probably also in Ṛig-Veda, x. 90, 9.

other similar collections no longer extant,[1] belong to an age more recent, and form with the Brâhmaṇas the secondary deposit in the stratification of Vedic literature.

The religion which is transmitted to us in these Hymns[2] is, in its principal features, this: Nature is throughout divine. Everything which is impressive by its sublimity, or is supposed capable of affecting us for good or evil, may become a direct object of adoration. Mountains, rivers, springs, trees, plants, are invoked as so many high powers.[3] The animals which surround man, the horse by which he is borne into battle, the cow which supplies him with nourishment, the dog which keeps watch over his dwelling, the bird which, by its cry, reveals to him his future, together with that more numerous class of creatures which threaten his existence, receive from him the worship of either homage or deprecation.[4] There are parts even of the apparatus used in connection with sacrifice which are more than sacred to purposes of religion; they are regarded as themselves deities.[5] The very war-chariot, offensive

[1] In all the ritualistic texts, even the most recent, we meet now and again with fragments of liturgy of the same nature and character, sometimes quite as ancient as the Hymns, and which do not occur in the Saṃhitâs of the Ṛig- and the Atharva-Veda as known to us.

[2] See J. Muir, Original Sanskrit Texts, vol. iv., 2d ed., 1873, and vol. v., 1870. We refer our readers, once for all, to this *exposé* as at once the most complete and the most reliable we possess of the Vedic religions. Max Müller, Ancient Sanskrit Literature, p. 525 *seq.* The same author's Lectures on the Origin and Growth of Religion, as illustrated by the Religions of India, 1878, pp. 193 *seq.*, 224 *seq.*, 259 *seq.* A. Ludwig, Die Philosophischen und Religiösen Anschauungen des Veda in ihrer Entwicklung, 1875; and Die Mantralitteratur und das Alte Indien (t. iii. of his translation of the Ṛig-Veda), 1878, pp. 257–415. A. Bergaigne subjects the mystic and religious ideas of the Ṛig-Veda to a searching analysis in a work still in course of publication, entitled, La Religion Védique d'après les Hymnes du Ṛig-Veda, t. i. (Bibliothèque de l'Ecole des Hautes Etudes, fascic. xxxvi.), 1878.

[3] Ṛig-Veda, vii. 35, 8; viii. 54, 4; x. 35, 2; 64, 8; ii. 41, 16–18; iii. 33; vii. 47, 95, 96; viii. 74, 15; x. 64, 9; 75; vii. 49; i. 90, 8; vii. 34, 23–25; vi. 49, 14; x. 17, 14; 97; 145. Atharva-Veda, viii. 7.

[4] Ṛig-Veda, i. 162, 163; iv. 38; i. 164. 26–28; iii. 53, 14; iv. 57, 4; vi. 28; viii. 101, 15; x. 19, 169; Atharva-Veda, x. 10; xii. 4; 5; Ṛig-Veda, vii. 55; ii. 42, 43; x. 165; i. 116, 16; 191, 6; vii. 104, 17–22; Atharva-Veda, viii. 8, 15; 10, 29; ix. 2, 22; x. 4.

[5] Ṛig-Veda, iii. 8; x. 76, 175; and in general the Aprî-sûktas; see, moreover, i. 187; i. 28, 5–8; iv. 58; Atharva-Veda, xviii. 4, 5; xix. 32,

and defensive weapons, the plough, the furrow which has just been traced in the soil, are the objects, not of blessing only, but of prayer.[1] India is radically pantheistic, and that from its cradle onwards. Nevertheless it is neither the direct adoration of objects, even the greatest, nor that of the obvious personifications of natural phenomena, which figures most prominently in the Hymns. Thus, Aurora is certainly a great goddess; the poets that praise her can find no colours bright enough or words passionate enough to greet this daughter of heaven, who reveals and dispenses all blessings, ushering in the days of the year and prolonging them to mortals. Her gifts are celebrated and her blessings implored, but her share in the cultus is small in comparison; it is not, as a rule, to her that the offerings go. Almost as much must be said of the deities Heaven and Earth, although they are still revered as the primitive pair by whom the rest of the gods were begotten. In the cultus they disappear before the more personal divinities; while in speculation they are gradually superseded by more abstract conceptions or by more recondite symbols. Of the stars there is hardly any mention. The moon plays only a subordinate part.[2] The sun itself, which figures so prominently in the myth, no longer does so to the same extent in the religious consciousness, or at most it is worshipped by preference in some of its duplicate forms, which possess a more complex personality and have a more abstruse meaning. The two single divinities of the first rank which have preserved their physical character pure and simple are *Agni* and *Soma*. In their case, the visible and tangible objects were too near, and, above all, too sacred, to be in any greater or less degree obscured or outshone by mere personifications. Nevertheless, means

9. The Rig-Veda, consecrated to the worship of the great gods, is comparatively meagre in supplying information on these imperfect and, at times, merely metaphorical deifications. On the other hand, more than the half of those portions which are peculiar to the Atharva-Veda are devoted to these lower forms of religion.

[1] Ṛig-Veda, iii. 53, 17–20; vi. 47, 26–31; vi. 75; iv. 57, 4–8.

[2] Ṛig-Veda, i. 24, 10; 105, 1, 10; x. 64, 3; 85, 1–5, 9, 13, 18, 19, 40.

were at length devised by which what was gross in the merely physical idea of a god Agni and a god Soma might be refined into more spiritual conceptions. They were invested with a subtle and complicated symbolism; they were impregnated, so to speak, with all the mystic virtue of sacrifice; their empire was extended far beyond the world of sense, and they were conceived as cosmic agents and universal principles.

Agni, in fact, is not only terrestrial fire, and the fire of the lightning and the sun;[1] his proper native home is the mystic, invisible heaven, the abode of the eternal light and the first principles of all things.[2] His births are infinite in number, whether as a germ, which is indestructible and ever begotten from itself, he starts into life every day on the altar from a piece of wood, whence he is extracted by friction (the *araṇi*), and in which he sleeps like the embryo in the womb;[3] or whether, as son of the floods, he darts with the noise of the thunder from the bosom of the celestial rivers, where the Bhṛigus (personifications of the lightning) discovered him, and the Açvins begat him with araṇis of gold.[4] In point of fact, he is always and everywhere the same, since those ancient days when, as the eldest of the gods, he was born in his highest dwelling, on the bosom of the primordial waters, and when the first religious rites and the first sacrifice were brought forth along with him.[5] For he is priest by birth in heaven as well as on earth,[6] and he officiated in that capacity in the abode of Vivasvat[7] (heaven or the sun), long before Mâtariçvan (another symbol of the lightning) had brought him down to mortals,[8] and before Atharvan and the Aṅgiras, the primitive sacrificers, had installed

[1] Ṛig-Veda, x. 88, 6, 11.

[2] Ṛig-Veda, x. 45, 1; 121, 7; vi. 8, 2; ix. 113, 7, 8.

[3] Ṛig-Veda, x. 5, 1; iii. 29; i. 68, 2; x. 79, 4, &c. Being born thus every day, he is called the youngest of the gods.

[4] Ṛig-Veda, ii. 35; iii. 1; ii. 4, 2; x. 46, 2; i. 58, 6; iii. 2, 3; x. 88, 10; 184, 3.

[5] Ṛig-Veda, i. 24, 2; iii. i. 20; x. 88, 8; 121, 7, 8; iv. i. 11–18.

[6] Ṛig-Veda, i. 94, 6; x. 110, 11; 150.

[7] Ṛig-Veda, i. 58, 1; 31, 3.

[8] Ṛig-Veda, i. 93, 6; iii. 9, 5; vi. 8, 4.

him here below as the protector, the guest, and the friend of men.[1] The later legends, in which the birth of the lightning, or the first generation of the sacred fire, is directly represented as a sacrifice, are in this respect only the legitimate development of these old conceptions. As lord and generator of sacrifice, Agni becomes the bearer of all those mystic speculations of which sacrifice is the subject. He begets the gods, organises the world, produces and preserves universal life, and is, in a word, a power in the Vedic cosmogony.[2] At the same time, as observation, doubtless, contributed to suggest, he is a sort of *anima mundi*, a subtle principle pervading all nature; it is he who renders the womb of women capable of conception, and makes the plants and all the seeds of the earth spring up and grow.[3] But at the core of all these high powers ascribed to him, he never ceases for an instant to be the fire, the material flame which consumes the wood on the altar; and of the many hymns which celebrate his praises, there is not one in which this side of his nature is for once forgotten.

Soma is in this respect the exact counterpart of Agni. Soma is properly the fermented drinkable juice of a plant so named, which has been extracted from its stalk under pressure after due maceration. The beverage produced is intoxicating,[4] and it is offered in libation to the gods, especially to Indra, whose strength it intensifies in the battle which that god maintains against the demons. But it is not only on earth that the soma flows; it is present in the rain which the cloud distils, and it is shed

[1] Ṛig-Veda, i. 83, 4, 5; 71, 2, 3; vi. 15, 17; 16, 13; x. 92, 10; vii. 5, 6; ii. 1, 9; 2, 3, 8; 4, 3-4; x. 7, 3; 91, 1, 2. He is called himself Aṅgiras, the first of the Aṅgiras.

[2] Ṛig-Veda, v. 3, 1; x. 8, 4: i. 69, 1. See Taitt. Saṃh., i. 5, 10, 2; Ṛig-Veda, vi. 7, 7; 8, 3; x. 156, 4.

[3] Ṛig-Veda, iii. 3, 10; x. 51, 3; i. 66, 8; iii. 26, 9; 27, 9; viii. 44, 16; x. 21, 8; 80, 1; 183, 3. In the Atharva-Veda he is identified with Kâma, Desire, Love; Ath.-Veda, iii. 21, 4. In the ritual he bears the surnames of Patnîvat, of Kâma, of Putravat: Taitt. Saṃh., i. 4, 27; ii. 2, 3, 1; ii. 2, 4, 4; see vi. 5, 8, 4.

[4] Ṛig-Veda, viii. 48, 5, 6; x. 119; viii. 2, 12.

beyond the visible world wherever sacrifice is performed.[1] This is as much as to say that, like Agni, Soma, besides the existence he assumes on the earth and in the atmosphere, has a mystic existence.[2] Like Agni, he has many dwelling-places;[3] but his supreme residence is in the depths of the third heaven, where Sûryâ, the daughter of the Sun, passed him through her filter, where the women of Trita, a duplicate, or at any rate a very near relation, of Agni, pounded him under the stone, where Pûshan, the god of nourishment, found him.[4] From this spot it was that the falcon, a symbol of the lightning, or Agni himself, once ravished him out of the hands of the heavenly archer, the Gandharva, his guardian, and brought him to men.[5] The gods drank of him and became in consequence immortal; men will become so when they in turn shall drink of him with Yama in the abode of the blessed.[6] Meanwhile, he gives to them here below vigour and fulness of days; he is the ambrosia and the water of youth; it is he who renders the waters fertile, who nourishes the plants, of which he is the king, infusing into them their healing virtues, who quickens the semen of men and animals, and gives inspiration to the poet and fervour to prayer.[7] He generated the heaven and the earth, Indra and Vishṇu. With Agni, with whom he forms a pair in closest union, he kindled the sun and the stars.[8] None the less is he the plant which the acolyte pounds under the stone, and the yellow liquid which trickles into the vat.[9]

[1] In the view of the Vedas, sacrifice is offered by the gods as well as by men; it is universal and eternal.

[2] Ṛig-Veda, i. 91, 4; ix. 36, 15.

[3] Ṛig-Veda, i. 91, 5.

[4] Ṛig-Veda, ix. 32, 2; 38, 2; 1, 6; 113, 3; i. 23, 13, 14.

[5] Ṛig-Veda, iv. 26, 6, 7; 27; 18, 13; viii. 82, 9; i. 71, 5; ix. 83, 4.

[6] Ṛig-Veda, viii. 48, 3; ix. 113, 7–11; viii. 48, 7; 79, 2, 3, 6; i. 91, 6, 7.

[7] Ṛig-Veda, ix. 8, 8; viii. 79, 2, 6; i. 91, 22; x. 97, 22; vi. 47, 3; i. 23, 19, 20; ix. 60, 4, 85, 39; 95, 2; 96, 6; 88, 3.

[8] Ṛig-Veda, ix. 96, 5; 86, 10; 87, 2; i. 93, 5.

[9] A. Kuhn has gone minutely into the ramifications of the leading myths that refer to Agni and Soma in his Memoir, Die Herabkunft des Feuers und des Göttertranks, 1859. For the symbolism of which these two gods are the subject, and for all that religion of sacrifice of which they are in some degree the centre,

In the other divinities the physical character is more effaced. Occasionally it is preserved only in the myth or in a limited number of attributes; and even in that case it is not always easy to determine it with precision. For the religious consciousness they are personal deities; and in general the greater the deity is the more pronounced and complex is the personality. *Indra*, he who of all these is invoked most frequently, is the king of heaven and the national god of the Aryans;[1] he gives victory to his people, and is always ready to take in hand the cause of his servants. But it is in heaven, in the atmosphere, that he fights his great battles for the deliverance of the waters, the cows, the spouses of the gods, kept captive by the demons. It is here that, intoxicated with the soma, he strikes down with his thunderbolt Vṛitra, the coverer, Ahi, the dragon, Çushṇa, the witherer, and a crowd of other monsters; that he breaks open the brazen strongholds of Çambara, the demon with the club, and the cave of Vala, the concealer of stolen goods; and that, guided by Saramâ, his faithful dog, and roused to fury by the song of the Aṅgiras, he comes to snatch from the cunning Paṇis what they have pilfered.[2] In these combats, which are now represented as exploits of a remote past, and again as a perennial struggle which is renewed every day, he is sometimes assisted by other gods, such as Soma, Agni, his companion Vishṇu, or his bodyguards the Maruts.[3] But he more frequently fights alone;[4] and, indeed, he has no need of assistance from others, so vast is his strength and so certain his victory.[5] Once only is he said to have been

see especially the work of A. Bergaigne already cited, La Religion Védique d'après les Hymnes, and the paper of the same author, Les Figures de Rhétorique dans le Ṛig-Veda, in Mémoires de la Société de Linguistique de Paris, t. iv. 96.

[1] Ṛig-Veda, i. 51, 8; 130, 8; ii. 11, 18; iv. 26, 2; viii. 92, 32, &c.

[2] Of the countless passages which refer to these struggles we shall mention only Ṛig-Veda, i. 32 and x. 108. For the basis of these myths and the expression given to them in the other mythologies, see the memoir of M. Breal, Hercule et Cacus, Etude de Mythologie Comparée, 1863.

[3] Ṛig-Veda, iv. 28, 1; ix. 61, 22; iii. 12, 6; i. 22, 19; iv. 18, 11; viii. 100, 12; iii. 47, &c.

[4] Ṛig-Veda, i. 165, 8; vii. 21, 6; x. 138, 6, &c.

[5] Ṛig-Veda, i. 165, 9, 10.

seized with terror, and that was after the death of Vṛitra, "when, like a scared falcon, he fled to the depths of space across and beyond the ninety and nine rivers;"[1] while even in this flight the later literature, which has preserved the memory of it, sees only an effect of remorse.[2] The fact is, that in India the struggle between the god and the demon is, and will always remain, an unequal one; it will give rise to an infinite number of myths; but this will not, as in Persia, issue in dualism. Indra, then, is pre-eminently a warlike god. Standing erect in his war-chariot, drawn by two fawn-coloured horses, he is in some sort the ideal type of an Aryan chieftain. But that is only one of the sides of his nature. As a god of heaven he is also the dispenser of all good gifts, the author and preserver of all life;[3] with the same hand he fills the udder of the cow with ready-made milk, and holds back the wheels of the sun on the downward slope of the firmament; he traces for the rivers their courses, and establishes securely without rafters the vault of the sky.[4] He is of inordinate dimensions; there is room for the earth in the hollow of his hand;[5] he is sovereign lord and demiurgos.[6]

Around him those divinities are grouped which seem to share in his empire, from the first, his faithful companions the *Maruts*, probably the bright ones, gods of storm and the lightnings.[7] When their host begins to move, the earth trembles under their deer-yoked chariots and the forests bow their heads on the mountains.[8] As they pass, men see

[1] Ṛig-Veda, i. 32, 14.

[2] The remorse of the brahmanicide, for the antagonist of Indra has become a Brahman: Mahâbhar., v. 228–569. The basis of this story is, however, of ancient date, Taitt. Saṃh., ii. 5, 1; ii. 5, 3; see vi. 5, 5, 2. Taitt. Saṃh., ii. 4, 12, Indra does not kill Vṛitra, but concludes a compact with him.

[3] Ṛig-Veda, iv. 17, 17; vii. 37, 3: He is the Maghavan, the munificent *par excellence*.

[4] Ṛig-Veda, i. 61, 9; iii. 30, 14; iv. 28, 2; ii. 15, 2, 3.

[5] Ṛig-Veda, i. 100, 15; 173, 6; vi. 30, 1; iii. 30, 5.

[6] Ṛig-Veda, ii. 12; i. 101, 5; iv. 19, 2; iii. 46, 2; ii. 15, 2; 17, 5; vi. 30, 5; viii. 96, 6.

[7] Twelve hymns of the first book addressed to the Maruts form the first volume (all that has appeared) of the translation by Max Müller.

[8] Ṛig-Veda, v. 60, 2, 3; viii. 20, 5, 6; i. 37, 6, 8.

the flashing of their arms and hear the sound of their flute-music and songs, with their challenge calls and the cracking of their whips.[1] Tumultuous though they are, they are none the less beneficent. They are dispensers of the rains, and from the udder of Pṛiçṇi, the spotted cow, their mother, they cause her milk to flow in the showers.[2] From their father, *Rudra*, they inherit the knowledge of remedies.[3] This last, whose name probably meant "the reddish one," before it was interpreted to mean "The Howler," is, like his sons, a god of storm. In the Hymns, which certainly do not tell us everything here any more than elsewhere, he has nothing of that gloomy aspect under which we find him become so famous afterwards. Although he is armed with the thunderbolt, and is the author of sudden deaths,[4] he is represented as pre-eminently helpful and beneficent. He is the handsomest of the gods, with his fair locks. Like Soma, the most excellent remedies are at his disposal, and his special office is that of protector of flocks.[5] He is a near relation of *Vâyu* or *Vâta*, the wind, with whom he is sometimes confounded,[6] a god of healing like him, and owner of a miraculous cow which yields him the best milk.[7] He is also similarly related to *Parjanya*, the most direct impersonation of the rain-storm, the god with the resounding hymn, who lays the forests low and causes the earth to tremble, who terrifies even the innocent when he smites the guilty, but who also diffuses life, and at whose approach exhausted vegetation begins to revive. The earth decks herself afresh when he empties his great shower-bottle; he is her husband, and it is through him that plants, animals, and men are capable of reproduction; and, as may always be

[1] Ṛig-Veda, i. 64, 4; viii. 20, 11; i. 85, 2, 10; 37, 3, 13.

[2] Ṛig-Veda, i. 37, 10, 11; 38, 7, 9; 64, 6; v. 53, 6–10; ii. 34, 10.

[3] Ṛig-Veda, i. 38, 2; ii. 34, 2; viii. 20, 23–26; ii. 33, 13.

[4] Ṛig-Veda, ii. 33, 3, 10–14; vii. 46.

[5] Ṛig-Veda, ii. 33, 3, 4; i. 43, 4; 114, 5; ii. 33, 2; vi. 74; i. 43; 114, 8; x. 169.

[6] Ṛig-Veda, x. 169. He is, like him, father of the Maruts: i. 134, 4; 135, 9.

[7] Ṛig-Veda, x. 186; i. 134, 4.

predicated of a god of storm, who has at his command both Agni and Soma under the forms of lightning and rain, he has a higher *rôle* and plays a part in the generation of the cosmos.[1]

By one of those peculiarities characteristic of the Vedic religions, nearly all the features which have just been mentioned as conspicuous in Agni, Soma, and Indra reappear in another divine personage of an origin apparently very different, *Bṛihaspati* or *Brahmaṇaspati*, as he is called, the lord of prayer. Like Agni and Soma, he is born on the altar, and thence rises upwards to the gods; like them, he was begotten in space by heaven and earth; like Indra, he wages war with enemies on the earth and demons in the air;[2] like all three, he resides in the highest heaven, he generates the gods, and ordains the order of the universe. Under his fiery breath the world was melted and assumed the form it has, like metal in the mould of the founder.[3] At first sight it would seem that all this is a late product of abstract reflection; and it is probable, in fact, from the very form of the name, that in so far as it is a distinct person, the type is comparatively modern; in any case, it is peculiarly Indian; but by its elements it is connected with the most ancient conceptions. As there is a power in the flame and the libation, so there is in the formula; and this formula the priest is not the only person to pronounce, any more than he is the only one to kindle Agni or shed Soma. There is a prayer in the thunder, and the gods, who know all things, are not ignorant of the power in the sacramental expressions. They possess all-potent spells that have remained hidden from men and are as ancient as the first rites, and it was by these the world was formed at first, and by which it is preserved up to the present.[4] It is this omnipresent power of prayer which

[1] Ṛig-Veda, v. 83; vii. 101; ix. 82, 3; 113, 3.

[2] Ṛig-Veda, ii. 24, 11; vii. 97, 8; ii. 23, 3, 18; ii. 24, 2-4; x. 68.

[3] Ṛig-Veda, iv. 50, 4; ii. 26, 3; 24, 5; iv. 50, 1; x. 72, 2.

[4] Ṛig-Veda, i. 164, 45; viii. 100, 10, 11; x. 71, 1; 177, 2; 114, 1; ii. 23, 17;

Brahmaṇaspati personifies, and it is not without reason that he is sometimes confounded with Agni, and especially with Indra. In reality each separate god and the priest himself[1] become Brahmaṇaspati at the moment when they pronounce the mantras which give them power over the things of heaven and of earth. The same idea, in a more abstract form, comes out in Vâc, the sacred speech, which is represented as an infinite power, as superior to the gods, and as generative of all that exists.[2]

If we combine into one all the attributes of sovereign power and majesty which we find in the other gods, we will have the god *Varuṇa*.[3] As is implied in the name, which is the same as the Greek *Οὐρανός*, Varuṇa is the god of the vast luminous heavens, viewed as embracing all things, and as the primary source of all life and every blessing.[4] Indra, too, is a god of the heavens, and these two personalities do, in fact, coincide in many respects. There is, however, this difference between them, that Indra has, above all, appropriated the active, and, so to speak, militant life of heaven, while Varuṇa represents rather its serene, immutable majesty. Nothing equals the magnificent terms in which the Hymns describe him. The sun is his eye, the sky is his garment, and the storm is his breath.[5] It is he who keeps the heavens and the earth apart, and has established them on foundations that cannot be shaken; who has placed the stars in the firmament, who has given feet to the sun, and who has traced for the

x. 11, 4; 90, 9. Prayer is the weapon of Bṛihaspati, ii. 24, 3, &c.; it is also that of the Aṅgiras. The brahman, the effective word, is *devakṛita*, the work of the gods, vii. 97, 3; compare the bellowing of Agni, of Varuṇa, of the celestial bull, the song of Parjanya and that of the Maruts.

1 Ṛig-Veda, iv. 50, 7.

2 Ṛig-Veda, x. 125.

3 The myth of Varuṇa and the whole of the conceptions which are connected with it are the subject of a study, as profound as brilliant, in the work of J. Darmesteter, Ormazd et Ahriman, leurs Origines et leur Histoire, 1877. See also the interesting monograph by A. Hillebrandt, Varuṇa und Mitra, ein Beitrag zur Exegese des Veda, 1877, and R. Roth, Die höchsten Götter des arischen Volkes, ap. Zeitschr. der Deutsch. Morgenländ. Gesellsch., t. vi. 70.

4 Ṛig-Veda, vii. 87, 5; viii. 41, 3.

5 Ṛig-Veda, i. 115, 1; 25, 13; Ath.-Veda, xiii. 3, 1; Ṛig-Veda, vii. 87, 2.

auroras their paths, and for the rivers their courses.[1] He has made everything and preserves everything; nothing can do harm to the works of Varuṇa. No one can fathom him; but as for him, he knows all and sees all, both what is and what shall be.[2] From the heights of heaven, where he resides in a palace with a thousand gates, he can discern the track of the birds through the air and of the ships over the seas.[3] It is from thence, from the height of his throne of gold on its foundations of brass, that he watches over the execution of his decrees, that he directs the onward movement of the world, and that, surrounded by his emissaries, he regards with an eye that never slumbers the doings of men, and passes judgment upon them.[4] For he is before all the upholder of order in the universe and in human society, and his sovereignty is the highest expression of law, both physical and moral.[5] He inflicts terrible punishments and avenging maladies on the hardened criminal;[6] but his justice discriminates between a fault and a sin, and he is merciful to the man that repents. It is also to him that the cry of anguish from remorse ascends, and it is before him that the sinner comes to discharge himself of the burden of his guilt by confession.[7] In other sections the religion of the Veda is ritualistic, and at times intensely speculative, but with Varuṇa it goes down into the depths of the conscience, and realises the idea of holiness.

It has sometimes been maintained that the Varuṇa of the Hymns is a god in a state of decadence.[8] In this view

[1] Ṛig-Veda, vii. 86, 1; viii. 41, 10; 42, 1; i. 24, 8; v. 85, 5; i. 123, 8; ii. 28, 4; v. 85, 6; vii. 87, 1.

[2] Ṛig-Veda, iv. 42, 3; i. 24, 10; 25, 14.

[3] Ṛig-Veda, i. 25, 10; viii. 88, 5; i. 25, 7–11.

[4] Ṛig-Veda, v. 62, 8; i. 25, 13; ix. 73, 4; vii. 49, 3; Ath.-Veda, iv. 16, 1–5.

[5] Hence his surnames of ṛitasya gopâ, the guardian of order, dhṛitavrata, satyadharman, whose decrees are irreversible and effectual.

[6] These are his *bonds:* Ṛig-Veda, i. 24, 15, &c. There is often mention of his wrath: i. 24, 11, 14; vii. 62, 4; iv. 1, 4; vii. 84, 2. Dropsy, in particular, was an infliction especially ascribed to Varuṇa: vii. 89; Atharva-Veda, iv. 16, 7.

[7] Ṛig-Veda, i. 25, 1, 2; ii. 28, 5–9; v. 85, 7, 8; vii. 86; 87, 7; 88, 6; 89.

[8] See the arguments for this in J. Muir's Original Sanskrit Texts, t. v. p. 116; see also Hillebrandt, Varuṇa und Mitra, p. 107.

we can by no means concur. That he filled small space in the public cultus at the time when these old chants were collected, is evident indeed from the small number of hymns to Varuṇa preserved in the collection. Still, though we might insist that the importance of a god is not always to be measured by the frequency with which his name is invoked in the ritual, an appeal to these few hymns is enough to prove that, in the consciousness of their authors, the divinity of Varuṇa stood still intact. In connection with no other god is the sense of the divine majesty and of the absolute dependence of the creature expressed with the same force, and we must go to the Psalms in order to find similar accents of adoration and supplication. Moreover, there are two hymns [1] in which a formal parallel is drawn between Varuṇa and Indra, the god who ought to have dethroned him, and in both places it is with Varuṇa on the whole that the supreme majesty remains. There is a third hymn,[2] it is true, where matters appear in a different light. In it we find Agni declaring that he quits the service of Varuṇa for that of Indra, the only true lord and master, and this is looked upon by some as authentic evidence that the worship of Varuṇa was superseded by that of Indra. This would be a very singular passage indeed, if it actually contained a chapter of religious history, all the more surprising that it bears the marks of such extreme antiquity. But it is not a page of history we must look for here; it is a page of mythology. Heaven is not always in a clement mood, and there was a time when Varuṇa was not solely just and good, when, alongside of myths representing his divine nature, there were others that expressed his demonic character, and in which heaven or Varuṇa was vanquished. The religious sentiment, in many respects so elevated, which appears in the Hymns, discarded the most of the myths of this class, as well as many others which were offensive to it; but it did not discard them all, and it could not prevent them

[1] Ṛig-Veda, iv. 42; vii. 82.

[2] Ṛig-Veda, x. 124.

surviving in a sort of latent state. In the passage in question, which is one of those that have passed in spite of the feeling against them, Varuṇa is not a god on the wane but a malign divinity; and that is a side of his nature the memory of which is kept alive in the Brâhmaṇas.

Varuṇa is the first of a group of deities with abstract names, such as *Mitra*, the friend, *Aryaman*, the bosom friend, *Bhaga*, the liberal, *Daksha*, the capable, *Aṃça*, the apportioner, which are only a splitting up and in some sort the reflection of his own being. They have no very defined existence, and, with almost the single exception of Mitra,[1] they are never invoked alone. They all, as is noticeable, tend in some degree to maintain the part of solar divinities; particularly is this the case with Mitra, the most conspicuous among them, and who, like his brother Mithra of the Zend books, becomes identified later on with the sun himself. Savitṛi also, a decidedly solar god, is often associated with them; and in one myth of unmistakably ancient date the sun is their brother, being born of an immature egg, which their mother has thrown away and sent rolling into space.[2] This mother is *Aditi*, immensity,[3] from whom they derive their name of *Aditya*, or sons of Aditi, an epithet applied sometimes also to Indra and Agni.[4] When the Hymns try to describe Aditi, they exhaust themselves in laborious efforts, and lose themselves at length in vagueness. In her the confused and imposing notion of a sort of common womb, a substratum of all existences, seems to have found one of its earliest expressions. In one passage she is "what has been born, and what will be born."[5] In another circle of ideas, a character quite similar is at times ascribed to the Waters, which are not only the divers manifestations of the liquid element, such as springs, rivers, rains, clouds,

[1] Ṛig-Veda, iii. 59.

[2] Ṛig-Veda, x. 72, 8, 9. Hence his name of Mârtâṇḍa.

[3] See Max Müller, Translation of the Ṛig-Veda, pp. 230–251, and A. Hillebrandt, Ueber die Göttin Aditi, 1876.

[4] Ṛig-Veda, vii. 85, 4; viii. 52, 7; x. 88, 11 (*âditeya*).

[5] Ṛig-Veda, i. 89, 10.

libations, but are also conceived of as the primitive medium in the womb of which is fashioned everything that exists.[1]

The transition from the Adityas deities to the solar deities is, as we have just seen, an imperceptible one. Of the latter, the most important are *Sûrya*, the sun, conceived directly as a divine being; he keeps his eye on men and reports their failings before Mitra and Varuṇa;[2] *Savitṛi*, the quickener, who, as he raises his long arms of gold, rouses all beings from their slumber in the morning and buries them in sleep again in the evening;[3] *Vishṇu*, the active, who is destined at a later period to such honour, the comrade of Indra, who paces along with long strides, and in three steps traverses the celestial spaces;[4] and *Pûshan*, the nourisher, who with his golden goad traces the track of the furrow, the good shepherd who loses not a single head of his cattle. He knows all roads, and these he is incessantly traversing on a chariot yoked with goats; he is the guide of men and of herds of cattle in their peregrinations, as he also is of the dead along the paths which lead to the abode of the blessed.[5] We need not insist on the qualities of clear-sightedness, sagacity, and ordaining power naturally common to all these deities in their character as beings related to the light and the sun. It will be observed, however, that they are conceived of, and especially treated, in a very personal manner, and in a way to suggest only very indirectly the luminary they represent, from which they are at times expressly distinguished;[6] and that, in fine, they express only the beneficent aspects of it. The harmful sun, the destroyer and devourer,—he, for example, whose wheel

[1] Compare such passages as Ṛig-Veda, vii. 47; 49 with x. 82, 5, 6; 109, 1; 121, 7, 8; 129, 1–3; 190, 1.

[2] Ṛig-Veda, i. 50; 115; vii. 62, 2, &c.

[3] Ṛig-Veda, ii. 38, &c.

[4] Ṛig-Veda, i. 22, 16–21; 154.

[5] Ṛig-Veda, i. 42; vi. 53; iv. 57, 7; x. 17, 3–6.

[6] See Ṛig-Veda, where, x. 149, 3, the sun is called the bird of Savitṛi; i. 35, 9, Savitṛi guides the sun; v. 47, 3, the sun is called a brilliant stone set in the sky; vii. 87, 5, it is the golden swing fabricated by Varuṇa.

Indra breaks in pieces,[1]—has given rise to myths, but he does not become a god as in the Semitic religions.

Ushas naturally takes rank next the sun; she is the Aurora, and the most graceful creation of the Hymns, a bright and airy figure that hovers on the uncertain borderland of poetry and religion, so transparent is the personification, and so uncertain are we whether it is to the object evoked that the poet addresses himself, or whether it is not rather God whom he adores in his works.[2] The case is quite different with regard to the two *Açvins*, the horsemen. It is not easy to explain either the reason of their name or their physical meaning. It is obvious that they are deities of the morning: they are the sons of the Sun and the betrothed of Aurora. On their three-wheeled chariot they make the circuit of the world every day; their whip distils the honey of the dew; it was they who revealed to the gods the place where the soma was hidden; and one part at least of the myths, in which they are always found succouring a person in distress, seems to be naturally explained by the deliverance, that is to say, the rising, of the sun out of darkness.[3] But neither does all this, any more than the comparison which has been drawn between them and the Dioscuri, render their origin much clearer. Nevertheless they rank among the divinities that are often invoked; they are dispensers of benefits, are possessed of invaluable remedies, and preside at generation.[4] By this last function they are allied to their maternal grandfather, *Tvashṭri*, the fashioner, who fabricated the thunderbolt of Indra and the cup of sacrifice, and whose special office it is to form the fœtus in the womb,[5] one of the most curious characters in the Vedic

[1] Ṛig-Veda, iv. 28, 2, &c.

[2] Nothing more charming than these hymns to Aurora is to be found in the descriptive lyrical poetry of any other people. Ṛig-Veda, i. 48, 113, 123, 124; iii. 61; vi. 64; vii. 77, 78.

[3] Ṛig-Veda, i. 34, 10; iii. 39, 3; viii. 9, 17; i. 118, 5; iv. 43, 6; i. 157, 3, 4; v. 76, 3; i. 116, 12; 119, 9. See A. Weber, Ind. Stud., v. 234; L. Myriantheus, Die Açvins oder arischen Dioskuren, 1876.

[4] Ṛig-Veda, i. 34, 3–6; 157, 5; x. 184, 2, 3; Ath.-Veda, ii. 30, 2. See Taitt. Saṃh., ii. 3, 11, 2.

[5] Ṛig-Veda, i. 32, 2; 20, 6; 188, 9; x. 10, 5; 184, 1; Taitt. Saṃh., i. 5, 9, 1, 2.

Pantheon, in a mythological point of view, but of slender account in a religious one. He has close affinities with Agni, of whom he is at times the father.[1] He has other children besides: *Saraṇyu*, the hurrying cloud, who has connection with Vivasvat, the sun, and *Viçvarûpa*, the many-fashioned, a monster with three heads, who is likewise a personification of the storm, and who expires under the blows of Indra.[2] He himself maintains a struggle with Indra, who ventures into his dwelling to ravish from him the soma. He is at once creator and evil-doer,[3] and the only power really invoked who partakes as much of the demon as of the god. As workman of the gods, he has the *Ṛibhus* as rivals, a set of genii, ordinarily three in number, who by their works attained to immortality. They are distinguished for having divided into four the one cup of sacrifice which Tvashtṛi had fashioned.[4] Here again what is nothing more than a myth has sometimes been taken for history; for we hear of the religious reform wrought by the Ṛibhus, and of their admission among the gods.[5] Notwithstanding their vague and hardly intelligible nature, they are frequently invoked, and they partake daily of the evening offering.

The solar myths naturally lead us to those which are connected with the life beyond the grave; for in India, as elsewhere, it is a solar hero who rules over the dead. *Yama* is, in fact, a son of Vivasvat, the sun.[6] He might have lived as an immortal, but he chose to die, or rather he incurred the penalty of death, for under this choice a fall is disguised.[7] He was the first to traverse the road from which there is no return, tracing it for future generations. It is there, at the remotest extremities of the heavens, the abode of light and the eternal waters, that he

[1] Ṛig-Veda, i. 95; 2; x. 2, 7.

[2] Ṛig-Veda, x. 17, 12; 8, 8, 9.

[3] Ṛig-Veda, iii. 48, 4; iv. 18, 3; x. 110, 9; ix. 5, 9; ii. 23, 17.

[4] Ṛig-Veda, iv. 35, 8; i. 20, 6.

[5] See Fr. Nève, Essai sur le mythe des Ribhavas, premier vestige de l'apothéose dans le Véda, 1847.

[6] Ṛig-Veda, x. 14, 1; 17, 1.

[7] Ṛig-Veda, x. 13, 4.

reigns henceforward in peace and in union with Varuṇa. There by the sound of his flute, under the branches of the mythic tree, he assembles around him the dead who have lived nobly. They reach him in a crowd, conveyed by Agni, guided by Pûshan, and grimly scanned as they pass by the two monstrous dogs who are the guardians of the road. Clothed in a glorious body, and made to drink of the celestial soma, which renders them immortal, they enjoy henceforward by his side an endless felicity, seated at the same tables with the gods, gods themselves, and adored here below under the name of *Pitṛis*, or fathers. At their head are, of course, the first sacrificers, the minstrels of other days, Atharvan, the Aṅgiras, the Kavyas, the Pitṛis by pre-eminence, equal to the greatest of the gods, who by their sacrifice delivered the world from chaos, gave birth to the sun, and kindled the stars.[1] It is not improbable there were some who thought it was they whom they saw sparkling at night in the constellations; for India, too, was aware of the old myth which conceives of the stars as the souls of the dead.[2] These, however, are very far from being the only representations that were given of the future life. As it was not always the custom to burn the dead, we find them conceived of as resting in the earth like a child on the lap of its mother, and dwelling for ever in the tomb, called in consequence "the narrow house of clay."[3] It was imagined, too, that when the body was on the eve of dissolution and returning to its elements, the soul went to tenant the waters or the plants.[4] This last conception, in which there is a sort of first rude idea of the theory of metempsychosis, occurs only in an exceptional

[1] Ṛig-Veda, ix. 113, 7–11; x. 135; 154; 14; 15; 16, 1, 2; 17. Compare Atharva-Veda, iv. 34, 2; Ṛig-Veda, i. 125, 5; 154, 5; x. 56, 4–6; 68, 11; 107, 1.

[2] Ṛig-Veda, i. 125, 6; x. 107, 2; see Taitt. Br., i. 5, 2, 5. The myths that relate to the seven Ṛishis (the stars of the Great Bear) and to Agastya (Canopus) are of ancient date: Ṛig-Veda, x. 82, 2; Çatap. Br., ii. 1, 2, 4; Taitt. Âr., i. 11, 1, 2; see besides Mahâbhâr., iii. 1745–1752.

[3] Ṛig-Veda, x. 18, 10–13; vii 89, 1.

[4] Ṛig-Veda, x. 58; 16, 3.

way in the hymns of the Ṛig-Veda. This notion seems to belong to religious beliefs of a lower type, which this collection despises, and the existence of which we shall have occasion to refer to after. Anyhow, the simple fact that the practice of incineration had become general presupposes a highly spiritualistic idea of death. The Hymns are much less communicative in regard to the destiny in store for the wicked. They either perish or go under the earth into deep and dismal pits, into which are cast along with them the demons, the spirits of deception and destruction.[1] The Atharva-Veda is cognisant of an infernal world,[2] but there is no description of hell, and we learn nothing of its torments.[3]

This very imperfect glance at the myths connected with the principal divinities will perhaps be enough to show out of what elements India has collected the objects of its worship. We shall not perform the same task for the other figures of the Pantheon. Not only would the mere enumeration of these be too tedious, since every object in the visible creation, as well as every idea of the mind, is capable of elevation to the rank of gods; they belong rather to the history of the myths than to that of religion. They are either abstract personifications, often very ancient indeed, such as *Purandhi*, abundance, *Aramati*, piety, *Asunîti*, blessedness, *Mṛityu*, death, *Manyu*, wrath (these two last being masculine); or deified objects, such as *Sarasvatî* and *Sindhu*, which are at once rivers and goddesses; or mere symbols, such as the different forms of the solar bird or the courser of the sun; or, in fine, ancient representations which have scarcely emerged from the penumbra of the myth, such as the *Gandharva*, *Ahi Budhnya*, the dragon of the abyss, *Aja Ekapâd*, the one-footed bounder

[1] Rig-Veda, iv. 5, 5; vii. 104, 3; ix. 73, 8.

[2] Atharva-Veda, xii. 4, 36.

[3] See, however, Atharva-Veda, v. 19, 3, 12–14, cited by M. H. Zimmer, Altindisches Leben, p. 420; and, in general, for the Vedic ideas on the future life, all chap. xv. of that excellent work. According to Benfey, Hermes, Minos, Tartaros, in the Memoirs of the Roy. Society of Göttingen for 1877, the conceptions of Tartarus and the Inferi are Indo-European.

or goat, *Gungû, Sinîvâlî, Râkâ*, goddesses who preside at procreation and birth, and who were early identified with the phases of the moon,—all indistinct figures, which are still invoked because their names occur in the old formulæ, though they no longer mean anything of any account for the religious sentiment. Expressions indicative of the gods in general also became at length proper names of certain classes of divine beings, such as the *Viçvedevas*, properly "all the gods,"[1] and the *Vasus*, the bright ones, of whom Indra or Agni is the chief. We shall have a better opportunity hereafter of considering a few of the more essential conceptions.

Among this crowd of deities,—of which there is often mention of thirty-three, or three times eleven,[2] once of three thousand three hundred and thirty-nine;[3] in the Atharva-Veda this last number is still further increased, the Gandharvas alone amounting to six thousand three hundred and thirty-three,[4]—there are some which cut a greater figure than the rest, but there is, properly speaking, no hierarchy. There is an interminable variety of ranks, and a confusing interchange of characters. This, to a certain extent, is a feature common to every religion depending directly on the myth. Myths are, in fact, formed independently of one another; they regard the same object in different aspects, and among different objects they seize the same relations. As they radiate from divers centres, they mutually interpenetrate each other and issue of course in a certain syncretism. If Greece, for example, had transmitted to us her ancient liturgies, we would, we may be sure, have found in them a very different state of things from the beautiful order which has been introduced by the light and profane hand of the muse on the classic Olympus. But in the Hymns

[1] We know that the most general name for the deity, *deva*, to which the Latin *deus* corresponds, signifies properly bright-shining or luminous.

[2] Ṛig-Veda, i. 45, 2; 139, 11. There are 35: Ṛig-Veda, x. 55, 3.

[3] Ṛig-Veda, iii. 9, 9.

[4] Âtharva-Veda, xi. 5, 2.

there is more than a simple want of classification. Not only "are there," as is somewhere remarked,[1] among these gods, who rule one another and are begotten from one another, "neither great nor small, neither old nor young, all being equally great," but the supreme sovereignty belongs to several, and we find at one time absolute supremacy, at another the most express subordination assigned to the same god. Indra and all the gods are subject to Varuṇa, and Varuṇa and all the gods are subject to Indra. There are kindred assertions made of Agni, Soma, Vishṇu, Sûrya, Savitṛi, &c.[2] It is somewhat difficult to arrive at an accurate conception of the mode of thought and feeling which these contradictions imply. They are no mere exaggerated expressions uttered in the fervour of prayer, for these would not have been collected and preserved in such numbers; neither does it seem possible to refer them to differences of epoch or diversities of worship. They form, in truth, one of the fundamental traits of the Vedic theology. As soon as a new god is evoked, all the rest suffer eclipse before him; he attracts every attribute to himself; he is the God; and the notion, at one time monotheistic, at another pantheistic, which is found in the latent state at the basis of every form of polytheism, comes in this way, like a sort of movable quantity, to be ascribed indiscriminately to the different personalities furnished by the myth. Another process by which this vague sense of the want of unity is relieved is by identifying one god with several others. There is, perhaps, not a single figure of note which has not given occasion to some such fusion. It is thus that Indra is in turn identified with Bṛihaspati, Agni, and Varuṇa; that Agni is said to be Varuṇa, Mitra, Aryaman, Rudra, Vishṇu, Savitṛi, Pûshan.[3] There is none, up to the formula so frequent in the Brâhmaṇas, "Agni is all the gods," which we do not meet with already in the

[1] Ṛig-Veda, viii. 30, 1. The contrary of this is said Ṛig-Veda, i. 27, 13.

[2] Ṛig-Veda, v. 69, 4; i. 101, 3; iii. 9, 9; ix. 96, 5; 102, 5; i. 156, 4; viii. 101, 12; ii. 38, 9.

[3] See a selection of passages in Muir's Sanskrit Texts, t. v. p. 219.

Hymns.[1] Doubtless this superior insight into the divine nature is not to be met with to the same extent in all the Vedic poets; with many of them, all that is said to their gods amounts to this, "Here is butter; give us cows;" but it exists in many of them, and not a few had the power of expressing it in language that we cannot but admire.

Thus the myth here is no more than a subordinate element, the mere substratum for a higher reality. It tends to return to what it originally was—a mere symbol. Its most definite features lose their sharpness, or continue to survive only in isolated allusions and ready-made phrases. In a developed and concrete form it becomes embarrassing, whether when it offers a conception of the gods which looks mean, gross, or even loathsome, or when it simply represents them in an aspect too human, too epic, and in a sense too familiar for the religious consciousness, now grown more exacting. The authors of the Hymns have thus discarded, or at least left in the shade, a great number of legends which existed previously, those, for example, which referred to the identification of Soma with the moon,[2] what was fabled of the families of the gods, of the birth of Indra, of his parricide, &c.[3] In this way a long list could be drawn up of what might be called the reticences of the Veda. In this connection it is particularly interesting to see how they have treated the myths which relate the manifold intermarrying that forms the basis of all mythologies, the union of a male divinity with a female being, conceived almost always as irregular, and very often incestuous. This union lies no less at the basis of a great number of representations in the Veda. All the gods there are conceived as begetters of offspring, males or

[1] With a slight variation, Ṛig-Veda, v. 3, 1.

[2] The myth which places the ambrosia in the moon appears to be Indo-European. Soma is identified with the moon, Ṛig-Veda, x. 85, 2–5. It is also as lunar god that he is the husband of Sûryâ, the daughter of Savitṛi, the sun conceived as a feminine deity, ib. 9, and that he presides over menstruation, ib. 41.

[3] Ṛig-Veda, iv. 18.

bulls; they are lovers of the *Waters*, the *Mothers*, the *Gnâs* (genetrices), of the *Apsaras*, the Undine class, of *Apyâ Yoshî*, the wife of the waters, who is capricious and wanton, and they are at once their sons and husbands. It would, however, be difficult to extract from the Hymns a chapter on the amours of the gods. With very few exceptions, everything is resolved into brief rapid hints, isolated features, or mere symbols. With the exception of Aurora, the goddesses here have only a featureless physiognomy, and the most conspicuous gods are hardly alluded to in these stories. Once only is Indrâṇi, the wife of Indra, the unchaste Venus;[1] once only is there mention made of the relations of Varuṇa with the Apsaras,[2] of whom, however, he is, agreeably to his origin, the true lover. In this capacity he gives place to the Gandharva, a being purely mythical.[3] In this there certainly appears a touch of moral delicacy, which it would be unjust not to acknowledge. In the dialogue between Yama and his sister Yamî,[4] for instance, the attempted incest is spurned, and yet it is almost certain that originally Yama yielded to the temptation. But when we consider how crude often the language of the Hymns is, we feel justified in affirming that this scruple was not the only one which induced the Vedic minstrels to pass hurriedly over these myths, and that in this matter we must also take into account their aversion to speak of the gods in too definite terms. Sometimes it seems, indeed, that this was the subject which chiefly occupied them; and it is not without a certain annoyance that we see them often striving to render themselves unintelligible, and in a manner to bury their ideas under a confusion of incongruous identifications. In this respect India already appears in the Veda what she has ever since continued to be. In the very first words she utters, we find her aspiring after the vague and the mysterious. It

[1] Ṛig-Veda, x. 86, 6. And the passage, besides, is interpolated.

[2] Ṛig-Veda, vii. 33, 11.

[3] Ṛig-Veda, x. 10, 4; 11, 2; 123, 5.

[4] Ṛig-Veda, x. 10.

would be unjust not to recognise often in this aspiration her very keen sense of the obscurity which hides from us the inner nature of things, and an anxious effort at times to penetrate that obscurity. There are many of those old songs in which, under confusion of thought and imagery, we think we still discern the trouble of a deeply affected soul both seeking truth and lost in adoration. But neither can we disguise from ourselves the fact that in this search for the obscure there is very frequently only affectation and indolence, and that already in the Veda, Hindu thought is profoundly tainted with the malady, of which it will never be able to get rid, of affecting a greater air of mystery the less there is to conceal, of making a parade of symbols which at bottom signify nothing, and of playing with enigmas which are not worth the trouble of trying to unriddle.

If now we try to sum up the theology of these books, we shall find that it hovers between two extremes; on the one side, polytheism pure and simple; on the other side, a species of monotheism, with several titularies, the central figure of which is, if I may say so, always changing places with another. Obviously the speculative spirit of the Vedic poets could not rest here; it was necessary for them to fix this floating idea, and in order to this very little remained for them to do. For a long while they had recognised it vaguely in the persons of Indra, of Agni, of Bṛihaspati, of Savitṛi, and they had had the splendid vision of it in Varuṇa. Instead of attaching it in turn to personalities intimately mixed up with the myth and the public cultus, and which in consequence were incapable of resolution, all they required to do was to transfer it to names more abstract, in order to realise as much of the personal monotheistic idea as India was ever to be able to receive. In this way arose *Prajâpati,* the lord of creatures,[1] *Viçvakarman,* the fabricator of the uni-

[1] Ṛig-Veda, x. 121, 10.

verse,[1] the *Great Asura,* the great spirit,[2] *Svayambhû,* the self-existent being (Atharva-Veda),[3] *Parameshṭhin,* he who occupies the summit (ibid.),[4] all so many names of the God of the gods. At the same time the pantheistic solution was arrived at in another way, by speculation, namely, on the origin of things. Varuṇa and his peers had made the world, that is to say, had organised it. But whence did they obtain the materials to fashion it?[5] To this question there was one reply, which must be very old, since it is Indo-European: The world was fashioned from the body of a primitive being, a giant, *Purusha,* dismembered by the gods.[6] Evidently this reply could not yield a satisfaction that would last; for whence came this Purusha, these gods themselves? and what was there before they were born? Here we ought to quote entire the celebrated hymn in which the self-existent substance, superior to every category and every antinomy, is affirmed as the first term of existence, with a depth of thought and an elevation of language which no school has ever surpassed.[7] In it arose *Kâma,* desire, and that was the first starting-point in the subsequent evolution of being. In this conception, the personal God, or, as we find him afterwards called, *Ka,* Who? is one of the terms, at times, indeed, the first term, in the evolution of the absolute, or *Tat,* This. It was *Hiraṇyagarbha,* "the golden embryo,"[8] who was the primary form. But already analysis shows a tendency to intercalate between him and the ultimate notion a certain number of principles or hypostatical beings, such as the Waters, Heat, Order, Truth, Desire, Time.[9] These two last especially became, in the Atharva-Veda, the centre of a vast system of symbols.[10]—When we consider these

[1] Ṛig-Veda, x. 81; 82.
[2] Ṛig-Veda, x. 177, 1; v. 63, 3, 7.
[3] Atharva-Veda, x. 8, 43, 44.
[4] Atharva-Veda, x. 7, 17; xix. 53, 9.
[5] Ṛig-Veda, x. 81, 2, 4.
[6] Ṛig-Veda, x. 90.
[7] Ṛig-Veda, x. 129.
[8] Ṛig-Veda, x. 121.
[9] Ṛig-Veda, x. 190; 82, 5; 129, 3, 4.
[10] Atharva-Veda, ix. 2; xix. 53, 54. For these personifications and other similar ones see the rich collection of passages in Muir's Sanskrit Texts, t. v. p. 350 *seq.*

speculations on the one hand, and the final doctrines of Persia and Scandinavia on the other, which are at once so definitively fixed and so much in harmony, the absence of everything like an eschatology is something surprising. These men, who meditated so much on the origin of things, appear never to have asked themselves whether they would come to an end, or how; and the Veda says nothing of the last times.

We should like to have some data in regard to the chronology of all these speculations, but on this point everything turns out to be extremely uncertain. From the fact that they are logically afterthoughts, and that, in the formulated state, they are almost all to be met with in one book of the Ṛig-Veda, which is unlike the rest, viz., the tenth, we conclude in a general way that they belong to the last epoch of Vedic poetry. This assumption may be correct, although we are not so satisfied in regard to it as people usually seem to be. The only proofs we have of a positive nature, those deducible from the language, are few and far between; and moreover it is precisely in the case in which the evidence of recency of composition is most complete, in that, viz., of the hymn to Purusha, that we find ourselves face to face with ideas of extreme antiquity. One point, however, may be reckoned certain: these more elevated conceptions have not directly done any injustice to the ancient divinities. Long after the epoch in which the most recent hymns were composed, Agni was still always the guest and brother of men, Indra the god whom they invoked in battle, and Varuṇa the executor of justice, whose fetters they dreaded; and if ever these figures fade away by degrees from the consciousness, it will not be in the presence of Prajâpati. The co-existence of things which seem to us to contradict and exclude each other is exactly the history of India, and that radical formula which occurs even in the Hymns, that "the gods are only a single being under different names,"[1] is one of those which is oftenest

[1] Ṛig-Veda, i. 164, 46; compare viii. 58, 2.

on her lips, and which yet, up to the present time, she has never succeeded in rightly believing.

Before quitting the Hymns, the only matter that remains for examination is the doctrine they teach us in regard to human duty, how they conceive of morality and piety, what sort of cultus they presuppose, and what ideas they attach to the observances of this cultus. The connection between man and the gods is conceived in the Hymns as a very close one. Always and everywhere he feels that he is in their hands, and that all his movements are under their eye. They are masters close at hand, who exact tasks of him, and to whom he owes constant homage. He must be humble, for he is weak and they are strong; he must be sincere towards them, for they cannot be deceived. Nay, he knows that they in turn do not deceive, and that they have a right to require his affection and confidence as a friend, a brother, a father. Without faith (*çraddhâ*), offerings and prayers are vain.[1] These are so many strict obligations due to the gods, on which the Hymns insist in a great variety of passages. They are less explicit, on the other hand, in regard to the duties which man owes to his fellows. In one passage, they praise acts of kindness towards all who are in suffering or in want;[2] in others, sorcery and witchcraft, seduction and adultery, are denounced as criminal;[3] and the last book contains a prayer with an exhortation to concord.[4] But in general it is only indirectly that we are able to estimate this part of their moral system. We must judge of it by the conception which they form of the gods, and, viewed in this connection, it will appear to bear the impress of unmistakable elevation of sentiment. We are not particularly told in what those *dharmans*, those *vratas*, or decrees of the gods, exactly consist, which they have established for the maintenance

[1] Ṛig-Veda, i. 104, 6; 108, 6; ii. 26, 3; x. 151. Indra and Agni in particular are often called father, brother, and friend.

[2] Ṛig-Veda, x. 117.

[3] Ṛig-Veda, vii. 104, 8 *seq.*; iv. 5, 5.

[4] Ṛig-Veda, x. 191; see x. 71, 6, for the curse upon the unfaithful friend.

of *satya* and *ṛita*, truth and order. But how could it be permitted to men to be bad when the gods are good, to be unjust while they are just, and to be deceitful when they never deceive? It is certainly a remarkable feature of the Hymns that they acknowledge no wicked divinities, and no mean and harmful practices. An enemy, indeed, is consigned in them to the divine wrath, but it is with the simple-hearted conviction that this enemy is impious. The few fragments of a different nature which have slipped into the collection[1] serve only to throw into greater relief this feature of the grand Vedic religions. They testify, in fact, that alongside of these there existed others of less purity, which the proud tradition of certain sacerdotal families managed for long to consign to oblivion. Banished by the Kaṇvas, the Bharadvâjas, the Vasishṭhas, the Kuçikas, and others, from their family cultus and that which they celebrated in honour of their kings and chieftains, these religious beliefs continued to subsist in the form of superstitions, and were finally collected in the Atharva-Veda. Some, it is true, are fain to see in them so many corruptions due to a later age. We do not deny that the collection of the Atharva-Veda does in fact contain a great number of passages of recent date, but there is much also of which the language does not differ from that of the Ṛig-Veda; and it involves in our opinion a mistaken judgment of human nature to be unwilling to admit that dissimilar conceptions may subsist together. It is a clear mistake, especially in regard to the mental state of a people with naturalistic religious beliefs, to conceive it possible there should have been an epoch in which it knew nothing of philtres, or incantations, or sorceries, or obscene practices, in which the mind would not be haunted with the fear of malignant spirits, and would not seek, by direct acts of worship, either to appease them or to turn their anger against an enemy. Now, a religion which, like that of the Ṛig-Veda, sees alongside of it practices like these and

[1] For example, Ṛig-Veda, x. 145, 159.

refuses to adopt them, is a moral religion. We must acknowledge, then, that the Hymns give evidence of an exalted and comprehensive morality, and that in striving to be "without reproach before Aditi and the Adityas,"[1] the Vedic minstrels feel the weight of other duties besides those of multiplying offerings to the gods and the punctilious observance of religious ritual, although we must admit also that the observation of these is with them a matter of capital importance, and that their religion is pre-eminently ritualistic. The pious man is by distinction he who makes the soma flow in abundance, and whose hands are always full of butter; while the reprobate man is he who is penurious towards the gods, the worship of whom is man's first duty.[2]

This worship resolves itself into two sets of acts—oblation and prayer. There is as yet no mention either of the devout rehearsal of sacred texts[3] or of vows properly so called, neither of ascetic practices, although the word *tapas*, which is properly heat, is already employed in some passages in the special sense of mortification,[4] this sense having become a common one in the Atharva-Veda; and we hear of the *Muni*, the ecstatic enthusiast, who lets his hair grow and goes quite naked or barely clad in rags of reddish colour (which, by the way, at a later date is the favourite colour with ascetics and also the Buddhist monks). He is considered to hold intimate communion with the gods, and there is a hymn in which the sun is celebrated under the form of a Muni.[5] But the true service of the gods is sacrifice accompanied with invocations. These invocations we still possess in part; the great majority of the Hymns are nothing else, and we have already stated in what respect the liturgy we find in them differs from that which was adopted at a later period, and which remains in use to this day. As for the sacrifice itself, we know few particulars

[1] Ṛig-Veda, i. 24, 15.

[2] Ṛig-Veda, viii. 31.

[3] On the contrary, a great value is attached to the "novelty" of the Hymns. There were, however, formulæ and *solemnia verba*: Ṛig-Veda, i. 164, 39; x. 114, 8; vii. 101, 1; ix. 33, 3; 50, 2; &c.

[4] Ṛig-Veda, x. 154, 2; 169, 2.

[5] Ṛig-Veda, viii. 17, 14; x. 136.

of the manner in which it was celebrated. Probably the ceremonial was much akin to that of the succeeding age, for a certain number of the observances prescribed in the books of ritual, and these at times very precise, appear to be Indo-Iranian. Of these there were great varieties, from the simple offering up to the great religious festivals. These last were very complicated observances; they required immense preparations and a numerous array of priests, singers, and officers at their celebration. The offerings were thrown into the fire, which bore them to heaven, to the gods. They consisted of melted butter, curdled milk, rice, soups, and cakes, and soma mixed with water or milk. This last kind of offering the gods, Indra in particular, were reputed to come and drink from a vat placed on a litter of grass before the fire. In the case of libations at least, the act of oblation was repeated thrice a day, at the three *savanas* of the morning, mid-day, and evening. Victims were also sacrificed, notably the horse, the sacrifice of which, the *Açvamedha,* is described at length.[1] The offering of the horse was preceded by that of a goat sacrificed to Pûshan.[2] A goat as a funeral victim was also consumed on the funeral-pile along with the carcase of the dead; it was the portion of Agni, who was thought to feast on it and then wrap the body of the dead in sacred flames that were painless.[3] They sacrificed besides to Indra and Agni bulls, buffaloes, cows, and rams.[4] In one passage Pûshan has a hundred buffaloes roasted for Indra, for whom Agni again roasts as many as three hundred.[5]

But if we possess only a very imperfect knowledge of the acts of sacrifice, we know better what ideas were attached to it. In the grossest sense, sacrifice is a mere bargain. Man needs things which the god possesses, such

[1] Ṛig-Veda, i. 162; 163, 12, 13.

[2] Ṛig-Veda, i. 162, 2, 3.

[3] Ṛig-Veda, x. 16, 4.

[4] Ṛig-Veda, v. 27, 5; x. 86, 14; 91, 14. Cows were slaughtered at nuptial ceremonies: Ṛig-Veda, x. 85, 13.

[5] Ṛig-Veda, vi. 17, 11; v. 29, 7; i. 116, 16, it is said that Ṛijrâçva sacrificed 100 rams to Vṛikî, the She-wolf.

as rain, light, warmth, and health, while the god is hungry and seeks offerings from man: there is giving and receiving on both sides.[1] Though nowhere expressly formulated, this idea nevertheless comes out in a great variety of confessions and certain unaffected materialistic touches.[2] To the religious sense, sacrifice is an act of affection and gratitude towards the gods, through which man renders thanks to them for their benefits, and hopes to obtain others in the future, either in this life or after death. But it is in no respect a mere act of oblation. To sacrifice is, over and above that, to stir up, actually to beget, two divinities of the first rank, the two principles of life *par excellence*, Agni and Soma. In the consciousness of the believer sacrifice then is a highly complex act; but before everything else it is a mystery, a direct interference with the phenomena of nature and the condition even of the normal course of things. Should it cease for an instant to be offered, the gods would cease to send us rain, to bring back at the appointed hour Aurora and the sun, to raise and ripen our harvests, because they would no longer incline to do so, and also, as is surmised sometimes, because they could not any longer do so.[3] And as it is to-day,

[1] The liturgical formulæ are at times very clear in this respect; for example, Taitt. Saṃh., vi. 4, 5, 6: "Does he wish to do harm (to an enemy)? Let him say (to Sûrya): Strike such an one; afterwards will I pay thee the offering. And (Sûrya) desiring to obtain the offering, strikes him." See, besides, this formula addressed to the libation-divider: "When filled, O divider! fly yonder; when well filled, fly back to us! As at a stipulated price, let us exchange force and vigour, O Indra! Give me, and I shall give thee; bring me, and I shall bring thee."—Taitt. Saṃh., i. 8, 4, 1.

[2] See, for example, the many passages where mention is made of the appetite of Indra, of the pleasure he has in filling his belly: Ṛig-Veda, ii. 11, 11; viii. 4, 10; 77, 4; 78, 7; x. 86, 13–15. The idea of the purely spiritual life of the gods, in particular that they neither eat nor drink (see Chândogya Up., iii. 6, 1, *seq.*), is foreign to the Hymns.

[3] The idea that it is from the offering the gods derive their strength recurs at every step in the Hymns: Ṛig-Veda, ii. 15, 2; x. 52, 5; 6, 7; 121, 7, &c. In the Atharva-Veda, xi. 7, the *Ucchishṭa*, the residue of the offering (nothing of the offering ought to be lost, and the priest alone has the right to eat what remains), is declared the first principle of all things. See Bhagavad-Gîtâ, iii. 11–16: "Cause by sacrifice the gods to prosper, and the gods will make you prosper. . . . From nourishment come beings, from rain nourishment, from sacrifice rain. . . . He who does not contribute some-

so it was yesterday, and so consequently was it as far back as the first of the days. Hence arose the myths which represent sacrifice as the first act in the cosmogony. It was by sacrifice—it is not said to whom—that the gods delivered the world from chaos, just as it is by sacrifice that man prevents it from lapsing back into it; and the dismemberment of the primeval giant, Purusha, whose skull was fabled to form the heavens and his limbs the earth, came to be regarded in India as the first act of sacrifice.[1] What is more, the gods being inseparable from the world, their existence must have been preceded by sacrifice; hence the singular myth which represents the Supreme Being as sacrificing himself in order to give birth to all other existences.[2] Placed thus at the origin of all things, and considered all along as the vital point in all the functions of nature, sacrifice became the centre of a vast system of symbols. The lightning and the sun are the sacred flame of it, the thunder is the hymn, the rains and rivers are the libations, the gods and the celestial apparitions are the priests, and so conversely. The ceremonial act itself, with its fine arrangement, is identified with the *ṛita*, the order of the world; and the altar is regarded as the womb of the ṛita, the mystic heaven from which Varuṇa and the great gods keep watch over the universe. All these notions, and many more besides, are mingled so

what to make this wheel turn is unworthy to live." It is said also in Manu, iii. 75, 76, "By sacrifice the house-master sustains this movable and immovable world. Cast into the fire, the offering goes into the sun; from the sun is produced the rain; from the rain the nourishment; from the latter the creatures are produced." The same passage occurs again in Maitri Up., vi. 37. The allegorical imagery, so common in the literature from the Upanishads onwards, in which universal production and life are likened to a series of sacrifices or libations, is connected with the same order of ideas. Chând. Up., iii. 16, 17; v. 4–8; Bṛih. Ar. Up., vi. 2, 9–14; vi. 4, 3. There is here a sort of second religion, a religion of *opus operatum*, a sort of ritualistic pantheism, in which the divine personalities fill only a subordinate part, and which from the era of the Hymns had deeply affected the consciousness. For information in regard to this side of the religious beliefs of the Veda, we would particularly refer to A. Bergaigne's work, already quoted, "La Religion Védique d'après les Hymnes du Ṛig-Véda."

[1] Ṛig-Veda, x. 90, 130.

[2] Ṛig-Veda, x. 81.

much in the Hymns, play so much one into another, that it is often impossible to tell in what sense we must accept the expressions which stand for them. And as it is with the rite, so it is with the invocation, the prescribed formula, and prayer. It is the expression which gives precision to the act, determines the object of it, and assigns to it in some sort its direction. It is, or in it lies, the hidden energy which gives it efficacy. This energy is the *brahman*, properly power of growth, invigoration, a word famous before every other, and the history of which is in a sense that even of Hindu theology. In the Hymns brahman is very often the name for prayer, and in this case it may take the plural, but it never loses its original meaning of force, of subtle and, in a sense, magical energy. Being the soul of sacrifice, the notion which is formed of it has naturally grown with that of sacrifice itself. It is the work of the gods; it is by it that they act; it is by it also that they are born and that the world has been formed.[1] What strikes us in these theories quite as much as the notions themselves is the prodigious elaboration which they have undergone, and that from the most remote antiquity; for here we cannot doubt that the ideas presented belong to the same date as that of the oldest hymns, to such a degree do they pervade all parts of the collection. These alone are sufficient to prove, if necessary, how profoundly sacerdotal this poetry is, and they ought to have suggested reflections to those who have affected to see in it only the work of primitive shepherds celebrating the praises of their gods as they lead their flocks to the pasture.

[1] Ṛig-Veda, x. 130; Atharva-Veda, xi. 5, 5; see Ṛig-Veda, vi. 51, 8, and the myths of Vâc and Brahmaṇaspati. Prayer was begotten in heaven. Ṛig-Veda, iii. 39, 2.

II.

BRAHMANISM.

I. RITUAL.

Gradual extension and general character of the religion of the Atharva-Veda, the Yajur-Veda and the Brâhmaṇas.—Changes introduced into the pantheon.—Still greater changes in the spirit and institutions.—The Brahman a member of a caste.—Formation of a sacred language and literature.—The Brahmacarya and the Brahmanical schools.—Ritualism and formalism : the rites come to the foreground and the gods retire into the shade.—Sketch of the cultus according to the Brâhmaṇas and the Sûtras.—The Gṛihya ritual : the ancient Smṛiti and the Dharma.—The Çrauta ritual : ishṭi and somayâga.—Aristocratic, expensive, and bloody character of this worship : animal sacrifice ; human sacrifice ; the anumaraṇa, or the suicide of the widow.—The authorised religion of the Brahmans recognised neither images nor sanctuaries.—Propagated, its exclusive spirit notwithstanding, among foreign races, in the Dekhan, and as far as the Sunda Islands : the Veda at Bali.

THE geographical region of the Hymns extends from the valley of Cabul to the banks of the Ganges, and perhaps beyond ; but the true country of their birth, that in regard to which they supply the most data, is the Punjâb.[1] In the age that follows, which we have now reached, we see the religions of the Veda advancing eastward, and gradually taking possession of the vast and fertile plains of Hindustan. From the epoch of the Brâhmaṇas their centre is no longer in the basin of the Indus, the tribes of which

[1] Its limits are these : On the west the Kubhâ (Ṛig-Veda, v. 53, 9 ; x. 75, 6), the Κωφήν of the Greeks, the river Cabul and its affluents, and the Gandhâris (Ṛig-Veda, i. 126, 7), a tribe of the valley ; the Rasâ, which corresponds with the Zend name of the Jaxartes, appears to be mythical in the Rig-Veda (Aufrecht, Morgenl. Gesellsch., xiii. 498). On

are, on the contrary, regarded with mistrust;[1] but on the Sarasvatî, in the Doâb, between the Jumna and the Ganges, and even farther east, on the Gomati and the Gogra. On the east and south they came into contact with the tribes which inhabit the shores of the Eastern Sea and the other side of the Vindhya mountains.[2] This change of place very considerably affected their organisation. The order of the priesthood asserted itself more rigorously. An event, besides, was not long in occurring which had a decisive effect on their destiny: the language of the old Hymns gradually ceased to be understood. From the epoch of the Brâhmaṇas it had become unintelligible to the multitude, and even obscure to the priests.[3] There arose thus a sacred language, and, in a narrow sense, sacred texts, to which it became more and more difficult, and finally impossible, to make any addition. From this moment these religions became, up to a certain point, stereotyped. They will doubtless continue to be still susceptible of modification in many respects, and especially of complication; but in the main they will be forced henceforth to subsist on their original capital; they will no longer be able to adapt themselves to great innovations; and the inevitable changes which time will bring will take place

the east, the Sarayu (Ṛig-Veda, iv. 30, 18; v. 53, 9), the modern Gogra, and the tribe of the Kîkatas (Ṛig-Veda, iii. 53, 14) in Bihâr. The authors of the Hymns had a certain acquaintance with the sea. For the geography of the Vedas, consult Vivien de Saint Martin (Etude sur la Géographie du Véda, 1859), Lassen Indische Alterthumskunde, i. 643 *seq.*, 2d ed., 1867), A. Ludwig (Die Nachrichten des Rig- und Atharva-Veda über Geographie, Geschichte, Verfassung des alten Indien, 1878), H. Zimmer (Altindisches Leben; die Cultur der Vedischen Aryer nach den Saṃhitâ dargestellt, 1879, ch. i.).

[1] Çatap. Br., ix. 3, 1, 18.

[2] Athar.-Veda, v. 22, 14; Aitar. Br., vii. 18, 2; viii. 22, 1.

[3] From this date we meet with prescriptions for the maintenance of the purity of the language among the Brahmans: Çatap. Br., iii. 2, 1, 24. The language of the Brâhmaṇas is already pretty much, indeed, the classical Sanscrit, and it differs from that of the Hymns more than the Latin of Lucretius does from that of the Twelve Tables. That the authors of these treatises only imperfectly understand these old hymns is obvious at every step, from their exegesis even, and their attempts at etymology. We must not, however, insist too much on this last argument; there is at bottom more fancifulness than real ignorance in these interpretations.

more and more beyond their pale, and assume, in consequence, an attitude opposed to them.

And, in fact, notwithstanding numerous modifications in detail, the theology of the Atharva-Veda, the Yajur-Veda, and the Brâhmaṇas is not at bottom very different from that of the Hymns. The pantheon is enlarged, it is true, by a certain number of subordinate figures. *Soma-Candramas*, the moon, the *Nakshatras*, or constellations,[1] the *Chandas*, or Vedic metres,[2] appear for the first time, or else proceed to play a more active part in the drama. At the same time, the door has been opened wide for the admission of a host of allegorical personifications, spirits, demons, and goblins of every shape and genealogy,[3] which, though unknown to the Hymns, are not, therefore, necessarily all of new creation; while, on the other hand, certain old mythic representations, which we find making a great figure in the Ṛig-Veda, show signs of retiring. Still the circle of the great divinities remains much the same, although we observe among them a more systematic organisation, and that not a few of them are in process of transformation. Prajâpati is now their unchallenged head, and the conception of a triad in Agni, Vâyu, Sûrya, the fire, the air, and the sun, as summing up the divine energies—a conception which we shall come upon again as we proceed—asserts itself more frequently. At the same time, the formalism which prevails in these writings tends to a multiplying of the number of the gods through the per-

[1] See A. Weber, Die Vedischen Nachrichten von den Naxatra, 2d part, in the Memoirs of the Academy of Berlin for 1861, p. 267 *seq.*

[2] See, among others, the beautiful myth of Gâyatrî going in the form of a falcon to ravish the Soma from the third heaven: Taitt. Saṃh., vi. 1, 6, 1–5; Taitt. Br., iii. 2, 1, 1; Aitar. Br., iii. 25–28. Compare Taitt. Saṃh., ii. 4, 3, 1. A. Weber has collected the most of the speculations of the Brâhmaṇas in reference to the Chandas in his memoir, Vedische Angaben über Metrik. in Ind. Stud., viii.

[3] See a lengthened enumeration of the spirits and goblins in Ath.-Veda, viii. 6, and the great number of exorcisms in relation to diseases considered as possessions; as, for instance, Ath.-Veda, ix. 8; in particular, in reference to Yakshma and Takman (see V. Grohmann, Mediciniscbes aus dem Atharva-Veda, in Ind. Stud., ix. p. 381 *seq.*). Compare also the prayer in deprecation of the demons which attack infancy in Pâraskara Gr. S., i. 16, 23, 24.

sonification of their attributes. Thus Agni Vratapati is not quite the same person as Agni Annapati, Agni Annavat, Agni Annâda; and these, in their turn, differ from Agni Kâma, Agni Kshâmavat, Agni Yavishṭha, &c. Soma is decisively confounded with the moon; he is the husband of the Nakshatras, the constellations of the lunar zodiac.[1] Yama is still always the king of the Pitṛis, but he is no longer so closely identified with the blessed life: the pious man hopes to go to *svarga*, which is rather the heaven of Indra and of the gods in general.[2] As for the wicked man, he will go into hell, where tortures, which are described at length, await him; or else he will be born again in some wretched state of being,—metempsychosis appearing in this way under the form of an expiation.[3] Asura, the old name of the divine powers, is henceforth applied only in a bad sense. The Asuras are now the demons,[4] and their struggle with the gods in general, which is one of the commonplaces of the Brâhmaṇas, only very remotely reminds us of the celestial battles celebrated in the Hymns. Aditi is most frequently identified with the Earth. Aditya is a name for the sun, and the Adityas, who begin now to be fixed at twelve, are once for all solar impersonations. Varuṇa passes into the status of a god of night, who is both hostile and cruel, and his empire is already confounded with that of the

[1] Taitt. Saṃh., ii. 3, 5, 1–3; compare ii. 5, 6, 4. In the Ṛig-Veda he is the husband of Sûryâ, x. 35, 9. Compare Ait. Br., iv. 7, 1.

[2] The recompense ordinarily guaranteed to sacrifice in the Brâhmaṇas is the enjoyment of the *svarga*, heaven, or the *salokatâ*, community of abode with such or such a god. The memory of the ancient sojourn of the blessed with Yama is not, however, completely forgotten. See the description of his palace, Mahâbhârata, ii. 311 *seq.* There are in the Upanishads very detailed descriptive accounts of the different worlds of the blessed: Bṛihadâr. Up., iv. 3, 31; Taitt. Up., ii. 8, and especially Kaushît. Up., i. 3–5.

[3] See A. Weber, Eine Legende des Çatapatha-Brâhmaṇa über die strafende Vergeltung nach dem Tode, in the Zeitsch. der Deutsch. Morgenl. Gesellsch., t. ix. p. 237. The same legend, according to the Jaiminîya-Brâhmaṇa, has been published by A. C. Burnell, A Legend from the Talavakâra Brâhmaṇa of the Sâma-Veda, Mangalore, 1878.

[4] Taitt. Saṃh, i. 5, 9, 2; Ait. Br., iv. 5, 1, represent them as powers of darkness or night.

Waters.[1] The gods in general tend to assume the place and form they will retain in the epic poetry. These specialisations, however, which, in an age more given to criticism than to poetry, are the necessary consequence of the vagueness of the conceptions that prevailed before, and which had all, besides, links of connection with the Hymns, are far from being steadily maintained, and the contrary tendency in the form of an unbridled syncretism is quite as common in these writings. The most serious novelty of this class (one which we shall come upon again as we proceed) appears in certain legends and fragments relegated especially to the Yajur-Veda, and which presuppose that the religion of Çiva is already in an advanced stage of development.

But if the theology of the religions of the Veda has not changed much, great changes, on the other hand, have taken place in their organisation, and even in their spirit. We have already insisted on the sacerdotal character of the Hymns; it is clear that from their time the offices of the priesthood constituted distinct professions, and that they were hereditary, although we are not able to say to what extent the heredity was fixed.[2] At the time of which we are now speaking, however, there is in this matter no longer room for doubt. The Brahman, the man devoted to prayer and the science of theology, is a member of a caste.[3] By means of a secret virtue which is transmissible only through the blood, he alone is qualified to celebrate the

1. Ath.-Veda, xiii. 3, 13; vii. 83, 1; Taitt. Saṃh., ii. 1, 7, 3; ii. 1, 9, 3; iii. 4, 5, 1; vi. 6, 3, 1–4; Taitt. Br., i. 6, 5, 6; Çâṅkhây. Br. in the Ind. Stud., ix. 358.

2. See J. Muir, On the Relations of the Priests to the other Classes of Indian Society in the Vedic Age, in the Journal of the Royal Asiatic Society, new series, vol. ii.; H. Kern, Indische Theorieen over de Standenverdeeling, 1871; and H. Zimmer, Altindisches Leben, p. 194 *seq.*; only this author, like the majority of German scholars, looks at the subject a little too much through the medium of the modern ideas of the Culturkampf.

3. See A. Weber, Collectanea über die Kastenverhältnisse in den Brâhmaṇa und den Sûtra, in Ind. Stud., t. x. The theory of the four castes, Brahmans, Kshatriyas, Vaiçyas, and Çûdras, who were brought forth respectively from the mouth, the arms, the thighs, and the feet of Brahmâ, is already formulated in the hymn of the Purusha, Ṛig-Veda, x. 90, 11, 12.

rites of religion with effect, and there are very few acts connected with worship which he has not appropriated the right to perform.✓ He for whom he officiates stands by in a more or less passive attitude, incapable in general of understanding what is said and done in his presence and for his benefit. Nay, the part the Brahman himself performs is reduced to a minimum; he no longer prays, he only says prayers. In order to vitalise by the word a set of ceremonies prescribed beforehand, he has only certain formulæ, all ready-made, to work with. Inspiration, the outburst of individual enthusiasm, has no more a place in the cultus he presides over, and the living springs of pious devotion seem all dried up. The great and only business now is to know the *brahman*,—that is to say, the sacred texts, their use, and the secret exegesis of them as handed down by tradition; to know the rites of religion with their hidden and mystic meanings.[1] The subjects of this knowledge, the rites, *i.e.*, as well as the texts, are conceived of as pre-existent, and represented at one time as of eternal ordination, at another as the institution of Prajâpati. Of those who, whether men or gods, make use of them for the first time, it is said that they "*see*" them;[2] revelation being thus conceived of not as a fact which takes place all at once, but as a series of successive facts. There were therefore no obstacles *a priori* to the introduction of new rites, and, in fact, the ceremonial, as well as the speculations of which it was the subject, continued to expand and grow in complexity, until the day when, as a new and opposite current set in, it reached a limit beyond which it could only become poorer and weaker instead of richer.

[1] Every indication in the Brâhmaṇas is invariably followed by the phrase, "Such or such a benefit will accrue to him who knows this." These secrets of knowledge are often nothing more than fantastical etymologies, for "the gods love the inscrutable," Aitar. Br., iii. 33, 6; Gopatha. Br., i. 1, &c.

[2] Hence the etymology which derives from the root *dṛiç*, to see, the word *ṛishi*. This, from the general signification of poet or inspired singer, which it has in the Hymns, came at length to assume the special sense of prophet or seer of a revealed text. This etymology is older than Yâska, who refers to it, Nirukta, ii. 11.

Up to a certain point this was true also of the liturgy; but in this case the fundamental changes which took place in the language interposed a barrier to the introduction of innovations at any earlier period. Amongst the causes which contributed to arrest the development of these religions and to reduce them to that form which we now designate by the name of Brahmanism, one of the most powerful was thus a change of language.[1]

To attain this complex science it became necessary there should be special instruction in it; and, in fact, the education of the brahman, the *brahmacarya*, is from that moment organised.[2] Instruction is no longer merely concerned with domestic traditions. The student travels to a distance, and attaches himself to now one, now another teacher of renown;[3] and the itinerant habits thus produced must have contributed not a little to imbue the Brahmans with the feeling that they formed a class by themselves, in the midst of the small tribes of people into which Aryan India was at the time divided. This apprenticeship, which was at the same time a noviciate in morals, was a very protracted one, for "science," they used to say, "is infinite."[4] To this discipline it is said Indra himself submitted for one hundred years under Prajâpati.[5] As it was not possible for all to take up every department of study, each of the several classes of priests had its separate discipline. In these schools, or *parishads*, as they were called, the Vedic collections originated and were formed—the Sâma-Veda, intended for the singers, and the Yajur-Veda, more especially adapted to the *adhvaryus*, or offerers of sacrifice, while the Ṛig-Veda and Atharva-

1 The Hindu theories on the origin, inspiration, and authority of the Veda are collected and discussed in vol. iii. of Original Sanskrit Texts by J. Muir, 2d ed., 1868. Ṛig-Veda, x. 90, 9, the ṛics, the sâmans, the chandas, and the yajus are produced from the sacrifice of Purusha.

2 See Atharva-Veda, xi. 5, in which the Sun organising the world under the direction of the supreme deity is described as a Brahmacârin under the orders of the Acârya.

3 Bṛihadâraṇyaka Up., iii. 7.

4 See the legend of Bharadvâja, Taitt. Br., iii. 10, 11, 3–5.

5 Chândogya Up., viii. 11, 3.

Veda, though compiled for less specific purposes, were indispensable, especially for those priests whose business it was to invoke the deity and to superintend the religious rites, the *hotṛis* and the *brahman*. Hence, finally and in particular, arose the Brâhmaṇas, which were, in their turn also, at a later date, to be accepted as oracles of revelation.

These last writings have preserved for us a faithful picture of the spirit which prevailed in these schools—a spirit which, it must be confessed, was singularly formal and destitute of all elevation of sentiment. There was no end of discussion, and the polemic was at times of a very lively sort; but all this activity was spent in trifles and subtleties. Of theology, properly speaking, there is very little indication in the Brâhmaṇas; no attempt is there made to put together anything of a nature the least akin to dogmatic orthodoxy. None of these men, constantly busied as they were with the service of the gods, appear to have surmised that there could be in regard to these gods authorised and unauthorised opinions; it would seem at times as if they themselves hardly believed in the existence of their deities, so mean and fantastic appear the comparisons which they apply to them; as, for instance, when they identify Vishṇu with the sacrifice, or Prajâpati, the supreme god, with the year.[1] Alongside of this extravagant symbolism there is also a strong Euhemerist tendency. It would in general be in vain to seek in the ritual portion of these writings that elevation and delicacy of religious feeling which we find in the Hymns. Instead of this, there is a dull lumbering display of a sort of professional cynicism. Sometimes the gods are represented as beings indifferent to every moral distinction, and we find stories unscrupulously related of them which are most indelicate, such as the

[1] Taitt. Saṃh., i. 7, 4, 4; Taitt. Br., i. 6, 2, 2, &c.; Aitar. Br., i. 1, 14. See, moreover, the confession that the notion of Prajâpati is obscure and confused, Taitt. Br., i. 3, 4, 4; i. 3, 8, 5; i. 8, 5, 6; and such expressions as "Agni is all the gods," "The Waters are all the gods." Taitt. Saṃh., ii. 6, 8, 3; Taitt. Br., iii. 2, 4, 3.

incest in many ways of Prajâpati with his daughter, and the frauds indulged in by Indra to the damage of his enemies, &c.[1] Religious rites are also prostituted to the achievement of criminal schemes; and we meet with cool directions to explain how, by the aid of certain manipulations, the priest may be able to compass the destruction of him who actually employs him and pays him,[2] although in other passages, indeed, this prostitution is expressly forbidden, and that under pain even of death.[3] We should go too far, however, if we were to conclude at once from this the fact of a wide-spread and increasing degradation of general mind and conscience. In reality, the general mind was not so degraded as it might at first seem, as we shall be able to satisfy ourselves when we come to examine the speculative doctrines which were discussed in some at least of these schools; while, on the other hand, we see from the rich collection of moral precepts which this literature, in spite of its general aridity, embraces, as well as from the more definite ideas of retributive justice after death which are here insisted on, that the moral code, instead of becoming poorer, had, on the contrary, become more precise and comprehensive. In judging of the Brâhmaṇas, we must make every allowance for that feebleness of style which is so marked a feature of them, as well as for the awkwardness natural to prose in so crude a state, in any attempt to express shades of thought of any delicacy; and, above all, we must always bear in mind their esoteric and strictly professional character.

The chief, and indeed the only, subject of these books is the cultus. Here the rites of religion are the real deities,

[1] Bṛihadâr Up., i. 3, 1–4. The same story with an expression of censure, Çatap. Br., i. 7, 4, 1–4; Aitar. Br., iii. 33, 1–3. In the Ṛig-Veda the myth is ascribed to no one by name, x. 61, 4–7; 31, 6–10.

[2] Taitt. Saṃh., i. 6, 10, 4; Aitar. Br., i. 25, 13; ii. 32, 4; iii. 3, 2–9; iii. 7, 8–10, &c. To provide against such a misdemeanour a particular ceremony has been instituted called the Tânûnaptra, by which all who take part in a sacrifice make themselves mutually responsible, Taitt. Saṃh., i. 2, 10, 2, and vi. 2, 2, 1–4; Aitar. Br., i. 24, 4–8.

[3] Aitar. Br., ii. 21, 2; ii. 28, 3; iii. 7, 7.

or at any rate they constitute together a sort of independent and superior power, before which the divine personalities disappear, and which almost holds the place allotted to destiny in other systems. The ancient belief, which is already prominent in the Hymns, that sacrifice conditionates the regular course of things, is met with here in the rank of a commonplace, and is at times accompanied with incredible details. If the gods are immortal, if they have ascended to heaven, if they have taken it by conquest over their seniors, the Asuras, it is because at the decisive moment they "saw" such and such a mantra or such and such a ritual combination.[1] Certain insignificant ceremonial arrangements are the reasons why the sun rises in the east and sets in the opposite quarter, why rivers flow in one direction rather than another, why the prevailing wind blows from the north-west, and why harvests ripen earlier in the south.[2] There are reasons quite similar to explain why trees when pruned shoot again from their stem, why animals are provided with bones, why the skull has eight or nine sutures, why people expose girls while they rear up boys, why women prefer men of a cheerful temper, &c.,[3] though it is not always easy to say how much pleasantry may lurk in such singular opinions. The efficacy of the rite, whether for good or for evil, is of course essentially due to magic, which resides in the rite itself. There is also much more stress laid on the accurate performance of these observances, and the qualification of the priest than the moral character of the believer. The least error in form may prove fatal, and it is only in a small number of cases that the act is pronounced valid in spite of the incapacity of the officiating priest;[4] while only two things are required of the believer—that he be persuaded of the efficacy of the

[1] Taitt. Saṃh., vi. 3, 10, 2; vi. 2, 5, 3, 4; vii. 4, 2, 1; i. 5, 9, 2, 3; Aitar. Br., ii. 1, 1, &c.

[2] Aitar. Br., 1, 7, 6–12.

[3] Taitt. Saṃh., ii. 5, 1, 4; vi. 3, 3, 3; see Atharva-Veda, viii. 10, 18; Taitt. Saṃh., vi. 1, 7, 1; Taitt. Br., iii. 2, 7, 3, 4; Taitt. Saṃh., vi. 2, 1, 4; vi. 5, 10, 3; vi. 1, 6, 6.

[4] Aitar. Br., ii. 2, 18; iii. 11, 4–16; i. 16, 40; ii. 17, 6.

rite, and that he be in a state of legal purity. It is only at a later period, in the Sûtras, that the exactly formulated doctrine appears, that in order to obtain the fruit of the sacrifice — the fruit *par excellence*, it is to be remarked, which is admission to heaven—it is necessary to practise in addition the moral virtues.[1]

It would be out of the question to attempt to describe here, even in quite a summary way, this cultus, which, as it has been transmitted in the Brâhmaṇas, and in the more recent manuals entitled *Sûtras*,[2] forms a body of ritual pro-

[1] See, for example, the classification of sins and virtues, Apastamba Dharma-S., i. 20, 1; i. 23, 6. Compare Gautama, viii. 22–25.

[2] These Sûtras are of two sorts: 1. *Kalpa-* or *Çrauta-Sûtras*, "which treat of ritual, of the ritual instituted by the Çruti, by the Veda;" these busy themselves exclusively with the ceremonies described in the Brâhmaṇas, with which they are closely connected. 2. *Smârta-Sûtras*, "which treat of the observances established by the Smṛiti, viz., tradition." These divide themselves into *Gṛihya-Sûtras*, "Sûtras regulating domestic ritual," and into *Dharma-Sûtras*, "Sûtras in relation to civil right and custom." Of this literature there are published:

1. Çrauta-Sûtras, those of Açvalâyana (Ṛig-Veda), the text and commentary in the Bibliotheca Indica; those of Lâṭyâyana (Sâma-Veda), the text and commentary, ibid.; those of Kâtyâyana (the White Yajus), in the edition of the White Yajus by A. Weber; the Vaitâna-Sûtra (Atharva-Veda), text and German translation by R. Garbe, 1878. Max Müller has translated and commented on the final section of the Çrauta-Sûtras of Apastamba (the Black Yajus) in the Zeitsch. d. Deutsch. Morgenl. Gesellsch., t. ix. p. 43, and R. Garbe has done the same work for the fifteenth section, ibid., vol. xxxiv. p. 319. A facsimile of an extensive fragment of the Çrauta-Sûtra of the *Mânavas* (another school of the Black Yajus) was published, with the commentary of the famous Mîmânsist doctor Kumârilabhaṭṭa, by the late Th. Goldstücker, 1861. The two last sections of the Kauçika-Sûtra (Atharva-Veda, which might be also conveniently reckoned in the following class) have been published, translated, and commented on by A. Weber in the Memoirs of the Academy of Berlin, 1858, p 344. Finally, G. Thibaut has published and translated in the Paṇḍit (Nos. 108–120, and new series, t. i.) the part of the Çrauta-Sûtra of Baudhâyana (the Black Yajus) with reference to the structure of the altar, the Çulva-Sûtra, and he has resumed the same subject while comparing the texts of Baudhâyana, Apastamba, and Kâtyâyana, in the Journal of the Asiatic Society of Bengal, t. xliv. p. 227.

2. Gṛihya-Sûtras: those of Açvalâyana, the text and commentary in the Bibliotheca Indica. The same text and German translation by F. Stenzler, 1864; those of Gobhila (Sâma-Veda), the text and commentary in the Bibliotheca Indica; those of Pâraskara (the White Yajus), the text and German translation by F. Stenzler, 1876–78; those of Çânkhâyana (Ṛig-Veda), the text and German translation by H. Oldenberg, in the Indische Studien, t. xv.

3. Dharma-Sûtras: those of Apastamba, text and extracts from the commentary, by G. Bühler, Bombay, 1868–71; those of Gautama, the text

bably the most stupendous and complex which has ever been elaborated by man. We must, however, try to ascertain our bearings in it once for all. The Brahmanical cultus comprehends, besides the great sacrifices—the only ones referred to in the Brâhmaṇas—a certain number of rites which these writings mention only casually, but which have been preserved to us in particular Sûtras under the title of domestic rites. We must not, however, affect to see in these last rites a domestic as opposed to a public cultus. Brahmanism knows no public cultus; each of its acts, as a general rule, has a purely individual reference, and is performed for behoof of a *yajamâna* (in certain exceptional cases there are several), that is to say, of a person who defrays the expense of it. With the *yajamâna* there is strictly associated only his wife, or the first of his wives, if he has several (the wife having no rights of worship of her own); and it is only indirectly, by means of certain attendant variations, that the benefit of the rite is extended to the rest of his family, to the people of his household, or to the body of his dependents.[1] In reality, this is not a case of two different cultuses, but of two different rituals. A certain number of acts, such as the institution and maintenance of the sacred fire, the daily offering to be made in this fire, and other matters besides, are common to both rituals; but in their domestic form they are more

alone, by F. Stenzler, 1876. These two collections of Sûtras have just been translated and commented on by G. Bühler, The Sacred Laws of the Aryas: Apastemba and Gautama, 1879, and form the second volume of the Sacred Books of the East, now publishing under the editorship of Max Müller. Gautama forms also part of a native collection of twenty-six codes of laws. entitled Dharmaçâstrasaṅgraha, and reprinted at Calcutta in 1876. The same collection contains an edition, slightly critical, of the Dharma-Sûtra of Vasishṭha (published also at Bombay with a commentary, 1878), and another of the Vishṇu-Smṛiti, which is the Dharma-Sûtra of the school of the Kâṭhaka (of the Black Yajus). For this last treatise see the monograph of T. Jolly (which also contains information on the Gṛihya-Sûtra of the Kâṭhakas, recently recovered at Kashmîr by G. Bühler): Das Dharmasûtra des Vishṇu und das Kâṭhakagrihyasûtra, in the Memoirs of the Academy of Munich for 1879. The same scholar has since published a complete translation of the Vishṇu Smṛiti: The Institutes of Vishṇu, translated, 1880, being vol. vii. of the Sacred Books of the East.

[1] See, for example, Aitr. Br., i. 30, 27, 28.

simple; they can be gone about with fewer preparations and a less numerous assemblage of priests; in particular, they can be performed by means of a single fire, whilst the acts celebrated according to the developed ritual require at least three of them. The domestic rites may be considered as the smallest number of observances incumbent on a chief of respectability and piety, and particularly on a Brahman. These rites are almost the only ones, in the main, which the Brahmans, who pride themselves on fidelity to their ancient usages, still observe in part to our own day. They comprehend: 1. The sacramental observances,[1] which the father either performs himself, or, if he is not a Brahman, sees performed for his children, from the day of conception till that in which the child, if he is a boy, passes under the authority of a master. 2. The initiation, in which the youth receives from his master or *guru*, along with the sacred cord, a knowledge of the principal mantras; in particular, the famous verse of the *Sâvitṛî*.[2] From this moment, which is considered as his spiritual birth, he is *dvija*, that is to say, is born a second time, and henceforth directly responsible for his acts.[3] This

[1] The Saṃskâras. These ceremonies are variously enumerated. Gautama, who includes under this denomination a complete list of all the religious acts, reckons them at forty (viii. 14–21); compare Manu, ii. 27, 28. But usually only the ten ceremonies of purification, binding on every Hindu of good caste, are so designated. 1. Garbhâdhâna, a rite which is to procure conception. 2. Puṃsavana has for its object to quicken the fœtus in the womb and to bring about the birth of a male child. 3. Sîmantonnayana, a ritual act which consists in parting the hair of the head of the woman during pregnancy. 4. Jâtakarman, a ceremony at birth: before cutting the umbilical cord, the new-born infant is made to taste honey and clarified butter from a gold spoon. 5. Nâmakaraṇa, the giving of the name. 6. Nishkramaṇa, when the child is first taken out to be shown the sun or the moon. 7. Annaprâçana, when it is for the first time presented with rice for food. 8. Cûḍâkarman, the tonsure, when only a tuft of hair is left on the top of the head. 9. Upanayana, initiation. 10. Vivâha, marriage. To this list is sometimes added the Keçânta or Godâna, when they celebrate the day on which the young man first shaves his beard; and the Pretakarman, funeral obsequies. The Saṃskâras are likewise prescribed, but without mantras, for women, with the exception of initiation, for which in their case marriage is substituted. Manu, ii. 66, 67; Yâjñav., i. 13.

[2] This mantra, which should be repeated several times a day, is usually (for there are several) the verse to Savitṛi, Ṛig-Veda, iii. 62, 10.

[3] Gautama, ii. 1–6.

initiation is a duty binding upon all free men.[1] He who evades it lapses, both himself and his race, into the condition of *vratya* or *patita*, that is, a person excommunicated, lost.[2] As a rule, it should be succeeded by a longer or shorter noviciate, consecrated to the acquirement of a knowledge of the Veda,[3] though it is evident that it properly concerned the Brahmans alone to occupy themselves with theological study. 3. There were the obligations resting on the master of the house; the institution, for example, of the domestic hearth, the rites of marriage, the daily offerings to the gods and to ancestors, the formalities to be observed towards guests and Brahmans, the daily repetition of the sacred texts, or at least of certain prayers, as well as of ceremonies of different sorts observable at stated days, funeral rites and funeral offerings (*Çrâddha*), considered as a debt which is transferred from one generation to another, and on the payment of which depends the happiness of the dead in the next life;[4] to which add a great number of acts of dedication or expiation, and the observance of occasional ceremonies. The practice of these

[1] Açvalây. Gr. Sûtra, i. 19, 8, 9; Pâraskara Gr. Sûtra, ii. 5, 39–43; Apastamba Dh. Sûtra, i. 1, 23–i. 2, 10; Manu, ii. 38–40; 168. There is no initiation for women, neither for the Çûdras, nor *a fortiori* for inferior grades.

[2] Manu, x. 20; 43; Apastamba, Dh. S., i. 1, 23-i. 2, 10, where we find indicated, at the same time, the conditions of reinstatement. Compare Manu, xi. 191, 192; Yâjñav., i. 38. The rite of excommunication is described, Gautama, xx.; Manu, xi. 182–188; Yâjñav., iii. 295–297. He on whom it falls is considered to be both civilly and religiously dead. In so far as reinstatement does not intervene, he is likened to the members of the lowest castes, with this difference only, that there is a limit to his degradation, whilst impurity of caste is indelible in the individual himself and his male descendants. In the female line, in the course of an unbroken succession of marriages with men of superior birth, caste gains in nobility by one degree at the end of the seventh generation. Apast. Dh. S., ii. 11, 10; Gautama, iv. 22; Manu, x. 64–65; Yâjñav., i. 96.

[3] Açvalây. Gr. Sûtra, i. 22, 3; Pârask. Gr. Sûtra, ii. 5, 13–15; Apast. Dh. Sûtra, i. 2, 12–16; Manu, iii. 1.

[4] In general this happiness depends on the good works of their descendants. The idea that the dead share in *puṇya* or *pâpa*, *i.e.*, the merit or demerit of the living, was early familiar to India. See, for example, Gautama, xv. 22; Manu, iii. 150. Almost all legal deeds of gift contain the formula that the gift is made "for the increase of the puṇya of the donor and that of his father and mother."

observances extends through the entire life of the faithful, unless, with the approach of decay, he, in observance of a more rigid custom, hands over the care of his household and his affairs to his son, when, renouncing henceforth all active business, he retires into solitude to prepare for death. The Sûtras, which preserve to us the details of this cultus, are not simple ritual treatises; their subject is the *dharma*, namely, duty in a larger sense, and their precepts respect alike established custom, civil right, and moral law. What is remarkable, we find here, among other matters, a theory and a very complete classification of moral transgressions. It is in this legislation, which constitutes the ancient *Smṛiti*, or traditional usage, and from which proceed at a later date the Dharmaçâstras, or codes of laws, such as that of Manu, that Brahmanism appears to best advantage; and, indeed, if we would do it justice, it is of importance that we should not forget the sound, solid, and practical morality which is laid down here.[1] The very ancient and always ingenious and suggestive symbolism which invests the majority of these usages is often of very great beauty; and from the whole there stands forth the image of a life at once grave and lovable, and which, though bristling somewhat with formalities, is nevertheless serviceably active, and nowise morose or inimical to joyfulness of heart.[2]

Quite as binding in theory, but doubtless of more limited observance in practice, are the acts of the developed ritual, which demand the kindling of at least three sacred fires.[3]

[1] The code of Manu, which is a kind of résumé of the Smṛiti, contains a perfect encyclopædia of moral teaching.

[2] The funeral and marriage ceremonies, as well as those connected with offerings to the Manes, as prescribed in this ritual, are the subject of three highly exhaustive monographs: Max Müller, Die Todtenbestattung bei den Brahmanen, in the Zeitschr. d. D. Morgenl. Gesellsch., t. ix.; E. Haas, Die Heirathsgebraüche der alten Inder nach den Gṛihyasûtra, with additions by A. Weber, in the Ind. Studien, t. v.; O. Donner, Piṇḍapitṛiyajña, das Manenopfer mit Klössen bei den Indern, 1870.

[3] A. Weber has commenced a general exposition of the Çrauta ritual, on the basis of the Kâtyâyana S., in the Indische Studien, t. x. and xiii. B. Lindner has made a special study

The institution of these fires, which should coincide with the close of the noviciate, forms by itself alone a ceremony of the first order, which is minutely described in the Brâhmaṇas, and certain details of which are repeated afterwards as integral parts of all the subsequent ceremonials. These are either *ishṭis*, which are characterised by offerings of cakes, soups, grain, butter, milk, honey, &c., or *somayâgas*, in which to the majority of the offerings afore-mentioned is added that of the soma. Of the ishṭis, one is of regular daily observance, the *Agnihotra*, which is celebrated morning and evening. The others recur at stated periods, such as the days of the new or full moon, the commencement of each of the three seasons, the return of the two harvests of spring and autumn. As regards the sacrifices of the soma, the rule is to celebrate one at least in the course of each year. The *Vâjapêya*, or strengthening beverage, the *Râjasûya*, or royal consecration, the *Açvamêdha*, or sacrifice of the horse, which are the princely sacrifices *par excellence*, are somayâgas. The offering of the soma, which is referred to as recurring constantly in the Hymns, thus turns out to be an exceptional event now; the reason is that of all these offerings it is the most expensive. Sometimes the rite of the soma, properly so called, apart from its preliminary and final ceremonies, lasts only a day, but ordinarily it takes several. When it takes more than twelve, it is a *sattra*, or session. There are sattras which last several months, a whole year, and even several years; in theory there are some which last 1000 years. But, whether short or long, these ceremonies require elaborate preparations and entail enormous expense. Every time the place where they are celebrated must be prepared

of the ceremony of consecration, which forms the introduction to every somayâga: Die Dîkshâ oder Weihe für das Somaopfer, 1878. The author has devoted particular attention to the recovery of the original meaning and form of the rite. A carefully elaborated monograph has just been published devoted to another ceremony of the same ritual, the Darçapûrṇamâsau, by A. Hillebrandt: Das Altindische Neu- und Vollmondsopfer in seiner einfachsten Form, 1880.

anew, with its double fence, its divers booths, and its altar of bricks of an extremely intricate construction.[1] Open table must be kept for the Brahmans, alms given at times, games organised, specially chariot races,[2] and gifts of cattle, gold, garments, and food distributed under the title of *dakshiṇâ*, or pay, among the numerous array of priests and assistants. The other rites likewise require the gift of a dakshiṇâ by way of present, but ordinarily it is less considerable. In general, the official cultus of Brahmanism is an aristocratic cultus, and is competent only to the chiefs of tribes and men of wealth and ability. Even the domestic ritual, when observed according to all the directions prescribed, implies at the least the possession of some little competency.

All these sacrifices are either binding, whether at stated times or on the event of certain occasions, or else voluntary, that is to say, performed at the instance of the believer for the fulfilment of certain specific vows. Each of them is celebrated in a series of acts of extreme complexity, and if we were to reckon up all the varieties specified in the texts, we would find they amounted to certainly more than 1000.[3] They are all accompanied

[1] See G. Thibaut, on the Çulva-Sûtras, in the Journal of the Asiatic Society of Bengal, t. xliv.

[2] See Taitt. Br., i. 3, 6.

[3] There are several classifications of the sacrifices. One of the commonest, and also the simplest, is that which is given, for example, by Gautama, viii. 18–20. 1. The seven kinds of Pâkayajñas, or little sacrifices; these are those of the domestic ritual: Ashṭakâ (the eighth day of the four winter months, from October–November to January–February), Pârvaṇa (the days of new and full moon), Çrâddha (funeral oblations), Çrâvaṇî, Agrahâyaṇî, Çaitrî, Açvayujî (the days of full moon from July–August, from November–December, from March–April, and from September–October). We may add the five daily oblations, called emphatically the five Mahâyajñas, or great sacrifices: oblations to the gods, the pitṛis, creatures in general, men and the ṛishis (acts of beneficence and hospitality and recitation of the Veda, these two obligations being regarded as yajñas—*i.e.*, oblations). 2. The seven kinds of Haviryajñas or ishṭis: Agnyâdhaya (the setting up of the sacred hearth), Agnihotra (the daily oblation in the three sacred fires), Darçapûrṇamâsau (ishṭis of the full and new moon), Agrayaṇa (the oblation of the first-fruits of the harvest), Çâturmâsya (at the beginning of each of the three seasons), Nirûḍhapaçubandha (the animal sacrifice, effected separately, not as an integral part of another ceremony), and Sautrâmaṇî (a ceremony which is usually an epilogue to certain somayajñas). 3.

with an entertainment provided for the Brahmans.[1] Originally they were themselves feasts, and they are so still in a symbolic sense; in token of which the participants, priests and yajamâna, consume each a small portion of the different offerings. Instead of the soma, the use of which is now the exclusive privilege of the Brahmans, another liquid is substituted to the same effect, in the case in which the yajamâna does not belong to the priestly caste.[2] This rite, which constitutes a real communion between the

The seven kinds of sacrifice of the soma: Agnishṭoma, Atyagnishṭoma, Ukthya, Shoḍaçin, Vâjapeya, Atirâtra, and Aptoryâma. These last cannot be characterised in few words; we shall therefore content ourselves with remarking that these names are not so much designations of ceremonies, properly so called, as they are norms to which the latter may be more or less referred. The same remark, though in a modified degree, applies to the two preceding groups. For a detailed exposition see A. Weber in the Ind. Stud., x. p. 322 *seq.*

[1] Apastamba Dh. S., ii. 15. 12.

[2] Ait. Br., vii. 28–32, and A. Weber in the Indische Studien, x. p. 62. There are, however, contrary indications (Çatap. Br., v. 5, 4, 9; in Weber, ibid., p. 12); and in epic poetry Somapa, drinker of the soma, remains as an attribute of the ancient kings. We believe we must see in this prohibition not so much a privilege to which the sacerdotal caste laid claim as an explanation from a Brahmanical point of view of a very simple fact, the neglect into which the use of the soma had fallen. In the Rig-Veda though there were from the date of it other spirituous beverages in use, such as the surâ (originally, as is like, a kind of cervisia; see Atharva-Veda, ii. 26, 5, and Taitt. Br., i. 7, 6, 9), the soma appears as a beverage in common and profane use. In the Brâhmaṇas, on the other hand, it seems to be employed exclusively in the service of religion. "The soma, it is said, is the sovereign nourishment of the gods; the surâ that of men." Taitt. Br., i. 3, 3, 2–3; see also injunctions such as Taitt. Saṃh. ii. 1, 5, 5–6. Might not this difference be due to a difference that had taken place in the quality of the beverage itself? There is, I am aware, a passage in A. Weber's writings somewhere, which we regret we cannot at present identify, in which he gives expression to his doubts as to the identity of the soma of the Rig-Veda and that of later times. For our part we think it would be very difficult to conclude that the beverage which the Hymns celebrate as delicious, which they describe as madhu, madhumat (honey, honied), and the immoderate use of which they testify to, is the soma of the Brâhmaṇas, which appears to have actually been the detestable liquor Haug tasted and describes (Aitareya Br., vol. ii. p. 489). This last is a sickening and purgative drug. Çatap. Br., iv. 1, 3, 6; Taitt. Saṃh., ii. 3, 2, 5–7; compare Taitt. Br., i. 8, 5, 5, and Sâyaṇa *ad locum*, Taittirîya-Sanhita, vol. ii. pp. 202, 203, edition of the Bibliotheca Indica. According to the same commentary, p. 406, it was vulgarly employed as a vomit. See on this subject H. Zimmer, Altindisches Leben, p. 276, who comes to the same conclusion. Perhaps it is not out of place to remark that in the later mythology it is not to Soma, but to another god, Varuṇa, that spirituous beverages are referred.

priests, the believer, and the gods, is the one of all the Vedic usages which has best survived; and we shall meet with it again in the majority of the sectarian religions. In fine, a great many of these sacrifices require animal victims. In the domestic ritual the act of sacrificing them is resolved for the most part into a purely symbolic act, but in the developed ritual it remained longer in force. Several ishṭis are very bloody. As regards the somayâgas, the rule is that there are none without *paçu*, that is to say, without victims; and in the case of some, the number of the victims required is such that if we were to interpret the texts literally, the classic hecatomb would appear as a bagatelle in comparison with these butcheries. There is reason to believe, however, that in these cases the sacrifice did not take place.[1] In the case of some, at any rate, there is the direct evidence of the texts that the animals, after having been brought formally to the altar, were in the end set at liberty. In general the more recent the texts are the more does the number of the symbolic victims increase and that of the real ones diminish; but even with these abatements the Brahmanical cultus remained for long an inhuman one.

Among these victims, which consist of all imaginable kinds of domestic and wild animals, there is one which recurs with an ominous frequency, viz., man.[2] Not only are there traces of human sacrifice preserved in the legends, as well as in the symbolism of the ritual, but this sacrifice is expressly mentioned and formally pre-

[1] In the Brâhmaṇas a tendency to a less bloody sacrifice already appears; see the legend given in Aitar. Br., ii. 8, and Çatap. Br., i. 2, 3, 6 (Müller, Ancient Sanskrit Literature, p. 420, and A. Weber, Zeitsch. d. D. Morgenl. Gesellsch., t. xviii. p. 262), according to which the *medha*, the property of the victim, passes in succession from the man to the horse, from the horse to the cow, from the cow to the sheep, from the sheep to the goat, from the goat to the earth, and finally into the barley and the rice, which thus contain the essence of all the victims, and constitute the best of the offering.

[2] A. Weber has exhausted this subject in his memoir, Ueber Menschenopfer bei den Indern der vedischen Zeit., in the Zeitsch. d. D. Morgenl. Gesellsch., t. xviii.; see also H. H. Wilson, on Human Sacrifices in the Ancient Religion of India, in his Select Works, t. ii. p. 247.

scribed. All the great somayâgas, as a rule, exact one or more human victims, and one of these is quite naïvely called the *Purushamêdha*, that is, the sacrifice of man. The texts speak differently in regard to these rites. At one time they represent them as fallen obsolete (in reference to one of them they have even preserved for us the name of him who was to celebrate it for the last time[1]); but they maintain them, as a rule, and protest against their abolition; at another time they conceive of them as purely symbolic acts; while at another they simply speak of them as usages in full force, and this in such a way that it is not always possible for us to assign to these discrepancies their connection chronologically. It is difficult to decide definitely among testimonies so conflicting, especially in view, on the one hand, of the silence of the Hymns (for we can see no indication of it in the sacrifice described in the hymn of the Purusha), and in view, on the other hand, of the doctrine, which we find growing in favour from that day, of the *ahiṃsâ*, or respect for all that has life. Must we see in these rites only a relic of primitive barbarism, the survival of one of those usages which the religion of the Hymns rejects? Are they to be viewed as an aberration in later times of the religious sense? Or is there not here only one of those merely theoretical extravagances with which this literature abounds, an extravagance that had arisen in certain morbid brains haunted with the idea that man, since he is the noblest of creatures, must also be the most prized of victims? The details supplied by the texts, however, are at times so precise, that it appears to us this last hypothesis, taken by itself, has small chance of turning out to be the true one. Notwithstanding the extremely slender trace of the practice in question to be met with in the Hymns,[2] the most pro-

[1] Çyâparṇa Sâyakâyana, according to Çatap. Br., vi. 2, 1, 39, was the last who consecrated the erection of the altar by the immolation of a human victim.

[2] A more precise one occurs in Ath.-Veda, xi. 2, 9, and is quoted by A. Weber in the Ind. Stud., xiii. p. 292. The whole passage is in the style of the Brâhmaṇas.

bable explanation seems to us to be that Aryan India did in fact profess and practise human sacrifice from the remotest times, but only as a rite that was exceptional and reprobated, and that to silence the reprobation with which it was regarded it required all the professional cynicism which displays itself so frequently in the Brâhmaṇas and the Sûtras, and the hazy indistinctness which results from their esoteric character.[1] On the other hand, a custom which is no less barbarous, but which continued to the present time, and could beyond a doubt reckon its victims by myriads, the immolation, viz., more or less voluntary, of the widow on the funeral pile of her husband, is not sanctioned by the Vedic ritual, although certain hints in the symbolism connected with funerals (particularly in the Atharva-Veda) come very near it, and in a measure foreshadow it.[2] In the Atharva-Veda we see the widow could marry again[3] under certain conditions, which in the course of time orthodox usage strictly debarred her from doing. The custom of the suicide of the *satî* is nevertheless very ancient, since, as early as the days of Alexander, the Greeks found it was observed among one of the tribes at least of the Punjâb.[4] The first Brahmanical testimony we find to it is that of the *Bṛihaddevatâ*, which is perhaps of quite as remote antiquity; in the epic poetry there are numerous instances of it. At first it seems to have been peculiar to the military aristocracy, and it is under the influence of the sectarian religions that it has especially flourished. Justice

[1] The Purushamedha of the old Brahmanism must be carefully distinguished from the human sacrifice which we shall meet with later on in the cultus connected with Durgâ.

[2] Ṛig-Veda, x. 18; Ath.-Veda, xviii. 3, 1 *seq.* It is precisely on Ṛig-Veda, x. 18, 7–8, as is known, where the widow is required to leave the funeral pile before the fire is applied to it, that the Brahmans insist in defending the usage as of divine ordination. See Colebrooke, On the Duties of a Faithful Hindu Widow, in his Miscellaneous Essays, t. l. p. 133, ed. Cowell; and H. H. Wilson, On the Supposed Vaidik Authority for the Burning of Hindu Widows, and his curious controversy on the subject with Râja Râdhâkânta Deva, in his Select Works, t. ii. p. 270.

[3] Atharva-Veda, ix. 5, 27–28.

[4] Lassen, Ind. Alterthumskunde, t. ii. p. 154; 2d ed., iii. p. 347, among the Καθαῖοι, Onesicrites in Strabo, xv. i. ch. 30.

requires us to add that it was only at a period comparatively modern that it ceased to meet with opposition.[1] It was we know finally abolished in the territory subject to the authority of Britain by Lord William Bentinck in 1829.

Up to this point we have said nothing either of images of the gods or of holy places. We cannot, however, altogether evade a question which has been often discussed, Was the religion of the Vedas an idolatrous one? The physical description given in the Veda of the gods, both great and small, is sometimes so precise, there are so many traits in it bordering on fetichism, and a very decided tendency to represent the deity by symbols, and, on the other hand, the human being, as soon as he conceives of his gods under a definite form, is so irresistibly tempted to realise that form in sensible objects, that it is difficult to believe that Vedic India did not worship images. We have no doubt, for example, that the systems of worship belonging to certain local and national divinities, in reference to which we have only indirect and very vague intimations, were at their origin thoroughly impregnated with idolatry and fetichism, as they afterwards continued to be, and that in this regard India has always had its figured symbols, its *caityas* (*i.e.*, sacred trees or stones), its places of frequent resort, its sacred caves and springs, that is to say, its idols and holy places. It would be, in our opinion, to make an undue use of the negative evidence we have, to conclude that all this is modern because the Vedic literature says nothing of it, or does so only at a very late date. Still, in spite of certain indications on which stress has sometimes been laid to prove the contrary,[2] we think that the Brahmanical cultus, properly so

[1] See A. Weber, Analyse der Kâdambarî (seventh age), in his Zeitsch. d. D. Morgenl. Gesellsch., t. vii. p. 585. The practice is proscribed in the Acâras of Malabar, ascribed to Çaṅkara, Ind. Antiq., t. iv. p. 256.

[2] See F. Bollensen, Die Lieder des Parâçara, in the Zeitsch. d. D. Morgenl. Gesellsch., t. xxii. p. 587; Ludwig, Die Nachrichten des Rig- und Atharvaveda über Geographie, Geschichte, Verfassung des alten Indien, pp. 32 and 50. On the question

called, was not affected by these usages, and that it was not idolatrous, and this because it could not be so. In fact, from the moment of our first acquaintance with it, we find it includes distinct sets of ceremonies, but it is not subdivided into distinct cultus systems. There is not one cultus for Agni, another for Indra, a third for Varuṇa, as there was elsewhere distinct systems of cultus for Zeus, Ares, and Apollo. Each of the acts of the Vedic ritual is a complex whole, addressed to a great number of gods, and, if of any significance, however little, to the entire pantheon. These rites did not then admit of images; no more did they admit of holy places. The place where they were performed was either the domestic hearth, which served as well for ordinary purposes, or an enclosure connected with the house, or else, for the great sacrifices, a special arena, as it were, the *devayajana*, a place essentially variable, the dimensions of which, as well as the situation, changed according to the nature and purpose of the ceremonies,[1] and the consecration of which, moreover, was considered at an end after the observance of each rite, since on every new celebration it required to be consecrated anew. Permanence, the very first characteristic, therefore, of a holy place, was altogether wanting, not to mention another equally essential, viz., community. The Vedic altar, in fact, was not a spot that was holy for all; like the sacrifice itself, it served a strictly personal purpose, and, far from uniting men, it isolated them rather. Two neighbours celebrating the same rite at the same hour must choose spots so far apart from each other that the sound of the prayer of the one could not reach the ear of the other.[2] Neither in such a cultus could there be thought

whether by the *çiçnadevas* of Rig-Veda, vii. 21 and x. 99, we must understand phallic idols, see J. Muir, Original Sanskrit Texts, vol. iv. p. 407, 2d ed.

[1] See on this subject Taitt. Saṃh., vi. 2, 6, 1–4.

[2] There must be no clashing between the mantras. Even the study of the Ṛig-Veda must be suspended whenever the song of the sâmans is heard, and, *vice versa*, the study and repetition of the sâmans must not be attempted in a place where the mantras of another Veda are being repeated. The probable

of places specially consecrated by the presence of the deity. At the very most, the religion of the Brâhmaṇas attaches a particular sanctity to the fords of the rivers (*tirtha*),[1] where people come to perform their ablutions (and pilgrims would one day resort), and to certain privileged regions,[2] such as the banks of the Sarasvatî, the Kurukshetra, or that forest of Naimisha, so celebrated later on in the epic poetry. But it has no knowledge either of pilgrimages or of holy places. Thousands of times in the Brâhmaṇas the sacred enclosure is compared to this lower world, in contrast with heaven; it is never regarded as forming a definite locality, and, as is somewhere said, "when consecrated by the holy word, the entire earth is an altar."[3]

It appears, then, there is a certain character of universality which it is of importance we should not overlook as a feature in this religion, which in other respects is so objectionably narrow. It is neither local nor even national, in the sense in which certain religions of Greece and Italy were. Thus, although it shows no tendency to proselytise, but the reverse, and although, as a rule, it regards as impure, and excludes from its mysteries as no better

reason for this prohibition is that the sâmans are the only mantras that are heard at a distance. The explanation Manu gives is that the sound of the sâmans suggests a taint of impurity. See Pâraskara Gr. S., ii. 11, 6; Apastamba Dh. S., i. 10, 17, 18; Manu, iv. 123, 124.

[1] Taitt. Saṃh., vi. 1, 1, 2, 3.

[2] See the legend of Mâthava Videgha, translated from the Çatap. Br. by Weber, in the Ind. Studien, t. i. p. 170 ss.; Ait. Br., ii. 19. The religious geography of Manu is summarised in ii. 17–24. Between the Sarasvatî and the Dṛishadvati (two small rivers to the north-west of Delhi, near Thanessar) is the Brahmâvarta, the abode of the brahman, within limits prescribed by the gods (see Ṛig-Veda, iii. 23, 4), to the east of which, as far as the Prayâga or confluence of the Ganges and the Yamunâ, extends the country of the Brahmarshis, the Brahmanic patriarchs. These two regions form Madhyadeça, the country in the middle, the cradle of the law and good custom. The space contained between the Himâlaya on the north, the Vindhya on the south, and the two western and eastern seas, is Aryâvarta, the abode of the Aryas. This country, which is the haunt of the black deer, is suitable for the celebration of sacrifice. (Compare Yajñav., i. 2.) Beyond these the land of the Mlecchas or barbarians stretches away, which is unfit for the celebration of the rites of religion, and where the regenerate must not even temporarily dwell. This is nearly the geography of the Brâhmaṇas. See Muir, Sanskrit Texts, ii. 397 *seq.*, 2d ed.

[3] Çatap. Br., iii. 1, 1, 4. Compare Taitt. Saṃh., vi. 2, 4, 5.

than a slave, the *mleccha*, the man of foreign speech and the barbarian, it will nevertheless make its way among these proscribed races. In fact, it is the peculiar possession of the Brahmans, and wherever the Brahman plants his foot, whether as a hermit, as the minister and the *protégé* of princes of his race, or as a simple tiller of the soil, though never as a missionary, it will enter in his train and root itself along with him. It will establish itself step by step along the slopes and on the plateau of the Dekhan, bringing along with it its sacred books, only partially and ill understood, but piously preserved, and an imposing array of prescriptions, so rigorous in appearance yet so flexible in reality. Thus will the time come when the Veda shall be oftener repeated and more commented upon in the Tamîl country, on the banks of the Kâverî, than upon those of the Ganges. It will be carried still farther—as far as the seas round Sunda to Java, and in particular to Bali, where it is said there still exists a redaction, conceivably tampered with,[1] but the study of which will be sure some day to bring to light curious revelations.

[1] See R. Friederich, An Account of the Island of Bali, in Journal of the Roy. As. Soc., new series, t. viii. p. 168. The alterations must be considerable, since, according to the author, these writings are in Çlokas and pure Sanskrit. The memoir of Friederich, continued in vol. ix. of the Journal, is full of curious information in regard to Brahmanism at Bali. The introduction of Hindu culture into the islands of the Archipelago is of ancient date, since even in Ptolemy the name for Java is Indian. Probably the Buddhists formed the first link in the chain. But the entire ancient history of these islands is obscure; the character of the oldest inscriptions is nearly the same as that which was in use on the Coromandel coast in the fifth century. See Kern, Over het Opschrift van Djamboe, in the Memoirs of the Academy of Amsterdam, 1877. According to the same scholar, it is from Cambodja that Hindu civilisation must have penetrated to the islands: Opschriften op oude Bouwwerken in Kambodja, ibid., 1879.

BRAHMANISM.

II. PHILOSOPHIC SPECULATIONS.

Part performed by the Brahmans in the elaboration of the philosophic doctrines.—The Upanishads.—These writings contain in a confused form the germs of the conceptions afterwards systematised in the Darçanas.—The atheistic, materialistic, or dualistic doctrine of the Sâṅkhya; the prakṛiti and the purusha.—The deistic Sâṅkhya.—The doctrine of the Vedânta: the âtman, the jîvâtman and the mâyâ.—The different systems mutually inoculate each other; the absolute idealism of the later Vedânta.—Practical side of the Upanishads: the saṃsâra and the doctrine of new births.—Theory of salvation: the yoga and the final emancipation.—Contempt for positive morality, the cultus, and the Veda.—Mystic observances.—Influences of these doctrines on the Hindu mind.—Reaction against the extravagant idealism; the Nâstikas or Cârvâkas: their denial of all metaphysics and morals.

WHILE the Brahmans were thus crowning their efforts with the erection, on the basis of an inadequate theology, of this stupendous system of rites, and with the realisation, if I may so speak, of the ideal of a religion composed entirely of observances, having its own end within itself, and well-nigh independent of the gods whom it served, they kept prosecuting at the same time, within the region of speculation, a work to all appearance very different, but at bottom pretty much akin, since it tended in the long-run to put philosophic conceptions in the place of those very gods which were in another department fading more and more away behind ritualistic conceptions. These two tendencies, which we become conscious of as early as the Hymns, were nevertheless opposed, and it is probable that they did not prevail in exactly the same centres. Indeed, there are traces of a certain antagonism between the men of the ritual and the men of speculation, an antagonism pretty much akin to that which at a later period still divided at times their respective successors, the mystic thinkers of the Vedânta and the casuists of the Mîmâṃsâ. In the domain of pure thought, too, the Brahmans were not the sole authorities, as they were indisputably in everything which affected the rites. Here they found rivals among all those who were capable of entertaining spiritual questions; and as they were the guardians of no orthodoxy, as they in no degree burdened themselves with the care of souls, and did not lay claim to the character of directors of consciences, they did not seek to disguise the fact that they had coadjutors in speculation. They have themselves preserved the record of kings condescending to teach them,[1] and of women mixing in their discussions and disconcerting their most celebrated doctors by the depth of their objections.[2] We cannot doubt, however, either the leading part the Brahmans took in the elaboration of the doctrines, or the gradual diffusion of these among all the schools of Brahmanism. A talent for controversy became one of the first conditions of theological distinction, of the *brahmavarcas*, and in the literature of each school greater or less scope was reserved for speculative exercitation.

The treatises which have preserved for us these old theorisings bear the name of *Upanishads*, or Instructions. Under this title there has been transmitted to us a voluminous literature, which is to a great degree apocryphal, and connected by date with all the epochs of the sectarian religions. There are Vishnuite Upanishads, Çivaite Upanishads, and mystic Upanishads of every kind, up to an *Allah Upanishad*,[3] intended to magnify the dream of a

[1] Bṛihadâr. Up., ii. 1; vi. 2; Chândogya Up., v. 3, &c.

[2] Bridhadâr. Up., iii. 6; iii. 8.

[3] Published by Râjendralâla Mitra in the Journal of the As. Soc. of Bengal, t. xl. p. 170. For the religious reforms attempted by Akbar, see Dabistan, ch. x. t. iii. p. 48 *seq.*, translated by Schea and Troyer. Compare H. H. Wilson, Account of the Religious Innovations attempted by Akbar, in his Select Works, t. ii. p. 379.

universal religion, that was fondly cherished by Akbar, the Mussulman emperor, at the end of the sixteenth century. The number of these documents catalogued up to the present day amounts to nearly 250.[1] But in this heterogeneous mass, which we will perhaps never succeed in classifying in an entirely satisfactory manner, there is a small number which form, or in reference to which it is established that they formed, an integral portion of a body of Vedic writings, almost always of a Brâhmaṇa. By adding one or two others of a more uncertain derivation, but of a character quite as antique, we obtain, at most, half a score of texts which may be regarded as

[1] For the different lists of these writings see A. Weber, Indische Literaturgeschichte, p. 171, 2d edition. At this date (1876) A. Weber had reached a total number of 235. Of this number, several, such as the Purushasûkta, the Çatarudriya, &c., are only fragments taken from different Vedic works. Our first acquaintance with the Upanishads is due to Anquetil du Perron, who, at the beginning of the century, published the Latin translation of a Persian version of fifty of these treatises: Oupnekhat id est secretum tegendum, opus continens antiquissimam et arcanam . . . doctrinam e iv. sacris Indorum libris excerptam, 1801–2, 2 vols. in 4to. In the analysis which he has given of this work (Ind. Studien, t. i., ii., and ix.), A. Weber has executed the translation over again, and published and commented on the texts contained in the collection of Anquetil. We owe to the same scholar an edition with a translation and commentary of the Râmatâpanîya Up. (Memoirs of the Academy of Berlin, 1864, p. 271), and another of the Vajrasûcî Up., attributed to Çaṅkara (idid., 1859, 227 *seq.*). The principal Upanishads have been published several times; the editions, however, that are most handy and most in favour are those of the Bibliotheca Indica, all of which are accompanied with commentaries, and some with translations. This collection comprehends, as far as it has gone, Bṛihadâraṇyaka, Châṇdogya, Îçâ, Kêna, Kaṭha, Praçna, Muṇḍaka, Mâṇḍûkya, Taittirîya, Aitareya, Çvetâçvatara, Gopâlatâpanîya, Nṛisiṃhatâpanîya, Shaṭcakra, Kaushîtaki, Maitri; besides 29 of the small Upanishads attached more particularly to the Atharva-Veda: Çiras, Garbha, Nâdavindu, Brahmavindu, Amṛitavindu, Dhyânavindu, Tejovindu, Yogaçikhâ, Yogatattva, Sannyâsa, Aruṇeyâ, Brahmavidyâ, Kshurikâ, Cûlikâ, Atharvaçikhâ, Brahma, Prâṇâgnihotra, Nîlarudra, Kaṇṭhaçruti, Piṇḍa, Atma, Râmapûrvatâpâniya, Râmottaratâpanîya, Hanumadukta - Râma, Sarvopanishatsâra, Haṃsa, Paramahaṃsa, Jâbâla, Kaivalya.

The principal Upanishads, those which have been commented upon by Çaṅkara, have been the subject of a work, very complete and highly meritorious in every respect, by P. Regnaud: Matériaux pour servir à l'Histoire de la Philosophie de l'Inde (it forms the xxviii. and xxxiv. fascicles of the Bibliothèque de l'Ecole des Hautes-Etudes), 1876-78. While we write, Professor Max Müller is engaged in publishing a translation of these very Upanishads. Vol. i. (which is the first of the series entitled Sacred Books of the East) contains Châṇdogya, Kêna, Aitareya, Kaushîtaki, and Içâ.

ancient Upanishads.[1] Of all this number there is not a single one, perhaps, of which the redaction is of a date anterior to Buddhism. Up to a certain point these are the most direct and trustworthy documents we have from which to construe the condition of things in which the new religion developed; but, taken together, these Upanishads embody a tradition much more ancient, and one which is connected without discontinuity with the very origin of the Brahmanical schools. In the Vedic literature they constitute the *Jñânakâṇḍa, i.e.*, the speculative section, in contrast with the rest of the Veda, known by the name of *Karmakâṇḍa, i.e.*, the practical section.

The doctrines committed to these books, some of which are selections rather than express treatises, do not form a homogeneous whole. Alongside of views which are really profound, and which give evidence of a singular vigour of thought, they contain a great number of allegories and mystic reveries, that bear either on mythology or ritual, and seem to involve quite a contrary conclusion. But even when rid of these parasitic elements, and reduced in compass to the part that is properly philosophical, they come far short of constituting a system. They have no connection among themselves, and in answer to the permanent problems of human thought concerning God, man, and the universe, they suggest several solutions which are radically opposed. These solutions are at the same time so elaborately worked up in certain of their parts that it is often difficult, and in a summary exposition such as ours almost always impossible, to determine exactly how much of an essential nature may have been added to them by the ages that succeeded. The principal task of those who have fallen heirs to this ancient wisdom will be to pick and sort in this confusion, to refer in some methodical way these incongruous elements to their separate systems,

[1] Bṛihadâraṇyaka, Chândogya, Kaushîtaki, Içâ, Kéna, Kaṭha, Praçna, Aitareya, Taittirîya, Muṇḍaka, Mâṇḍûkya. Anyhow, the majority of probabilities is in favour of these texts.

and to invent for each of these systems an appropriate and definite mode of exposition. In this way we shall obtain at least three of the different systems or *darçanas* (Sâṅkhya, Yoga, and Vedânta), which, fixed to an indefinite period and to the number of six principal ones, in manuals called Sûtras, will be found to constitute the official philosophy of India.[1] But outside the school, this country will nevertheless remain at heart attached to the manner of philosophising found in the Upanishads. To that its sects will come back again one after another; its poets, its thinkers even, will always take pleasure in this mysticism, with its modes of procedure, at once so vague and so full of contradictions. In speculation, as in everything else, eclecticism, pushed to the extreme of confusion, seems to be the very method of Hindu thinking.

We shall now give, in a summary form, an analysis of such of the doctrines of the Upanishads as are more especially connected with the history of religion; and that we may not be obliged to return farther on to the same subject, we shall indicate at the same time the essential developments they have undergone in the systems properly so called. So far as the Upanishads deal with purely objective philosophy, which they seldom do, their ideas are easily classified and reduced to known categories. Their cosmogony, for instance, and we may add that of the Brâhmaṇas in general, only develop the solutions of which we have already a glimpse in the Hymns. At one time it is a first being conceived as a person,

[1] The most solid and reliable general exposition of the philosophic systems of the Hindus is to this day that executed by H. T. Colebrooke in his famous memoirs, On the Philosophy of the Hindus, read from 1823–27 at the meetings of the Royal Asiatic Society, published in vols. i. and ii. of the Transactions, and reprinted in the author's Miscellaneous Essays. The fundamental Sûtras of the six principal systems, Sâṅkhya, Yoga, Nyâya, Vaiçeshika, Mîmâṃsâ, and Vedânta, have all been published at different times, in particular from 1851–54 in the editions of Allâhâbâd and of Mirzapore, in which the text is accompanied with an English translation. With the exception of the Yoga-Sûtras, they are also edited, texts and commentaries, in the Bibliotheca Indica. The edition of the Mîmâṃsâ - Sûtras is, however, not finished.

Prajâpati, viz., or an equal (once we find Mṛityu,[1] or Death), who, tired of his solitude, "emits," that is to say, draws forth from himself, everything that exists, or who begets it, after having divided himself in two, the one half male, the other half female.[2] At another time, this first personal and creative being is represented as himself proceeding from a material substratum:[3] in the mythic form, he is *Hiraṇyagarbha*, the golden embryo, *Nârâyaṇa*, "he who reposes on the waters," and *Virâj*, the resplendent, who issued from the world-egg. In both of these cases we have to do with uncertain pantheistic conceptions, which practically resolve themselves into that pale and shallow deism which India has often confessed with the lips, but which has never won the homage of her heart. Besides these two solutions there is still a third. Instead of organising itself under the direction of a conscious, intelligent, divine being, the primary substance of things is represented as manifesting itself directly without the interposition of any personal agent, by the development of the material world and contingent existences.[4] It is then simply, and by whatever name it may be dignified, the *asat*, the non-existent, the indeterminate, the indistinct, passing into existence—chaos, in other words, extricating itself from disorder by its own energies. When systematised, this solution will on one side have its counterpart in the metaphysics of Buddhism, while on the other it will issue in the Sâṅkhya philosophy. The latter, in fact, admits a primary material cause, the *prakṛiti*, one, simple, eternal, essentially active and productive, the source of intellectual energies, as well as of visible and tangible matter, of intelligence, consciousness, and the senses,

[1] Bṛihadâr. Up., i. 2.

[2] Gopatha Br., i. 1; Bṛihadâr. Up., i. 4; Chândog. Up., vi. 2; Praçna Up., i. 4; vi. 3; Aitar. Up., i. 1; Çvetâçvat. Up., vi. 1. This emission is very frequently represented as a sacrifice. See besides Taitt. Saṃh., ii. 1, 1, 4. In the Çatap. Br., x. 5, 3, the first principle is *manas, i.e.,* thought.

[3] Nṛisiṃhatâp. Up., i. 1; Çatap. Br., xi. 1, 6, 1; Taitt. Saṃh., v. 6, 4, 2; vii. 1, 5, 1.

[4] Chândog. Up., iii. 19; Taittir. Up., ii. 1; ii. 7.

as well as of the subtle elements which compose the higher organisms and the grosser elements of which bodies are formed. Outside of this material development, the Sâṅkhya admits only of individual souls, all equal, eternal, and indestructible, essentially unmodifiable and passive, producing nothing and doing nothing. The prakṛiti energises and manifests itself in order to unite with the soul or the *purusha* (for this word, borrowed from certain old dualistic myths, and signifying properly the male, occurs always in the singular, in contrast with the prakṛiti, although the purusha is essentially multifold, and there is no supreme soul). The part performed by the soul is confined to contemplating these manifestations, to giving itself up to this union in which the existence of individual beings is realised, to experiencing its pleasures and disgusts, until the day when, fully satiated, and recognising itself as radically distinct from matter, it breaks partnership with it and returns to its primeval liberty. In this system there is room for beings of every kind, superior and inferior to man; for if all souls are equal, all the modifications of the prakṛiti with which they may unite, are not so. But there is hardly need to add that these beings, in so far as they are capable of reciprocal actions, are all finite, and that, philosophically viewed, the system is atheistic. And therefore, at a later date, when we shall find a certain orthodoxy take shape, it will appear in the religious literature (where it has all along played a prominent part) only in combination with other doctrines, which, with more or less of logical warrant, will introduce into it the idea of God. In the most ancient Upanishads, on the other hand, in which the ideas that have come out in the Sâṅkhya are already in general favour, as well as in Buddhism, where they predominate, the system is not yet a dualistic one.[1] We do not yet find opposed to the prakṛiti a purusha radically distinct: everything

[1] In the more recent Upanishads, on the other hand, it is no longer so. The Çvetâçvatara Up., for instance, is in point of doctrine exactly on the same level as the Bhagavad-Gîtâ.

issues indiscriminately from the same blind and dark root, and we have to do in the passages where these ideas are asserted only with a materialistic and atheistic explanation of the universe.

There is in these treatises still a fourth solution, which to such an extent eclipses all the rest that it may be considered as the philosophy proper of the Upanishads, viz., the pure pantheism which is destined to assume its ultimate form in the system of the Vedânta. But this master doctrine is exactly the one which there is most risk of distorting when we attempt to reduce it to any accepted metaphysical formula. In fact, it is not with a simple *a priori* conception that we have to do here; pure speculation here depends on subjective theories, and we here for the first time come upon it endeavouring to construe God and the universe by starting from man. A minute analysis too would be necessary in order to guard against misapprehension. At bottom, all the efforts of these theosophists tend towards one single aim, which has been that of all mystic pantheists, the real identity, namely, of subject and object, of man and God. But their manner of arriving at it here is so peculiar—they start from such a distance, with data that are so innocently assumed, and which they never dream of verifying by the way, they make so many digressions, they halt so long at certain stages and move on so rapidly at others—that in order to follow them aright it would be necessary to traverse the whole road along with them; and that would be a long journey indeed. We shall try to indicate, anyhow, the point from which they embark, and their point of landing.[1]

They appear to have started from the idea that the principle of life which is in man, the *âtman*, or self (for the word was especially in use as a reflex pronoun, so that "to know the âtman" and "to know one's self" were synonymous), is the same as that which animates nature.

[1] In the exposition which follows we suppress the references; otherwise we should require to adduce the half of the ancient Upanishads.

This principle in man appeared to them to be the *prâṇa*, the breath; the air, or something more subtle than air, the ether, being the âtman in nature. Or else the âtman was a small being, a homunculus, a *purusha*, which had its seat in the heart, where it was felt stirring, and from which it directed the animal spirits. Here it sat at its ease, for it was not larger than the thumb. It could even make itself still smaller, for it was felt making its way along the arteries, and could be distinctly seen in the small image, the pupil, which is reflected in the centre of the eye. A purusha, quite similar, appeared with dazzling effect in the orb of the sun, the heart and eye of the world. That was the âtman of nature, or rather it was the same âtman which thus manifested itself in the heart of man and the sun; an invisible opening at the top of the skull affording a passage for it to go from the one dwelling-place to the other. Gross as these conceptions are, they have nevertheless served as a point of departure for one of the most imposing and subtle of the systems of ontology yet known in the history of philosophy; and not only have they formed its point of departure, but what is much more surprising, they continued to form one of its principal axioms. To arrive at their doctrine of identity, or, as they call it, *advaita*, *i.e.*, of non-duality, the Hindu theosophists have more than others been reduced to make large demands on the spontaneous sweep of the thought. They had not the resources of a subtle psychology at their service to establish it in a more learned manner, nor those hypotheses concerning ideas, the logos, or the pure reason, that legacy from Greek philosophy from which other mystic sects have profited so much. Thus they have never for once, even when they must have seemed to them perplexing, given up those old popular ideas, of which pre-intimations occur already in the Hymns,[1] and to which assent was given without reflection

[1] The purusha seated in the heart occurs in Ṛig-Veda, x. 90, 1. Compare Athar.-Veda, x. 8, 43.

from mere force of habit. Up to the last they will go on speculating about the âtman breath and ether, the âtman-purusha of the heart, the eye, and the sun.

On the other hand, the point at which they have arrived is this: the âtman is the one, simple, eternal, infinite, incomprehensible being, assuming every form, and itself without any, the only, yet immovable and immutable agent, the cause of all action and all change. It is both the material and efficient cause of the world, which is its manifestation, its body. This it draws from its own substance, and again absorbs into it, not by necessity, however, but by an act of its own will, as the spider spins forth and draws back into itself the thread of its web. From it proceed and to it return all finite existences, just as sparks leap from the furnace and fall back into it again, whilst the multiplicity of these existences no more affects its own unity than the formation of the foam and the wave affects that of the sea. More subtle than an atom, greater than the greatest of existences, it has nevertheless a dwelling, the cavity of the heart of every man. It is there that it resides in its fulness, and that it rests rejoicing in itself and its works. This direct and material immanency of the absolute being in the creature, which is the unreasoned and mystic assumption of the system, is also its connecting bond. Thanks to this fact, man has power over the âtman. By intense meditation, aided by operations in which a fanciful physiology plays a prominent part (for there is not a little materialism at the bottom of all these conceptions), he has only to make his soul literally re-enter his heart again in order to bring it into contact with the supreme unity, and enable it to be conscious of itself in that unity. Here, it is true, there arose some puzzling questions. What room would there be for this soul, this individual âtman, this *jîvâtman* identical with the *paramâtman*, the supreme âtman, and yet distinct, capable of self-consciousness in it and yet ignorant of it? How concede personality to it in presence of the absolute being? How deny this to it without imputing to that being ignorance, error, and weakness? What becomes of the theory of one sole agent, alongside of the assumption that it is in the power of the soul to initiate its return to the âtman? For it is the soul which goes to the âtman, not the âtman which brings it back to itself; and the notion of grace, with which India will become familiar at a later date, is as good as foreign to the primitive Vedânta.[1] These are difficulties, and there are others besides, which the authors of the Upanishads are not the only people who have had to face; and it is not astonishing that they have not resolved them. They describe the states of the jîvatman; they enumerate its organs; they show it involuted in a succession of concentric material envelopes, more and more dense, which constitute its organs, and restrict in different degrees its sphere of action and range of knowledge.[2] As the image of the sun is distorted and deceptively multiplied in agitated water, so the jîvâtman has only distracted and mistaken conceptions. It sees only diversity, makes the distinction of *me* and *thee*, and perceives nothing beyond; but by meditation, conducted according to the rules of true science, it can dissipate all these vain images; it sees then that there is only an âtman, and that this âtman is itself. If the point is to show it in action, it is spoken of as a distinct reality given in experience; if, on the contrary, the subject is its relation to the paramâtman, the said reality disperses, and all particularity is treated as pure illusion. In this way the different aspects of the problem are confusedly exhibited, but the problem itself is by no means resolved. No more do the Sûtras, in which the old Vedânta received its final form, resolve this problem. The author or authors of these Sûtras,

[1] To the best of our recollection it occurs distinctly formulated only in a single passage common to the Kaṭha Up., ii. 23, and to the Muṇḍaka Up., iii. 2, 3: "This âtman can be obtained neither by means of the Veda nor by force of understanding, nor by great knowledge; he whom it chooses, that one obtains it; it chooses the person of that one as its own." See Bhagavad-Gîtâ, xi. 53.

[2] Taittir. Up., ii. 2–8, and the long description, Maitri Up., ii. 5-iv. 2.

who have imposed on themselves the knotty task of presenting in a didactic and methodic shape the apocalyptic visions of the Upanishads, and who, except in the cases in which they by main force refer to the Vedânta certain passages that are in fact inspired by a totally different philosophy, have discharged this task with a truly noble fidelity, do, in fact, concede to the individual soul and to finite beings in general a practical experimental existence, but they deny to them reality in the absolute sense of the term. Thus they come at length to maintain, for instance, the existence of a personal God,[1] of an Içvara or Lord, distinct both from the world which he governs and from the Absolute, a notion which is not unfamiliar to the ancient Upanishads, but foreign, as it could not help being, to passages purely Vedântic. But, for all that, the doctrine of being taught in the Vedânta Sûtras, although it is more elaborated, does not perceptibly differ from that of the old texts. It is only in the philosophy of the sects, in what may be called the new Vedânta, in certain Upanishads of more recent date, in the *Bhagavad-Gîtâ* and in the *Vedânta Sâra,* that an attempt will be made to formulate with any exactness a radical solution. In this system, the finite world does not exist; it is the production of the *Mâyâ,* of the deceptive magic of God, a mere spectacle where all is illusion, theatre, actors, and piece alike, a "play" without purpose, which the Absolute "plays" with himself.[2] The ineffable and the inconceivable is the only real.

The doctrine of illusion is not, however, peculiar to the Vedânta; it affected the core of the Sâṅkhya philosophy as well. The prakṛiti of this last was identified with the Mâyâ; and the purusha, from the manifold which it was in

[1] See Pramadâ Dâsa Mitra, "A Dialogue on the Vedantic Conception of Brahma," in the Journ. of the Roy. As. Soc., t. x. p. 33. Compare Çaṅkara on the Vedânta Sûtra, iv. 3, 7 *seq.*, p. 1119, ed. of the Bibliotheca Indica. For the doctrine of Çaṅkâra see F. H. Windischmann, Sancara, sive de Theologumenis Vedanticorum, Bonnæ, 1833; and especially A. Bruining, Bijdrage tot de Kennis van den Vedânta, Leiden, 1871.

[2] See Bhartṛihari, iii. 43, ed. Bohlen.

the original system, became the one and the absolute being. Under this new phase, the Sâṅkhya and the Vedânta differ only in terminology and the details of exposition. The Bhagavad-Gîtâ, for instance, and several Upanishads,[1] are connected as much with the one system as with the other. Or rather, for it matters little how we expound and denominate things which we deny, there is in these writings only one system, pure idealism, very closely related to the other extreme, pure nihilism. The Sâṅkhya and the Vedânta, in their twofold form, will almost by themselves alone meet all the demands made upon the metaphysical systems of the Vishnuite and Çivaite religions. Of the four other great official systems, the *Yoga* is rather a manual of mystic exercises than a philosophy; the *Nyâya* (logic and criticism) and the *Vaiçeshika* (the physical theory of the world) treat too remotely of religious matters to find place here; and, finally, the *Mîmâṃsâ* is only the extension, in the form of a critical examination, of the ritualistic literature of the Brâhmaṇas and the Smṛitis. It is opposed to speculation; it recognises the gods only so far as they are specially mentioned in the liturgical formulas, and several of those who profess to teach it[2] explicitly refuse to concede the Vedic quality, that is to say the quality of revealed scripture, to the *Jñânakâṇḍa, i.e.*, to everything which does not bear directly upon the cultus.

It would be to give a quite imperfect idea of the Upanishads, however, if we emphasised only the purely metaphysical side of them. These singular books, though of a character so heterogeneous, are still more practical than speculative. They address themselves more to man as man than to man as thinker; their aim is not so much to expound systems as to teach the way of salvation.

[1] For example, the Çvetâçvatara Up.

[2] The school of Prabhâkara. See Satyavrata Sâmaçramin's notes in his edition of the Sâma-Veda, vol. i. pp. 2, 4, Bibl. Indica. In regard to this atheistic and merely ritualistic school, see moreover Burnell's Classified Index of the Sanskrit MSS. in the palace at Tanjore, ii. 84.

They are pre-eminently exhortations to the spiritual life, perplexed and confused indeed, but delivered at times with a pathos that is both lofty and affecting. It seems as if the whole religious life of the period, which we miss so much in the ritualistic literature, had become concentrated in these writings. Notwithstanding their pretensions to mystery, they are in the main works that aim at proselytism, but a proselytism prosecuting its task within a limited circle. The tone which prevails in them, especially in their manner of address and in the dialogue, in which there is at times a touch of singular sweetness, is that of a preaching which appeals to the initiated. In this respect nothing in the literature of the Brahmans so much resembles a Sûtra of Buddhism as certain passages of the Upanishads, with this difference, however, that for elevation of thought and style these passages far surpass all that we as yet know of the sermons of Buddhism. When that remarkable man, Râmmohun Roy, who undertook at the beginning of this century to reform Hinduism, expressed his belief that if a selection were made from the Upanishads it would contribute more than any other publication to the religious improvement of his people, he was not the victim of an altogether groundless delusion. It is on this, the religious and practical side of the Upanishads, that we have still to say a few words.

After the brief sketch which we have given above of the doctrine of these books, it is hardly necessary to say that, in the view of their authors, the separated condition of the soul, which is the cause of mental error, is also the cause of moral evil. Ignorant of its true nature, the soul attaches itself to objects unworthy of it. Every act which it performs to gratify this attachment entangles it deeper in the perishable world; and as it is itself imperishable, it is condemned to a perpetual series of changes. Once dragged into the *samsâra*, into the vortex of life, it passes from one existence into another, without respite and without rest. This is the twofold doctrine of the *karman*, *i.e.*, the act by which the soul determines its own destiny, and of the *punarbhava*, *i.e.*, the successive re-births in which it undergoes it. This doctrine, which is henceforth the fundamental hypothesis common to all the religions and sects of India, is found formulated in the Upanishads for the first time. In the most ancient portions of the Brâhmaṇas it appears of small account, and with less range of application. The faith we find there seems simply to be that the man who has led an immoral life may be condemned to return into this world to undergo here an existence of misery. Re-birth is only a form of punishment; it is the opposite of the celestial life, and tantamount to the infernal. It is not yet what it is here, and what it will continue to be eventually, the state of personal being, a state which may be realised in endlessly diverse forms of being, from that of the insect up to that of the god, but all of equal instability, and subject to relapse.[1] It is impossible to fix the period at which this old belief found in the new metaphysical ideas the medium favourable to its expansion; but it is certain that from the end of the sixth century before our era, when Çâkyamuni was meditating his work of salvation, the doctrine, such as it appears in the Upanishads, was almost complete, and already deeply rooted in the popular conscience. Without this *point d'appui* the spread of Buddhism would hardly be intelligible.

As the state of separation and ignorance is for the soul a fallen state, so the cessation of that state, the return to unity, is salvation. As soon as the soul has acquired the perfect immediate certainty that it is not different from the supreme âtman, it no longer experiences doubts or desires. It still acts, or rather the consequences of its previous actions still act for it, almost as the wheel of the potter continues to revolve when the workman has ceased to turn it. But as water passes over the leaf of the lotus without wetting it, so these acts no longer affect the soul. It attaches itself no longer to anything; it no longer sins;

[1] Bṛihadâr. Up., iv. 4, 5, 6; vi. 2, 16; Chândog. Up., v. 10, 3–8; Muṇḍaka Up., i. 2, 10, &c.

the "bond of the karman" is broken; unity is virtually restored. This is the *yoga*, the state of union. He who brings it about, the *yogin*, is a sovereign being, over whom nothing perishable has power any more, for whom the laws of nature no longer exist, who is "emancipated"[1] from this life. Death even will be able to add nothing to his bliss; it will only abolish what already no longer exists for him, the last appearance of duality. This will be the final deliverance (*moksha*), the complete and final absorption into the one only being; or as, by borrowing an expression from Buddhism, we shall find it expressed at a later date, this will be the extinction, *Nirvâṇa*.

The practical consequence of such a doctrine as this can be only a morality of renunciation, and to underrate, if not to scorn, every established cultus. There is consequently very little mention of positive duties in the Upanishads. The essential matter is to stifle desire, and the ideal of the devout life is that led by the *Sannyâsin*, "of the man who has renounced everything, the anchorite."[2] In the Smṛitis and in the Codes of laws, which have preserved for us the requirements of a morality at once more worldly and more real, this kind of life is ordinarily permitted only to old people after a well-spent life.[3] But the

[1] Chândog. Up., iv. 14, 3; v. 24, 3; Kaṭha. Up., vi. 14, 15, 18; Çvetâçvat. Up., ii. 12–15. In general, the ancient Upanishads describe the beatitude of the âtman and the final emancipation rather than the *jîvanmukti*, emancipation from this life. What is noticeable, they keep silence in regard to the *siddhis*, or supernatural faculties (such as the gift of ubiquity, the power of flying through the air, &c.), which the Yoga and also the Vedânta Sûtras (iv. 4, 17–21, p. 1150, ed. of the Bibl. Ind.) ascribe to the jîvanmukta.

[2] Bṛihadâr. Up., iii. 5, 1; iv. 4, 22; vi. 2, 15; Kaṭha Up., vi. 14; Muṇḍaka Up., i. 2, 11; iii. 2, 6.

[3] After they have discharged the "three debts" to the ṛishis (in the study of the Veda), to the manes of their ancestors (by begetting a son), and to the gods (by performance of the sacrifices), Manu iv. 257. The question, which has never been rightly settled, is debated at length, Apastamba Dh. S., ii. 23, 3–ii. 24, 15. See, on the one hand, Gautama iii. 1; on the other, Manu iv. 35–37 and Yâjñav. iii. 57. The rule generally accepted is that a dvija must pass through the four successive stages of student (brahmacârin), householder (gṛihastha), anchorite (vanaprastha), and ascetic (sannyâsin). These are the four *âçramas*. The Vanaprasthas, "inhabitants of the forest," the ὑλόβιοι of the classic authors, formed a set of colonies devoted to a contemplative life, and practising a parti-

Upanishads do not seem to pay respect to these restrictions,[1] from which, moreover, ardent natures must have easily shaken themselves loose. Buddha, according to the legend, had not reached his thirtieth year when he quitted his family; and in the most ancient Upanishads we see, what is much more alien still to the spirit of Brahmanism, that a wandering religious life was embraced even by women.[2] On the other hand, the extravagances of asceticism occupy small space and find slender favour in these treatises. They prescribe renunciation and contemplation indeed; but mortifications, prolonged fastings, nudity, all held from that time in very high honour, are base practices which their theosophy disdains. The standpoint from which they regard these observances appears to be that of Buddhism, which condemns them. There is not any more mention of those insane and cruel penances which we see exalted so much, for instance, in the epic poetry, the hideous spectacle of which the majority of the Hindu sects have up to our own day been so fain to parade; and yet it is probable that these extravagances had their adepts from that time. The companions of Alexander noticed the existence of them among the Sannyâsins of the Punjâb in the fourth century;[3] and we know, by the account of the death of Calanos, which Plutarch has preserved for us,[4] that the custom of religious suicide dates from a period as early.

cular ritual. Here the master lived, surrounded by his wife and disciples, but in the observance of chastity (Çakunt, act i.). For the sannyâsin the matrimonial tie was entirely broken (Bṛihadâr. Up., iv. 5). He lived alone without any fixed abode, and was no longer bound down to practise any observance of the cultus (Sannyâsa Up. and Aruṇeya Up., ed. of the Biblioth. Indica, p. 34 and 39).

[1] See, for example, Chândog. Up., ii. 23, 1.

[2] Chândog. Up., iv. 4, 2. The passage is doubtful, but compared with such scenes as Bṛihadâr. Up., iii. 6 and 8, it seems to support our interpretation. See the testimony of Nearchus in Strabo xv. 1, cap. lxvi.

[3] Strabo xv. 1, cap. lxi., lxiii. The Smṛiti prescribes these observances only as an expiation for certain definite faults. They are condemned in a general way, Bhagavad Gîtâ, vi. 16; xvii. 5, 6, 19.

[4] Plutarch, Alexander, lxix.; Strabo, xv. 1, cap. lxxiii. See the suicide of Zarmanochegas at Athens under Augustus, Strabo, ibid. 1, cap. lxxiii. Suicide is condemned in a general way by the Smṛiti: Apastamba Dh. S., i. 28, 17; Manu, v. 89; Yâjña-

As for the traditional cultus, it is clear that the tendency of the philosophy of the Upanishads is to destroy it. It is no more directly assailed than the established morality; but no one expects to attain the supreme good through it, any more than through the discharge of the ordinary duties of life. Sacrifice is only an act of preparation; it is the best of acts, but it is an act, and its fruit, consequently, perishable. Accordingly, although whole sections of these treatises are taken up exclusively with speculations on the rites,[1] what they teach upon this point may be summed up in these words of the *Muṇḍaka Upanishad:* "Know the âtman only, and away with everything else; it alone is the bridge to immortality."[2] The Veda itself and the whole circle of sacred science are quite as sweepingly consigned to the second plane.[3] The Veda is not the true *brahman;* it is only its reflection; and the science of this imperfect brahman, this *çabdabrahman*, or brahman in words, is only a science of a lower order. The true science is that which has the true brahman for its subject, the *parabrahman* or supreme brahman; that is to say, the âtman which reveals itself directly in the human heart. This employment of the old name for prayer, afterwards for the revealed Veda, brahman in the neuter, to designate the Absolute, an application of it which we observe here for the first time, and into which the primitive sense of energy still enters so conspicuously, was not altogether new, since we find it already in the Atharva-Veda.[4] But it is from the date of the Upanishads that it passes into general use, and it is in them first that,

valkya, iii. 154; and probably, where the modes most generally adopted are enumerated, Gautama, xiv. 12. Compare Megasthenes in Strabo, xv. 1, cap. lxviii. But it is prescribed as an expiation for certain crimes: Apastamba Dh. S., i. 25, 2–7, 12; i. 28, 15; Gautama, xxii. 2, 3, &c. Even in this case it is condemned by Hârîta, cited by Apastamba, i. 28, 16.

[1] For example, the sections i., v., vi. of the Bṛihadâr. Up., and i., ii., iii. of the Chândog. Up.

[2] ii. 2, 5. See Bhagavad-Gîtâ, xviii. 66.

[3] Chândog. Up., vii. 1; Muṇḍaka Up., i. 1, 4, 5. See Bhagavad-Gîtâ, ii. 45; ix. 21.

[4] x. 7, 17, 24, 32; x. 8, 1, &c.

with or without attributive, it is, to the exclusion of almost every other, accepted in this sense. At the same time the practice arose of designating by Brahmâ in the masculine, the personal God, the first manifestation of the Absolute, the Prajâpati of the ancient texts, the creator and grandsire (*Pitâmaha*) of all existences.

But this science of the true brahman is not one of those which can be taught by words. The admission of the doctrine of identity is already doubtless something, but it is only the point of departure. At first it was thought enough to possess the perfect notion, the thorough and permanent certainty of this identity; but soon more was required. It was maintained that the soul must have an immediate perception of it, and feel itself in union with the Absolute. It is here that this haughty theosophy collapses and pays the penalty of its disdain of all practice and observance. For long special powers of vision were ascribed to dreams [1] and ecstatic phenomena. They were believed to afford a means of communication with the invisible world and with the deity; they were conceived to be the true philosophic method, the way to the Yoga and salvation. There is, therefore, in the Upanishads, especially in those of less antiquity, a complete theory given of the ecstatic state and the means of inducing it; [2] such as a protracted bodily stillness, a stupifying fixity of look, the mental repetition of strange sets of formulæ, meditations on the unfathomable mysteries contained in certain monosyllables, such as the famous *om*, which is the brahman itself, suppression of the breath, a succession of sleep-inducing exercises, by which they fancied they charmed the vital spirits into the thought, the thought into the soul, concentrated this last entirely

[1] Already, in Ṛig-Veda, viii. 47, 14.

[2] Kaṭha Up., iii. 13. The two first sections of the Çvetâçvatara Up. and the 6th of the Maitrî Up. (described, it is true, as *Khila* or supplement by the commentary of Râmatîrtha, p. 77, ed. of the Bibl. Ind.) are entirely taken up with these exercises. In the Garbha Up., 4, the fœtus already prepares for this in the maternal womb.

in the brain, and thence conveyed it back into the heart, where the supreme âtman holds his seat. It is useless, however, to dwell on these processes, to which a strange physiology may lend a certain appearance of singularity, but which reappear again in almost the same terms in the stock-in-trade of many other sects of the enlightened. They have been collected and expounded *ex professo* in the system which more particularly bears the name of *Yoga*. Conscientiously observed, they can only issue in folly and idiocy; and it is, in fact, under the image of a fool or an idiot that the wise man is often delineated for us in the *Purâṇas*, for instance.[1]

We are not required to judge here of the speculations of the Upanishads, nor to insist more at large on the conclusions to which this first attempt at the philosophy of the absolute would inevitably lead. It is only too evident how little disposed this system is to subject itself to the test of experience, how much it fosters spiritual pride, that sin of the race with which the Greeks were so struck when they first came into relation with the Brahmans;[2] how, even when stripped of its extravagances, it tends to enervate the conscience, and what a melancholy idea, in short, it presupposes of life. This last aspect of the matter has often been insisted on; and in these aspirations after a state which, in our view, is very much akin to annihilation, some would have heard the wail of a people unhappy and tired of life. This is an explanation which we, for our part, think must be accepted with extreme reserve, even in regard to Buddhism, which has, however, been much more inclined to the pessimist theory of life. The premises once assumed, the metaphysical deductions

[1] See the legend of King Bharata, Vishṇu P., ii. ch. xiii. t. ii. p. 316 of the translation by H. H. Wilson, ed. Hall; and the vow of folly, the "unmattavrata," ibid., i. ch. ix. t. i. p. 135.

[2] See the narrative of the interview of Onesicritus with the Brahmans in Plutarch, Alexander, lxv.; Strabo, xv., cap. lxiv., lxv.; Megasthenis Fragmenta, pp. 140, 141, ed. Schwanbeck. Compare the legend of Raikva, Chândog. Up., iv. 1 and 2.

follow with somewhat of the rigour of fate; and even if we ventured to seek them there ever so little, they must follow from the primary assumptions of the system, which have nothing in common with disgust of life. These doctrines, therefore, appear to us to be from the first much more instinct with the spirit of speculative daring than the sense of suffering and weariness. It is, nevertheless, true that they are far from wearing a serene aspect, and that, notwithstanding their unquestionable sublimity, they have had in the end a depressing effect upon the Hindu mind.[1] They have accustomed him to recognise no medium between mental excitement and torpid indifference, and they have in the end impressed upon all he produces a certain monotonous character, compounded of satiety and ungratified zeal. For (and it is the last remark which we have to make here) these doctrines will not only be transmitted in the school as a philosophic system, but all the aspirations, good and bad, of the Hindu people will henceforth find in them their fit expression. They will supply to all the sects a theological science of a high order. Some will be inspired by them as with an ideal, and under their inspiration will arise at intervals a set of works of incomparable elevation and delicacy of sentiment, while others will drag them down to their own level, and treat them as a repertory stored with commonplaces. The less religious will borrow from them the externals of devotion; the baser sort and more worthless will wrap themselves up in their mysticism and appropriate their formulæ. It is with the word brahman and deliverance on his lips that the alchemist will form to himself a religion of his search for the philosopher's stone, that the votaries of Kâlî will slaughter their victims, and certain of the Çivaites will give themselves over to their riotous revels. It is not easy to explain declensions so profound as these, happening alongside of such works as

[1] See P. Regnaud, Le Pessimisme Brâhmanique, in Annales du Musée Guimat, vol. i.

the *Bhagavad-Gîtâ*, the *Kural*, and even certain portions of the *Purâṇas;* and no literature so demonstrates as this does the vanity of mysticism and its inability to found anything that will prove durable. The number of times that minds of no ordinary stamp have in this way tried to reconstruct the work of the Upanishads is truly prodigious. The majority of these attempts differ from each other only in certain details of facts, and we shall not have any need even to enumerate them. What may be said of all of them is, that they are always, and very drearily too, telling the same story over and over again; at the outset an effort full of spirit and instinct with lofty aims, followed soon after by an irredeemable collapse, and, as final result, a new sect and a new superstition.

It is, therefore, not surprising that in the course of those idle, barren discussions, rugged good sense has at times had its revenge, and that to such day-dreams it has been able to reply with scepticism, scoffing, and cynical negation. As early as the Ṛig-Veda, we find mention of people who denied the existence of Indra.[1] In the Brâhmaṇas the question is sometimes asked if there really is another life;[2] and the old scholiast Yâska, who is ordinarily supposed to have lived in the fifth century before Christ, finds himself obliged to refute the opinion of teachers of much more ancient date than himself, who had pronounced the Veda to be a tissue of nonsense.[3] This vulgar scepticism, which must not be confounded with the speculative negations of the Sâṅkhya and Buddhism, whose sneering attitude contrasts so forcibly with the timorous spirit of the modern Hindus, appears to have reckoned at one time a goodly number of adherents. The most ancient designation we find applied to them is that of Nâstika (a derivative of *na asti, non est*), "those who deny."[4] They

[1] Ṛig-Veda, ii. 12, 5; viii. 100, 3, 4.

[2] Taittir. Saṃh., vi. 1, 1, 1; Kaṭha Up., i. 1, 20.

[3] Nirukta, i. 15, 16.

[4] Specifically, "who deny a future life." Compare the eloquent passage directed against them, Bhagavad-Gîtâ, xvi. 6, *seq.;* and J. Muir's Metrical Translations from Sanscrit Writers, pp. 12–22, 1879.

appear to have formed associations, more or less avowed, under the title of *Cârvâkas* (from the name of one of their teachers) and *Lokâyatas*, or "secularists." Like other sects, they had their Sûtras, ascribed, doubtless in derision, to Bṛihaspati, the *guru* or preceptor of the gods. Their doctrine is representedas an absolute scepticism, and their morality, which has been preserved to us in certain *çlokas*, or couplets written with much *verve*, and ascribed to the same Bṛihaspati, is a simple call to enjoyment: "So long as life lasts, delight thyself and live well; when once the body is reduced to ashes, it will revive no more." [1]

[1] Sâyaṇa has devoted to the Cârvâkas the first chapter of his Sarvadarçanasaṅgraha; the greatest part of this chapter will be found, as translated by Cowell, in the new edition of the Miscellaneous Essays of Colebrooke, t. i. p. 456. The "false science of Bṛihaspati" is denounced, Maitrî Up., vii. 9. The authors of the Kâçikâ Vṛitti, who were probably Jainas, ascribe this ill-conceived system to the Buddhists. Max Müller, in the Academy for the 25th September 1880, p. 224. The Buddhists, on the other hand, father it upon the Brahmans. Milindapañho, p. 10.

BRAHMANISM.

III. DECLINE.

The Brahmans, custodiers of the Veda and tradition.—Formation of an orthodox Brahmanical literature, popularly accessible : Itihâsa, Purâṇa, Codes of Laws.—Monotheistic tendencies : Brahmâ.—From the time of Çaṅkara especially, Vedântism becomes more and more the sole orthodox exponent of speculative Brahmanism.—Modifications introduced into the ancient cultus : the doctrine of ahiṃsâ and the abolition of animal sacrifice.—Gradual decay of the ceremonial observances of the ancient ritual.—The Vedas ceased to be studied : revived study of them due to European scientific interest in them.

THE religion which we have just expounded is properly Brahmanism, the religion of the Brahmans. Very different from those which we have still to examine—some of which, Buddhism and Jainism, broke off from them at the first, while others, the different forms of Vishnuism and Çivaism, were adopted by them and flourished under their guidance, but never belonged to them to such an extent that they could not dispense with their service—the latter is very much their work and property. It would not have arisen without them, it could not subsist without them, and without them it would have disappeared, leaving us some defaced memorials perhaps, but certainly not a single authentic testimony ; and just this has been the secret of the vigour and continued existence of their caste, so feeble and worthless as an organisation, that it always retained the consciousness of its mission as the guardian of tradition. Notwithstanding the zeal with which they have thrown themselves into theosophy and the devotional systems of the sects, notwithstanding the leading and divinely authoritative part, as it were, they have managed to play in connection with the new religions,[1] they have never ceased to watch over this ancient trust. It is probable that several centuries before our era many of them had adopted, alongside of their own peculiar doctrines, religious beliefs of different origin, and it will be our business, as we proceed, to notice particularly some of the religious forms due to these compromises. In their theoretical studies, however, which are conformable to their traditional customs and their ancient literature, they have on the whole remained faithful to the accepted theoretic of the past; and this not only among the Mîmânsists, who were tradition incarnate, but even among the Vedantins, who had very many more points of affinity with all the innovations. It is the very same cultus at bottom that we find described successively in the Brâhmaṇas, the Sûtras, the Prayogas, and other treatises that are still more modern. The Smṛitis, although of different dates, contain for the most part nothing sectarian. When Patañjali, who is, however, the reputed author of the Yogasûtras, the most eccentric of the philosophical systems, pleads in the introduction to his Mahâbhâshya (in the second century before Christ) the claims of grammatical studies, he takes up exactly the same ground as the ancient Yâska, that, viz., of the Vedic exegesis.[2] Çaṅkara in the eighth century, Sâyaṇa in the fourteenth, were Vaishṇavas, and even reputed to have been incarnations of Vishṇu, though of this there is not much evidence when they comment, the one on the Vedântasûtras and the Upanishads, and the other on the whole of the great Vedic collections.[3] In the

[1] With Çatap. Br., ii. 2, 2, 6, and Manu, xi. 84, compare such passages as Bhâgavata-Pur., iii. 16, 17. A modern verse of a proverbial cast says, "The entire world depends on the gods, the gods depend on the mantras, the mantras depend on the Brahmans; the Brahmans are my gods." J. A. Dubois, Mœurs des Peuples de l'Inde, t. p. 186, and O. Böhtlingk, Indische Sprüche, No. 7552, t. iii. p. 607, 2d ed.

[2] Mahâbhâshya, i. 1, 1, pp. 1–5, ed. Kielhorn.

[3] The commentary of Sâyaṇa on the Atharva-Veda, which, at one time

philosophical treatises, a conspicuous element is polemic against the different doctrines of the sects, but it is one which is strictly scholastic. Even in the great reaction on the offensive against Buddhism, which was begun in the Dekhan in the seventh and eighth centuries by the schools of Kumârila and of Çaṅkara,[1] and in which sectarian passions played, in reality, a decisive part, there is nothing in the authentic documents anyhow that have been studied till now but what appears to be resolvable into simple metaphysical discussions. If we confined ourselves to this literature, we would say that Brahmanical India has never, outside of its Veda, recognised anything but some philosophical systems, and we could hardly realise the existence of those powerful religious movements which are revealed to us in the epic poetry, in profane literature, and in the immense mass of writings belonging to the sects. Never indifferent to the interests of the present, and with very

affirmed, at another denied to exist, had become more than suspected (Burnell, Vaṃçabr., p. xxi.; Haug in the Zeitsch. der Deutsch. Morgenl. Gesellsch., xviii. p. 304; Max Müller, in the Academy, 31st January 1874), has just been discovered. See the letters of Shankar Pandurang Pandit, Max Müller, and G. Bühler, in the Academy of the 5th and 12th June 1880. The Atharva-Veda, which is completely unknown to-day in the South, the native region of Sâyaṇa, and which as early as the seventeenth century was considered lost (Burnell in the Indian Antiq., viii. 99, and Classified Index of the Tanjore MSS., i. 37), was certainly known favourably there before, since use is made of it in the Apastamba Dharma-Sûtra, which in all probability was composed in Southern India. G. Bühler, Sacred Laws of the Aryas, i. pp. xxv. and xxx. For information about Sâyaṇa see Burnell, especially Vaṃçabrâhmaṇa, preface, p. v. *seq.* He was principal chief (jagad-guru) of the Smârtas Brahmans, and died in 1386 at the monastery of Çriṅgeri in the Mysore. Burnell has advanced the hypothesis, by no means improbable, that Sâyaṇa and Mâdhava, who are reputed to be brothers, and divide the honour of producing the majority of these commentaries, are in reality one and the same personage.

[1] For the age of Kumârila Bhaṭṭa, see Burnell, Sâmavidhânabrâhmaṇa, introd., p. vi. Çaṅkara Acârya is generally placed in the eighth century; perhaps we must accept the ninth rather. The best accredited tradition represents him as born on the 10th of the month of Mâdhava (April–May) in 788 A.D. Ind. Studien, t. xiv. p. 353. Other traditions, it is true, place him in the second and the fifth centuries. Ind. Antiq., i. 361, vii. 282. The author of the Dabistân (ii. 141), on the other hand, brings him as far down as the commencement of the fourteenth.

imperfect resources on the whole at their disposal, the Brahmans have thus, during more than twenty centuries, preserved their ancient heritage with a fidelity for which not only modern science, but India also, owes them no small gratitude. For if in the midst of this flood of dreamy speculations there has been anything vitally serviceable in the past history of this people, it is the continuity of the pure tradition of Brahmanism, in spite of its fondness for routine and its disregard of the lessons of experience, the exclusiveness of its creed, and its profound want of charity. No sectarian movement has on the whole produced anything of such solidity as the old Smṛitis, anything so independent and so purely intellectual as certain philosophic Sûtras. The *vaidika,* who knows by heart and teaches to his disciples one or several Vedas, which he still understands at least in part, is superior to the sectarian *guru,* with his unintelligible mantras, his amulets, and his diagrams; the *yâjñika,* who possesses the complex science of ancient sacrifice, must be ranked above the illiterate attendant of a temple and an idol; and the *agnihotrin,* who, while diligent in his own business, keeps up his sacred fires, and, with his wife and children, conforms to the prescriptions of his hereditary ritual, is a more serviceable and moral being than the fakir and even the Buddhist monk.

We shall not attempt to trace Brahmanism in its decline through that long period during which it was only one of the phases of that many-shaped Proteus called Hinduism, and in the course of which it came to be so intimately mixed up with the sectarian religions that we can now only separate it from them by an act of abstraction. There are certain points, however, which it is important we should notice.

Almost all ancient religious literature was esoteric, or became so at length. The Veda was more or less so by right, since it could be transmitted only by oral instruction, from which women and the menial class were strictly excluded,[1] and which in the end was addressed only to the Brahmans. The books connected with it were so in point of fact;[2] for they either presuppose a knowledge of the Veda, or else their form is such that only the initiated could understand them: no profane person would have been able to read a Sûtra, for example. The art of writing having become general, and regard being had, perhaps, to the practice common among the sects, attempts were made, without trespassing on the sacred domain of the Veda, to reproduce under a more accessible form such doctrines as were of more general interest than others. We think we must instance the majority of the Upanishads as the first attempt that was made in this direction, particularly the small ones, which are of a character specially adapted to the common intelligence. Other monuments of this literature have perished, or have only come down to us very materially altered, such as the old epic and legendary collections, the ancient Itihâsa and the ancient Purâṇa, so often referred to, and of which certain unsectarian portions of the Mahâbhârata may give, perhaps, some idea. At a later period the numerous *Dharmaçâstras*, or codes of laws, such as those of Manu, of Yâjñavalkya, and others,[3] were drawn up

[1] The Upanayana, the presentation of the pupil to the master, is confined by the whole Smṛiti to the male children of the dvijas, *i.e.*, of the members of the three superior castes, which have not by their negligence forfeited their right to initiation. The Çûdra is expressly excluded (Apastamba Dh. S., i. 1, 5). In this respect, there can be no doubt, it would be more interesting to know to what extent the non-Brahmans availed themselves of their right. But the Smṛiti does not concern itself much with any except the Brahmans, and what it says of the other castes is almost always to be distrusted. In all probability the communication of the Veda resolved itself for them, and even many of the Brahmans, into a simple formality.

[2] They themselves besides openly profess to give an esoteric doctrine. See Nirukta, ii. 3, 4 (a passage which we find again in Manu, ii. 114, 115, 144, and Saṃhitopanishad, 62, iii.); Manu, i. 103; ii. 16; xii. 117.

[3] For different lists of the Dharmaçâstras see Stenzler, Zur Literatur der Indischen Gesetzbücher, in the Ind. Studien, t. i. p. 232. There are published up to the present time in critical editions and easily accessible: Manu, or Mânava-Dharmaçâstra, which has been published a great many times (among others

with this very object. These are compilations comparatively modern, very few of which date before our era, and some of which are much more recent, though all are very old in respect of the foundation they rest on. In this way there arose a purely Brahmanical literature, without any sectarian admixture, accessible to everybody, and kept alive uninterruptedly to our day; and as this literature was produced at times in the names of the most revered among the ancient sages, some of its productions were not long in eclipsing the scholastic originals. The code of Manu, for instance, ascribed to the mythical ancestor and legislator of the human race, ranked at the head of the Smṛitis, and immediately next to the Veda.

It is in these books that the most decided stress is laid on the *rôle* of Brahmâ (mas.), the creator, the father of gods and men, a figure majestic indeed, but somewhat pallid, as all the products of speculation are, and ill qualified to dispute the supremacy with his formidable rivals that had their origin in the popular beliefs. Unknown to the ancient cultus—although his prototype, Prajâpati, filled a pretty large space in it—he does not appear to have occupied more space in the new systems of worship; and many sanctuaries as there are in India, we know of only one of

by Gr. Ch. Haughton, 1825, and A. Loiseleur Deslongchamps, 1830–33), and reproduced in many languages, since the celebrated translation by Sir William Jones, 1794. Yājñavalkya, text and translation into German by A. F. Stenzler, 1849. The Mitāksharā, a treatise on jurisprudence, composed at the end of the eleventh century, and several times edited in India, is based on the code of Yājñavalkya. Nārada, an English translation by J. Jolly, 1876: the text has not appeared. A collection of twenty-six of these texts has been reprinted by Jîvânanda Vidyâsâgara, under the title of Dharmaçâstrasaṅgraha, 2 vols., Calcutta, 1876. To these publications may be added the compendiums or digests compiled by the Paṇḍits: The Code of Gentoo Law, 1776 (compiled by order of Warren Hastings, and translated into English by Halhed, has been translated into French and German); and the Digest of Hindū Law on Contracts and Successions by Jagannâtha Tarkapañcânana (translated by Colebrooke, 1798, reprinted in 1801 and in 1864). Of a character somewhat different, although from the same source, is the new Digest of Bombay, drawn up according to the decisions of Çâstrins, or native jurists attached to the law courts of the Presidency, by R. West and G. Bühler, 1867.

these, that of Pushkara, near Ajmeer, in Râjastan, which is exclusively dedicated to him.[1] It is likewise in these books that the theory of the four ages of the world (*yuga*), and of the gradual triumph of evil, as well as that of the successive creations and destructions of the universe, following each other in the lapse of immense periods, is expounded for the first time in any exact manner.[2] The doctrines which refer to the life beyond the grave, especially those which refer to hell, or rather purgatory (for there are no eternal torments), assume their final form. Besides, no effort is made to raise again the old deities after the many blows dealt at them in succession by ritualism, theosophy, and sectarian devotionalism. Indra and his peers are the gods of the cultus; outside of that they are very subordinate powers; who watch like guardians over the different regions of the world (*lokapâla*), and to whom man may, by science and penance, become the equal, if not the superior.[3]

[1] The worship of Brahmâ is, however, minutely described in the Bhavishya-Purâṇa, Aufrecht, Oxford Catalogue, pp. 30, 31.

[2] See R. Roth, Der Mythus von den fünf Menschengeschlechtern bei Hesiod und die Indische Lehre von den vier Weltaltern, 1860. This pessimist theory is expressed by the allegory of the Cow of Dharma, which stands over four feet in the first age, over three in the second, over two in the third, and over one in the present age. The developed theory of the four ages contains numerical data which refer to astronomy, either Chaldean or Greek. See Biot, Etudes sur l'Astronomie Indienne et Chinoise, p. 30 *seq.*

[3] Just as the ancient gods retain their rank in the ritual portion of these books, so they also preserve it often in the legends of the epic poetry, of the Purâṇas, identically those ones, too, whose sectarian character is most pronounced. See on this subject the interesting monographs of A. Holtzmann: Agni nach den Vorstellungen des Mahâbhârata, 1878; Indra nach den Vorstellungen des Mahâbhârata, in the Zeitschr. d. D. Morgenl. Gesell., xxxii. p. 290; Die Apsaras nach dem Mahâbhârata, ibid., xxxiii. p. 631; Arjuna, ein Beitrag zur Reconstruction des Mahâbhârata, 1879. But in all these writings the devas, so to speak, disappear as soon as the question becomes one of speculation or the cosmogony. According to Manu they came into existence along with men and inferior beings, although after the production of the elementary principles and the demiurgic powers, the Manus and the Prajâpatis, personages who, taken separately, belong nearly all to the ancient literature (being for the most part Vedic ṛishis), but who are new in this character, and so grouped in classes, Manu, i. 5–8. This cosmogonic mythology occurs again in the epic and all the Purâṇas, with an endless number of variations in detail, but such as do not affect the system, which remains the same at bottom. The principal difference is that in the Purâṇas it is subordinated to the great sectarian divinities, and, above all, enlarged to a prodigious

Through their eclectic and monotheistic tendency, these books contributed to the formation of a certain orthodoxy in the bosom of Brahmanism. On the one hand, the Veda was accepted more than ever as an absolute authority,[1] which was the less to be challenged in theory that it was so slightly troublesome in practice; on the other hand, the recognition of a personal god and a divine providence, with which the Brâhmaṇas and the Upanishads at times dispense so easily, became by degrees a settled dogma. Under whatever name he might be worshipped, and whatever metaphysical explanation might be given of his nature, it was necessary to confess an Içvara, a Lord, and humble one's self before him. The Sâṅkhya, which denied this notion, was pronounced guilty of impiety. The Mîmâṃsâ, which ignored it, was also looked upon with suspicion,[2] in spite of its severe traditionalism; and it was obliged to introduce it at the beginning of its creed. The Vedânta alone, by that prescriptive right which the idealistic systems have always enjoyed, of reconciling a particular system of devotion with a metaphysical system which seems to require its exclusion, evaded at times the necessity of recognising in terms a god who was self-conscious and distinct from the world. In the *Atma-*

extent as respects at once amount of detail and exaggeration. Thus, with reference to the Manvantaras or the reign of a Manu, as everything changes from one of these periods to another, things, men, and gods, it becomes an amusement to draw up an inventory of each, not only such as are considered to have passed, but even those which are still to come. See, for instance, the first chapters of book viii. of the Bhâgavata P., and book iii. of the Vishṇu Purâṇa.

[1] It is not till this period of decline that there appears to have been any thought of subjecting the whole of the Vedic literature, the Çruti, and everything connected with it, to a definitive classification, and to draw up in systematic form the subject-matter. This is attempted in the Prasthânabheda of Madhusûdana Sarasvatî, and the Caraṇavyûha, one of the pariçishṭas or supplements to the White Yajus, published in succession by Professor Weber in the Indische Studien, vols. i., ii. Yet, notwithstanding these attempts, this literature has never been formed into a canon, in the strict sense of the word, such as that of the Buddhists or Jainas, the different families of Brahmans having by preference always adhered each to their hereditary Veda.

[2] By Varâha Mihira (sixth century) the Mîmânsists are likened to the Buddhists, Ind. Studien, xiv. p. 353.

bodha[1] (knowledge of the âtman), ascribed to Çaṅkara, although it is a work adapted to the instruction of the vulgar, there is mention only of the neuter and impersonal brahman. But as soon as thought, resting from speculative effort, comes to make use of formulas that are less precise, the Vedânta has to submit in its turn to the common rule, and speak the language of deism. Thanks to that elasticity which enabled it to satisfy all kinds of piety, this system ended by absorbing into itself all the others in the religious domain. Commencing specially with the vigorous impulse which it received from Çaṅkara, who appears to have been the first to introduce into the school a cenobitic organisation,[2] it gradually became almost the only speculative exponent of Brahmanism. The whole modern literature, which aims at instruction and propagandism, draws its inspiration from it, and in our days the majority of learned Brahmans—a minority on the whole, to whatever sect they may belong otherwise—more or less profess Vedântism.[3]

It would be interesting to inquire into the state of the cultus of Brahmanism during the same period, and to trace it in its gradual disappearance. But on this point we have no accurate information; one thing is certain, it never merged in any of the sectarian systems. Not only do the orthodox writings, such as Manu, prohibit Brahmans from serving in connection with temples and idols, and officiating in popular ceremonials, but books as decidedly sectarian as the epic poems, and even certain

[1] Translated and commented on by F. Nève in the Journal Asiatique, t. vii. 6th series. See, moreover, F. H. H. Windischmann, Sancara, sive de Theologumenis Vedanticorum, 1833.

[2] See Burnell, Vamçabrâhmana, introd., p. xiii. These cenobites differed considerably from the ancient Hylobioi. They lived together in *maṭhas*, or monasteries, the sexes being always separated and devoted to celibacy. They formed regular religious orders, similar to that of Buddhism; and in the different sectarian religions, among whom the institution became especially flourishing, they constituted a sort of clergy, of which the old Brahmanism knew nothing. The Brahmans, it cannot be too often insisted on, were a hereditary body of sacred individuals, but they formed no clergy.

[3] Compare, for the seventeenth century, the testimony of the author of the Dabistân, ii. p. 103.

Purâṇas (Mârkaṇḍeya-P., Vishṇu-P., Brâgavata-P.) hardly refer to any except the ancient ceremonies. It is only in the Tantras, the Purâṇas which are akin to them, certain Upanishads, technical manuals and compilations—that is to say, in writings composed for a very special purpose—that we find any precise indications of the sectarian ritual. It would appear that in the esteem of even Brahmans who have been most intimately connected with the new religion, the cultus of these religions was never more than a special devotion, a rendering of a system of acts of homage, a *pûjâ*, which was radically different from the *yajña*, the sacrifice of tradition. The doctrines were intermingled; the rites remained distinct. Of the ancient observances, it was not unnaturally those of the domestic ritual which at once held out best and varied most. We shall mention only the most significant of these innovations, the revolting custom of *anumaraṇa*, which required that the widow should be burned on the same pile with the body of her husband.[1] As for the great Brahmanical cultus, attested as it was by a more learned tradition, it was less threatened with the chance of change than that of desuetude. This cultus was extremely complicated and burdensome, and as early as the Brâhmaṇas compromises had to be resorted to.[2] Without offence to the ancient theory, matters were so adjusted that its observances became easier in practice. As a general rule, the more modern a ritual treatise is, the more detailed it is, and in appearance more exacting; but the more it at the same time multiplies dispensations and means whereby, while the rule is observed, the expenses are lessened. A whole class of writings, the Vidhânas, the origin of which is besides very ancient, have no other object than to direct

1 The place where a *satî* has thus devoted herself is sometimes marked by a *cippus*, bearing engraven on the upper part two footprints, one large and the other small, the one in the track of the other, and directed to the same quarter.

2 See, for example, Taitt. Saṃh., i. 6, 9, where the benefits of the great somayâgas are ascribed to the *ishṭis* of the simplest kind.

in the observance of a kind of cultus at a reduced rate, which should procure the same advantages as the great sacrifices.[1] The immolations which were incompatible with the precept of *ahiṃsâ, i.e.*, respect for everything that has life, a consequence of the doctrine of metempsychosis, and also of the more gentle philosophy diffused by Buddhism, were by degrees abolished, and the liberation of the victim, or the substitution in its stead and place of a figure made of flour paste, both of which were at first matter of sufferance, became at length matter of requirement. The *dânâ,* that is, the making of presents to the Brahmans, whether in the form of donations in land[2] or in gifts of any other kind (one of these offerings consisted in giving its own weight in gold and silver[3]), became gradually the most meritorious of pious works, endowed with an efficacy far superior to that of sacrifice.[4] At the same time, Brahmanism admitted of a great

[1] Two Vidhânas have been published up to the present time: that of the Sâma-Veda by Burnell, The Sâmavidhânabrâhmaṇa, 1873; and that of the Ṛig-Veda by R. Meyer, Ṛigvidhânam, Berlin, 1878.

[2] A considerable and daily increasing number have reached us of these deeds of gift engraved on copper plates, and granted by kings, ministers of state, and vassal princes. The majority of the ancient inscriptions consist of documents of this sort, and it is by means of these that we are enabled to construe bit by bit the positive history of India. The most of them are granted in favour of Brahmans; only a small number are in the name of members of the laity.

[3] This sort of gift is called *tulâ*, "a balance." In an inscription of the twelfth century it is said of a king of Canoje that he celebrated the tulâ rite a hundred times. Râjendralâla Mitra, Notes on Two Copperplate Grants of Govindacandra of Kanauj, in Journ. As. Soc. of Bengal, t. lxii. See also the Vṛihat-Parâçarasmṛiti in the Dharmaçâstrasaṅgraha, vol. ii. p. 232, edition of 1876.

[4] There is a very considerable literature connected with the dâna. The little text entitled Bṛihaspatismṛiti (published in the Dharmaçâstrasaṅgraha, i. p. 644 *seq.*), and the whole of book viii. of Vṛihat-Parâçarasmṛiti (ibid. ii. p. 215 *seq.*), treat exclusively of it. It is also the subject of a great portion of the Bhavishyottâra Purâṇa (Aufrecht, Oxford Catalogue, p. 35), and of the whole of the second section or Dânakhaṇḍa of the Encyclopædia of Hemâdri, the Çaturvargacintâmaṇi (thirteenth century, in course of publication in the Bibliotheca Indica). The tulâ rite is described in the 150th chapter of the Purâṇa and the 6th of the Dânakhaṇḍa. It is right, however, we should remark that there is throughout the literature referred to a twofold doctrine on this subject. On the one hand, the excellence of the dâna is extolled, and the *pratigraha*, the right to receive it, is regarded as one of the most precious privileges of the Brah-

number of such observances as pilgrimages, ablutions in the Ganges, &c., of which the ancient books know nothing, and which in Manu even are not held in high esteem.[1] Of all these changes the literature gives us ample account. What it does not tell us is the place which this cultus still held in reality. From coins and inscriptions we know that the great sacrifices, such as the açvamêdha, the vâjapêya, and the paundarîka, &c., were still celebrated during the early part of the middle age.[2] Then from the eighth century these testimonies become extremely rare, and there is no more reference, except in a general way, to subsidies supplied to the Brahmans for the performance of their rites.[3] The Mussulman conquest, which extended permanently over a great portion of the territory, must have accelerated this decadence by drying up in vast provinces the spring of these princely liberalities; and it is probably to this epoch we must assign the disappearance of important ritual texts which were still in existence in the middle age, and which have since been lost.[4] The

mans; on the other, those are censured who accept gifts, especially at the hands of a king. See A. Weber in the Ind. Stud., x. p. 55 *seq.* Contradictions exactly similar occur in regard to the position of the *purohita*, the domestic chaplain of a prince or a grandee, a rank which is at one time exalted above every other, and at another represented as worthy of no honour. A. Weber, ibid., p. 99 *seq.*; J. Muir, Sanskrit Texts, i. pp. 128 and 507, 2d ed.; and Ind. Antiq., vi. p. 251 *seq.*). The Brahman must not earn his livelihood by the altar as by a trade; he must not sell his services or accept the situation of a servant for wages. There is in all this a conflict between the ideal and the pride of asceticism and the desire of worldly power, two passions equally dear to the Brahmanical caste.

[1] Manu, viii. 92.

[2] Coins and inscriptions of the Guptas; inscriptions of Ajaṇṭâ, the Pallavas, and the ancient Calukyas and Kadambas of the Dekhan. In the inscriptions of Gujarât (dynasty of Baroch, Calukyas, Valabhîs, of the fifth and sixth centuries), on the contrary, only ceremonies of the domestic ritual are specified. Journ. of the Roy. As. Soc., i., new series, pp. 269, 276; Ind. Antiq., vii. pp. 70, 72; viii. p. 303; Journ. of the Roy. As. Soc., Bombay, xi. 344, 345. The chief document of all, the great inscription of Nânâghât, is still unedited. See Journ. of the Roy. As. Soc., Bombay, xii. 405.

[3] In the professedly sectarian inscriptions, the gift is made directly to the god, that is, to the sanctuary.

[4] This gradual desertion is discernible in the last great effort of the ancient theology, in the Commentaries of Sâyaṇa. This is one of those learnedly compiled works which have no root in actual life, epitomise the past, and have no future.

somayâgas, which we know have been celebrated in our own century, may be counted off upon the fingers.[1] The agnihotrin Brahmans, who maintain the three sacred fires, are now reduced to a small number, and the ancient noviciate, the brahmacarya, through which an acquaintance with the texts and the rites is acquired, no longer enlists more than a very few recruits.[2] Advancement lies elsewhere—in the study of logic, jurisprudence, and grammar,[3] and the youth go to acquire a knowledge of these in colleges organised after the English fashion, rather than in the *tols* or the *maṭhas* of the Brahmans. In 1829, Wilson reckoned up as still existing twenty-five of these institutions, with 600 pupils, at Nadiyâ, the chief seat of native science in Bengal. In less than forty years after, the number of institutions was reduced to a half, and that of the pupils to a fourth;[4] and what applies to Bengal applies to nearly every place else, in the extreme south, in the Mahratta countries, and even at Benares. In the religious field, the interest centres in the modern works of sectarian Vedantism. The ancient theology, since it no longer corresponds to a faith and has ceased to be a lucrative profession, is everywhere visibly on the wane. Few now busy themselves with procuring new copies of the ancient books, as the old copies get destroyed; and although there are still in India many thousands of Brahmans who know by heart the principal texts of the Veda, we may say that European science has not arrived too soon to gather together this antique inheritance, at the

[1] The last, which was celebrated at Poona, in the Mahratta country, took place as far back as 1851; it lasted six days. Haug in the Zeitsch. d. D. Morgenl. Gesell., xvi. p. 273.

[2] The "upanayana," the gift of the sacred cord, the communication of the Sâvitri, &c., being sacraments, are still observed, especially in the case of Brahmans; but all these ceremonies, which the Smṛitis distribute on an average over twelve years, usually take no more than some days.

[3] In a curious register of the members of a literary assembly held in the twelfth century at Kashmir, more than thirty pandits being present, there are found only four vaidikas. G. Bühler in the Journ. of the Roy. As. Soc., Bombay, vol. xii., extra number, p. 50.

[4] Hunter, A Statistical Account of Bengal, vol. ii. p. 109.

very moment when it was about to fall escheat. The kind of revival of Vedism which has manifested itself in these last days in the publication of texts, and even in efforts at a practical return to ancient orthodoxy, patronised as it is by divers *Dharmasabhâs* (associations for the maintenance of the law), is itself only a consequence of the work, begun nearly a century ago, by Sir William Jones; and it forms a movement with which, certain appearances notwithstanding, the taste for archæology, the reawakening of the national spirit, and politics even, have more to do on the whole than religion.

III.

BUDDHISM.

Buddhism the most direct and deliberate repudiation of Brahmanism; in what sense it is also the most ancient.—Literature of Buddhism: the Tripiṭaka.—Buddha, his life and death: date of the Nirvâṇa.—Difficulty in defining the Master's own personal teaching.—Anti-theological and little given to speculation, primitive Buddhism atheistic and occupied exclusively with the problem of salvation.—Its Four Noble verities.—The Nidânas or conditions of existence.—Existence, as it is essentially perishable; the skandhas, the karman, and the new births. —Nirvâṇa, absolute annihilation.—Negations of Buddhism: issue in nihilism in the school of Nâgârjuna.—Affinities with the Sâṅkhya and the Vedânta.—The rapid advance of Buddhism and the causes in explanation: the personality and the legend of Buddha.—Spirit of charity and propagandism.—Preaching of and training in its principles, and direction of the conscience.—Formation of a Buddhist mythology: the Buddhas and Bodhisattvas.—Organisation of Buddhism. —Institution of monasticism and a clergy: the Saṅgha.—Buddhism and caste.—Wealth of the religious order and magnificence of the cultus.—Political circumstances favourable to Buddhism: establishment of the great monarchies.—Açoka and the Buddhist missions.—Domination abroad: cosmopolitan spirit of Buddhism.—Decay and total extinction of Buddhism in India.—Has it been unable to withstand persecution?—Fanaticism in India.—Kumârila and Çaṅkara.—The real causes of the downfall of Buddhism its internal vices, which have disabled it from competing with the sectarian religions.

As we pass to the younger religions which have developed in the train of Brahmanism, the first of these which presents itself to us is Buddhism, not because it has been proved to be the most ancient, but because it attained a separate independent existence before any other, and is in a way a direct offshoot from the old stock, while its rivals have rather been engrafted into it like parasitic plants. Buddhism presents, in fact, a twofold aspect. On the one hand, it is a Hindu phenomenon, a natural product, so to speak, of the age and social circle that witnessed its birth. When we attempt to reconstruct its primitive doctrine and early history, we come upon something so akin to what we meet in the most ancient Upanishads and in the legends of Brahmanism, that it is not always easy to determine what features belong peculiarly to it. On the other hand, it asserts itself from the first as an independent religion, in which a new spirit breathes, and on which the mighty personality of its founder has left an indelible impress. In this sense, Buddhism is the work of Buddha, just as Christianity is the work of Jesus, and Islam that of Mahomet. From the date of the death of the Master, we feel ourselves face to face with a body of doctrines, and an institution with a life of their own, and the history of which is connected with that of the contemporary religions only in an indirect and quite external way. This history we shall not attempt to relate here, neither shall we venture to sketch in a general outline the immense development of the dogmas, the institutions, and destinies of this system. We shall hardly be able to touch on the questions which arise in connection with the sources of this history of Buddhism, the various related traditions, so widely different from one another, the duplicate form in which its sacred literature appears, preserved at first in Sanskrit in the North, and in Pâli in the South, and more or less faithfully reproduced at a later period in the majority of the languages of High and Eastern Asia.[1] We shall have no occasion to refer,

[1] The collection of the sacred books of Buddhism bears the name of Tripiṭaka (in Pâli, Tipiṭaka), "the three baskets," * since it is formed of three minor collections: that of the Vinaya, or the discipline, which especially respects the clergy; that of the Sûtras, or sermons of Buddha, containing the general exposition of doctrine; and that of the Abhidharma, or the metaphysics of the system. This division is traditional rather than logical, and the definitions are exact only in a quite general way. For other divisions see Burnouf, Introd. à l'Hist. du Bouddh. Ind., p. 48, and the communications of R. Morris and Max Müller in the Academy of the 21st and 28th August 1880, pp. 136 and 154. These writings have been preserved in two comparatively original

* An expression which seems to presuppose the existence of written texts, but which, according to V. Trenckner, Pâli Miscellany, part i. p. 67, would, on the contrary, harmonise very well with the Buddhist tradition of a long purely oral transmission of the canon.

except in passing, to the biography of its founder, its different metaphysical systems, its morals, its ecclesiastical

redactions, but neither of them in the Mâgadhi dialect, the primitive language of the Church. One of them is in Pâli, and passes current in Ceylon and India beyond the Ganges; the other is in Sanskrit, and was discovered some fifty years ago in Nepâl by B. H. Hodgson. The comparative study of these two redactions has made little progress as yet, and the question of their relative age and authority is far from being decided. In general, the probabilities are in favour of the Pâli redaction, which anyhow has the advantage of having been fixed ever since the fifth century by the commentaries of Buddhaghosha, and which appears to have better preserved the distinction between the ancient writings and the more recent productions; but in opposition to the often sweeping assertions of Pâli scholars (see, *e.g.*, Childers's Dictionary of the Pâli Language, p. xi.), respect should be had to the objections and judicious reservations formulated by E. Senart (Notes sur quelques Termes Buddhiques, in the Journ. Asiat., 1876, viii. p. 477 *seq.*), as well as to the elements of ancient popular poetry, pointed out by the same scholar (Essai sur la Légende du Buddha, ib., 1874, iii. pp. 363, 409 *seq.*), and by H. Kern (Over de Jaartelling der Zuidelijke Buddhisten, p. 23 *seq.*), in the Gâthâs of the developed Sûtras of the North; that is to say, in what, since Burnouf, has come to be regarded as the most modern portion of the Sanskrit collection and the canonical literature in general. Both redactions have been translated into a certain number of foreign languages, and by these, according as they have adopted the one or the other, and regard the Sanskrit or the Pâli as the sacred language, the Buddhist population is distinguished into Buddhists of the North and Buddhists of the South. To the Buddhism of the South belong Ceylon, Burmah, Pegu, Siam; while Nepâl, Tibet, China, Japan, Annam, Cambodja, Java, and Sumatra are or were connected with the Buddhism of the North. Analyses of this literature will be found, for the Pâli Tipiṭaka, in Spence Hardy's Eastern Monachism, p. 166 *seq.*; in the Pâli Dictionary by Childers, p. 506, and in Rhys Davids' Buddhism, p. 18 *seq.*; for the Nepâl collection, in the Memoirs of B. H. Hodgson (Asiatic Researches, xvi., Trans. of the Roy. As. Soc., ii., Journ. of the As. Soc. of Bengal, v. and vi., reprinted in the collection of his Essays, 1874, Nos. 1, 2, 3, and 8); and especially in Burnouf's Introduction à l'Histoire du Bouddhisme Indien, which is entirely devoted to the collection of Nepâl. Consult also E. B. Cowell and T. Eggeling, Catalogue of Buddhist Sanskrit Manuscripts in the Possession of the Royal Asiatic Society (Hodgson Collection), in the Journ. of the Roy. As. Soc., new series, viii. For the Tibetan collection, see the Analyses of Csoma of Körös in the Journ. of the As. Soc. of Bengal, i., and the Asiatic Researches, xx.; for the Chinese collection, see S. Beal's The Buddhist Tripiṭaka as it is known in China and Japan, a catalogue and compendious report published for the India Office, 1876. The information collected by W. Wassiljew, Der Buddhismus (see in particular, p. 87 *seq.* and 157 *seq.*), refers at once to the Tibetan and the Chinese collections.

Of the Abhidharma we possess up to the present time only extracts and fragments. For the Sûtras, which are better known, see *infra*. It is only the Vinaya that it has till now been proposed to publish entirely, the first volume of which, a third of the whole, has just appeared, with a scholarly preface. H. Oldenberg, The Vinaya Piṭakam, one of the Principal Buddhist Holy Scriptures, in the Pâli Language, vol. i., The Mahâvagga, 1879. The second volume has since appeared, containing the Cullavagga, 1880.

organisation, its discipline and cultus, its mythology and sacred writings, its schools, its heresies, and its councils, and its probable or possible influence upon other beliefs, such as Manicheeism and different sects of Christianity. In a word, we shall touch on its doctrine and its history only in so far as we shall find it necessary to explain its fortune and to indicate the place which belongs to it in the religious development of India.[1]

[1] General works on Buddhism:—Contemporary with the works of Abel Remusat and J. J. Schmidt on the religions and literatures of High and Eastern Asia, and those of Csoma de Körös on Tibetan Buddhism (Journ. of the As. Soc. of Bengal, i.; Asiatic Researches, xx.), the direct study of Indian Buddhism commences with the discovery and examination of the Buddhist books of Nepâl by B. H. Hodgson, 1828–1837. His Memoirs, reprinted in 1874, "Essays on the Languages, Literature, and Religion of Nepâl and Tibet," were followed closely by the works of G. Turnour on the Pâli literature and the Singhalese chronicles: The Mahavaṃso, with Translation, and an Introductory Essay on Pâli Buddhistical Literature, vol. i., 1837; and Journ. of the As. Soc. of Bengal, vii., 1838. The first work, which contains the ancient part, the thirty-three first chapters of the Mahâvaṃsa, or the "Great Chronicle" of Ceylon, has not been continued, but a redaction, a little earlier, of the same materials, the Dîpavaṃsa, "The Chronicle of the Isle," has just been published, text and English translation, by H. Oldenberg: The Dîpavaṃsa, an Ancient Buddhist Historical Record, 1879. These two works, which record the origin of Buddhism and the Singhalese Annals to the end of the third century A.D., were probably compiled about the fourth or fifth century, from documents preserved in the monasteries of Ceylon, the most ancient books of history which India has left to us. In 1844 E. Burnouf introduced a new era in regard to these studies by the publication of his Introduction à l'Histoire du Bouddhisme Indien (reprinted in 1876), followed in 1852 by Le Lotus de la Bonne Loi, traduit du Sanscrit et accompagné de vingt et un Memoires relatifs au Bouddhisme. Then there come in order of date, R. Spence Hardy, Eastern Monachism, an Account of the Origin, Laws, Discipline, and Sacred Writings . . . of the Order of Mendicants founded by Gotama Buddha, compiled from Singhalese MSS., 1853, reprinted 1860. By the same, A Manual of Buddhism in its Modern Development, translated from Singhalese MSS., 1853, reprinted 1860, and again in 1880. C. F. Köppen, Die Religion des Buddha, 2 vols., 1857–1859. W. Wassiljew, Der Buddhismus, seine Dogmen, Geschichte und Literatur, first part (all that has appeared), translated from the Russian, 1860; a French translation by La Comme, 1865; very important for Indian Buddhism, though drawn exclusively from Thibetan and Chinese sources. A. Schiefner, Târanâtha's Geschichte des Buddhismus in Indien, aus dem Tibetischen übersetzt, 1869: the author wrote at the beginning of the seventeenth century. To these works must be added R. C. Childers, A Dictionary of the Pâli Language, 1875, some articles of which are genuine monographs, and which furnishes on a great number of points valuable information borrowed from works often hardly accessible. Among popular works it is proper to cite in the first rank J.

We have only legendary data, deeply infected with mythical elements, in regard to the life of the remarkable man who, towards the close of the sixth century before our era, laid the foundations of a religious system which, under a form more or less altered, constitutes, even in our own day, the faith of more than a third of the inhabitants of the globe.[1] He belonged to the family of the Gautamas, who were, it is said, the line royal of the Çâkyas, a Rajpoot clan, which was settled at the time on the banks of the Rohiṇî, a small affluent of the Gogra, about 137 miles to the north of Benares. When twenty-nine years of age, he quitted his parents, his young wife, and an only son, who had just been born to him, and became a sannyâsin. After seven years of meditation and internal struggles, he announced himself as in possession of the perfect truth, and assumed the title of Buddha, the awakened, the enlightened. During forty-four years more, he preached his doctrine on both banks of the Ganges, in the province of Benares and in Behar, and entered Nirvâṇa at the advanced age of eighty.[2] The date of his death, which is differently

Barthélemy Saint-Hilaire, Le Bouddha et sa Religion, 2d ed., 1862, and especially a recent little work (date not given, but which must be 1877) by T. W. Rhys Davids, Buddhism, being a Sketch of the Life and Teachings of Gautama, the Buddha, published by the Society for Promoting Christian Knowledge. We can only in a very general way refer here to the many labours of J. d'Alwis, S. Beal, L. Feer, Ph. E. Foucaux, D. J. Gogerly, Max Müller, A. Schiefner, E. Schlagintweit, A. Weber, H. H. Wilson. In fine, Ch. Lassen, last not least, has also done much to promote these studies in his great work, Indische Alterthumskunde, 1847–74.

[1] The most recent statistics give 470,000,000 as the total number of the Buddhist population. T. W. Rhys Davids, Buddhism, p. 5.

[2] The biography of Buddha :—Ph. E. Foucaux, Rgya-Tcher-Rol-Pa, ou Dévelopment des Jeux ; Histoire du Bouddha Sakya-Mouni, publié et traduit du Tibétain, 1847–1860, 2 vols. 4to. It is the Tibetan version of the following :—The Lalitavistara, or Memoirs of the Early Life of Çakya Sinha, edited by Râjendralâla Mitra, Calcutta, 1853–77 (Biblioth. Indica). This text, the only one of the Sanskrit books of Nepâl edited as yet (we have only a translation of the Lotus of the Good Law), carries on the life of Buddha as far as the commencement of his apostleship. Another of these texts, devoted also to the legend of Buddha, the Mahâvastu, will be shortly published by E. Senart. S. Beal, The Romantic Legend of Sâkya-Buddha, from the Chinese, 1875, translated from the Chinese version of the Abhinishkramaṇasûtra, or a narrative of the call and retreat of Buddha. A. Schief-

reported in the different traditions of Buddhism, and by all inaccurately, has been determined with a probability, in our opinion, little short of certainty, only in recent times, through the discovery of three new inscriptions of the Emperor Açoka.[1] From these texts it follows that the thirty-seventh year of the reign of this prince was reckoned as the 257th from the decease of the Master, and this in Maghada, the native country of Buddhism. When adjusted to our chronology, this date makes the Nirvâṇa take place on one of the years which fall between 482 and 472 before Christ.[2] It is the first date that we meet with

ner, Eine Tibetische Lebensbeschreibung Çakyamuni's, 1849. The original was written in 1734. All these works belong to Northern Buddhism. The following are drawn from Southern sources:—R. C. Childers, The Mahâparinibbâna Sutta, Pâli text and commentary, in the Journ. Roy. As. Soc., vols. vii. and viii., new series. It contains the narrative of the last days and death of Buddha; the translation, interrupted by the author's death, did not appear. V. Fausböll, The Jâtaka, together with its Commentary, vol. i., 1877. The introduction of the commentary contains a detailed biography of Buddha, omitting the closing years. P. Bigandet, vicar apostolic of Ava and Pegu, The Life or Legend of Gaudama Buddha of the Burmese, Rangoon, 1858, 2d edition, 1866; a 3d edition is in preparation; a French translation by V. Gauvain, 1878. H. Alabaster, The Wheel of the Law, 1872, from Siamese sources. In fine, we could not refer to the life of Buddha without mentioning the beautiful work of E. Senart, Essai sur la Légende du Buddha, son Caractère et ses Origines, 1875 (which appeared in the Journal Asiatique, 1873–75). A new edition is in preparation. We venture to think that the author goes a little too far in the way of mythic explanation; but, after this book, it can be no longer any idea of writing the life of Buddha, as it is given, for instance, in the work of Barthélemy Saint-Hilaire, cited above.

[1] These celebrated inscriptions, engraven on rocks and pillars in different places of Northern India, from the valley of Cabul as far as the peninsula of Gujarât, and from the frontiers of Nepâl to the mouth of the Mahânadî in Orissa, contain, in the form of edicts or proclamations, religious and moral directions addressed by the Emperor Açoka to his subjects. Deciphered successively by J. Princep, Norris, and Dowson, and elucidated by the works of Burnouf, Lassen, Wilson, Kern, and Bühler, they have been collected and published anew by General A. Cunningham in his "Corpus Inscriptionum," and they are at this very moment being subjected to thorough re-examination by E. Senart in the Journal Asiatique, 7th series, vol. xv. 287, 479; xvi. 215. These are the most ancient epigraphic texts of India. From their mentioning the names of Greek princes contemporary with Açoka, they with absolute certainty confirm the identity of Candragupta, the grandfather of this prince, and the Sandrocottus of the classic historians, an identity which constitutes the fundamental assumption connected with the ancient chronology of India.

[2] The question of the date of Nirvâṇa has been principally treated by Ch. Lassen, Ind. Alterthumsk, ii. p. 53, 2d ed.; A. Cunningham, Bhilsa

in the history of India, and, if we except those which depend on it, the ten centuries which are to follow do not supply altogether half a dozen more.

The doctrines of Buddha are better known to us than the details of his life, but they are far from being so in any exact manner. In the documents in which there is, on the whole, still the most chance of finding the echo of his word, in the Pâli *Suttas*, these memorials, judging from what has been published of them till now,[1] are so seriously altered by the lucubrations of an age of formalism and scholasticism (the language of these documents, the Pâli, being more recent than the dialects in which the inscriptions of Açoka were drawn up towards the end of the

Topes, p. 74, 1852; Jour. As. Soc. of Bengal, 1854, p. 704; and Corpus Inscrip. Indic., p. iii. *seq.*; Max Müller, Ancient Sanskrit Literature, p. 263; N. L. Westergaard, Ueber Buddha's Todesjahr, German translation, 1862; H. Kern, Over de Jaartelling der Zuidelijke Buddhisten, 1873. T. W. Rhys Davids, On the Ancient Coins and Measures of Ceylon, 1877, p. 38 *seq.*, in the new edition of Marsden's Numismata Orientalia. It has been, if not decided, at all events brought nearer a final solution, by the discovery, due to General A. Cunningham, of the new inscriptions. G. Bühler, Three New Edicts of Açoka, in the Ind. Antiq., vi. 149, and vii. 141; and A. Cunningham, Corpus Inscriptionum Indicarum, vol. i. pp. 20–23, pl. xiv.

The masterly discussion to which these texts have been subjected by Bühler has certainly not availed to do away with all uncertainty. We have ourselves taken certain exceptions in our criticism in the Revue Critique of the 1st June 1878; others have been taken by Senart, Journal Asiatique, May–June 1879, p. 524. But in spite of its absolute rejection by Pischel, Academy, 11th August 1877, and by Rhys Davids, Ancient Coins and Measures of Ceylon, p. 57 *seq.*, and the objection, which is a very grave one indeed, started by H. Oldenberg, The Vinaya Piṭakaṃ, i. p. xxxviii., we think that the conclusions of Bühler hold good, that these inscriptions emanate from King Açoka, that they reckon from the era of the Nirvâṇa, and they give for the death of Buddha the date which was accepted in the third century B.C. in Magadha.

[1] Fr. Spiegel, Anecdota Pâlica, 1845; L. Feer, Études Bouddhiques, in the Journal Asiatique, 1866–78; R. C. Childers, The Kuddakapâṭha, Pâli text with translation, in the Journ. of the Roy. As. Soc., vol. iv., new series; The Mahâparinibbânasutta, ibid., vols. vii. and viii., by the same author; P. Grimblot, Sept Suttas Pâlis tirés du Dîgha-Nikâya, 1876; Coomara Svamy, Sutta Nipâta, or the Dialogues of Gotama Buddha, translated, 1874; R. Pischel, The Assalâyanasuttaṃ, edited and translated, 1880. E. Burnouf has translated several Pâli Suttas in the Lotus de la Bonne Loi. Of the works of Gogerly, now so very scarce, on this part of the Buddhist writings, some have passed into the posthumous work of Grimblot. For the Dhammapada and the Jâtaka, see *infra*. A considerable number of Sûtras have been, moreover, published or

third century before Christ), that, as regards the form at least, the instructions of the Master may be considered as lost.[1] There are sparks in this monkish literature, but never flame; and it is certain that it was not by strange

translated from the books of the North by E. Burnouf (in the Introduction à l'Histoire du B. I.), S. Beal, A. Schiefner, L. Feer, &c. To these publications have recently been added: Max Müller, On Sanskrit Texts Discovered in Japan, and Cecil Bendall, The Megha Sûtra, in Journal of the Roy. As. Soc., new series, xii. p. 153 and 286 (1880). Of the great Sûtras peculiar to this literature, we possess the Lalitavistara in Sanskrit (ed. Râjendralâla Mitra), in Tibetian, and in French (ed. Foucaux), and the Lotus de la Bonne Loi in French (translated by Burnouf). An edition of the Mahâvastu by Senart is in the press.

[1] For the age and origin of the Pâli, so much controverted, see Westergaard, Ueber den ältesten Zeitraum der Indischen Geschichte, p. 87, who derives it in the third century before Christ from the dialect of Ujjayinî; Kern, Over de Jaartelling der Zuidelijke Buddhisten, p. 13 *seq.*, who considers it an artificial language akin to the Çaurasenî of the dramas, and elaborated about the beginning of the Christian era; Oldenberg, The Vinaya Piṭakaṃ, vol. i. p. xlix. *seq.*, who, on the other hand, thinks he finds in it a dialect of the Eastern Dekhan. There has been no less discussion respecting the origin and growth of the Buddhist canon. The authorities of the North and the South agree in referring the redaction, or at least the composition (for certain testimonies make mention of a pretty prolonged oral transmission), to a first council which must have met at Râjagṛiha immediately after the death of the Master. This redaction, according to the authorities of the South, must have been revised and restored to its original purity by the doctors of the second council, which the tradition of the North ignores, held at Vaiçâlî a hundred years after Nirvâṇa, under the first Açoka or Kâlâçoka. Finally, a last revision, with some additions to boot, such as the Kathâvattu (Dîpavaṃsa, vii. 56), must have been made 118 years later by the third council, held at Pâṭaliputra under the great Açoka, or Dharmâçoka Priyadarçin. The tradition of the North, on the other hand, ascribes the third redaction to a council held at Kashmîr under the Turanian king Kanishka towards the beginning of the Christian era. These facts have been differently interpreted by criticism. Lassen admits that we possess documents contemporary with the first council, but that the Sanskrit canon was finally fixed only by the Kashmîr council (Ind. Alterth., ii. 86 and 856 *seq.*, 2d ed.), which is also Burnouf's opinion (Introd. à l'Hist. du Bouddh. Ind., p. 579). Perhaps a complete examination of the Chinese collection may enable us to come to a closer agreement on the matter. Senart thinks that the council of Pâṭaliputra was the first to attempt to fix the dogma and the canon (Essai sur la Légende du Buddha, p. 514 *seq.*). Kern is of opinion that we must rest satisfied with affirming that the Pâli canon, pretty much as we have it, must have been in existence in Ceylon some time before the redaction of the commentaries of Buddhaghosha in the fifth century (Over d. Jaartelling, p. 25). The most recent attempt at solution, and the one which at the same time aims at the greatest precision, is that of Oldenberg. During the first century, he thinks, Buddhism had only two sorts of writings, Vinaya and Dharma, discipline and doctrine; the redaction of the greater part of

harangues like these that the "Lion of the Çâkyas" carried captive men's souls. The basis of his teaching has doubtless held out better than the form. But when we think of the kindred questions which arise in connection with the origin of Christianity, in which the traditional element, however, became stereotyped much earlier, we will readily understand that, if it is easy to distinguish between a primitive Buddhism and the doctrines grossly altered which first saw light at a later date, it is surely advisable to use some precaution in speaking of the Buddhism of Buddha himself. With these reservations, we proceed to indicate as briefly as we can the fundamental doctrines of the religion established by Gautama.

The two characteristics which strike us at once in primitive Buddhism, and which certainly belong to the teaching of the Master, are the absence of every theological element and a conspicuous aversion to pure speculation. Buddha does not deny the existence of certain beings called Indra, Agni, Varuṇa; but he thinks that he owes nothing to them, and that his business does not lie with them. Neither does he think of arraying himself against the revealed tradition; he passes it by. The Veda, which his Church will one day in terms reject, was summed up at this epoch in the practice of religious observances, and

the Vinaya and the origin of the Sûtrapiṭaka was prior to the council of Vaiçâlî; the completion of the Vinaya, the development of the collection of the Sûtras, and the commencement of that of the Abhidharma befell in the period which separates this council from the succeeding one. The rest of the literature was subsequent to the reign of Açoka (Vinaya Piṭakaṃ, i. p. x. *seq.*). It is not possible to be precise in a matter so obscure, and of all Oldenberg's propositions the most certainly true seems to be the last (see Jacobi, in Zeitsch. d. D. Morgenl. Gesellsch., xxxiv. p. 184). From the time of Açoka Buddhism had a literature, but, strictly speaking, no canon; that is a point which in our opinion results forcibly from the inscription of Bairât (Babhra), on whatever supposition to which recourse may be had to identify the writings enumerated in this inscription with parts of the collections now in our possession. For these identifications see Burnouf, Lotus de la Bonne Loi, p. 710 *seq.*; Kern, Over de Jaartelling, p. 39; Oldenberg, Vinaya Piṭakaṃ, i. p. xl.

with these Çâkyamuni,[1] by embracing the life of an anchorite, naturally broke all connection. His position, then, in reference to the established religion is not much different from that of many of his contemporaries. He seems to think, as they do, that it is an affair of the Brahmans to try and move the celestial powers by the ritual observances, and obtain from them benefits which he for his part does not value a rush. His work, for his part, is entirely a layman's; and as he recognises not a god upon whom man depends, his doctrine is absolutely atheistic. As for his metaphysics, it is pre-eminently negative. He does not busy himself with the origin of things; he takes them just as they are, or as they appear to him to be; and the problem to which he incessantly returns in his conversations is not that of being in itself, but that of existence. Still more than in the Vedânta of the Upanishads, his doctrine is confined to the question of salvation.

The scheme of this doctrine is expounded in the "four noble truths." First, the existence of pain: to exist is to suffer. Second, the cause of the pain: this cause is to be found in desire, which increases with the gratification. Third, the cessation of pain: this cessation is possible; it is obtained by the suppression of desire. Fourth, the way which leads to this suppression: this way, which comprehends four stages or successive states of perfection, is the knowledge and observance of the "good law," the practice of the discipline of Buddhism and its admirable morality. The end of this is Nirvâṇa, extinction, the cessation of existence.

The conditions of existence are summed up in the theory of the Nidânas, or the twelve successive causes, each of which is conceived to be the consequence of the one which precedes. These are:—First, ignorance; second, the predispositions of mind which determine our acts, or more simply action, the *karman;* third, consciousness; fourth, individuality; fifth, sensibility; sixth, the contact

[1] Properly, "the solitary of the Çâkyas."

of the senses with objects; seventh, sensation; eighth, desire or "thirst;" ninth, clinging to existence; tenth, existence; eleventh, birth; twelfth, old age and death, or suffering.[1] These terms, of which, however, there have been various interpretations, simply answer to facts, states, or conditions of finite existence; they do not, in primitive Buddhism anyhow, represent substances or entities. The first, for instance, is not, as it became afterwards, both non-cognition and the incognisable; it simply denotes the state of ignorance, the fact of assuming for real what is not. Neither are they always presented in the same order, and it is probable that this order did not always imply a rigorous and continuous concatenation from cause to effect. Thus it is evident that the series extends to several existences, and that the same facts recur, but regarded from a different point of view. Activity, for instance, ought not to be conceived as absolutely preceding existence; and it is not less evident that the tenth and twelfth conditions are at bottom the same, and that the third, seventh, eighth, and ninth only explicate what is already implicit in the second.

As regards the being which undergoes existence, it is viewed as a composite being, resulting from the *skandhas*, or the aggregates. These aggregates, which in the case of the human being amount to five[2] (they are fewer in number for other beings), along with a hundred and ninety-three subdivisions, exhaust all the elements, all the material, intellectual, and moral properties and attributes of the individual. There exists nothing apart from these, either fixed principle, or soul, or simple or permanent sub-

[1] For the twelve Nidânas see E. Burnouf, Introduction à l'Histoire du Bouddhisme Indien, p. 491, and the account of R. C. Childers in the new edition of the Miscellaneous Essays of Colebrooke, vol. i. p. 453.

[2] These are Rûpa, form, material attributes; Vedanâ, sensations; Sañjña, notions, abstract ideas; Saṃskara, faculties and dispositions of the mind; Vijñâna, reason, judgment. See Burnouf, Introduction à l'Histoire du B. I., pp. 475, 511; Wassiljew, Buddhismus, p. 94; Rhys Davids, Buddhism, p. 90, and the Pâli Dictionary of Childers, pp. 198, 405, 453, 457 561, 562, 576.

stance of any kind. They unite and arrange themselves so as to form a several being, undergo incessant modification along with it, and dissolve at its death; the individual, being throughout a compound of compounds, entirely perishes. The influence of its karman alone, of its acts, survives it, and through this the formation of a new group of skandhas is immediately effected; a new individual rises into existence in some other world,[1] and continues in some degree the first. It matters not that this substitution is so rapid that practically no account is taken of it, since Buddha, for instance, and the saints that have attained omniscience, are represented as recalling and speaking of their previous existences, as if they had retained their identity in passing from the one to the other. It is nevertheless true that the Buddhist, strictly speaking, does not revive, but that another, if I may say so, revives in his stead, and that it is to avert from this other, who is to be only the heir of his karman, the pains of existence that he aspires to Nirvâṇa. Such, at any rate, is the doctrine of the Pâli books; not merely of the small number of them that have as yet been published, but of the entire orthodox literature of Southern Buddhism, according to the opinion of scholars of the highest authority who have had the opportunity of studying it in the country itself.[2] Was this doctrine as explicitly formulated in the instruction of the Master? We take leave to doubt this. On the one hand, the Sanskrit books of the North appear to concede something permanent, an *ego* passing from one existence to another.[3] On the other hand, one could hardly explain, it seems, how Buddhism, not content with having annihilation accepted as the sovereign good, should have from the first rendered its task more difficult still by in the end representing the pursuit of this good as a pure act of charity. But in no

[1] Among these worlds are the heavens and the hells, of which the Buddhists, as well as the Brahmans and Jainas, admit a great number.

[2] Spence Hardy, Gogerly, Bigandet, Childers, Rhys Davids.

[3] Burnouf, Introd., p. 507.

way can this vaguely apprehended and feebly postulated *ego* be compared, for instance, with the simple and imperishable soul of the Sâṅkhya philosophy. It is not independent of the skandhas, as the latter are of those elements which are analogous to them; the principles, viz., that spring from the development of the prakṛiti. It becomes extinct, on the contrary, when the skandhas happen to fail. But, indeed, whatever difficulty there may be in extricating on this matter the exact idea of the founder from under the elaborate scholasticism of several centuries, if there is a conclusion which asserts itself as having been that of Buddhism at all ages, which follows from all that it insists on and from all that it ignores, it is that the "way" conducts to total extinction, and that perfection consists in ceasing to exist.[1] By the removal of the first of the twelve causes, viz., ignorance, the possibility of all that which follows next is prevented, viz., the karman and all that depends on it. From the moment of death there will be no further formation of new skandhas, and the individual will have disappeared entirely and without return. Such is the dogmatic logical

[1] The bibliography of the opinions that have been expressed on the doctrine of Nirvâṇa would by itself alone supply matter for a lengthened article. As it is the principal doctrine of Buddhism, there is reference to it in most of the works enumerated above. Of special treatises we shall mention Max Müller, On the Original Meaning of Nirvâṇa, in Buddhism and Buddhist Pilgrims, 1857; The Introduction to Buddhaghosha's Parables, by the same author, 1869; Barthélemy Saint-Hilaire, Sur le Nirvâṇa Bouddhique, 2d ed. of Le Bouddha et sa Religion, 1862; R. C. Childers, in the article Nibbânam in the Dictionary of the Pâli Language, p. 265; J. D'Alwis, Buddhist Nirvâṇa, Colombo, 1871; Ph. E. Foucaux, in the Revue Bibliographique, 15 juin 1874; Introduction to the French translation of Bigandet's Life of Gaudama, by the same author, p. v., 1878; O. Frankfurter, Buddhist Nirvâṇa, and the Noble Eightfold Path, Journal of the Royal Asiatic Society, vol. xii. (new series), p. 548 *seq.* From these last texts (three Sûtras extracted from the Saṃyutta Nikâya), as well as from several others besides, it appears Nirvâṇa is also predicated of the state of perfect calm, in which all passion and every movement of egoism are extinct, and in this sense it is obvious it can be attained in the present life. But it seems no less evident that it is so used only metaphorically, the condition of Nirvâṇa being taken for Nirvâṇa itself. From all we know of the Buddhist ontology, the state which is described to us in these texts can only be provisional and must come to an end.

conclusion, which is not weakened by the fact that it is not always found expressed in all its severity, and that, in ordinary belief especially, it has been subjected to all sorts of processes of attenuation. The imagination even of an Asiatic has some difficulty in settling down to the idea of annihilation. Thus the Chinese pilgrims Fa-Hian and Hiouen-Thsang, who visited India respectively in the fifth and seventh centuries,[1] and were orthodox believers in the complete Nirvâṇa of Buddha, nevertheless speak of miracles, and even apparitions of his, as if he had not ceased to exist; and it is beyond a doubt that with many of the Buddhists of former days Nirvâṇa was only what it is with the majority of them to-day, a sort of eternal repose or negative state of blessedness. This does not hinder Buddhism from being doctrinally the confession of the absolute vanity of all things, and, as regards the individual, an aspiration after non-existence.

This vanity of all existence would, even if it had not been reiterated so often by Buddha, follow logically from the simple theory of the Nidânas. The first of the twelve causes, viz., ignorance, which consists in taking for real that which is not, evidently implies the non-reality of the world, not as a substance—the thing in itself being outside the range of primitive Buddhism—but of the world such as it appears to us. The objects which we see have no proper reality, and, as we have just remarked, exactly the same is taught in the doctrine of the Pâli Suttas respecting the subject which sees them. One's

[1] Foė Koue Ki, ou Relation des Royaumes Bouddhiques; Voyages dans la Tartarie, l'Afghanistan et l'Inde à la fin du iv. siècle, par Chi-Fa-Hian, translated by A. Rémusat, reviewed by Klaproth and Landresse, 1836. S. Beal, The Travels of the Buddhist Pilgrim Fah-Hian, translated with Notes and Prolegomena, 1869. St. Julien, Voyages des Pèlerins Bouddhistes, t. i.; Histoire de la Vie de Hiouen-Thsang et de ses Voyages dans l'Inde, . . . translated from the Chinese, 1853, t. ii. and iii.; Mémoires sur les Contrées Occidentales, par Hiouen-Thsang, translated from the Chinese, 1857–59, a work of great importance, not only for the history of Buddhism, but for that of ancient India in general. S. Beal is preparing an English translation of the narrative of Hiouen-Thsang. The work of C. J. Neumann, Pilgerfahrten Buddhistischer Priester von China nach Indien, aus dem Chinesischen übersetzt, 1833, did not extend beyond the first volume.

individuality is only a form, an empty appearance. Ῥεῖ τὰ πάντα, everything is only a flux of aggregates, which are interminably uniting and disuniting, an immense flood, of which we do not seek to know the beginning, and from which we can escape only by Nirvâṇa. When once the system reached this point, only a negation remained to be formulated, but one of a purely ontological order, the negation, namely, of substance itself. This last step was taken in the school founded by Nâgârjuna, about a century before our era, at a time when the doctrine of Çâkyamuni, which was at first speculative only to a small extent, had given rise to a vast and complex labyrinth of metaphysical conceptions.[1] In this school, which was called that of the Madhyamikas, Buddhism resolves itself into a pure nihilism. It actually became, what the Brahmans reproached it with being, the *çûnyavâda*, "the system of the void." This, beyond a doubt, was not the teaching of Buddha, but it is not to be denied that it is its direct continuation.

Now, if we compare this doctrine with the contemporary speculations of the philosophy of the Brahmans, we cannot but be struck with their common family likeness. Atheism, scornful disregard of the cultus and tradition, the concep-

[1] For the different Buddhist schools and their doctrines, see, in particular, W. Wassiljew, Der Buddhismus, *passim.* To this speculative industry there corresponds a mythological development of no less account, which has gone on increasing until, in China and Japan, it has ended with making Buddhism one of the most fantastic and grossly idolatrous religious systems to be met with in the world. Of the figures of this pantheon, which poetry never seems to have irradiated with a single ray, some are of speculative origin, such as the Adibuddha, the primordial and sovereign Buddha, akin to the brahman of the Vedânta; others, such as the myriads of Buddhas and Bodhisattvas, have been formed by the endless multiplication of certain elements of primitive Buddhism; while others still have been borrowed from Brahmanism and the sectarian religions, particularly Çivaism and the systems of worship connected with the female divinities. This complicated Buddhism is usually designated by the term "*Mahâyâna*," "the Great Vehicle," by contrast with the more sober doctrine of the primitive age, styled the *Hînayâna*, or "the Little Vehicle." It is especially represented in the great Sûtras as peculiar to the literature of the North, the late redaction of which cannot well be called in question, although they appear to contain, especially in their versified portions, popular elements of very high antiquity.

tion of a religion entirely spiritual, a contempt for finite existence, belief in transmigration and the necessity of deliverance from it, the feeble idea of the personality of man, the imperfect discrimination, or rather the confusion of material qualities and intellectual functions, the affirmation of a morality with its sanction within itself, are so many characteristics which we find, differently emphasised, however, in Buddhism and the Upanishads. If we go further, and take the systems of Brahmanism one by one, we find that it is with the Sâṅkhya that the doctrine of Çâkyamuni has *prima facie* most resemblance. On several essential points the conclusions are the same, and the analogies become exceedingly striking when we descend to particulars. Evidently the two systems have grown up side by side, and have borrowed mutually from one another. We question, however, whether the true origin of Buddhism is to be sought in this quarter. The Sâṅkhya, as well under the confusedly materialistic form which it has in the oldest Upanishads, as under the dualistic form which it assumed at a later period, is a solid system, but little susceptible of developments and modifications of any depth. It is especially very little given to sentiment, and it cannot be from it that the pessimism was derived which is stamped so deeply on all the conceptions of Buddha. On the other hand, we can hardly admit that this hatred of existence was directly inspired, as the legend suggests, by the spectacle of the miseries of life. Experience teaches that there is almost always a metaphysical shipwreck connected with the rise of such great sorrows as these, and in our own days it is close upon the collapse of great idealistic systems that we see very similar ideas become current among us. When speculation, after having undermined the idea of reality in sensible objects, feels forced to confess that the transcendental object is going also, there remains only the alternative of scepticism or the philosophy of despair; one is either a Cârvâka or a Buddhist. It is, then, in an idealistic system, in the primitive Vedânta, but in a Vedânta which has lost all faith in the brahman, that we think the point of departure for the ideas of Buddha must be sought. We must believe in the Absolute in order to feel as deeply the emptiness and imperfection of finite things; we must have believed in it, and have found the vanity of this belief, in order to ignore it with a resolution as calm and inflexible.

Two centuries and a half after the death of its founder, Buddhism became the official religion of Açoka the Maurya, the most powerful monarch in India, whose immediate authority extended from the valley of Cabul to the mouths of the Ganges, and from the Himâlaya to the south of the Vindhya mountains; and by this time its missionaries had penetrated into the Marhatta and Dravidian countries, and taken root in Ceylon. This rapid progress was certainly not owing either to its dogmas, which were anything but attractive, and at bottom of no great originality, or even to the unquestionable superiority of its morality; and if it had had no other means of action, its success would be one of the most puzzling problems of history. But besides its doctrines and precepts, Buddhism had its institutions and its spirit of discipline and propagandism, a quite new art of winning and directing souls; it had, especially, Buddha himself, and his memory, which remained a living one in the Church. We cannot, in fact, ascribe too much in the conquests of Buddhism to the personal character of its founder and to the legend regarding him. Brahmanism, in which everything is impersonal, whose most revered sages have left behind them only a name, has nothing to oppose to the life of Buddha, which, however imperfectly historical as regards facts, has certainly preserved to us the physiognomy of the Master, and the ineffaceable image of him transmitted by his disciples. These narratives, drawn up as they are in that frightful Buddhist style, the most intolerable of all styles, form, nevertheless, one of the most affecting histories which humanity has ever conceived; and it is a well-known fact that even in our Western world, into which they had penetrated by means of copies in Greek, they furnished the subject of a popular legend, which for long supplied matter of an edifying kind to the nations of Christendom.[1] In any case, these have gained more souls for Buddhism than its theories respecting existence and Nirvâṇa. To meditate on the perfections of Buddha, to admire him, to love him, to confess and feel one's-self saved by him, were new sentiments, unknown to Brahmanism; and singular it is that it was thus a religion without God which first introduced India to a sense of the inner delights of devotion. So long as Buddhism preserved the monopoly of these sentiments, it grew and multiplied, and its existence will be threatened from the day when the neo-Brahmanic religions, particularly Vishnuism, shall, in their turn, take advantage of these sentiments, and turn them against it.

To comprehend this better, we must be able to take our stand before this legend of Buddha; we must set clearly before us the admirable figure which detaches itself from it, that finished model of calm and sweet majesty, of infinite tenderness for all that breathes and compassion for all that suffers, of perfect moral freedom and exemption from every prejudice. The ideal of the Brahman, elevated as that is, is egoistical; it is to save himself, and to save himself alone, that he aspires at perfection. It was to save others that he who was one day to be Gautama disdained to tread sooner in the way of Nirvâṇa, and that he chose to become Buddha at the cost of a countless number of supplementary existences.[2] The Brahman has got the length, too, of in theory professing goodwill towards

[1] The romance of "Barlaam and Josaphat."

[2] This is the act of the Great Renunciation, the Great Resolution. The legend ranks that of Gautama under Buddha Dîpaṅkara, four asaṅkhyeyas and a hundred thousand kalpas before his last birth. See Jâtaka Commentary, ed. Fausböll, i. p. 13. The asaṅkhyeya is the number represented by one followed by 140 ciphers. The kalpa or mahâkalpa is the immense period which separates one destruction of the world from the next.

all other creatures; but among his own fellows there are many whom he spurns with horror, and contact with whom defiles him. Buddha knows that man is defiled only by sin, and the very Caṇḍâla, who is less than a dog, is received by him as a brother. The morality of Buddhism, which, if we analyse it precept by precept, does not differ essentially from that which may be drawn from the Brahmanical books, thus appears to a high degree original, and entirely pervaded by a new spirit, if we consider it in the life of its founder. To imitate Buddha was in some respect a higher law, which gave to the new religion many admirable disciples. The memory of these disciples was in its turn no less piously preserved than that of the Master, and Buddhism thus acquired an incomparable collection of legends, a "Life of the Saints," which, for delicacy and charm of religious sentiment, yields only to that which should be one day produced by Christianity.[1]

To imitate the Master, that was before everything else to carry on his work; it was to propagate like him the good doctrine. This last was not, like Brahmanism, a system of thaumaturgy; it included none of those recipes which a man may be tempted to store by for himself, because they assure him of temporal advantage, the possession of which he grudges his neighbour. It was the good news for all, destined to pass from mouth to mouth, and which there is as much satisfaction in disseminating as in knowing. Buddhism was then a religion to be propagated, the first on record in history. It is in it first that we come upon the notion of conversion, as well as a special term to designate it.[2] Its weapon of war was that which the Master had already employed, preaching in the vulgar tongue. To that, besides its legends and biographies, was added by degrees a quite popular literature, of collections of parables

[1] Burnouf has translated some of the most beautiful of these legends in his Introduction à l'Histoire du Buddhisme Indien.

[2] In Pâli *sotâpatti*, in Sanskrit *srotaâpatti*, "the entrance into the current."

and semi-religious, semi-profane stories, the subject of which is often taken from the earlier existences of Buddha, and which form one of its most original creations.[1] Wherever it entered, it adopted the idiom of the country.[2] If in certain countries, such as Ceylon, Burmah, and Siam, it came at length to possess a sacred language, its canonical books were nevertheless translated and expounded to the people in their vernacular, very different in this respect from the Veda of the Brahmans, where the form is as sacred as the substance, and which, when translated into another dialect, or even simply committed to writing, is the Veda no longer.

Naturally a mission to convert implied the duty of watching over the work of conversion, of upholding the good doctrine, exhorting to good conduct, of stirring up piety, of coming to the help and support of weakness. Buddhism, then, had a cure of souls. The distinction between orthodoxy and heresy, painful instruction in correct opinions, the direction of consciences, the pastoral art, are of Buddhist creation; and perhaps we ought to

[1] The *Jâtakas*, "births." On these narratives, the official number of which is 550, see L. Feer, in the Journal Asiatique, t. v. and vi., 1875. A certain number of Jâtakas have been published between 1861 and 1872 by V. Fausböll, J. Minayef, and J. D'Alwis. Since then Fausböll has undertaken the publication of the entire collection, in co-operation, with a view to translation, at first with R. C. Childers, then, after the premature death of that scholar, with T. W. Rhys Davids. The first vol. of the text appeared in 1877: The Jâtaka, together with its Commentary, being Tales of the Anterior Births of Gotama Buddha. A second vol. of the text, as well as the first vol. of the translation of Rhys Davids, appeared, the one in 1879, the other in 1880. Besides the Jâtakas, Buddhism has produced other collections of tales and fables, of which St. Julien has published a specimen from a Chinese collection: Contes et Apologues Indiens inconnus jusqu'à ce jour, 2 vols., 1860. See L. Feer, Le Livre des Cent Légendes (Avadaña Çataka), in the Journ. Asiat., 1879, t. xiv. p. 141 *seq.*, 273 *seq.* See also the tales published and translated from the Tibetian and Mongol by A. Schniefner and B. Jülg. It is known that the literature of fable goes in great part as far back as Buddhist sources. See Th. Benfey, Pantschatantra; Fünf Bücher Indischer Fabeln, t. i., 1859.

[2] And that in virtue of a positive precept early ascribed to Buddha himself: J. Minayef, Grammaire Pâlie, p. xlii., translated by St. Guyard; and Oldenberg, The Vinaya Piṭakaṃ, i. p. xlviii.

ascribe the institution of a profession of faith and that of confession to the Master himself.[1]

One thing certainly may be traced to him, and that is the manner in which the mission of Buddha was conceived. It is hard to say to what extent Çâkyamuni was a visionary. But unless we refuse all credit to the testimonies we have of him, we must admit that, after years of struggle, and at the close of a decisive crisis in his life, he possessed, and believed he possessed, a revelation of the absolute truth; that he pretended to teach, not a personal doctrine without tradition and precedents, but the immutable eternal Law, such as it had been proclaimed from age to age by infallible seers, the Buddhas of past times, of whom he was the successor; that in his eyes, in fine, his coming, as well as theirs, was no mere accident, but a predestined and necessary event. On this subject there was eventually formed, and that very early, an entire mythology. A list was drawn up of as many as twenty-four predecessors of Gautama; by and by they became too numerous to reckon, and *Bodhisattvas* or Buddhas of the future without number peopled the worlds and the different degrees of existence. Of these saviours to come the Southern Buddhists mention in a special way only one, Maitreya, who is to be the next Buddha. The churches of the North, on the other hand, confess several, who, from the first centuries of our era, have been the objects of a genuine cultus. The religion of Çâkyamuni, so bald at first, had in this way not merely the appearance of being traditional; it had its patrons even, or, to speak more correctly, its gods.

[1] See J. F. Dickson, The Pâtimokkha, being the Buddhist Office of the Confession of Priests, Pâli text and translation, in the Journal of the Royal As. Soc., t. viii., new series. The briefest and most universally accepted statement of the creed of Buddhism is the celebrated formula: Whatever conditions proceed from a cause, the causes of them Tathâgata hath proclaimed, and the obstruction of them too hath the great Çrâmaṇa proclaimed. This formula, which we meet with thousands of times on monuments of every kind and description, served from an early period to consecrate votive offerings and charms. Tathâgata, "he who is gone away like" (the other Buddhas), and the great Çrâmaṇa, "the great ascetic," are titles of Buddha.

It is not only by its doctrines, however, and all its tendencies that Buddhism became thus early, and in opposition to Brahmanism, a compact and militant religion; it was so besides, and especially in virtue of the institutions he established. Çâkyamuni secured to his work, in fact, the most efficient of all the instruments for propagandism in preparing the way for monachism. It is certain that it was his aim to found something quite different from a school. His disciples are not pupils who come to be instructed under a master, with the intention of parting from him one day, and going to live each after a plan and for a purpose of his own. They form a congregation whose object is to realise the perfect life, a true religious order, into which by and by members were admitted only after the performance of certain vows and a profession of faith, and from which they durst not draw back without becoming renegades. We cannot stop to describe the Buddhist *Sañgha*.[1] We shall, therefore, have nothing to say here of its skilfully contrived scheme of discipline, its simple yet powerful hierarchy, its rules of enlistment, guarded by legal precautions which bear evidence of a singularly cautious policy, the order of women, which in course of time came to be added,[2] or its relation to the community of laymen, which was not long in being formed under its direction, and which, restricted to minor duties, constituted the second

[1] The Sañgha is the third term of the Triratna, of the three jewels, the Buddhist trinity, of which the two others are Buddha and the Dharma or the Law. See the inscription of Bairât, l. 2, in Cunningham's Corpus Inscr. Indic., pl. xv. The formula of conversion to Buddhism is taking refuge with Buddha, the Dharma, and the Sañgha. For the organisation of the Sañgha, see especially Burnouf, Introd. à l'Histoire du Bouddh. Ind., p. 234 *seq.*, and R. Spence Hardy, Eastern Monachism. From Buddhist monachism there developed in Tibet, towards the end of the middle age, the Lamaic hierarchy, for which consult C. F. Köppen, Die Religion des Buddha, 1859, t. ii., and E. Schlagintweit, Buddhism in Tibet, 1863.

[2] See the elegant little work of Mrs. Mary Summer, Les Religieuses Bouddhistes depuis Sakya-Mouni jusqu'à nos jours, with a preface by Ph. E. Foucaux, 1873. As early as the edicts of Açoka, the Bhikhunis, the nuns, figure alongside of the Bhikhus, the monks: inscription of Bairât, l. 7, in Cunningham's Corpus Inscr. Indic., pl. xv.

element in the Church.[1] Still less shall we try to determine how much in this organisation may be considered as the work of the founder himself. Tradition not unnaturally refers the whole to him; and it is hardly necessary to say that its voice in the matter cannot be admitted. Buddhism certainly had not at its rise the constitution which we see it had in the time of Açoka; and here, as in other organisations, it is the opposition encountered from without and the struggle waged with heresy within which gave form and fashion to the Church.[2] Still, on the other hand, we cannot, as we think, reject entirely the evidences which go to prove that the Saṅgha was in action from the date of the Master's death, as an ecclesiastical body already established on a solid basis, under the direction of the chief disciples and elders, or *sthaviras.*[3] In any case, it had this as its distinctive characteristic from the commencement, that it was open to all without exception, not only to the classes who were entitled to instruction at the hands of the Brahmans, but also to those who were excluded from it, whether because they happened to be reduced to a more or less servile

[1] R. C. Childers, The Whole Duty of the Buddhist Layman, a Sermon of Buddha, in the Contemporary Review, March 1876. See the Sigâlovâda-Sutta, Grimblot, Sept Suttas Pâlis, p. 297.

[2] The Buddhists usually reckon up seventeen as the number of the heresies that arose in the bosom of the Church in the second century after Nirvâṇa (Dîpavaṃsa, v. 16–54), and six as that of the hostile sects founded by the "six false teachers," the Tîrthyas of the Northern books (Prâtihârya-Sûtra in Burnouf's Introduction à l'Hist. du Bouddh. Ind., p. 162), the Titthiyas of the Pâli scriptures, all represented as having been contemporaries of Buddha: Sâmaññaphala-Sutta in Burnouf's Lotus de la Bonne Loi, p. 448 *seq.*, and Grimblot, Sept Suttas Palis, p. 113 *seq.* See also Childers, Pâli Diction., p. 511; and T. D'Alwis, Buddhism, its Origin, History, and Doctrines, Colombo, 1862. Nevertheless, in the Milindapañha, p. 4, they are made contemporaries of King Milinda, whom the same book (p. 3) places 500 years after Nirvâṇa.

[3] There is certainly a historical basis in the therâvalis, or lists of teachers (Pâli *thera* = Sanskrit *sthavira*), which have been transmitted to us, *e.g.*, Dîpavaṃsa, v. 69–107. See the discussion in regard to this list by Rhys Davids, Ancient Coins and Measures of Ceylon, p. 46 *seq.*, and G. Bühler, Ind. Antiq., viii. p. 148 *seq.* The lists preserved by the Northern Buddhists are much more open to suspicion. See Lassen, Ind. Alterthumsk., ii. p. 94, 2d ed.; Wassiljew, Der Buddhismus, p. 42 *seq.*; and S. Beal, Ind. Antiq., ix. 148.

position, or because, adverse to the restraint of the settled usages of society, they preferred of their own will a life of freedom in a state of excommunication. Buddha repelled no one, and within the circle of his disciples there were no other distinctions than those of age and merit. We must not, however, conclude from this that the Buddhist order drew its proselytes directly, and in the country of its birth, to a great extent from among the classes that were spurned as impure. The kind of life led by the majority of these populations, the force of prejudice even, and, we will say, of prejudice in many cases not without reason, of which they were at all times the object, and especially the presence in the order of numerous Brahmans, all conspire to render such a supposition as that the reverse of tenable. It was only at a later date, when a body of laymen of greater and greater account began to gather round the Church, it was especially when the latter began to spread far and wide among peoples of foreign blood and manners, that Buddhism reaped the full benefit of the free and lofty conception of a human fraternity which had fashioned itself together in the heart of its founder. To estimate to what extent the liberty of action it asserted for itself on this new field was superior to that of Brahmanism, one instance will suffice. While Buddha teaches that "his law is a law of grace for all,"[1] the Vedânta Sûtras declare that a Çûdra, who has no right to the Veda, is just as little entitled to receive and practise their teaching; in other terms, that in his actual condition he is incapable of effecting his salvation. And this proposition is expressly maintained in his commentary by Çaṅkara,[2] who was, however, a man of the South, and who probably wrote this work of his in the South, that is to say, in a country where more than nine-tenths of the population were regarded by the Brah-

[1] Burnouf, Introd. à l'Hist. du Bouddh. Ind., p. 198.

[2] Çaṅkara on the Vêdânta Sûtra, i. 3, 34–38, p. 325, ed. Biblioth. Ind.

mans as pure Çûdras. It is evident that Brahmanism, in order not to die of exhaustion, was condemned to violate constantly its own peculiar principles, while Buddhism, on the contrary, in order to spread wider, had only to practise its.

Must we go further than this and see, as is often done, in the institution of the Sañgha and in primitive Buddhism in general, a reaction against the régime of caste and the spiritual yoke of the Brahmans? To show that this is nothing better than a fiction of romance, we should require to examine what this régime of caste might possibly be in the sixth century before our era, and up to what extent the claims made by the Brahmans might appear oppressive. This is not the place to enter into the examination of this new question. We shall confine ourselves to the remark that there is not a shadow of evidence that the social problem was ever agitated among the semi-agricultural, semi-pastoral tribes in the midst of which Buddha spent his life, or that there was any thought of disputing the right of the Brahmans, which, indeed, was at bottom their great privilege, to be the bearers of the Veda, and by claim of blood to be the ministers of certain religious rites. Neither as regards these rights do we even know to what extent they were observed by the people, and we have the best reasons for thinking that they were not even in general use among the populations among which the Brahmanic gotras had for long and in great numbers founded settlements. One fact more is enough to discredit this theory; it is that Buddhism, at the time when it was dominant, never in the slightest interfered with caste in the countries where it happened still to exist; and not only did it not do so—it was it which in all probability imported caste into countries where it did not yet exist, viz., into the Dekhan, Ceylon, the isles of Sunda, and wherever a considerable number of Hindu people followed in its train.

The truth is, that Buddhism carried in itself the denial,

not of the régime of castes in general, but of the caste of the Brahmans, and this without respect to any doctrine of equality, and without, for its part, having any thought of revolt. Thus it is quite possible that the opposition which existed remained for long an unconscious one on both sides. Apparently their paths did not touch or cross each other. Buddha never arrogated to himself the right to teach the mantras or to officiate in an act of sacrifice; the Brahmans on their side never laid claim to the exclusive right of property in speculations that bore on salvation. Çâkyamuni would have been only following their example, if he had confined himself to denying the supreme efficacy of the Veda and the rites. Even in repudiating for himself and his disciples the observance of all cultus whatever, he did not even then place himself necessarily in hostility with the Brahmans; and so long as the community was composed of persons who, after the example of the Master, had renounced the world, it was very easy for it to avoid the sensation of a rupture. But this was no longer possible when it had gathered round it a body of laymen, who naturally sympathised with its indifference in regard to the ancient rites, when, by force of circumstances, it had been led to set tradition against tradition, and to substitute for the old cultus a new one of a quite different nature, consisting only in spiritual exercises and moral exhortations, and over which the Brahmans could not lay claim to any right. Especially was it no longer possible when they had to share along with it the liberality of kings and the great. From that moment a vehement antagonism arose, and the sacerdotal caste, assailed at once in its functions and its revenue, must have felt that it was its very existence that was threatened. The Brahmans nevertheless continued to resort to the Buddhist Saṅgha, for they never formed a compact body governed by common interests, and from that day they probably no longer all lived by ministering at the altar. Besides, for a long while they furnished the new religion with its chief teachers; the name brahman remained a title of honour among the Buddhists, and in Ceylon it was given to kings. But, as a distinct class, invested with a special religious privilege, there was no status for them in the Church.[1]

When the Saṅgha was finally organised—and it certainly was so long before Açoka—Buddhism was found to be in command of an admirable body of military. The Buddhist religious, the *bhikshu, i.e.*, the mendicant, is not, like the Brahman, a worker of miracles, a mediator between man and the deity; he is first a penitent, and afterwards, if he is capable of it, a scribe, a preacher, a director of conscience, a teacher of the faith, and at times a first-rate missionary. Humble by profession, possessing nothing, without family, without interests other than those of the order, he goes wherever his superiors send him. Personally the bhikshu has taken the vow of poverty and lives on alms;[2] but the order has possessions, it is rich, and the origin of its wealth is of very ancient date, if, as its traditions, which are noways improbable, allege, it is true that some of the donations in land were made to it as far back as the lifetime of Buddha. Very different from the gifts conferred on the Brahmans—which are always made to the individual, and among whom the most insignificant domain, even if it is given to a corporation, is always divided

[1] A polemic against caste forms the subject of the Vajrasûci of Açvaghosha, first edited for Wilkinson by Soobajee Bapoo, with a reply in defence of caste by the Brahmanical editor, Bombay, 1839; a new edition, with translation by Weber, in the Memoirs of the Academy of Berlin for 1839; and of the Assalâyana-Sutta, edited and translated by R. Pischel, 1880.

[2] From an early date, however, the rule seems to have admitted of exceptions and compromises. Açoka, for instance, on entering the order, certainly did not renounce the world. There were doubtless affiliations effected which amounted to nothing more than a simple formality, as is the case still in Burmah and Siam. In an inscription at Junnar (Kern, in Ind. Stud., xiv. p. 394), some bhikshus figure as donors, so that they must have retained property. In those of Kuḍâ there appear in the same character certain *religieuses* (pravrajitikâ, which seems here to be synonymous with bhikshuṇî), one of whom is actually a matron. Jacobi in Ind. Antiq., vii. 254, 256, Nos. 2 and 9. These inscriptions belong to the first centuries of our era. In the Sañcî inscriptions there are also many bhikshus and bhikshuṇîs among the donors. Cunningham, Bhilsa Topes, p. 235 *seq.*

into as many portions as the corporation has members—the Buddhist foundations remain undivided; they accumulate and are utilised in their entirety to the common advantage. In proportion as it thus increased in wealth Buddhism grew more and more sumptuous. It needed immense monasteries to shelter its legions of monks, commemorative monuments to mark the spots which, it was believed, the Master and the saints had rendered sacred by their presence, edifices, richly decorated, in which to deposit their relics, and chapels in which to erect their images. The cultus remained simple. It consisted in the repetition of a sort of office, acts of faith and homage, offerings of flowers, keeping a few lamps burning before the image or the shrine of Buddha;[1] but the style was grand. Everything leads to the belief that these "mendicants" were the first builders in India. The most ancient and stupendous ruins we meet with everywhere are of piles reared by their hands.[2] The underground temples, the monasteries excavated in the rock, are their workmanship;[3] and we find their mark in the substructures of

[1] The worship of images first appears at a rather recent date on the Buddhist monuments. The first sacred objects to which we find acts of homage rendered are symbols, such as the *cakra*, the wheel of the Law, the *Bodhi* tree, and especially the *Dagop* (Dhâtugarbha), a cupola-shaped structure intended to contain relics, and which in the ancient sanctuaries occupies exactly the place of the altar in Christian churches. At a later date it is replaced by images of Buddha, a substitution which, according to J. Burgess (Cave Temples, p. 180), is subsequent to the fourth century after Christ. The representations of Buddha, however, which we find on the coins of Kanishka (Von Sallet, Die Nachfolger Alexander's des Grossen in Baktrien und Indien, p. 191, and pl. vi. 1), do not permit us to doubt that images of the Master were worshipped as early as the first century of our era.

[2] See, for example, A. Cunningham, The Bhilsa Topes, or Buddhist Monuments of Central India, 1854; and The Stûpa of Bharhut, a Buddhist Monument ornamented with numerous Sculptures illustrative of Buddhist Legend and History, 1878. The greater part of the nine vols. of Reports on the Operations of the Archæological Survey of India by the same author, 1871–80, refers to Buddhist monuments. See besides J. Fergusson, History of Indian and Eastern Architecture, 1876; and Tree and Serpent Worship, 1873; the monographs, for the most part richly illustrated by J. Burgess, on the holy places of Elephanta, Junnar, Elurâ, Ajaṇṭâ; and the recent publication by the same authors, The Cave Temples of India, 1880.

[3] The number of these underground structures of which we have any account up to the present time in different parts of India exceeds 1000, eighty per cent. of which are of Buddhist origin.

almost all the great sanctuaries of Hinduism. It was for them especially that those sculptors, those painters, the forlorn hope of Greek art, appear to have laboured, who for a brief space afforded to India some glimpse of plastic beauty at once faithful and true.[1] While Brahmanism, the most materialistic of all cultuses, has kept to the last to its primitive tools, its penthouses of bamboo, its turf-clods and grass-blades, and a few vessels of wood, it was this religion, at once the most abstract and the most bald, that by a singular contrast was the first to think of impressing the imagination by appealing to the sense of sight.

We cannot trace the history of Buddhism without discovering, moreover, that its success was quite as much due to events that favoured it as to its own inherent aptitudes. The period of its extension coincides, in fact, with that of a profound change which came over the political condition of India. In connection with the empire of the Achemenides and the Greek domination, the government of the small states cleared the way for great monarchies, based on military and administrative centralisation, and which were not long in extending far beyond the confines of Brahmanism. These monarchies very soon saw what a powerful and pliant auxiliary they had in these militant communities, at once disconnected with everything and ready to conquer everything, humble in presence of the secular power, always disposed to call in its assistance in their affairs and quarrels, sufficiently organised to give a

[1] The isolated, and perhaps the most interesting, specimens of this art found at Mathurâ, in the Punjâb, in the valley of Cabul, are scattered up and down in the museums of Calcutta and Lahore, and in the India Museum. They have never been the subject of a work that reviewed the whole, and only a small number have been published, in, for instance, the Journ. of the Asiat. Soc. of Bengal, xliv. 214; Ind. Antiq., iii. p. 158; Cave Temples, p. 138. T. Fergusson, ibid., p. 90, is of opinion that Hindu sculpture reached its zenith in the fourth century, in the bas-reliefs of Amarâvatî. On the other hand, Byzantine art, even in Ravenna and at Mount Athos, has nothing to show superior to certain pictures in the caves of Ajaṇṭa, which appear to be of the sixth century. J. Burgess, Notes on the Bauddha Rock-Temples of Ajanta, 1879, in the 9th number of the Archæological Survey of Western India, and Cave-Temples of India, p. 280 *seq.*

hold on them and to be of service to it, not enough to excite any distrust; something, in short, like the mendicant Orders without the Pope. The most powerful of these empires, that of the Mauryas, which arose by reaction against the Macedonian aggression, was the work of a soldier of fortune of humble birth, a Çûdra in the opinion of the Brahmans. There was, therefore, a sort of natural affinity between this dynasty and Buddhism, which was, like it, an offspring of yesterday—like it, at variance with tradition, and caring as little as it for differences of race, manners, and creed. Thus these princes were pre-eminently friendly to it. Candragupta, the founder of the dynasty, is reported to have protected it. Açoka, his grandson, raised it to the rank of a state religion, and held sway over it.[1] Two of his children, a son and a daughter, were influential members of the Sañgha, and he himself was admitted a member of it at the close of his reign. This son was appointed chief of the mission by which Buddhism was introduced into Ceylon, and, according to the legend, he became the head of the Church there. It was by Buddhist missions, in like manner, that the powerful emperor came into relation with the kings of the Dekhan, over whom he appears to have exercised a kind of protectorate. Without distrusting in any way the sincerity of Açoka, we may remark that Buddhism alone lent itself to this close and fruitful alliance of faith and statecraft.[2]

When the power of the Mauryas began at length to decline, the north-west of India passed for several centuries under the sway of foreign princes, Greeks, Parthians, and Turanians. These last, who set about the conquest of the

[1] See the part which the Mahâvaṃsa (v. p. 42) makes him play at the council held in his reign, a part perfectly in keeping with the imperial patronising tone of his letter to the assembly of the clergy of Magadha, which the inscription of Bairât (Babhra) has preserved for us. Cunningham, Corpus Inscr. Indic., pl. xv.

[2] For the Buddhist missions see Lassen, Ind. Alterthumsk., vol. ii. p. 246, 2d ed. Dîpavaṃsa, ch. viii.; Mahâvaṃsa, ch. xii., xiii., p. 71 *seq.*

country by invasion, were able, towards the beginning of our era, to unite together all the countries on the north of the Vindhya. From this long thraldom the religion of Çâkyamuni was still the only one to reap benefit. Brahmanism was hostile, and held no parley with the stranger;[1] the popular religions, although less exclusive, were also intensely Hindu; Buddhism alone was cosmopolitan. The literature of the Cingalese has preserved for us a curious work, in which the Greek king Menander is represented as a zealous convert,[2] and the reign of the Turanian emperors, especially that of Kanishka, coincides perhaps with the period when the fortune of Buddhism in Hindustan was at its height. On the one hand, it must have met with a ready welcome from the uncivilised hoards that issued from the North in the train of the conquerors, and who settled in great numbers in the countries to the west of the Ganges. On the other hand, as the authority of these princes extended over both slopes of the mountains, this opened up for it roads into the North, into Afghanistan, Bactriana, China, and Thibet, just as the piety and policy of Açoka had opened up for it those into the South.

We do not know to what extent the reaction which led to the restoration of independence was directly injurious to it. The national dynasties, so far as appears by inscriptions, were much more Vishnuite or Çivaite than Buddhist; but Buddhism was fairly treated by them, and shared in their acts of liberality. It is clear, however, that its

[1] Alexander was obliged to treat the Brahmans with severity, because they drove the people to resistance and revolt. Plutarch, Alexander, ch. lix., lxiv. A vague acquaintance with these facts occurs again even in Shahrastâni's (twelfth century) Religionspartheien und Philosophenschulen, translated by Haarbrücker, ii. 374.

[2] The Milinda Pañha, "The Questions of Milinda." Spence Hardy has given numerous extracts from them in his "Eastern Monachism" and his "Manual of Buddhism." It is now edited: The Milindapañho, being Dialogues between King Milinda and the Buddhist Sage Nâgasena. The Pâli text, edited by V. Trenckner. What Plutarch says, De Gerendæ Reipub. Præcept (ch. xxviii.), of the way in which the different towns disputed for the remains of the body of Menander seems also to testify in favour of the Buddhism of that prince.

best days are now past. It has no longer to do with the ancient Brahmanism, but with rivals that were formidable in a very different way—the religions of Çiva and Vishṇu—and in this new struggle the advantages are on the side of the adversary. At the beginning of the fifth century, indeed, the Chinese pilgrim Fa-Hian found it still flourishing in the different parts of India. In the seventh, on the other hand, it appears in the accounts of Hiouen-Thsang in a state of decay. In the eleventh, it has still footing in some of its great sanctuaries in the provinces of the West;[1] in those of Magadhâ, at Gayâ, the land of its birth, we meet with traces of it even as late as the fourteenth;[2] and Buddhist dynasties appear to have subsisted in Behâr and towards the mouths of the Godâvarî until the end of the twelfth century.[3] Then we hear no more of it. The Brahmans continue still to argue a good deal against the Bauddhas; and Sâyaṇa in the fourteenth century still assigns to them the second place in his "General Review of the Systems." But it is difficult to say whether these arguments are addressed to real opponents, or whether they are not rather mere scholastic exercises.[4] Confined to the island of Ceylon, the valleys of Nepâl, and the districts which border on Burmah, Buddhism in

[1] Even the characters imprinted on the Buddhist clay seats found in great quantities in the grottoes of Kaṇheri, near Bombay, do not appear to date beyond the thirteenth century. Journ. of the Roy. As. Soc., Bombay, 1861, pl. vii. Albirouni in the eleventh century, in Reinaud's Mémoire sur l'Inde, p. 89, and Shahrastani in the twelfth century, translated by Haarbrücker, t. ii. p. 358, speak of the Buddhists as still existing in India.

[2] Inscription of Gayâ in A. Cunningham's Archæological Survey of India, vol. iii. pl. xxxv., and Corpus Inscrip. Indicarum, p. v. These places, besides, continued to be an object of pilgrimage for Buddhists from abroad; see the Burmese inscription of the fourteenth century, Archæological Survey, vol. i. p. 8.

[3] A. Cunningham, Archæological Survey, vol. iii. pp. 119, 121; P. Goldschmidt, in the Ind. Antiq., vi. 328.

[4] When Abul Fazl visited Kashmir (in the end of the sixteenth century), there were still some old men there who professed Buddhism, but he confesses he did not once fall in with a teacher of that religion; and yet the court of Akbar was a place of resort for learned men belonging to all the different schools of religious belief. He does not appear to know at what period the Buddhists had disappeared from India, and merely says "it was a long while ago." Ayeen Akbari, translated by Fr. Gladwin, Calcutta, 1786, t. iii. p. 158.

our days has completely disappeared from India proper. Its only memorials are the innumerable ruins which it has left behind over the whole surface of the peninsula, perhaps also a few groups of sects, viz., Vishnuites such as the Vaishṇavavîras of the Dekhan, and Çivaites like the Kâṇphâṭas of Hindustan, who have long abjured or forgotten their origin, but who still keep Buddhist saints in their calendar.

How are we to account for this total extinction of Buddhism in the country that witnessed its birth, and in which it flourished so long? Although it is in general more difficult to account for the decay of religions than their rise and growth, the disappearance of this one appears to have been so rapid, and is, in fact, so complete, that nothing, one would think, should be easier than to determine the causes of it. Such, however, is the obscurity which still veils many phases of the past history of India, that we can on this matter form only conjectures, and of only a quite general character too. The cause, persecution viz., to which we are apt to assign the first place, is exactly the one which, in the existing state of our knowledge, appears the least probable. No evidence of any serious weight has as yet been adduced to prove that Buddhism has ever been, either before its triumph or in the days of its decline, the object of rigorous measures directed against it with any unanimity of purpose and on any considerable scale. On the contrary, the most reliable documents, the coins and inscriptions, bear evidence of a toleration exceptionally generous on the part of the civil powers.[1] Not only do the princes of the same dynasty profess the most diverse religious creeds, but the same

[1] The coins of the Turanian princes of the first century are Çivaite and Buddhist ones; their inscriptions are Buddhist ones, and perhaps also Jainist. The Andhrabhṛitya kings, who, if we may judge from their names, were supporters of the ancient cultus, appear in their inscriptions at Nánághât, Nâsik, and Ajaṇṭâ, at once as practising the rites of Brahmanism and as patronising the Buddhists with gifts. Among the Guptas, Candragupta is a Brahmanist, like the other princes of the dynasty on the pillars of Behâr and Bhitari, and a protector of Buddhism and the Buddhists in the inscriptions of Sañcî. The kings

prince often distributes his bounties among several sects; and we might give a pretty long list of kings who, though they did not embrace Buddhism, were among its benefactors. Several of the monarchs, for instance, whom Hiouen-Thsang speaks of as professed patrons of the Church, appear to have been in reality adherents of one or other of the neo-Brahmanic religions. At a later date, even at the time when absurd legends represent Çaṅkara as exterminating the Buddhists from the Himâlaya to Cape Comorin, we read of Vishnuite princes who belonged to Vishnuite dynasties making donations to a sister religion of Buddhism, that of the Jainas, whom the Brahmans detested quite as much;[1] and these testimonies are not contradicted by the contemporary literary documents.[2] Not that India has been innocent of religious fanaticism. On the contrary, she was early familiar with it, and, under the form of exclusivism, practised the most

of Valabhî were Çivaites and Vishnuites, and we see them for nearly a century making donations to a Buddhist monastery founded by a princess of their family. Inscrip. in the Ind. Antiq., iv. 105, 175; vi. 15; vii. 67; Journ. of the Roy. As. Soc. of Bombay, xi. p. 361. Prof. Kern is of opinion that the accounts of the persecutions which the Buddhists must have had to undergo are to be classed with the tales of "My Mother the Goose." Over de Jaartelling der Zuidelijke Buddhisten, p. 43.

[1] The inscriptions of the Calukyas of the sixth and eighth century, in the Ind. Antiq., v. 69; vii. 106, 112. One of their vassals in the eleventh century built at one and the same time a temple of Jina, another of Çiva, and a third of Vishṇu, ibid., iv. 180. Even as late as 1119, a Çilâhâra prince of the Western Dekhan made gifts at once to Çiva, Buddha, and Arhat (= Jina), Journ. of the Roy. As. Soc., Bombay, xiii. p. 7. The Cera princes of the Gaṅgâvamça were Vishnuites, and their donations, until the tenth century, are made indifferently to Brahmans and Jainas, Ind. Antiq., i. 363; ii. 156; v. 136, 138; vi. 102; vii. 104, 112.

[2] See, for example, the rôle of the Buddhist priestess in the Mâlatî and Mâdhava of Bhavabhûti, the characters, or the mention of Buddhist characters, which occur in the Mṛicchakaṭikâ, in the Mudrârâkshasa, in the Daçakumâracarita, and the Nâgânanda (this Buddhist drama of the seventh century has been translated into English by Palmer Boyd, 1872, and into French by A. Bergaigne, 1879). See, besides, Varâha Mihira, Bṛihat Saṃhitâ, lviii. 44, 45; lx. 19. Moreover, the accounts in the Râjataraṅginî, if they at times give evidence of a certain animosity against the Buddhists, do not by any means exhibit them in the light of persons excommunicated and beyond the pale of Hindu society. Even in the 12th century we find a Buddhist religious figuring among the favourites of Harshadeva, king of Kashmir; Râjataraṅg., vii. 1100.

odious kind of it without any mercy.[1] At a later period she was no stranger to the excesses of propagandism, and it would seem that it is Buddhism she has to thank for her first lesson in this particular. It was not for nothing that the latter, in spite of its gentle spirit, showed itself a Church with universal pretensions and power of political adaptation. Even the proceedings connected with its erection into a state religion by Açoka appear to have been accompanied, if not with violence, at any rate with coercion, as is evident from the expressions ascribed to that prince. In less than two years, he says, "The gods who were worshipped as true divinities in Jambudvîpa (in India) have been rendered false; and this result is not the effect of my greatness, but of my zeal."[2] Up to the present time, there is nothing from a Brahmanic source to match this testimony, so significant in its brevity. From an early period, and long before that of the Brahmans, is the literature of the Buddhists of a violent temper, openly aggressive, and replete with tales of cruelty; and even in the work of the good Hiouen-Thsang we meet at every step with the naïve expression of the most cordial hatred, and that, too, on the part of a soul of the gentlest temper. The Brahmans, it is true, were not slow in retaliating in the same vein. The religions of the sects, not less eagerly zealous in their propaganda than Buddhism, were fanatical to an intense degree.[3] The disciples of Kumârila and Çaṅkara, organised into military orders, constituted themselves the rabid defenders of ortho-

[1] The true Brahmanical fanaticism is that which inspired the narrative of Râmâyaṇa, vii. ch. 74–76, where Râma cuts off the head of a Çûdra whom he surprises performing penances forbidden to his caste.

[2] Inscript. of Sahasrâm, of Rupnâth and Bairât, in the Ind. Antiq., vi. 156, and Corpus Inscrip. Indic., pl. xiv. Compare with this the institution of the Dharmamahâmâtras, a set of officials specially charged with the inspection and direction of everything connected with religion. Fifth edict of Girnanar, reproduced at Kapurdigiri, Khâlsi, and Dhauli, in the Corpus Inscrip. Indic., i. 71, and the pillar edict of Delhi, ibid. p. 115.

[3] The mere fact of entering a Buddhist sanctuary is in the Vṛihannâradîya Purâṇa reckoned in the number of the sins for which there is no forgiveness. Aufrecht, Oxford Catalogue, p. 10.

doxy on the ground of tradition and speculation. That, in these manifold struggles, other weapons than those of persuasion were employed; that the leaders of parties did not scruple at times to compass their ends by the physical force mediation of some râja, or by stirring up against their adversaries the passions of the mob; that the Buddhists in particular, as they became weaker, were subjected to many vexatious annoyances, and that their enemies, in their eagerness to appropriate their property and their sanctuaries, did not always wait until the last possessors had left, is what we must frankly admit. But there is a great difference between such local broils as these and a general mustering of forces on the field with a view to wholesale persecution; the possibility of an enterprise of this nature is out of the question in the divided state, political and religious, of India at that time. Everything, on the contrary, tends to prove that Buddhism became extinct from sheer exhaustion, and that it is in its own inherent defects we must especially seek for the causes of its disappearance.

In fact, there is no doubt whatever that Buddhism has been smitten with premature decrepitude. From the great deeds which it has done, from the new ideas which it has disseminated in the world, from the numberless lives of devotion which it has inspired, we feel assured that there was once a time when it must have been fresh with youth and full of vigour; but we have, in truth, no direct evidence of the fact. With the exception of certain admirable stanzas,[1] and some legends of striking beauty, notwithstanding their imperfect redaction, all it

[1] Particularly those of the collection entitled Dhammapada. The Pâli text, with a Latin translation and copious extracts from the commentary of Buddhaghosha, was published at Copenhagen by V. Fausböll, 1855. It has been translated into German by A. Weber, Zeitschr. d. Deutsch. Morgenl. Gesellsch., t. xiv.; into English by Max Müller, in his Introduction to the work of H. T. Rogers, Buddhaghosha's Parables, translated from the Burmese, 1869, and by S. Beal (on the Chinese text), Scriptural Texts from the Buddhist Canon, commonly known as the Dhammapada, 1878; into French by F. Hû, 1878.

has left us bears the stamp of senility. It cannot claim an assignable place either in poetry or Hindu science; nowhere has it been able to give birth to a national literature, or rise above the popular tale and the chronicle. Many causes have contributed to reduce Buddhism to this monotonous and helpless mediocrity, and it would not be difficult to discover some of these even in the teaching of Çâkyamuni, in his disrelish for the supernatural, in his ideas as too abstract for a sensual people with an exuberant imagination, in his morbid way especially of laying down and resolving the problem of life. We shall instance here only one of these causes, because it has, in our opinion, been the most direct and effectual, the very institution to which this creed must have owed its rapid triumphs at first; we refer to its monasticism. Some are at times fain to regard Buddhism as a spiritual emancipation, a kind of Hindu Reformation; and there is no doubt that in certain respects it was both. But in substituting the Sañgha for the caste system of Brahmanism, it created an institution far more illiberal, and formidable to spiritual independence. Not only did all the vitality of the Church continue concentrated in a clergy living apart from the world, but among this clergy itself the conquering zeal of the first centuries gradually died away under the influence of quietism and the discipline enforced. The *vihâras,* in spite of the laxity of morale which too clearly prevailed, continued, no doubt, to afford a shelter for sentiments of humble and sincere piety and the practice of the most heart-affecting virtues. But all boldness and true originality of thought disappeared in the end in the bosom of this spirit-weakening organisation. The intellectual powers were exhausted in scholastic discussion or lulled to sleep in the midst of idle routine, and a time came at length when it ceased even to give birth to heresies. The Buddhism of Ceylon has not changed much since the time of Buddhaghosha (in the fifth century), and that of Nepâl, or rather of Hindustan, could devise no better means of prolonging life than by effecting a sort of fusion with Çivaism.[1] It was in this state of apathy, when it had, so to speak, outlived itself, that Buddhism had to enter into competition with the neo-Brahmanic sects, which were in constant process of new birth, at each new transformation rushing into the arena of debate with the zeal of neophytes. When we consider that the majority of these sects gave battle with its own weapons; that they preached, like it, the religious equality of all men; that over against the figure of Buddha they set figures, less perfect doubtless, but quite as personal, quite as capable of stirring up a passionate devotion of legendary deities, such as Mahâdêva, Kṛishṇa, Râma, to say nothing of their goddesses; when we consider that they knew at least as well as it how to appeal to the senses with their temples, their images, their pompous and stagy festivals, and that they possessed, moreover, a splendid system of fable, while it had only been able to cloak itself in an abstract artificial mythology; when, in addition to this, we consider, in fine, that they had at their head the Brahman and at their service the popular poetry, that their religious beliefs formed one body, so to speak, with the national legend, and recalled all the glorious and heroic memories of the ancient epic, we shall very easily understand how Buddhism had to go to the wall. To have been made sure of a longer life, it would have required the return to life of the first apostles of its faith, and it had only *bonzes*.

But while it was disappearing as a Church, it did not

[1] On this point see B. H. Hodgson, Essays on the Languages, Literature, and Religion of Nepâl and Tibet, ed. 1874, particularly the essay x. p. 133 *seq.*; Burnouf, Introduction à l'Hist. du Boud. Ind., p. 546 *seq.*; Köppen, Die Religion des Buddha, vol. ii., and the brief but compact Memoir of Paṇdit Bhagvanlâl Indraji, The Bauddha Mythology of Nepâl, given as an appendix by J. Burgess in No. 9 of the Archæological Survey of Western India, p. 97 *seq.* This fusion must have been pretty thorough before writings could become common to the two religions, for example the Pragnottararatnamâlâ (published in Sanskrit, in Tibetan, and in French, by Ed. Foucaux, La Guirlande Précieuse des Demandes et des Réponses, 1867, and by A. Weber in the Memoirs of the Academy of Berlin for 1868, p. 92 *seq.*), ascribed to Çaṅkara.

take along with it the germs which it had for long had the opportunity of disseminating, and it left the very religions which succeeded in smothering it more or less pervaded by its spirit. There is no doubt that there is in Sanskrit literature, or, to speak more correctly, in the literature of the Hindus, an under-current, as it were, of Buddhist ideas. If we take, for example, the fable of the Mahâbhârata, we shall see how different the spirit in which it is treated is from that in which it was conceived; and we should find a more striking instance still if we went back to the poetry of the Râmâyaṇa. There are here accents of an ardent charity, of a compassion, a tenderness, and a humility at once sweet and plaintive, which ever and anon suggest the action of Christian influences, and which, in any case, contrast singularly with the pride and want of feeling—fruits of the spirit of caste—with which that literature is nevertheless replete. Quite as remarkable in this respect is the change which has taken place in the religious observances of this people, the gradual discontinuance of sacrifice to the advantage of almsgiving, pious deeds, and the worship of latreia; especially that aversion to the shedding of blood which has more and more restricted the practice of animal sacrifice, and which turned up eventually in that whimsical exaggeration of charity towards brutes in the erection of hospitals in their behalf[1] in a country where there are none for men. It would be to make a false use of historical coincidences to affect to see dimly in all these facts the direct action of Buddhism; but we cannot nevertheless deny that they belong to a movement inspired by ideas to which Buddhism had given the most effective expression.

[1] Heber, Narrative of a Journey through the Upper Provinces of India, 1824–25, ch. xxv.

IV.

JAINISM.

Canonical literature of the Jainas as yet little known.—Striking resemblance between Jainism and Buddhism: the Jinas and the mythology of the Jainas.—Cultus.—Rejection of the Veda and caste.—Clergy and lay community.—Chief divisions of the Jainas.—Asceticism, metaphysics, and moral system.—The Jina and the Buddha of the present age: the Nirvâṇa of the Jina.—Uncertain character of Jaina tradition.—The Nirgrantha Jñatiputra.—Whatever the date of its origin, Jainism historically more recent than Buddhism.—Present condition of Jainism.

BEFORE we proceed to the sects of new Brahmanism, we have still to speak of a religion closely allied to Buddhism, and one of the least known among those which have performed an important part in the past of India—the religion of the Jainas. Not that we are absolutely without documents bearing on the history and the doctrines of Jainism. We possess, among others, a manual of the twelfth century, the *Yogasûtra*,[1] which gives a summary of its morals; the *Kalpasûtra*, a translation of a biography of its founder, which professes to date as far back as the sixth century;[2]

[1] E. Windisch, Hemacandra's Yogasûtra, ein Beitrag zur Kenntniss der Jaina Lehre, in the Zeitsch. d. Deutsch. Morgenl. Gesellsch., vol. xxviii. p. 185. L'Abhidhânacintâmaṇi, a lexicon, by the same author, of synonyms, edited by O. Böhtlingk and Ch. Rieu, 1847, contains also a good deal of information in regard to the Jainas.

[2] Stevenson, The Kalpasûtra and Nava Tatva, Two Works Illustrative of the Jaina Religion and Philosophy, translated from the Magadhi, 1848. H. Jacobi has since published the text of the first, with a learned introduction, The Kalpasûtra of Bhadrabâhu, edited with an introduction, notes, and a Prâkṛit-Sanskṛit glossary, 1879. The pretended author, Bhadrabâhu, must have lived, according to the tradition of the Çvetâmbaras, in the fourth century B.C.; but the redaction we have dates at most only from the commencement of the sixth century after our era. The Digambaras reject the Kalpasûtra as apocryphal. See the introduction of Jacobi, pp. 10 *seq.*, 20 *seq.*, 30.

some extensive extracts from another work of biography and legend, the *Çatruñjaya-mâhâtmya*,[1] which is assigned to the same period, but which has probably been recast in the thirteenth or fourteenth century, and sundry specimens of the *Stotras*, or the lyric poetry of the Jainas.[2] But, with the exception of a single fragment of the *Bhagavati*,[3] we do not possess another of their canonical texts; and we are still always obliged to refer to Brahmanical sources to obtain a general view of their system. Now, these are interested exclusively in the speculative side of the doctrines, and, moreover, they supply us with no data to enable us to distinguish epochs in their development. On the other hand, we happen to know that the Jainas form several distinct sects, very widely separated from one another, differing even in regard to the number and the selection of their canonical books, the *Agamas*.[4] In these circumstances, it would be rash to venture to expound and criticise in detail a system which as yet is known to us only in a sort of abstract way, and in regard to the historic development of which we are absolutely in the dark.[5]

[1] A. Weber, Ueber das Çatruñjaya Mâhâtmyam, ein Beitrag zur Geschichte der Jaina, 1858. The biography of the Jina is here connected with the glorification of the holy mountain Çatruñjaya, in the peninsula of Gujarât. Bühler holds this work to be quite apocryphal, Ind. Antiq., vi. 154.

[2] H. Jacobi, Zwei Jaina-stotra, in the Ind. Stud., xiv. p. 359, and The Kalpasûtra, p. 13; Joh. Klatt, Dhanapâla's Ṛishabhapañcâçikâ, in the Zeitsch. d. D. Morgenl. Gesell., xxxiii. p. 445. Besides, H. Jacobi has published, with a translation and a commentary, the legend, very curious in a historical point of view, of one of the fathers of the Jaina Church, Das Kâlakâcârya-Kathânakam, in the Zeitsch. d. D. Morgenl. Gesell., xxxiv. p. 247 *seq.*

[3] A. Weber, Ueber ein Fragment der Bhagavatî; ein Beitrag zur Kenntniss der heiligen Litteratur der Jaina, two parts, 1866–67, in the Memoirs of the Academy of Berlin. An edition of the Bhagavatî began to appear in Bombay, in 1877, under the editorship of Abhayadeva, in a collection intended to include all the sacred writings of the Jainas. We must now add the Nirayâvaliyâ Suttam, which contains the five last of the twelve Upângas, and which S. Warren has just edited, 1880. Perhaps there is better to come, but as far as yet published it is wretchedly poor literature.

[4] G. Bühler in the Ind. Antiq., vii. 28; H. Jacobi, Kalpasûtra, p. 14; S. J. Warren, Over de Godsdienstige en Wijsgeerige Begrippen der Jainas, p. 7; A. C. Burnell, in the Ind. Antiq., ii. 354. See ibid., iii. 129.

[5] Besides the works mentioned already, consult for a general review

Viewed as a whole, Jainism is so exact a reproduction of Buddhism that we have considerable difficulty in accounting for both their long-continued existence by each other's side, and the cordial hatred which seems always to have separated them. The Jainas are the followers of *Jina*, the "victorious," as the Bauddhas are of Buddha, the "awakened" one. A Jina (this term, which is common to the two sects, along with many others, being among the Buddhists one of the many synonyms of Buddha) is a sage who has reached omniscience, and who comes to re-establish the law in its purity when it has become corrupted among men. There have been twenty-four of these Jinas, the last Jina included, who was of the royal race of the Kâçyapas. As the Jainas maintain that Gautama Buddha was a disciple of their founder, this number exactly corresponds with that of the twenty-four predecessors of Buddha, the last of whom is a Kâçyapa as well. These Jinas succeeded each other at immense intervals of time, their stature and their term of life always decreasing from the first Ṛishabha, who was 3000 feet in height and lived eight millions of years, until Vardhamâna, the last, whose age and stature did not exceed those of actual humanity.[1] These fancies, which, along with many others, we meet with in Buddhism,[2] especially in that of the low epochs, with this difference, however, that their more mature elaboration and arrangement must almost always be credited to the side of the Jainas, go to prove that at a very late date the two religions still exercised a certain influence on one another. Like the Buddhas, the Jinas became veritable deities and the direct objects of worship.

of the Jainas and their doctrines, Colebrooke, Miscellaneous Essays, vol. ii. p. 174 (1807), and vol. i. p. 402 (1826); to this last article Prof. Cowell has added, at p. 444, a minute analysis of chap. iii. of the Sarvadarçanasaṅgraha, where Sâyaṇa expounds the system of the Jainas. H. H. Wilson, Select Works, vol. i. p. 276. Lassen, Ind. Alterthumsk., vol. iv. p. 755. S. J. Warren, Over de Godsdienstige en Wijsgeerige Begrippen der Jainas, 1875.

[1] See the detailed list in the Ind. Antiq., ii. 134.

[2] See Jâtaka Commentary, ed. Fausböll, i. 29 *seq.*

They have at their side the Çâsanadêvîs,[1] goddesses, who execute their commands, and who remind us of the Çaktis of the neo-Brahmanic religions, and the like of which we meet with also among the Buddhists of the North, in the persons of *Târâ* and the other goddesses of the Sanskrit books of Nepâl. Their images, which are at times colossal, especially in the Dekhan,[2] are to be seen in great numbers in the sanctuaries of the sect, which has done a great deal in the way of building, and whose structures are almost all distinguished by a style of their own and of great elegance. Next to the Jinas rank their immediate disciples, the *Gaṇadharas*, who receive homage in the character of guardian saints, and a great number of deities which the Jainas have borrowed one by one from the Hindu pantheon, but which have no share in the regular cultus. The cultus itself is pretty much akin to that of the Buddhists. There are the same offerings, the same acts of faith and homage; the use of little bells is common to both of them, and the women enjoy the same rights as the men. In both, confession is practised, great importance is attached to pilgrimages, and four months in the year are more especially given up to fastings, the reading of sacred books, and spiritual meditations.

The Jainas, like the Buddhists, reject the Veda of the Brahmans, which they pronounce apocryphal and corrupt, and to which they oppose their own *Aṅgas*, as constituting the true Veda. They are quite as little disposed to tolerate the existence of a sacerdotal caste, although at present the clergy, in some of their communities at least, are recruited from certain families in preference to others, and, it appears, from the Brahman caste itself. Besides, they observe the rules of caste among themselves as well as in their relations with those who dissent from them, but, like several Hindu sects, however, without attaching any religious significance to it. In general, and although

[1] A. Weber, Çatruñjaya Mâhâtmyam, p. 24.
[2] Ind. Antiq., ii. 129, 353; v. 37.

we do not exactly know what was in this respect the practice of the Buddhists in India even, they appear to have separated themselves less from Hinduism than the Buddhists did, and, in fact, they profess to be Hindus. They have taken a much more active part in the literary and scientific life of India. Astronomy, grammar, and romantic literature owe a great deal to their zeal. This did not prevent a serious animosity springing up between them and the Brahmans, which was marked at times in Gujarât and in the extreme South, among other places, by somewhat bloody episodes.[1]

Like the Buddhists, they are divided into a clerical body and a lay—into *Yatis* or ascetics, and into *Çrâvakas* or simple hearers; but the monastic system appears to have been developed to a less degree among them. At present their Yatis form sorts of colleges, kept up at the expense of the communities, but the members of which no longer subsist on alms, and they no longer admit, as they formerly did, an order of women. They are divided into two principal sects—the *Çvetâmbaras*, or "the white gowns," and the *Digambaras*, or "those who are clothed in air," that is to say, who go naked—designations these which have passed from the clergy to the laity as well. The Çvetâmbaras hold, in general, the first rank, but the Digambaras, who are also more specifically denominated the *Nirgranthas*, *i.e.*, "those who have cast aside every tie," appear to be the more ancient; at least this last title occurs already in the inscriptions of Açoka,[2] and in all probability as a designation of the Jainas. Both sects are mentioned in certain inscriptions of Mysore, which go back as far probably as the sixth, perhaps the fifth, century;[3] and there is similar evidence of their presence

[1] G. Bühler, in the Ind. Antiq., vi. 186; Lassen, Ind. Alterthumsk, vol. iii. p. 240; R. Caldwell, A Comparative Grammar of the Dravidian Languages, introduction, pp. 89, 138.

[2] Eighth edict of Delhi, l. 5, in the Corpus Inscrip. Indic., pl. xx. The tradition of the Digambaras places the schism of the Çvetâmbaras towards the end of the first century A.D. Jacobi, Kalpasûtra, p. 15.

[3] The inscriptions of the ancient Kadambas, in the Ind. Antiq., vi. 23–32; vii. 33–37; in this last docu-

at Canoje in the seventh.[1] Their respective relations recall those subsisting between the Buddhist sects of the Great and the Little Vehicle; that is to say, in spite of considerable differences, they are rather rivals than declared enemies. To this division another, as among the Buddhists, has come to be added—that of the Jainas of the North and the Jainas of the South—which, though simply geographical in its origin, has extended in the end to the doctrines taught, the question of the canon of scripture, and the entire body of the traditions and usages.[2] The Digambaras Yatis no longer practise nudity nowadays, except during their meals, when they take these in common. But it is evident that the practice must have been more rigidly enforced at former times; and Hesychius, in the third century, was doubtless well informed when he translated ***Γέννοι*** by ***Γυμνοσοφιστάι***.[3] This evidence, joined to many others, such as the practice of depilation, seems to imply that at first one of the leading differences between Jainas and Buddhists was that the former professed a more rigorous asceticism than the latter. No Hindu sect has carried *ahiṃsâ* farther, *i.e.*, respect for and abstinence from everything that has life. Not only do they abstain absolutely from all kinds of flesh, but the more rigid of them drink only filtered water, breathe only through a veil, and go sweeping the ground before them for fear of unconsciously swallowing or crushing any invisible animalcule. In regard to all these matters, primitive Buddhism had much fewer scruples. The extravagances of asceticism, nudity in particular, were expressly condemned by Çâkyamuni. Some of his disciples even broke partnership with him on that score; and we know

ment the revenue of a village is divided between the Çvêtapaṭas (Çvetâmbaras) and the Nirgranthas. See also Journ. of the Roy. As. Soc. Bombay, xii. 321.

[1] Bâṇa, in F. E. Hall, Vâsavadattâ, Pref., p. 53.

[2] Ind. Antiq., ii. 354; iii. 129.

[3] In Varâha Mihira's (sixth century) Bṛihat Saṃhita, lx. 19, ed. Kern, Nagna, "naked," is the official designation of a Jaina Yati.

that according to tradition he himself died from a fit of indigestion after dining on pork. In regard to another observance, equally repudiated by Buddha, religious suicide, to wit, the Jainas differ; one of their canonical books condemns it, the Bhagavatî emphatically affirming that "suicide increases life."[1] But, on the other hand, inscriptions that have been collected together from sanctuaries in the Dekhan leave no doubt as to the frequent practice of this custom among the Jainas of the South during a long period of the middle age.[2]

It is always to Buddhism that we are referred back when we come to examine the general doctrine of the Jainas. The essential points, such as the idea of the world and the philosophy of life, are nearly the same in both. Like the Buddhists, the Jainas are atheists. They admit of no creator; the world is eternal; and they explicitly deny the possibility of a perfect being from all eternity. The Jina became perfect; he was not always so. Like the Buddhists of the North, this denial has not prevented them, or at least some of them, from returning to a sort of deism; and just as in the books of Nepâl we see an *Adibuddha*, a supreme Buddha, arise, so we find in the monumental inscriptions of the Dekhan a *Jinapati*, a supreme Jina, entitled the primary creator,[3] and that in contradiction to the most explicit declarations extracted from their most authorised writings. All beings are divided into two classes, animate and inanimate. Animate beings are composed of a soul and a body, and their souls, being radically distinct from matter, are eternal. This is one of the very few essential points in which the doctrinal system of Jainism deviates from that of Buddhism. On the other hand, it is in very close affinity with the Sâṅkhya conception; and it explains in a quite similar way how the soul, which is pure intelligence, is nevertheless a prey to illusion, and condemned on that account to

[1] A. Weber, Ueber ein Fragment der Bhagavatî, 2d part, p. 267.

[2] The inscriptions of Çravaṇa Belgola, in the Ind. Antiq., ii. 322; iii. 153.

[3] Ind. Antiq., vii. p. 106, l. 51.

submit to the yoke of matter through an infinite succession of existences. It is, therefore, not the fact of existence which is the evil in the eyes of the Jainas; it is life which is bad; and Nirvâṇa is with them, not the annihilation of the soul, but rather its deliverance and its entry into a blessedness that has no end. The way to Nirvâṇa is naturally revealed by the Jina. The means of reaching it constitute the Triratna, the "three jewels:" first, the perfect faith, or faith in the Jina; second, the perfect science, or the knowledge of his doctrine; third, perfect conduct, or the strict observance of his precepts. Under a form, at first sight perceptibly different, we at once recognise here the Triratna of the Buddhists, viz., Buddha, the Law, and the Saṅgha. Thus we detect in these two systems throughout a constant effort, as it were, not to appear to have too close a connection with each other—a fact which, still more than their open collisions, proves their close relationship. The development of the "perfect conduct," for instance, is the exact counterpart of the moral teaching and discipline of Buddhism. Only, if we except a small number of points, such as the classification of merits and of sins, which is the same, everything is transposed; the same things are called by different names, and the same names denote different things. We might say they are two mosaics of different design but composed of similar pieces. As matter of detail, we may observe that the Digambaras agree with the Buddhists in maintaining that women have not the capacity of attaining Nirvâṇa, while the Çvetâmbaras teach that they have.[1]

[1] The canon of the Digambaras is very different from that of the Çvetâmbaras (G. Bühler, in Ind. Antiq., vii. p. 28), and as little is that of the Digambaras of the South the same as that of the Digambaras of the North (Burnell, ibid., ii. p. 354). For the canon of the Çvetâmbaras of the North, the only one of which anything is known, see the lists of Bühler (in Jacobi, The Kalpasûtra, p. 14), Klatt and Jacobi (in the Zeitsch. d. D. Morgenl. Gesellsch., xxxiii. pp. 478, 693). This canon includes forty-five Agamas or texts composing the law, viz., eleven Aṅgas (these are the sacred books *par excellence*, collected, according to tradition, in the fourth century B.C. by the Saṅgha of Pâtaliputra; the Bhagavatî is one of the Aṅgas); twelve Upâṅgas, or auxiliary trea-

In this also the former appear to have adhered more faithfully to the original doctrine. Finally, the denial of the objective reality of the conceptions of the mind, which is one of the fundamental doctrines of the Buddhists, has its counterpart in the probabilism of the Jainas. The latter maintain, in fact, that we can neither affirm nor deny anything absolutely of an object, and that a predicate never expresses more than a possibility. Hence the Brahmans, who call the Bauddhas *Çûnyavâdins*, that is, "those who affirm the void," designate the Jainas by the term *Syâdvâdins*, *i.e.*, "those who say perhaps."

But the attempt to trace the parallelism of the two religions becomes really perplexing when we pass to their traditions, to those especially which concern their respective founders. The legend of Vardhamâna, or, to apply to him the name which is most in use, Mahâvîra, "the great hero," the Jina of the present age, presents so many and so peculiar points of contact with that of Gautama Buddha, that we are irresistibly led to conclude that one and the same person is the subject of both.[1] Both are of royal birth; the same names recur among their relatives and disciples; they were born and they died in the same country and at the same period of time. According to the accepted reports, the Nirvâṇa of the Jina took place in 526 B.C., that of Buddha in 543 B.C.; and if we make allowances for the uncertainty inherent in these data (since we know that the real year of the death

tises (one of them, the Sûryaprajñapti, which treats of astrology and calculation, has been the subject of an extended analysis on the part of A. Weber in the Ind. Stud., x. p. 294 *seq.*); ten Prakîrṇakas, or miscellanea; eight Chedas, or sections, fragments; and four Mûlasûtras, or fundamental Sûtras. The Jainas themselves admit that all this literature is of secondary formation; that from the second century after the death of the founder, all their ancient books (the fourteen Pûrvas) were lost, and that the canon now accepted was made up only at the commencement of the sixth century A.D., by the Sâṅgha of Valabhi, under the direction of Devarddhigaṇin. This redaction itself seems to have undergone since that time notable alterations. Jacobi, The Kalpasûtra, pp. 14 *seq.*, 30.

[1] See A. Weber, Ueber das Çatruñjayamâhâtmya, p. 2; H. Kern, Over de Jaartelling der Zuidelijke Buddhisten, p. 28.

of Buddha fell between 482 and 472 B.C.), the two dates may be considered as identical.[1] Coincidences quite similar occur in the course of the two traditions. Like the Buddhists, the Jainas claim to have been patronised by the Maurya princes. The former had Açoka for patron; the latter speak of Sampadi, his grandson, in the same connection, and even of his grandfather, Candragupta, who, according to the traditions of the South, must have been a Jaina ascetic.[2] A district which is a holy land for the one is almost always a holy land for the other, and their sacred places adjoin each other in Behar, in the peninsula of Gujarât, on Mount Abû in Râjastan, as well as elsewhere. If we collate together all these correspondences in doctrine, organisation, religious observances and traditions, the inference seems inevitable that one of the two religions is a sect, and, in some degree, the copy of the other. When, in addition to this, we think of the manifold relations which there are between the legend of Buddha and the Brahmanical traditions, relations which are wanting in the legend of Mahâvîra; when we reflect, moreover, that Buddhism has in its behalf the testimony of the edicts of Açoka, and that from that time, the third century before our era, it was in possession of a literature some of the titles of which have been transmitted to us,[3] while the most ancient testimonies of an unquestionable nature in favour of Jainism do not go farther back than the fifth century after Christ (for the mention of the Nirgranthas in the edicts of Açoka amounts only to a probability, and the application to the Jainas of an inscription of Mathurâ of the first century is doubtful);[4] when we

[1] For the various computations current among the Jainas, see Jacobi, The Kalpasûtra, pp. 8 and 30. One of them gives for the death of Mahâvîra a date which differs only by about a dozen years from the *true* date of the death of Buddha; the other, which is borrowed from the tradition of the Digambaras, gives a date only two years different from the official but *false* date of the Singhalese Nirvâṇa. These are very surprising coincidences.

[2] Ind. Antiq., iii. p. 155.

[3] The inscription of Bairât in the Corpus Inscrip. Indic., pl. xv.

[4] A. Cunningham, Archæological Survey, vol. iii. p. 35. The nudity of the figure is perhaps not decisive in favour of a Jaina origin. See, however, ibid., vol. i. p. 94.

reflect further that the chief sacred language of the Buddhists, the Pâli, is almost as ancient as these edicts, while that of the Jainas, the *ardha-mâgadhî*, is a prâkrit dialect obviously more recent;[1] when we add to all this the conclusions, very uncertain, it is true, in the present state of our knowledge, which are furnished by the internal characteristics of Jainism, such as its more mature systematisation, its tendency to expatiate, and the pains it is always taking to demonstrate its antiquity, we shall feel no hesitation in admitting that, of the two, Buddhism is the one which is best entitled to the claim to originality.[2] We are bound to add, however, that Professor G. Bühler, the scholar who is best acquainted with the still unedited literature of the Jainas of the North, thinks he has come upon data to prove that the traditions concerning Mahâvîra point back to a real personage distinct from Gautama Buddha, and nearly contemporary with him, whose real name must have been the Nirgrantha Jñâtiputra, *i.e.*, the ascetic of the Jñâtis, Jñâti denoting a Rajput tribe to which the Nirgrantha must have belonged.[3] This fact, if it were per-

[1] For the age of the Jaina writings, see now H. Jacobi, Kalpasûtra, Introd., p. 15.

[2] Colebrooke had adopted the contrary conclusion, Miscellaneous Essays, vol. ii. p. 276, ed. Cowell. H. H. Wilson, on the other hand, did not think the Jainas more ancient than the eighth or ninth century, Select Writings, vol. i. p. 334.

[3] Ind. Antiq., vii. p. 143. H. Jacobi, who shares with Bühler the honour of this discovery, has since expounded it with a greater array of details, Kalpasûtra, p. 6. From this investigation it follows that, at the period of the redaction of the Kalpasûtra, the Jainas, in fact, acknowledge the Nirgrantha Nâtaputta as their founder (the Jñâtiputra of the books of Nepâl, Nâyaputta in Jaina prâkrit), one of the six Titthiyas or false teachers, whom the Buddhist books make contemporary with Buddha (see *supra*, p. 123). We only require to ascertain what this tradition is worth, and to what extent it is independent of that of the Buddhists, which, in its turn, on this particular point of the six Titthiyas, is none the less artificial. Pending the more profound study of ancient Jaina literature, of which, thanks to G. Bühler, the library of Berlin now possesses a nearly complete collection, and the results of which will throw fresh light on the subject, we must confess that the data collected by Jacobi do not appear to us altogether to confirm the authority of Jaina tradition, and that in adding new coincidences to those which we know already, they tend rather to strengthen the suspicion that there is much that is borrowed in the alleged Jaina original. Compare, however, the recent observations of Jacobi in the Indian Antiquary, ix. p. 158, especially the curious parallelisms to which he draws attention

fectly established, would evidently be of great weight, and only a few more such would suffice to modify greatly the preceding conclusions. But by itself alone it can prove neither the authenticity of the biography of the Jina, nor, in particular, the originality of Jainism, which, viewed in the light of the affiliation of the doctrines, we must continue to regard, till further proof be forthcoming, as a sect that took its rise in Buddhism.

At what period did this sect attain a really independent existence? To answer this question we must first be able to determine the character of primitive Jainism, and that is a problem which we will be able to face only after we have obtained access to the canonical books of the sect. Up to the present time, our sources of information on the matter are limited to external testimonies. We have seen already that the Nirgranthas, from the inscriptions of Açoka, in all probability concerned, if not the Jainas, at all events the ancestors of existing Jainism. From its philological characteristics, the sacred language of the sect would take us back for the origin of its literature to a later epoch by several centuries—to the beginning of our era. From the date of the fifth century, on the other hand, we find the Jainas in fixed settlements at the very extremity of the peninsula; and it is to them and the Buddhists, who had, however, preceded them in these districts, that the first literary culture of the Canarese and Tamîl languages can be traced. In the seventh century, in the time of Hiouen-Thsang, they were the dominant sect in the Dekhan. At the present time they are much reduced in number (to about half a million), and as a Church they are fallen into decay. They still always collect, however, in remarkable groups in the South, where they in general

between the opinions which the Buddhist books ascribe to the Nirgrantha and doctrines in vogue among the Jainas. According to these recent researches, the accurate orthography of the name must have been Jñâtṛiputra. Jacobi is disposed also to believe now that Mahâvîra was only the reformer of the sect, and that the latter in reality dates back as far as Pârçvanâtha, the Jina before the last, if not still farther.

practise agriculture, and in Western Hindustan, where they prefer to devote themselves to commerce, and where communities of them, which are for the most part wealthy, hardly present any traces of their primitive asceticism. In almost all the large towns, from Lahore to Bombay and Calcutta, we meet with them settled as traders or bankers, and the particular aptitude they show for traffic constantly reminds us of the conspicuous part which merchants, goldsmiths, and shipowners play in the legends and inscriptions of Buddhism. In Behar, the country of their birth, where the sanctuary of Pârasnâth (a vulgar form of the word Pârçvanâtha, the Jina before the last) is to this day an object of pilgrimage,[1] they have almost entirely disappeared as a settled population.[2] It would be easy to form conjectures to explain the survival of these Jainas, in contrast with the very different fate of the Buddhists. We shall hazard only one such. Whatever may be the date of the first rise of Jainism, its appearance as a religion is later than that of Buddhism, and from a historical point of view it is more recent. It was thus able to hold on till the period of the Mahommedan domination, the effect of which was to arrest the propagation of Hinduism, and which, while it evidently contributed to the religious, political, and social dismemberment of the nation, everywhere showed itself conservative of minorities, small associations, and small churches.

[1] See Hunter, A Statistical Account of Bengal, vol. xvi. p. 216.

[2] Remnants, for most part extremely degenerate, and of which some have lost all recollection of their origin, are scattered about under the name of Sarâks, Sarâvâks (= Çrâvaka), in the districts south-west of Bengal and the tributary states dependent on it. Hunter, *op. cit.*, vol. xvi. p. 381, vol. xvii. p. 291.

V.

HINDUISM.

Sect the very essence of Hinduism.—Place which the Veda and ancient tradition hold in it.—Part which the Brahmans play in it : as having adopted while they control the new religions, though these have never been entirely subject to them.

THE sectarian or neo-Brahmanic religions, which we embrace under the general designation of Hinduism, and which are at the present time professed by about 180,000,000 people[1] in British India, Nepâl, Ceylon, Indo-China, the Sunda Isles, at the Mauritius, at the Cape, and as far as the West Indies, where they have been imported by the Coolies, do not form a whole as homogeneous as ancient Brahmanism, still less Buddhism and Jainism. In spite of the efforts made at different periods and from different points of view to reduce them to a kind of unity, they have steadily resisted every attempt to group them systematically. They constitute a fluctuating mass of beliefs, opinions, usages, observances, religious and social ideas, in which we recognise a certain common ground-principle, and a decided family likeness indeed, but from which it would be very difficult to educe any accurate definition. At the present time it is next to impossible to say exactly what Hinduism is, where it begins, and where it ends. Diversity is its very essence, and its

[1] According to the census of 1872, the population of British India amounted to 245,000,000, of whom 140,000,000 were Hindus. In this number were not included the half-naturalised populations, who are socially excluded from Hinduism, but who, in a religious point of view, cannot be entirely separated from it.

proper manifestation is "sect," sect in constant mobility, and reduced to such a state of division that nothing similar to it was ever seen in any other religious system. In the past this dividing process, doubtless, was carried on to a less degree; still, however far we go back, we are led to fancy, if we do not find, a state of things which must have more or less resembled what we witness to-day. Hence, in the investigation to which we have still to subject these beliefs, we must abandon all idea of carrying our analysis as far as the sectarian element, although that is the only real thing at bottom; but not to lose ourselves in a waste of detail or an enumeration of particulars without meaning, we shall be obliged to keep to generalities, and to treat them in categories.

We have already had frequent occasion to characterise the relation of these religions to those which preceded them, or those whose development was contemporary with theirs. Like that of Buddhism, their rise was in general due to the unsatisfactory nature of the old Brahmanical theology, the divinities of which had gradually retired and disappeared behind a host of abstractions too subtle to affect the conscience of the masses. But in taking this step they did not, like the sect of Çâkyamuni, openly sunder all connection with the past. They, on the contrary, claim to be its continuation, or rather they represent themselves to be that very past unchanged and unmodified. The most of them profess to be based on the Veda, with which at bottom they have almost nothing in common, and which they virtually superseded by a quite different literature, but to which, in spite of protestations to the contrary which they sometimes let drop,[1] they nevertheless continue to appeal to as

[1] For instance, in the Mahâbhârata, i. 269, it is said that when the gods put into the balance on the one scale the four Vedas, and on the other the Mahâbhârata alone, the latter outweighed the former. The Agni-Purâṇa, i. 8–11, declares that it is the revelation of the supreme brâhman, of which the Veda is only the inferior expression. The Bhagavad Gîta does not adopt a different style of speaking, ii. 42–45; ix. 21. This is an echo of the Upanishads.

their highest authority. And to a certain extent there is truth in this profession. They have always drawn liberally from this old store, borrowing from it in part their formulæ, usages, legends, and even doctrines, almost always spoiling what they appropriate from it, but also attaining at times, in their more learned forms, a more or less partial assimilation with that system. The cultus peculiar to them, for instance, is radically distinct from the cultus of Brahmanism; yet is this last not, therefore, entirely set aside. At bottom, it is true, they despise it, and will extinguish it in the end. But when it is their interest to do so, they boast of its excellence. In Bhagavad-Gîtâ, Kṛishṇa declares expressly that he regards every religious act which is done in faith as addressed to himself.[1] Thus it is possible to be at once an orthodox Brahmanist and a zealous sectary.

The traditional and to a certain extent mixed character of the majority of these religions is naturally accounted for by reference to the fact that it was the Brahmans who took the leading part in their formation. Except in what concerns the authority of the Veda, upon which their own claim to the primacy depended, the latter were by no means such uncompromising conservatives as some are disposed to represent them. As they formed the intellectual and religious aristocracy of the nation, they must, on the contrary, have felt more keenly than others the unsatisfactory nature of doctrines so antiquated; and so, in fact, we find them at the head of all new movements. Here, besides, they had an obvious interest in not repudiating beliefs which gave them an advantage in contending against the progress of Buddhism, so much more formidable to them otherwise. In any case, and whatever their motives may have been, they threw themselves into the movement with ardour. Almost the whole literature of these religions is more or less their work; and among the founders of the sects, the memory of whom is

[1] Bhagavad Gîtâ, ix. 24, 25; vii. 20–23.

preserved in the pages of history, there are few which have not belonged to their caste. Nor did they merely content themselves with being the theologians of the new cultus systems; they were also their ministers. In spite of the prohibitions of the Smṛitis, many of them became the attendants on the temples and the idols, as well as the priests, the guides, and the contractors in pilgrimages and local devotions. Only it is of importance to remark that the old prohibition has never been revoked, and that even in our day those who exercise these functions form so many inferior classes, whom the Brahmans of high caste, even though they share in their beliefs, despise, and whose right to wear the sacred cord they more or less contest.

We have in this an indication which goes to show that, if the sacerdotal caste played a very considerable part in the development of these religions, the latter have never been either at first or since entirely dependent on it. And this indication is not the only one. The most ancient section of the sectarian literature, which in its existing form is certainly the work of the Brahmans, did not always belong to them. The Mahâbârata and several Purâṇas are put into the mouth of profane bards;[1] and although they are styled the fifth Veda,[2] no exception was ever taken to the translation of them into the vulgar dialects.[3] If we except the *mantras*, or the formulæ strictly so called, in which the sense of the words is everything, the sects have no sacred language. Popular songs, sung in all the dialects of India, have, on the

[1] The Sûtas, the equeries. See what E. Burnouf says, Bhâgavata Pur., vol. i., Pref. p. xxv.

[2] Châdog. Up., vii. 1, 2; Mahâbhârata, iii. 2247.

[3] All these translations are very free, the majority even being reproductions rather than genuine versions. Contrary to what happened at an early date with regard to the Veda, the formalism of the letter has never been carried very far in connection with this literature. It constitutes none the less in all other respects a genuine sacred literature. In Nepâl, for example, it is still the custom, before the courts of justice, to place the Harivaṃça on the head of the witnesses if they are Hindus, the Pancarakshî or the Koran if they are Buddhists or Mussulmans: B. H. Hodgson, Miscellaneous Essays on Indian Subjects, vol. ii. p. 226, ed. 1880.

contrary, been one of their principal instruments in the propagation of their systems; and among the authors of those songs, styled *dâsas*, that is, slaves of the god whom they celebrate, there have been and still are many of low caste. The *Kural* of Tiruvalluvar,[1] that admirable collection of stanzas in the Tamîl language, which is instinct with the purest and most elevated religious emotion, and the authority of which the Brahmans accept without reservation, is the work of a Pareiya.[2] There are legends which represent Vâlmîki, the author of the Râmâyaṇa, as a Koli, that is to say, a member of one of the most despised aboriginal tribes on the Bombay coast. Vyâsa, the greatest name connected with the epic and sectarian poetry, the mythical author of the Mahâbhârata and the Purâṇas, must have been, according to the testimony of these works, himself a Brahman of extremely questionable purity,[3] and similar traditions are in circulation respecting the celebrated Çaṅkara.[4] While we would not attach undue weight to these traditions, we may be allowed to plead the fact of their persistency. If we compare them with the doctrine of a larger fraternity professed in the main by the majority of these religions, as well as with the facts that not even in our time, any more than that of the old Smṛitis, have these cultuses fallen entirely into the hands of the Brahmans, that certain sacerdotal functions, in the South especially, are assigned by preference to men of the people, and that the *Gurus* themselves, the spiritual chiefs, may be members of another caste (in recent times this part has even been assumed by women[5]),

[1] C. Graul, Bibliotheca Tamulica, vol. iii., Der Kural des Tiruvalluver, ein Gnomisches Gedicht über die drei Strebeziele des Menschen, 1856; G. de Du Mast, Maximes des Courals de Tirout-Vallouvar, or the Moral Doctrine of the Parias, 1854.

[2] R. Caldwell, A Comparative Grammar of the Dravidian Languages, Introd., p. 131, 2d ed. Tiruvalluvar signifies the saint (tiru = Sanskrit çrî) Valluvar. The Valluvar are the pûjâris or priests of the Parias.

[3] He was the illegitimate child of a Brahman and a young girl of impure caste of the fisher class, a Dâsakanyâ, a slave-girl, as she is called, Bhâgavata Pur., ix. 22, 20.

[4] Ind. Antiq., vii. 286.

[5] See farther on for Mîrâ Bâî (sixteenth century), Sahaji Bâî (eight-

we shall see at once that we are here on ground obviously different from that of the old Brahmanism, and that a certain unmistakable popular element is a characteristic feature of these religions. An investigation into the character of their theology will conduct us to the same conclusion.

eenth century): more recently still the Kartâbhâjs of Bengal had a female head, Hunter, Statistical Account of Bengal, vol. i. p. 74.

HINDUISM.

I. THE HINDU SECTS—THEIR GREAT DEITIES.

The common characteristic of the sectarian religions, the supremacy they assign to new divinities of popular origin, identified with Rudra-Çiva and with Vishṇu.—Çaivas and Vaishṇavas.—Growing importance of Rudra in the Veda: the Çatarudriya.—Çiva, Devî, and their surroundings.—Advent of Vishṇu to the supremacy coincident with the first appearance of Kṛishṇa.—Vishṇu and Lakshmî.—Theory of the Avatâras.—Myths and cycle of Kṛishṇa.—Myths and cycle of Râma.—Though formed of the same materials as those of the ancient religion, the new divinities are of a more obstinate personality, with a marked tendency to monotheism.—Different combinations of these divinities among themselves, and with elements supplied by ancient theology and speculation: the Trinity, Brahmâ-Vishṇu-Çiva.—Its theoretic and literary character.—The true objects of the sectarian theology, Vishṇu and Çiva, with their feminine counterparts.—A fourth term introduced into the Trinity.—The Trinity reduced to two terms: Harihara.

THE characteristic common to the majority of these religions is the worship of new divinities exalted above all the rest, and the highly concrete and intensely personal conception of which comes out in sundry descriptions of a biographical nature. These divinities are identified either with Çiva, who is himself connected with the Vedic god Rudra, or with Vishṇu; and according as it is the one or other of these which is raised to the supreme rank, the religions are called Çivaite or Vishnuite, and their respective followers styled *Çaivas* or *Vaishṇavas.* The genesis of these religions is involved in extreme obscurity. The Vedic writings chance upon them, and, as it were, go alongside of them, during the very period of their formation; but they treat them more or less as alien, and the details which they have preserved for us are calculated rather to stimulate our curiosity than to satisfy it.

Of the two principal divinities, *Çiva*, "the propitious," although his name hardly occurs in the Vedas, is still the one whose genesis can be most easily traced.[1] Already in the Atharva-Veda we see an increasing importance attached to the part played by Ṛudra, the old deity of the storm, the father of the Maruts, who is fated to be absorbed one day by Çiva. He is invoked as the master of life and death; and we find those aspects of his character which inspire terror and strike dread are exalted in preference to that beneficence of nature which most distinguishes him in the Hymns of the Ṛig. He is more frequently identified with Agni, the Fire, conceived as an element of destruction.[2] By his side appear *Bhava*, "the prosperous," and *Çarva*, "the archer," both of whom are destined to merge in the person of the new god; and *Kâla*, or "time," which produces and devours all things, and which shall also become one of the elements or "forms" of Çiva, is invoked as the first principle of all that exists. In the Yajur-Veda the identification of Rudra with Agni has began to prevail. He receives the names of *Içâna*, *Içvara*, "the Lord," and *Mahâdeva*, "the great god." At the same time, we first meet with the legends that relate his birth, his triumphs over the Asuras, whose Tripura he destroys, the "triple city," viz., of earth, air, and heaven, as well as others which exhibit him breaking into the

[1] Dr. J. Muir has devoted the whole of the fourth volume of his "Sanskrit Texts" (2d ed., 1873) to the history of the two great sectarian deities. We cannot do better than refer the reader once for all to the rich collection of passages which he has collected from the Saṃhitâs of the Ṛig- and the Atharva-Veda, the Brâhmaṇas, the Mahâbhârata, the Râmâyaṇa, and the Purâṇas. The reader will also find collected together here the opinions of the principal scholars who have occupied themselves with this subject, Lassen and A. Weber among the chief.

[2] Agni is one of the names of Çiva, Taitt. Saṃh., i. 4, 36. Compare Taitt. Ar., iii. 21.

midst of the gods and taking violent possession of the offerings made in sacrifice to them. Çiva will fall heir to all this, as well as those accounts which shall form the basis of his biography, and that kinship with the Fire which, in the Mahâbhârata even, is one of his "forms." There will remain traces, moreover, of this relationship in most of such names of his as are also names of Agni; in such names of his feminine counterpart as are names of the flames or "tongues" of Agni; in the obscure epithet *Tryambaka,*[1] "he who has three mothers," where there is perhaps a reminiscence of the triple birth of Agni; in several legends, for instance in that of Skanda, the god of war, who is at once his son and Agni's; and, in fine, in one of his principal symbols, the trident, which is an emblem of the lightning. In another of his attributes, the third eye, which he wears in the middle of his forehead, and from which there bursts forth a flame which is one day to devour the world, we recognise both the eye of the Cyclop and the vestige of an ancient affinity with the sun. Still, however imposing the part assigned to Rudra in these texts, not only does he not attain to sovereignty, he does not even rise above the ordinary level of the gods. In these different data there is nothing beyond the ordinary amount of the syncretism of the Brâhmaṇas; and if they supply certain elements in the character of Çiva, they are far from an adequate explanation of his being. It seems to us, on the contrary, that this explanation is suggested by another text, apparently of modern date, although it is found in all the recensions of the Yajur Veda; we refer to the *Çatarudriya,* the hymn to the hundred Rudras.[2]

[1] Already Ṛig-Veda, vii. 59, 12 (= Ath. Veda, xiv. 1, 17; Vâj. S., iii. 60; Taitt. S., i. 8, 6, 2¹, in a verse added afterwards, and for which there is no pada. The MSS. of the commentary of Sâyaṇa vary in regard to this verse. Some pass it over in silence; those who explain it render *tryambaka* by "producer of the three worlds," or by "father of the three gods, Brahmâ, Vishṇu, and Rudra," or, which is the usual explanation, "by him who has three eyes." The Nirukta, xiv. 35 (pariçishṭa), and the Rigvidhâna render it simply by Rudra, Mahâdêva.

[2] Taitt. S., iv. 5, 1–11; Vâj. S., xvi. 1–66; Kâṭhaka, xvii., 11–16.

In this piece, which is one of those invocations in the form of litanies so frequent in the more recent literature, Rudra appears with all the characteristics of a deity of purely popular origin, in vital relation with all the aspects of the rough and troubled life which has from time immemorial distinguished India. He and his *gaṇas*, the "troops" under his command,[1] are invoked as protectors of the house, the fields, the herds, and the roads. He is the patron of craftsmen, of cartwrights, carpenters, smiths, potters, hunters, and watermen, and is himself a crafty merchant; but he is also the head of the armies, the god of the brave, of foot-soldiers, and of those who fight in chariots, of all those who live by the bow, the sword, and the spear. It is his cry which echoes in the thick of battle, and his voice which resounds in the war-drum.[2] Being a soldier, he is a bandit; for in the East the two are nearly the same. He is the patron of thieves, of freebooters, of brigands, of all those who go forth by night in troops and live on plunder. He is also the god of beggars and fakirs, of those who wear long and matted hair, and of those who shave the head. By himself, or by the numberless spirits at his beck, he is omnipresent, in the houses, and in the fields, in the rivers, and in the fountains, in the wind and the passing cloud, in the grass as it springs up, in the tree as it grows green, in the leaf as it falls. But his dwelling is especially in forests and solitary places, and he reigns over the mountains. We can conceive nothing more lifelike[3] than the figure which stands out from this piece of rude realism, but nothing, at the same time, less Brahmanic. In this interminable

The piece forms also a special Upanishad. It is translated by A. Weber, Ind. Stud., ii. 32, and by J. Muir, Sanskrit Texts, iv. 322.

[1] The gaṇas are themselves called Rudras. Their number is differently estimated; the Bhâgavata Purâṇa, vi. 6, 17, reckons them at tens of millions.

[2] See Atharva-Veda. v. 21. On the coins of the Indo-Scythian kings Çiva is represented with a drum. Lassen, Ind. Altherthumsk., vol. ii. pp. 839, 841, 2d ed.

[3] This remark applies, in general, moreover, to the character of Rudra in the Atharva-Veda and in the Brâhmaṇas. It seems that this god has here more body, so to speak, than the others.

array of epithets, in which we already meet with almost all the designations of Çiva, there does not occur a single expression bearing on ritual, not a single allusion to a sacred custom. This Rudra, who "manifests himself to neatherds and water-carriers," is already pretty much the Çiva whose cultus will by and by be celebrated without Brahmans, and whom his detractors will reproach with being the god of Çûdras and people of no account.[1] Doubtless he does not appear here as a sovereign divinity, but he is as one destined to become such, and we already forecast the reasons which must have determined the Brahmans to choose him from so many others in order to elevate him to this rank. They will have only to adopt him entirely, only, so to speak, to infuse their theology and their metaphysics into this rude figure, yet so real in the popular consciousness, and he will become in reality Mahâdeva, the great god.[2]

This adoption was *un fait accompli* several centuries before our era. In the Mahâbhârata, which, however, in its existing redaction, is conceived in the interest of Vishnuism, the cultus which we find most widely spread is that of Çiva.[3] He is the Dionysos of Megasthenes, who relates that he was worshipped especially upon the mountains, the rival cultus of Hercules or Krishṇa being thenceforth dominant in the plain of the Ganges.[4] He is raised far above the general run of the gods; with his followers he is the greatest of all; with everybody he is one of the greatest, who has none equal or superior to him, except

[1] Muir, Sanskrit Texts, iv. p. 377; Vasishṭha-Smṛiti, quoted by Banerjea, Nârada-Pañcarâtra, Pref., p. 5.

[2] The hypothesis recently revived by Wurm, Geschichte der Indischen Religion, that Çiva is a non-Aryan deity, or, to be more precise, a Dravidian, is inadmissible. All we can say is (and the same thing is true of Vishṇu), that under more than one local Mahâdeva lies concealed an old aboriginal worship, but these substitutions have not at all affected the general conception of the god. For some of his feminine counterparts a foreign derivation is more probable. See *infra*, p. 204.

[3] Lassen, Ind. Alterthumsk., i. 922; Muir, Sanskrit Texts, iv. 283.

[4] Megasthenes, Indica, p. 135, ed. Schwanbeck; Lassen, Ind. Alterthumsk., i. 795, 925. This interpretation of the passage from Megasthenes has been contested by A. Weber, Ind. Stud., ii. 409.

Brahmâ or Vishṇu. He sits enthroned on Kailâsa, the fabulous mountain of the North, beyond Himavat, surrounded and waited on by the *Yakshas*, and a great number of spirits of different forms, who receive their orders from his adopted son, Skanda, the god of war, and the fosterchild of the Pleiades; from *Gaṇeça*, the "chief of the troops," the god with the elephant's head, the inspirer of cunning devices and good counsel, afterwards the patron of letters and of learned men; from *Kubera*, the god of treasures; from *Vîrabhadra*, "the venerable hero," the personification of fury in battle, whose cultus is widespread in the Dekhan, and who is regarded at times as a "form" of Çiva himself. His birth is variously represented, but in reality he is eternal; he is *Mahâkâla*, endless time, which begets and devours all things.[1] As procreator, his symbols are the bull and the phallus, as well as the moon, which serves for his diadem. As destroyer, he is clothed in terrible "forms;" he is armed with the trident, and wears a necklace of skulls. He is identified with *Mṛityu*, "Death;"[2] and his old surname, *Paçupati*, "Lord of herds," acquires the ominous meaning of "Master of human cattle," perhaps that of "Master of victims," for he is, more than any other god, cruel, and exacts a bloody cultus.[3] He is the chief of the *Bhûtas*, of the *Piçâcas*, of mischievous spirits, of ghouls and vampires, that frequent places of execution and those where the dead are buried, and he prowls about with them at nightfall.[4] There is an orgiastic side to his nature: he is *Bhairava*, the god of madly frantic folly, who, clothed in the blood-stained skin of an elephant, leads the wild dance of the tâṇḍava.[5] But

[1] Under this form he had a celebrated sanctuary at Ujjayinî in Mâlava, Meghadûta, 35.

[2] Several of his attendants, such as Bṛiṅgin and Kâla, are represented in the form of skeletons, as, for instance, at Bâḍâmi and Elurâ. Indian Antiq., vi. 359; Cave Temples, p. 433 *seq.*, and plate lxxii.

[3] Atharva-Veda, xi. 2, 9; Açvalâyana Gr. S., iv. 8; Pâraskara Gr. S., iii. 8; Mahâbhârata, in Muir's Sanskrit Texts, iv. 284, 288.

[4] Bhâgavata Pur., iii. 14, 22 *seq.*

[5] See Meghadûta, 37. Câmuṇḍâ, one of the terrible forms of Devî, is depicted also in the 5th act of Mâlatî-Mâdhava.

he is also *par excellence* the god of asceticism and austerities. He is the chief of the Yogins; like them, he goes naked, his body smutty with ashes, his long hair plaited and gathered up in a knot on the crown of his head. The legends are full of his appalling mortifications, and they relate how, with a single glance of his Cyclop eye, he reduced to ashes *Kâma,* Cupid, who had dared to bring trouble into his breast. By his side sits enthroned *Umâ,* "the gracious," the daughter of Himavat, whom we meet with already in some Vedic passages as the wife of Rudra, while *Ambikâ,* "the good mother," who is now identified with her, is found there only as the sister of the god. Like her husband, of whom she is the exact counterpart, she has many names and assumes many "forms." She is worshipped as *Devî,* "the goddess," *Pârvatî,* "the daughter of the mountains," *Durgâ,* "the inaccessible," *Gaurî,* "the bright one," *Satî,* "the devoted wife," *Bhairavî,* "the terror-inspiring," *Kâlî,* "the black one," *Karâlâ,* "the horrible one," and under no end of other designations, which express her twofold nature as goddess of life and goddess of death.

If the Vedic literature supplies certain data from which we are able to frame some idea of the way in which the character of Çiva was formed, and to infer the probable coexistence therewith of his cultus as a popular religion, it has, on the other hand, preserved for us no similar intimations in regard to his rival, the sectarian *Vishṇu.* Vishṇu, the ancient personification of the sun, is, it is true, already in the Hymns a deity of the first rank, and in several passages we find him invested with a species of sovereignty; but that is a distinction which he shares in common with other deities, and which even the later writings appear very rarely to remember. When the sun is invoked as supreme god, it is by other designations in preference, under that of Savitṛi, for instance; in the Atharva-Veda, under that of Rohita, "the red,"[1] while at a later date the

[1] xiii. 1.

adherents of the strictly solar religious systems will worship him under those of Sûrya and Aditya. Neither in the numerous legends collected in the Brâhmaṇas, and which have preserved so many characteristic traits connected with the fate of the gods, do we find that Vishṇu is preparing to undergo transformation or assume a more imposing *rôle*. These legends relate with greater fulness of detail the old myth which represents him as traversing or conquering the three worlds in three strides;[1] they represent him as the personification of sacrifice, and in this regard they speak of his violent death,[2] a feature which accords well with a solar divinity,[3] and which occurs again in the final catastrophe that befalls Kṛishṇa. But they know nothing of the theory of the Avatâras, and in none of these accounts, any more than in the liturgy or the ritual (of course exceptive here of compilations so recent as the last book of the "Taittirîya Araṇyaka"), there is not the least trace of even a first step on the part of Vishṇu to the supreme rank. In the epic poetry, on the contrary, in the Mahâbhârata, Vishṇu is in full possession of this honour. But, at the same time, there comes into view a hero, a man-god, Kṛishṇa, who is declared to be an incarnation of his divine essence; and this figure, which is absolutely unknown to the Veda, is, beyond all doubt, a popular divinity. From this we think we must conclude that there is a connection between the attainment of supremacy by Vishṇu and his identification with Kṛishṇa; and we are led to ask the question whether Kṛishṇa was likened to Vishṇu because the latter had come to occupy the first rank, or whether the supremacy of the Brahmanic god was not rather the result of his fusion with the popular god? Of these two hypotheses, the latter appears to me

[1] For a quite peculiar form of this myth see Çatap. Br., i. 2, 5, 1–7.

[2] T. Muir, Sanskrit Texts, iv. p. 122 *seq.*

[3] Allusion is often made to the death of the sun; see, for example, Taitt. S., i. 5, 9, 4; i. 5, 4, 4. Yama, the first who deceased, is a solar character.

to be the most probable.[1] We have already seen that the Veda does not lead us to anticipate the supremacy of Vishṇu. Neither does it appear to us to be very ancient in the Mahâbhârata, which, in general, is concerned with Vishṇu only in so far as it is with Kṛishṇa. Here the most widely spread cultus is in the main that of Çiva, and even in those episodes of this essentially eclectic poem which have been least remodelled, the supreme figure is

[1] We are here obviously departing from the common opinion which inclines to the notion of a slow indeed, and chronologically determinable development in the deification of Kṛishṇa, and we may say the same for Râma. This view is usually made to rest on the parts of the Mahâbhârata and the Râmâyaṇa, where Kṛishṇa and Râma are *still* represented as simple heroes, where they are not *yet* identified with the supreme being. In our opinion these words "still" and "yet" are made too much of. Not only in their supplementary parts, but in the whole of the existing redaction, the two poems belong to the epoch of the full development of the theory of the Avatâras, and their heroes are at once truly men and truly gods. For the contrary view, see especially Weber, Kṛishṇajanmâshṭamî, p. 316; Die Râma-tâpanîya Upanishad, p. 275; Ueber das Râmâyaṇa, at the beginning. Neither can we attach so much weight as is usually done to the absence of all reference to Kṛishṇa, which Burnouf was the first to point out (Introd. à l'Hist. du Bouddh. Ind., p. 136), in what he conceived to be the most ancient part of the Buddhist writings. That is a mode of arguing which, considering the time it took to fix the Buddhist canon, is very apt to carry us a little too far. On this principle we must also regard the divinity of Kṛishṇa as of later date than the text we have of Manu (not to mention other books of the kind), which yet is acquainted with both the Greek and the Chinese. Kṛishṇa often appears in the developed Sûtras of the North, and has even already undergone in them quite peculiar transformations. In the Lalitavistara he is mentioned once among the number of the greatest deities (pp. 148, 149 of the edition of the Bibl. Ind.); but usually he is the chief of the black demons; and Mâra, the great enemy of Buddha and his mission, is called the ally of Kṛishṇa (ibid., pp. 175, 376, 379, &c.). All these passages, the last of which implies a declared hostility to Krishnaism, are met with in Gâthâs, texts the authority of which recent researches tend to re-establish. After all the affinities pointed out in Senart's work, "La Légende du Buddha," it appears to us, on the other hand, that Buddhism is itself the evidence of the ancient, quite mythical, and divine origin of the legend of Kṛishṇa. The Jainas, as is their wont, have worked up a whole system on that basis. With them Kṛishṇa is the ninth of the black Vâsudevas, who, with the nine white Balas, the nine Vishṇudvish, or enemies of Vishṇu, the twelve Cakravartins, or universal monarchs, and the twenty-four Arhats, form their sixty-three Çalâkapurushas: Hemacandra, Abhidhânacintâmaṇi, ed. Boehtlingk and Rieu, p. 128. There are, as regards Kṛishṇa, however, traces of several different attempts to introduce him into the Brahmanic pantheon, especially those which make him proceed from a hair of Vishṇu, or which identify him and Arjuna with Nara and Nârâyaṇa.

not yet either Çiva or Vishṇu, but Indra, the ancient god of the heavens. It seems, then, that there is but little scope left for the development of a purely Vishnuite religion, the less that the cultus of Kṛishṇa appears to go back to a pretty remote date. "Kṛishṇa, the son of Devakî," is mentioned once at least in a Vedic writing, which represents him purely and simply as the disciple of a sage,[1] and this absolutely Euhemerist representation appears already to be less original than that which we see in the epic. From the date of the second century before our era, the story of Kṛishṇa was the subject of dramatic representations similar to those connected with the festivals in honour of Bacchus and our ancient mysteries.[2] Besides, there is good ground for regarding this personage as the Indian Hercules, the worship of whom Megasthenes found prevailing in the valley of the Ganges at the beginning of the third century before Christ. If these conjectures are well grounded, the two great sectarian divinities must have originated in nearly the same way. According to these, the religion of Vishṇu must be the more recent, but, like that of his rival, it must be the result of the adoption by the Brahmans, and the fusion with one of their old deities, of some popular gods; in the particular case of Kṛishṇa, of a hero who was probably at first the *kuladevatâ*, the ethnic god, of some powerful confederation of Rajpût clans.[3]

Once elevated to the supreme rank, Vishṇu becomes more and more estranged from his ancient solar character, a reminiscence of which survives only in certain symbols, such as the *discus*, the *cakra*, which is his weapon of war, and the bird *Garuḍa*, which serves him as a steed, and remains the object of a cultus.[4] He sits enthroned in Vaikuṇṭha, his paradise, along with his wife *Çrî* or *Lakshmî*, the goddess

[1] Chândogya Up., iii. 17, 6.

[2] Mahâbhâshya, in Ind. Stud., xiii. 353.

[3] Lassen, we believe, was the first to suggest this popular origin of the worship-systems of Çiva and Vishṇu. Ind. Alterthumsk., t. i. 925, t. ii. 441.

[4] For the myth of Garuḍa, an amplification of the old figure of the solar bird, see Mahâbhârata, i. 1239–1545.

of beauty, pleasure, and victory. Retiring gradually to a mysterious distance, he assumes the functions which formerly belonged to Brahmâ; he is identified with Hiraṇyagarbha, especially with Nârâyaṇa, the oldest of all beings, who, carried on the coils of *Çesha* or *Ananta*, the serpent "without end," the symbol of eternity, appeared at the beginning of things floating above the primordial waters. According as he sits awake, or sinks back into mystic slumber, he gives birth to creation or draws it back again into himself; and it is from his navel that the lotus of gold springs, whence issue Brahmâ and the demiurgic gods. But it is not so much by himself that he interposes in the affairs of the world and receives the homage of men, as by means of his incarnations. These are very numerous; for Kṛishṇa, which is probably the most ancient of them, is not the only figure under which he manifests himself in this lower world. "Every time," as he says in the Bhagavad Gîtâ, "that religion is in danger and that iniquity triumphs, I issue forth. For the defence of the good and the suppression of the wicked, for the establishment of justice, I manifest myself from age to age."[1] This is the theory of the *Avatâras*, or the "Descents," which is not only a characteristic of Vishnuism, but which indicates a new and distinctly defined phase in the religious development of India. In fact, by permitting the worship of the deity under a series of hypostases no longer abstract, such as those which the ancient theology had conceived, but such as were highly concrete, highly personal, and, what is better still, human, they resolved in a new manner the old problem, so often attempted, of reconciling aspirations after a certain monotheism with an irresistible tendency to multiply forms of worship. In a way which surpasses the clumsy device of divine genealogies, or the conception of different "forms" of the same god, which still prevails in the Çivaite religions, it responded by its elasticity and its affection for mystery to all the instincts

[1] iv. 7, 8.

of this people, who are at once so sensual, so superstitious, and so speculative, with an equal appetite for subtle theosophy and coarse exhibitions, and who have never been able either to rest satisfied with faith in one god or to reconcile themselves to the worship of many. An Avatâra, in the highest and fullest sense of the word (for all Avatâras have not this meaning), is not a transitory manifestation of the deity, still less the procreation, by the connection of a god with a mortal, of a being in some sense intermediate; it is the presence, at once mystic and real, of the supreme being in a human individual, who is both truly god and truly man, and this intimate union of the two natures is conceived of as surviving the death of the individual in whom it was realised. In short, it is a mystery, to the contemplation of which minds speculatively endowed will be able to devote themselves at their leisure, while the vulgar will be content to find here such cheap gratification to their religious instincts as anthropomorphism, or even zoomorphism, combined with the grossest idolatry, may afford. Of these Avatâras there is one only which is founded on a myth originally proper to Vishṇu, that of the Brahman Nain, who recovered for the gods the three worlds usurped by the Asuras, by persuading their chief to grant him the space traversed by three of his steps, and who, in his three celebrated strides, immediately went bounding away over earth, heaven, and hell. The rest are of diverse origin. Alongside of Vedic legends, but which in the Veda (as elsewhere) are referred to other gods, especially to Prajâpati, those, for instance, of the tortoise, which supports the earth, of the boar, which draws it from under the waters, of the fish, which guides the ark in which Manu escapes the deluge,[1] there are others the development of which belongs more particularly to the epic poetry and the

[1] The Vedic legend of the Deluge according to Çatapatha-Brâhmaṇa, has been published and commented on for the first time by A. Weber, Ind. Stud., i. 161.

sectarian Upanishads, such as the legend of *Nṛisiṃha*, the "Man-lion," a form under which Vishṇu tears in pieces a demon-despiser of the gods, or that of *Paraçurâma*, that is, "Râma with the hatchet," a terrible Brahman of the race of Bhṛigu, who in three-times-seven assaults exterminated the impious race of the Kshattriyas. Thus this theory supplied a convenient framework for connecting with Vishṇu a good part of the ancient fable, and into which even there were introduced at a later period a great number of figures more or less historic. It is thus that a way was opened to Buddha, in whose person the Lord appeared in this lower world to consummate the ruin of the wicked by seducing them with false doctrines.[1] It is thus too that the hope of a national revenge received its expression in *Kalkin*, an avenger who was one day to put an end to the domination of the Mlecchas, the barbarians, and that the majority of the *Gurus*, or founders of sects, were either after or even during their lifetime regarded by the faithful as Avatâras of the Most High. Thus the number of these "Descents" is differently stated;[2] they are reckoned at 10, 12, 22, 24, 28, and soon they are declared to exceed all reckoning.[3] Reduced thus to a system, these successive manifestations of restorers of the law present an unquestionable analogy with the succession of the different Buddhas. They are distinguished into complete incarnations, in which the deity is entirely present, and into partial incarnations (*aṃçavatâras*), in which appears only a part of his being. Çrî usually "descends" at the same time as her husband, and incarnates herself in female form. In fine, from Vishṇu this power passed to other gods, and there are few figures in the pantheon of whom we are not able to affirm some

[1] Agni Pur., xvi. 1–5; Bhâgavata Pur., i. 3, 24; Gîtagovinda, i. 13. In the Vishṇu Pur., iii. ch. xvii. and xviii., it is the Jainas, perhaps, that are referred to. Kapila, the author of the Sâṅkhya system, is an incarnation of Vishṇu as well, in the Bhâgavata Purâṇa, i. 3, 10; iii. 24.

[2] Mahâbhârata, xii. 341, 12941; Bhâgavata Pur., i. 3, 5–26; Agni Pur., i.–xvi.; Gîtagovinda, i. 5–17; the official number is 10.

[3] Bhâgavata Pur., i. 3, 26; Agni Pur., xvi. 12.

such manifestation.[1] From these indications alone, it is already obvious that many of these Avatâras are more connected with the mythology than the religious history. Somé appear to be simply poetic fables, although it is somewhat difficult to make allowance for this distinction at this distance of time.[2] Others are pious legends, in which we recognise at times the echo of some local cultus, and which have contributed to nourish some special devotions, but do not seem to have finally assumed the shape of distinct religions. But it is otherwise with the Avatâras of Kṛishṇa and of Râma, which, with accessory figures, compose two vast cycles, in which Vishnuism found its true divinities.

Considered in his physical derivation, *Kṛishṇa* is a figure of complex quality, in which there mingle at length myths of fire, lightning, and storm, and, in spite of his name (Kṛishṇa signifying the "black one"), of heaven and the sun. By a singular coincidence, which we can only indicate here, but which sheds a curious light on the quasi-fermentation process which appears to have taken place among the religious elements at work in India, several centuries before our era we meet with the majority of these myths again, often accompanied with a striking similarity of detail, in the legendary biography of Buddha.[3] As a character in the epic, on the contrary, and as he is accepted by Vishnuism, Kṛishṇa is a warlike prince, a hero, equally invincible in war and love, very brave, but above all very crafty, and of a singularly doubtful moral character, like all the figures, however, which retain in a marked way the mythic impress. The son of *Vasudeva* and *Devakî*, under which we recognise concealed the ancient pair, the celestial man and the Apsaras,[4] he was born at Mathurâ, on the Yamunâ

[1] See the Mahâbhârata, i. 2638–2796, where all the heroes of the poem are represented as incarnations of gods or demons.

[2] In the Mahâbhârata, for example, and also in Pâṇini (iv. 3, 98), there are indications of an ancient worship of Arjuna quite analogous to that of Kṛishṇa.

[3] These relations are fully illustrated in the learned work of E. Senart, La Légende du Buddha, son Caractère et ses Origines, 1873–1875.

[4] Vasudeva appears to be synonymous with the simple Vasu, which is an old name for the celestial genii, "the bright ones," and Devakî, which signifies at once "the divine

between Delhi and Agra, among the race of the Yâdavas, a name which we meet with again at a later period in history as that of a powerful Râjput tribe. Like those of many solar heroes, his first appearances were beset with perils and obstructions of every kind. On the very night of his birth his parents had to remove him to a distance beyond the reach of his uncle, King Kaṃsa, who sought his life, because he had been warned by a voice from heaven that the eighth son of Devakî would put him to death, and who consequently had his nephews the princes regularly made away with as soon as they saw the light. In the Veda, the sun, in the form of Mârtâṇḍa, is the eighth son born of Aditi, and his mother casts him off, just as Devakî, who is at times represented as an incarnation of Aditi, removes Kṛishṇa. Conveyed to the opposite shore of the Yamunâ, and put under the care of the shepherd *Nanda* and his wife *Yaçodâ*, he was brought up as their son in the woods of Vṛindâvana, with his brother, *Balarâma*, "Râma the strong," who had been saved as he was from massacre. The latter, who has for his mother at one time Devakî herself, at another time another wife of Vasudeva, *Rohiṇî*, "the red" (a mythical name also applied now to Aurora, now to a star), and who is reputed to be an Avatâra of Çesha or Ananta, the serpent without end, which serves as a bed to Vishṇu, appears to be an ancient agricultural deity, that presided over the tillage of the soil and the harvest. He is armed with a ploughshare, whence his surname, *Halabhṛit*, "the plough-bearer," and his distinctive characteristic is an ungovernable passion for bacchanalian revels, inebriation, and sensual love. The two brothers grew up in the midst of the shepherds, slaying monsters and demons bent on their destruction,

one" and "the gambler," recalls the nymph of the waters, the woman-cloud, deceiving and many-formed, *Viçvarûpâ*, who in the Veda is the wife of Vivasvat. A. Weber was the first, we believe, to point out the etymological play which there is in the name Devakî: Kṛishṇajanmâshṭamî, p. 316. See Senart, *op. cit.*, in the Journ. Asiat., 1874, t. iii. p. 374 *seq.*, 421 *seq.*

and sporting with the Gopîs, the female cowherds of Vṛindâvana. These scenes of their birth and infancy, these juvenile exploits, these erotic gambols with the Gopîs, this entire idyll of Vṛindâvana, which recalls the myths of the youth of Indra and Agni, became in course of time the essential portion of the legend of Kṛishṇa, just as the places which were the scene of them remain to the present time the most celebrated centres of his worship. Arrived at adolescence, the two brothers put to death Kaṃsa, their persecutor, and Kṛishṇa became king of the Yâdavas. He continued to clear the land of monsters, waged successful wars against impious kings, and took a determined side in the great struggle of the sons of Pâṇḍu against those of Dhṛitaṛâshṭra, which forms the subject of the Mahâbhârata. In the interval he had transferred the seat of his dominion to the fabulous city of *Dvârakâ*, "the city of gates," the gates of the West, built on the bosom of the Western sea, and the site of which has been since localised in the peninsula of Gujarât. It was there that he was overtaken, himself and his race, by the final catastrophe. After having been present at the death of his brother, and seen the Yâdavas, in fierce struggle, kill one another to the last man, he himself perished, wounded in the heel, like Achilles, by the arrow of a hunter. Notwithstanding the amiable character with which the Muse has delighted to invest Kṛishṇa (and Vishnuism, in contrast with Çivaism, shows a disposition in general to magnify this feature), there is, accordingly, something sad, and even cruel, at the basis of his legend. It is in a smiling mood that he presides over all these acts of destruction, that he sees the end of his people approaching, and that he prepares for it, for it is for this he came; and it was to relieve the earth of the burden of a proud race, become too numerous, that he was incarnated in the womb of Devakî. Though less fierce than Çiva, Vishṇu is nevertheless, on one side of his character, an inexorable god; he, too is that Time which devours everything.

This brief analysis of the legend of Kṛishṇa can give no idea of the astonishing fulness of the myths which have contributed to its formation. There is here, as there is indeed in the epic poetry in general, a prodigious after-crop of fable, which, though preserved in memorials of comparatively modern redaction, is nevertheless for most part very ancient, and the body of which, taken as a whole, shows at any rate how far the ancient Brahmanism is from having transmitted to us completely the mass of old beliefs and traditions peculiar to India. Thus we have been obliged to pass by without mention the numerous figures which form the pantheon peculiar to Krishnaism, and which have almost been identified, on the one hand, with Brahmanical divinities, of which they are conceived to be incarnations, and, on the other hand, with the abstract conceptions of speculation. In this way the whole fable of the Mahâbhârata has been, so to speak, absorbed by Vishnuism, and the cultus of the five sons of Pâṇḍu, which we meet with to-day as far as the extreme South, has become a sort of appendage to the worship of Kṛishṇa. Of his innumerable wives[1] we shall mention only *Rukmiṇî*, the Avatâra pre-eminently of Çrî, and mother of *Pradyumna*, "the shining one," himself the incarnation of *Kâma*, the god of love, whose worship, spread very widely in the Middle Age,[2] was thus connected with Vishnuism, just as those of Skanda, the god of war, and Gaṇeça, the patron of letters, were more specially connected with the Çivaite religions.

The cycle connected with Râma is more limited than the one we have just analysed. It has been preserved for us chiefly in the *Râmâyaṇa*, which is a more homogeneous

[1] 16,000 in round numbers. Agni Pur., xii. 31.

[2] The Bhavishyottara Purâṇa devotes at least three chapters (chaps. 75, 79, 120) to his worship: Aufrecht, Oxford Catalogue, pp. 34, 35. His festival, which was also that of Vasanta, the spring, is one of the favourite themes of dramatic poetry: Çakuntala, act vi.; Mâlatî-Mâdhava, act i.; Ratnâvalî, act i. In the Matsya Purâṇa, where it is also described, Kâma is identified with Krishṇa himself. Aufrecht, Catalogue, p. 39.

work, and more artistically conceived than the Mahâbhârata, and the origin of which is much less ancient. Although classed in the fabulous history of India in an epoch more remote than Kṛishṇa, Râma appears to be a more recent figure, at least as an Avâtara of Vishṇu. His mythical import is much more indistinct, and his special cultus, which is known to us only through sectarian Upanishads and works belonging, beyond a doubt, to modern literature, appears not only to have developed later, but to have been less widely diffused. The Mahâbhârata has devoted a long episode to the legend about him:[1] he is the hero of more than one celebrated poem, but he did not obtain the honour of a Purâṇa[2] to himself; and even in our day, although the devotion to Râma is pretty general, the number of those who worship him in preference to any other god is comparatively small.

Like Kṛishṇa, Râma is a hero, an exterminator of monsters, a victorious warrior. But idealised by the poetry of a more fastidious age, and one less affected by the myth, he is at the same time, what we cannot maintain in regard to the enigmatic figure of the son of Devakî, the finished type of submission to duty, nobility of moral character, and of chivalric generosity. Though the eldest son and heir of Daçaratha, king of Ayodhyâ, *i.e.*, modern Oude, he declines the throne out of respect for an imprudent promise which his father made to his stepmother, and he submits to voluntary exile for fourteen years in the depths of the woods. He is followed thither by one of his brothers, *Lakshmaṇa*, who is, like himself, an incarnation of Vishṇu, and has a share in the cultus paid him, just as Balarâma has in that of Kṛishṇa, and also by his wife *Sîtâ*, the daughter of Janaka, king of Mithilâ, who had been born from a furrow traced round the altar. In this last trait we recognise the Sitâ, the "furrow," already deified in the Hymns, and the goddess of the same name, wife of Indra,

[1] Mahâbhârata, iii. 15872–16602.

[2] The legend respecting him is specially developed in the Padma Purâṇa. Aufrecht, Catalogue, p. 63.

who in the domestic ritual is invoked at the time of tillage and seed-sowing.[1] Perhaps there is here the indication of an original identity of the son of Daçaratha with Râma Halabhṛit, or "the plough-bearer," belonging to the cycle of Kṛishṇa. In a legend of the Black Yajus, Sîtâ, daughter of Savitṛi, is united in love with Soma. Now Soma, the king of the plants and the god of fecundity, was identified from that day with the Moon, and the reminiscence of a connection between the Daçarathide and the Moon appears to have been exactly preserved in the name *Râmacandra*, "Râma-Lunus," by which he is at times distinguished from his namesakes. These are very weak indications; if we ventured to follow them, they would lead, as respects our hero, to an agricultural deity, to a lunar god presiding over the labours of the field and dispensing joy and abundance. This derivation would agree well both with the name Râma, which signifies the Joy-bringer, and with the description which is given of his reign as a sort of golden age.[2] But, with this single exception, nothing else of those peaceful promising beginnings has remained in the part enacted by the son of Daçaratha, whose vicissitudes rather remind us of those that befall the solar deities. Sîtâ, moreover, has retained of her rustic nature only the name, or the legend that refers to her birth. In the Vishnuite religions she is the Avatâra of Çrî, and the ideal type of the wife.—The exiles have taken the road to the great forests of the South. Here Sîtâ is borne away by the king of the demons, *Râvaṇa*, who carries her off beyond the seas to Lañkâ, the island of Ceylon. Râma recovers trace of her ravisher. He forms an alliance with Sugrîva, the king of the monkeys, the inhabitants of those solitudes, and distinguished among whom is *Hanumat*, "with the strong jaws," the son of the Wind, the god-monkey, whose cultus is to this day one of the

[1] Ṛig-Veda, iv. 57, 6, 7; Pârask. Gr. S., ii. 17; Kauçikasûtra, in A. Weber's Zwei Vedische Texte über Omina und Portenta, p. 368.

[2] For these relations see especially A. Weber, Die Râma-tâpanîya Upanishad, p. 275.

most widely spread in India. At the head of a countless host of quadrumanæ the son of Daçaratha invades Laṅkâ, after having constructed across the sea a dyke, the ruins of which are still to be seen in the long chain of reefs which seem to connect Ceylon with the neighbouring continent. Laṅkâ is taken, Râvaṇa slain, and Sîtâ restored to her husband, who returns with her to reign in Ayodhyâ. After long years, during which the world enjoyed an unparalleled felicity, Râma is separated anew from her, but this time by an act of his own will, because he yields to unjust suspicions. This second separation is, according to a proceeding familiar to the myths, at bottom only a repetition of the first. It is terminated by a final reconciliation, after which Sîtâ returns to the bosom of the earth, from which she had come forth long before. Before disappearing she restored to Râma his two sons, that they might continue the line of solar kings in Ayodhyâ.

We shall not proceed farther with this list of materials which have been at the service of the neo-Brahmanic religions. Even a summary examination is enough to show how little these materials differ at bottom from those which we see were made use of in the most ancient documents. Here, as there, we are in the presence of divine personalities, which are resolvable into myths of Nature-worship, and these myths, in their turn, resolve into the same physical phenomena. We have indicated, by way of example, only a small number of these relations; others will come to light, perhaps, of themselves in our exposition; to specify them all would be an endless task. But if India has thus resumed in these religions the work of its remotest past, it has this time arrived at very different results. The divinities of ancient Brahmanism remained undisguisedly mythical. The piety of the Vedas always shrinks from too concrete representations, and behind its gods it never ceased to recognise the natural forces of which they were the expression. Thus under the first efforts of reflection these gods, of themselves as it were, dissolve in pantheism.

The new types, on the contrary, although formed of the same elements, are of a less pliant personality. They were not adopted by the theology of the learned till after they had undergone transformation in the epic, and had taken on distinctly defined features, of which the most mystic devotion will never be able to divest them completely. Even Çiva, who has retained more of the antique, and to whom the amalgam, so to speak, of his different *forms* has imparted something of a vague and monstrous nature, is nevertheless a god with a biography; we know his habits, his favourite seats, and the exact spot where he performed such and such a feat; and in several respects his personality is not much more indistinct than that of the Zeus of Homer. As regards the principal incarnations of Vishṇu, in them the anthropomorphism is perfect; they are figures quite as distinctly defined as Hercules or Theseus. Thus the tendency of these divinities is not, like that of the ancient ones, towards a pantheism more or less physical or abstract—although speculation, in appropriating them, must reduce them to its pantheistic formulæ—but always towards a certain personal monotheism, or, if we prefer to say so, towards an organised polytheism under a supreme god, and which will approach monotheism in different degrees, and at times near enough to be confounded with it.

Of the different combinations to which speculation was thus led, there is one that is connected more closely than the rest with the prior conceptions of Brahmanism: it is that of the Hindu *Trinity*, in which Çiva and Vishṇu are associated with Brahmâ in a way to form along with him the threefold impersonation of the supreme Brahman. This constitutes, in some degree, a solution midway between the ancient orthodoxy in its final form and the new religions; it is at the same time the most considerable attempt which has been made to reconcile these religions to one another. That is to say, in our regard it does not seek to show a first stepping-stone, as it were, towards the sectarian beliefs, the existence of which, on the contrary, it presupposes; it is simply an eclectic explanation of these beliefs made from the point of view of Brahmanism. And, in point of fact, the Trinity, in which Creuzer thought he had discovered the primitive dogma of India,[1] has not, up to the present time, been pointed out in any writing which can be accepted as of date anterior to the development of the sectarian systems of worship.[2] The idea, it is true, of associating the gods in groups of three is very ancient in India. Examples of it occur as early as the Hymns.[3] At a later date, we often find in the Brâhmaṇas the idea expressed, that there are in reality only three gods, Agni, Vâyu, and Sûrya,[4] that is to say, a divinity for the earth, fire; another for the atmosphere, the wind; and a third for the heavens, the sun; and the old scholiast Yâska, who reproduces this division, completes it by a curious distribution of the principal figures in the pantheon into one or other of these three categories.[5] It is probable that the dogma of the sectarian Trinity found a point of support in this ancient triad, as well as in some other old ternary conceptions; but it differs from these too much to be directly derived from them. Here, in fact, the point is not, as formerly, a cosmographic distribution of the deified forces of nature, but a threefold evolution of the divine unity. The Brahman, the Absolute, manifests himself in three

[1] *Symbolik*, t. i. p. 568, 2d ed.

[2] The *Maitry Upanishad*, in which we meet with it distinctly formulated (v. 2), is a work interpolated to such a degree that we must reject it as modern, although we find it engrossed in a Brâhmaṇa. There is still less reason to attach any weight to such testimonies as that of Amṛitavindu Up., 2, or those of Nṛisiṃha Up., collected in Ind. Stud., ix. 57.

[3] Ṛig-Veda, i. 23, 6, 7; 24, 41; vii. 62, 3; viii. 18, 9; x. 124, 4, 126; 158, 1; 185. Compare the *tisro devîḥ*, the three goddesses, i. 13, 9; 194, 8; ii. 35, 5; iii. 4, 8; ix. 5, 8; x. 70, 8; 110, 8. Agni himself composes a triad.

[4] Taitt. Saṃh., vi. 6, 8, 2 = Çatap. Br., iv. 5, 4; Taitt. Ar., i. 21, 1; Bṛihaddevatâ in Ind. Stud., i. 113. For other references to the Çatap. Br., see Weber, Zwei vedische Texte, p. 386.

[5] Nirukta, vii. 5; 8–11. The arrangement of the Hymns in several books of the Ṛig-Veda, and also that of Naighaṇṭuka 5, are made on the same principle. Compare also Ait. Br., i. 1, 1.

persons, Brahmâ, the creator; Vishṇu, the preserver; and Çiva, the destroyer, It is in them that he becomes capable of action, and that he partakes of the three "qualities" of goodness, passion, and darkness, subtle principles that pervade everything, and in which the ancient Sâṅkhya philosophy sums up the energies of Nature. Each of these persons is represented by one of the three letters, *a*, *u*, *m*, the combination of which forms the sacro-sanct syllable *om*, the symbol of the Absolute. As a theological commonplace, the dogma of the Trinity has passed into all the sectarian literatures, but the significance of it as a religious belief has been much exaggerated. In its comparatively orthodox form especially, in which Brahmâ is regarded as the first of three equal persons, it appears never to have been very popular. Yet we find figured representations of this triad which are of pretty high antiquity;[1] and as India is pre-eminently the country where nothing is lost, we see as late as the fifteenth century a king of Vidyânagara in Mysore dedicating a temple to it.[2]

But usually, when the sectarian writers accept the notion of the triad, they interpret it in a manner more conformable to their own respective predilections. One of the persons, either Çiva or Vishṇu, is immediately identified with the supreme being, and the other two, Brahmâ especially, are reduced to act a subordinate part. This subordination is, of course, susceptible of various grades, and it is not unfrequently seen to change in the course of one and the same writing. But, in general, considerable stress is laid on it; sometimes even it is expressed in terms which imply a very marked grudge at the members thus sacrificed, and a real condemnation of their

[1] Among others, at Elephanta and at Elurâ. See this last as given by Burgess in Cave-Temples, pl. lxxv. fig. 2. Fergusson thinks these images belong to the eighth century.. Ibid., p. 467.

[2] Lassen, Ind. Alterthumsk., t. iv. p. 181. See, Ind. Antiq., viii. 22, 23, the analysis of another inscription of the Dekhan (at the commencement of the twelfth century), containing a donation to a sanctuary of the god Traipurusha ("the threefold person") and his wife Sarasvatî.

cultus. Thus the triad is, with most of the sects, only a formula, nearly without any meaning. Brahmâ figures in it only to make up a number; and there is no real change of view involved, either when, renouncing the ternary combination, they sometimes leave him entirely out of account, or when they add a fourth person to the other three, as in the *Brahmavaivarta Purâṇa*, in which Kṛishṇa is superadded to the Brahmâ- Vishṇu- and Çiva-Trinity.[1] In reality, there are present only Vishṇu and Çiva, or, more exactly, if we should probe the sectarian consciousness, only the "incarnations" of the former and the "forms" of the latter, comprehending in both cases the manifestations of their respective feminine counterparts. These are the real elements of the sectarian theology, the two poles, as it were, between which it moves. Usually it pronounces, if not with clearness, then with passionate emphasis enough, between the two rivals; on one side the god, on the other at most his lieutenant, who is almost always the first of his devotees. In the most pronounced forms of the religion of Vishṇu, who is still in the main the more accommodating of the two, Çiva is only the *gurur gurûṇâm*, the doctor of the doctors, a sort of superhuman prophet of Bhagavat, of Vishṇu the Most High.[2] The god who is found reduced in this way to the character of satellite does not therefore cease to be glorified, but his majesty is borrowed, and it is understood that the homage which is paid to him goes in the end to him who is above him. Viewed thus, in the extreme expressions of them, the neo-Brahmanic religions form two groups clearly opposed and even inimical to one another; but in practice this opposition is almost always softened down by compromises. The jealous ardour with which the militant

[1] H. H. Wilson, Select Works, vol. iii. p. 99. In the Nṛisiṃha Upanishad, in like manner, all the three persons of the Trinity are subordinated to Nṛisiṃha. All the sects at bottom do the same; their fourth term (the turîya) is still a person, and they no sooner assert the Absolute than they limit it by the most concrete forms.

[2] This is the character he maintains, for instance, in the Nârada Pañcarâtra, i. 9, 31, 38-42, 46, &c.

portion of the sects ordinarily maintain the exclusive title of their god to supremacy and adoration, and which has been expressed more than once in violent conflicts,[1] is seldom shared in by the mass of the people. As a general rule, a Hindu pays homage to a favourite deity, most frequently one of the forms of Vishṇu, Çiva, or Devî, in the *mantra*, or mystic formula of invocation (which he must keep secret), of which he has been initiated by a *guru*, a divinity to whom he applies in his extreme need, whom he will invoke at the moment of death, and in whom he hopes for his salvation. But with this leading devotion he is always ready to connect an indefinite number of others, no matter of what origin. It may be that this devotion of his choice has come of itself to be superinduced in his case on some local superstition, or the hereditary cultus of a *kuladevatâ*, a family god belonging perhaps to a quite different religious cycle; and if he has any tincture of philosophy at all, he will find the means besides of combining with all this a considerable dash of abstract unitarian mysticism. It is thus that among the Câlukyas, who have ruled in the Dekhan from the fifth to the twelfth century, and who had Vishṇu for kuladevatâ, some at least professed Çivaism,[2] and that the majority of the others show in their inscriptions a great zeal for the cultus of Skanda and his mothers, who belong to the Çivaite pantheon. This eclecticism, which is in some respect peculiar to the individual, very slightly dogmatic, and in no case conventional, like that which appears in the literature, was singularly fostered besides by the speculative mysticism, the vague notions of which had percolated slowly through all the layers of society. An adept in the Vedânta or the Yoga was not obliged to subordinate

[1] See the outrage perpetrated in 1873 by three Çivaite devotees on the Vishṇu of Pandharpur, Ind. Antiq., ii. 272; iv. 22. In 1640, at Hurdwar, a celebrated resort for pilgrims on the Upper Ganges, Çivaite and Vishnuite Sannyâsins, fought a bloody battle. Dâbistân, ii. 19, translated by Shea and Troyer.

[2] See Vikramânkacarita, iv. 58, ed. Bühler.

Vishṇu to Çiva or Çiva to Vishṇu; he could, if he chose, see the only Being in both. "One god, Çiva or Vishṇu!" exclaims Bhartṛihari, who was a Çivaite, in one of his stanzas.[1] Another Çivaite, Abhinavagupta, has commented on the Bhagavad Gîtâ,[2] which is in a way the gospel of Kṛishṇa. Çaṅkara, who appears to have inclined rather to Vishnuism, is claimed alike by the Çaivas and Vaishṇavas; and even in our day the Smârta Brahmans ("orthodox observers of the Smṛiti") in the Dekhaṅ, who are reputed to be his direct heirs, take part in the sectarian devotions without formally declaring themselves in favour of any. In Hindustan it is the same with the majority of the members of the upper and educated classes. Thus there have been sects who, instead of choosing between the two great divinities, have associated them together in a common cultus. Alongside of the god who is three and one there is thus the god who is two and one, Harihara (Harihara, that is, Vishṇu-Çiva—though the pure Çivaites interpret this name as "Çiva (the master) of Vishṇu"), and he, from a simple mystic formula, which was all he was at first, has come in the end to be a perfectly concrete figure with a mythology of his own. As the object of a special and well-defined cultus, he appears to be of somewhat recent date. It is only since the tenth century that the invocation *ex æquo* of Çiva and of Vishṇu is found attested with a certain emphasis in the inscriptions.[3] Harihara himself does not appear in them before the end of the thirteenth. We would feel bound to name a much earlier date, however, if we could be sure, on the one hand, that the hymn in his honour which is contained in the *Harivaṃça*[4] formed part of the original redaction of this poem (there already existed one of that name in the sixth

[1] iii. 30, ed. Bohlen. Çiva is a "form" of Vishṇu (or the reverse) in several Purâṇas; for example, in the Vṛihannâradîya P., in Aufrecht's Oxford Catalogue, p. 10.

[2] G. Bühler in the Journ. of the Roy. As. Soc., Bombay, vol. xii., extra number, p. 76.

[3] See the inscriptions in the Ind. Antiq., vi. 51; v. 342; Journ. of the Roy. As. Soc., Bombay, xi. 267, 276; xii. 25.

[4] Ch. clxxxi.

century),[1] and if we could be sure, on the other hand, that the sculptures in the great hypogeum at Bâḍâmi, in which this god is one of the figures,[2] were contemporary with the institution of this sanctuary, which is of the sixth century as well. However this may be, his cultus is found to be wide spread in the Dekhan from the date of the fourteenth century, particularly in Mysore; and Harihara is at the present time one of the most popular deities of the Tamîl country.[3]

[1] A Harivamça is mentioned, Vâsavadattâ, p. 93, ed. F. E. Hall.

[2] Ind. Antiq., vi. 358. The author of the article, J. Burgess, the discoverer of these caves, appears to have no doubt on this point. Compare his "Cave-Temples," p. 406.

[3] See F. Foulkes, The Legends of the Shrine of Harihara, Madras, 1876. Not to interrupt our exposition of the religions of Çiva and Vishṇu, which constitute the true substance of Hinduism, we refer our readers to the details given pp. 252 *seq.*, respecting the other deities of the sectarian Pantheon, which are usually subordinate, but some of which, such as Gaṇeça, have had their peculiar sects, and one of which, the sun namely, has at times attained the rank of a supreme divinity.

HINDUISM.

II. THE SECTS, THEIR HISTORY AND DOCTRINES.

Obscurity of the ancient and most interesting portion of this history.—Absence of a chronology, and want of accurate information, notwithstanding the array of documents.—The Mahâbhârata, the Râmâyaṇa, the Purâṇas.—The positive history of the sects does not commence till the eleventh or twelfth century, by which time they are capable only of reassertion.—Ancient Vishnuism : idealism of the Bhâgavad Gîtâ, and its influence on the entire ulterior development.—Moderate idealism of the Pâñcarâtras or Bhâgavatas.—The schools and sects of Çaṅkara, Râmânuja, and Anandatîrtha.—Ancient Çivaism, its preference for the Sâṅkhya metaphysics.—Pâçupatas and Mâheçvaras.—The doctrine of grace among the Çaivas.—The Çakti, or the female principle : the Çaktas and their twofold rite of the right hand and the left hand : human sacrifices, magical and obscene rites.—Idealistic Çivaism : Tridaṇḍins and Smârtas.—The Kashmir school of the Pratyabhijñâ.—Great Çivaite religions of the Dekhan : Basava and the Lingâyits.—The Sittars and the alchemists : Arab influences.—The Çivaite sects of the North : the different orders of Yogins.—Extravagance of asceticism and moral degeneracy.—Apparent decrease of Çivaism.—Doctrine of salvation and the means of it : Jñâna or gnosis : above it Bhakti or faith.—Is this Bhakti such as it at first appears in Vishnuism, something borrowed from Christianity ?—Jesus and Kṛishṇa, alleged reciprocal influence of the two religions small in reality.—Results of the doctrine of Bhakti ; splitting up of sects and idolatry.—Refinements of Quietism and Mysticism.—The doctrine of grace among the Vaishṇavas.—In consequence of his very elation Bhakti leads back to formalism.—Bestowed on the Guru, who is deified, and at length the only authority of the sect, it becomes a new cause of schism.—Vishnuism becomes an erotic religion : sects of Caitanya, Vallabhâcârya, and others.—Mystic and pietistic communities.

FROM what precedes it is easy to see that the different ways of connecting or combining the persons of the gods, which occupy so great a space in the literature, and one of which, at least, the Trinity, has had a certain celebrity among ourselves, constitute in reality only a subordinate point in the theology of the sects, and the decision of which they have left more or less to individual predilection. Their proper work lies elsewhere, in the doctrinal conception which each has formed to itself of its principal god, and in the practical consequences which they have severally deduced from it. These form the real data for their history, and consequently for that of the religions of India, for more than two thousand years. Unhappily an entire half (and that the most interesting part) of this history is enveloped in deep obscurity. On some points there is abundance of detail, but there is absolutely no chronology. On other points the facts themselves are wanting. The great epic poem of the *Mahâbhârata,* which is in the main the most ancient source of our knowledge of these religions, is not even roughly dated; it has been of slow growth, extending through ages, and is, besides, of an essentially encyclopedic character.[1] The *Ramâyaṇa,* which is pre-eminently a work of art, in which an elevated religious and moral spirit is allied with much poetic fiction, leaves us in equal uncertainty.[2] The same is true of the eighteen principal *Purâṇas,* not one of which is dated, which almost all quote from one another, and the period of the redaction of which embraces perhaps a dozen centuries.[3] Neither have we

[1] For the Mâhâbhârata and its different redactions, see especially Lassen, Ind. Alterthumsk., i. 1004; ii. 494, 2d ed. The editions most common are that of Calcutta, 4 vols. 4to, 1834-39, and that of Bombay, folio, 1863. A would-be French translation by H. Fauche, which embraces the eight first cantos, appeared in 10 vols., 1863–70.

[2] See A. Weber, Ueber das Râmâyaṇa, 1870 (Memoirs of the Academy of Berlin). The Râmâyaṇa has been edited and translated into Italian by G. Gorresio, 11 vols., 1843–67. A French translation by H. Fauche has appeared in 9 vols., 1854–58. The edition of Schlegel, with Latin translation, 1829-30, has not been finished. There are several native editions of the Râmâyaṇa; among others, that of Calcutta, 1859, and that of Bombay, 1859.

[3] For the Purâṇas in general see H. H. Wilson, Analysis of the Purâṇas, in Journ. of the Roy. As. Soc., vol. v. (1838), reproduced in his Select Works, vol. iii.; it comprises only six of these works: Brâhma, Padma, Agni, Brahmavaivartta, Vishṇu, and Vâyu. By the same author, Preface to the translation of the Vishṇu Purâṇa (1840), as well as the numerous comparative notes attached to the translation. These notes have been completed by F. E. Hall in the new edition (1864–77). A. Weber, Verzeichniss der Sanskrit-

succeeded in fixing the age of the sectarian *Upanishads*, some of which are of all the more value that they are not eclectic, like the majority of the preceding writings; nor can we determine that of the *Bhakti Sûtras* and of the *Nârada Pañcarâtra*,[1] both so important with respect to the development of Vishnuism and the doctrine of faith. An obscurity greater still rests on the *Sûtras*, the *Agamas*, and the *Tantras*, which contain the dogmas and the ritual of the Çaivas, especially all that has respect to the cultus of the Çaktis, the female divinities. Of all this voluminous and complex literature, the dated works of which do not go farther back than the eighth century, we know up to the present time only some titles and some extracts,[2] to which we must add the *résumé* of the Çivaite metaphysics—a theoretic one, and in no respect historical—which Sâyaṇa in the fourteenth century inserted in his "General Synopsis of the Systems."[3] We may be permitted

Handschriften der K. Bibliothek zu Berlin, 1853, pp. 127–148. Especially Th. Aufrecht, Catalogus Codicum MSS. Sanscriticorum quotquot in Bibliotheca Bodleiana adservantur, 1859, pp. 7–87. The work of Vans Kennedy, Researches into the Nature and Affinities of Ancient Hindu Mythology, 1831, rests principally on the Purâṇas.

The two Purâṇas most celebrated, the Vishṇu P. and the Bhâgavata P., are well known, the one by the translation of H. H. Wilson, 1840 (2d. ed. 1864-77), the other by the edition and the translation of E. Burnouf, comprising only books i.–ix. (M. Hauvette-Besnault is at present engaged in the publication of the three last), 3 vols. 1840–47. Of both there exist several native editions. The collection of the Bibliotheca Indica comprehends the Mârkaṇḍêya P., published by K. M. Banerjea, 1862; the Agni P., by Râjendralâla Mitra, 1873–79, 3 vols.; and the Vâyu P., commenced by the same editor. There are besides native editions of the Mastya P., the Linga P., the Brahmavaivartta P., the Kûrma P., &c., and fragments (principally Mâhâtmyas) of several others. Besides the eighteen principal Purâṇas, there are reckoned eighteen Upapurâṇas, or secondary Purâṇas, the enumeration of which is given in Wilson's preface to the translation of the Vishṇu-P., p. lxxxvii., new edition. The official lists of the Purâṇas and Upapurâṇas are far from including all the works which lay claim to these titles, and it is for the present next to impossible to get up a critical bibliography of this literature.

[1] Published in the Bibliotheca Indica, the first by R. Ballantyne, 1861; the second by K. M. Banerjea, 1865. The Bhakti Sûtras are later than the Bhagavad Gîtâ, which they quote, Sûtra 83.

[2] The most minute information we have in regard to the Tantras will be found in Aufrecht's Oxford Catalogue, pp. 88–110.

[3] The Sarvadarçanasaṅgraha, published several times in India, among others in the Bibliotheca Indica.

to question whether we shall ever succeed in establishing for this first period of the sectarian religions a chronological chain with the least pretension to accuracy; for the difficulty seems inherent in the very nature of the documents, which are for the most part impersonal works, in which the apocryphal and the fraudulent at times flourish to an unconscionable extent. In these circumstances, the data, so valuable otherwise, which are supplied by foreign sources, such as Greek, Chinese, and Arabic,[1] by certain secular writings fairly dated, and especially by inscriptions, might themselves lead to illusions, unless used with precaution. Nothing warrants us, for instance, in referring to the *Pâñcarâtras*, mentioned in the seventh century by Bâṇa and Kumârila, the doctrines expounded in our Pañcarâtra, or in identifying the Bhâgavatas which figure in the inscriptions from the end of the second century, on the one hand with those of the Mahâbhârata, and on the other hand with those against whom Çaṅkara argues. Even from the writings of this last master we gain nothing to speak of towards the history of the sects, because he confines himself in his discussions to the investigation of certain metaphysical points, of which it is next to impossible to recover either the historical filiation or the religious form. There is a work, it is true, on which reliance has sometimes been placed, and which, in fact, if we might make use of it, would yield us more than mere hints in reference to the epoch of this celebrated man, and something like a statistic account of the sectarian opinions then prevalent. We refer to the *Çaṅkaravijaya*, "The Triumphs of Çaṅkara," in which Anandagiri, the disciple of Çaṅkara, is presumed to relate at length the polemics maintained by the master against

[1] See Renaud, Fragments Arabes et Persans relatifs à l'Inde antèrieurement au xi. siècle, 1845, and Mémoire Geographique, Historique et Scientifique sur l'Inde antèrieurement au xi. siècle d'après les Ecrivains Arabes, Persans et Chinois, 1849; Lassen, Geschichte des Chinesischen und Arabischen Wissens von Indien, at the end of vol. iv. of the Indische Alterthumskunde; E. Rehatsek, Early Moslem Accounts of the Hindu Religions, in the Journ. of the Roy. As. Soc., Bombay, xiv.

forty-eight different sects. But since the work has been published,[1] it is enough to compare it with the authentic polemic of Çaṅkara, especially with his commentary on the second book of the Vedânta Sûtras, to feel satisfied that that is only an apocryphal romance of no worth in regard to the eighth century. Some other compositions on the same subject, the existence of which has been pointed out, are quite as untrustworthy.[2] Till we receive farther light on the subject, we must therefore rest content with this, that during a space of a thousand years and more, there is, for the sectarian religions, only a sort of internal chronology of extreme vagueness, and more or less matter of conjecture. Their positive history hardly commences till we come upon the heads of the schools of the twelfth century (for the Çivaism of Kashmir a little earlier, viz., the ninth),[3] that is to say, till an epoch when each creed had, as regards its essential principles, already more than once spoken its final word.

In fact, these very sects, which have lived such an intense and varied life, and which have up to our own time shown such capacity to modify and continually readjust their organisation, their practices, and their spirit, were early obliged to repeat and reassert the same theological principles, as these had been furnished to them by the ancient speculations of Brahmanism. They appropriated these abstract formulæ to themselves, at one time applying them as they were, at another modifying them in such a way as to make them quadrate more with religious sentiments cast in a different mould from those which had inspired the authors of the old Upanishads and the redactors of the Darçanas; for obviously neither the impersonal Brahman and the single substance of the Vedânta,

[1] In the Bibliotheca Indica by Jayanârâyaṇa Tarkapañcânana, 1868.

[2] See F. E. Hall, A Contribution towards an Index to the Bibliography of the Indian Philosophical Systems, 1859, pp. 167, 168.

[3] Thanks especially to the reports brought lately from Kashmir by G. Bühler, and recorded by him in vol. xii., extra number, of the Roy. As. Soc., Bombay.

nor Nature, fertile but blind, the first cause of the Sâṅkhya, corresponded with the new objects of devotion. The Vedânta had to recognise more or less explicitly a god distinct from the world; and with this view it was necessary it should either deny the reality of the world by developing to the utmost the theory of illusion, of *Mâyâ*, or renounce its fundamental dogma of *Advaita*, or nonduality, of ἓν καὶ πᾶν. As for the Sâṅkhya, it had to transmute itself into a deistic system. These solutions, of which we have already made mention several times, but the true origin of which, it appears, must be sought here in the sectarian religions, have received a twofold expression: the one technical, in writings which for the most part are still known only at secondhand, and in which, as in almost all the productions of Hindu scholasticism, the precision of the formulæ is often in direct ratio to the vagueness of the doctrines; the other literary and poetic, in works in which there prevail usually endless confusion and dogmatic incoherency, but also in which mysticism asserts itself at times with a sublimity of sentiment of no ordinary kind.

Nowhere does this last character appear to better advantage than in the celebrated work which contains probably the oldest dogmatic exposition we possess, not only of Vishnuism, but of a sectarian religion in general, the *Bhagavad Gîtâ*, "The Song of the Most High." In this poem, which is interpolated as an episode in the Mahâbhârata,[1] Kṛishṇa, who is identical with the supreme being, himself reveals the mystery of his transcendent nature. The doctrine, as is generally the case with Vishnuism, is essentially unitarian, that is to say, Vedantic, although extensive use is made in it of the nomenclature and conceptions of the Sâṅkhya. Kṛishṇa is the absolute being in human form, immutable and alone; the world

[1] Mahâbhârata, vi. 830–1532. Since the time of the translation of it by Ch. Wilkins in 1785, this book has been frequently published, and there are translations of it now into all the languages of Europe.

and himself in his mortal form are the production of his Mâyâ, his deceptive magic; he alone is real, and those who are conscious of being one with him have peace and safety. The same doctrine, but not so pure and less elevated in point of conception as well as in point of form, reappears in several Krishnaite Upanishads. It is found applied to the religion of Nṛisiṃha, of Vishṇu conceived as man-lion—a sect of which there is not much mention elsewhere—in the *Nṛisiṃhatâpanîya-Upanishad*, and to the religion of Vishṇu-Râma in the *Râmatâpanîya-Upanishad*. If Çaṅkara, the great champion of the orthodox Advaita, professed a sectarian doctrine, it was that. It is from it in the main that the *Kural* of Tiruvalluvar draws its inspiration, as do also the songs of his sister Auvaiyâr, those gems of ancient Tamîl literature. We shall meet with it again in Çivaism. It plays an important part in the Vishnuite Purâṇas, especially in the *Bhâgavata Purâṇa* which has consecrated to its service a power of composition of such range and fulness as at times to remind us of the inspired language of the Bhagavad Gîtâ. Finally, the great influence exercised by these two works has rendered it familiar to all the modern sects, at least in Hindustan, and in the north of the Dekhan. It has infused itself deeply into the popular poetry, and we meet with its formulæ in Bengal in the *Kîrtans* of the followers of Caitanya, as well as among the Marhattas in the songs of Tukarâma, or in the Punjâb in the *Adigranth* of the Sikhs.

But it is clear, too, that such a tenet must not be too closely pressed, when the subject in debate is the faith of the great mass of the people. Even speculative people, with their accustomed power of thought, find it difficult to lay hold of it, and are often baffled with the language, even in treatises which affect scholastic rigour of statement. Much more is this the case in the mystic effusions of a poetry which is not hampered by the fear of contradicting itself, and which aims less at convincing the mind than at overpowering it, by affecting it with a sort of vertigo. Thus it is often difficult to distinguish this doctrine from another of equally ancient tradition, but the systematic exposition of which we find only in more recent documents. We refer to the doctrine of the Pâñcarâtras, or, as they are at times called more generally, the Bhâgavatas.[1] These, it is said, regarded the world and the souls of individuals, the *jîvas*, as emanations from the Supreme Being, destined to be absorbed anew in him, but constituting, during the intermediate term, beings at once real and distinct from God. Çaṅkara, to whom we owe the first intimation we have of this doctrine, says that it was conceived in contradiction to the Veda by Çâṇḍilya;[2] and, in fact, there is very clearly an allusion to it in the *Bhaktisûtras*,[3] which have reached us under the name of Çâṇḍilya. All through the Vishnuite literature there occur passages, and very numerous they are, which are in perfect keeping with it; but none of the ancient books (we cannot consider the *Nârada Pañcarâtra*[4] such) in which it was specially expounded have come down to us. In a historical point of view we know little of it. The Mahâbhârata presupposes a close connection between the Pâñcarâtras and the Bhâgavatas,[5] whose perfect faith in one only god it extols, a faith which must have been imported to them from abroad, from Çvetadvîpa, "The White Island," a sort of Atlantis situated in the extreme north, beyond the Sea of Milk.[6] More recently, in the

[1] They are treated of in the 4th section of the Sarvadarçanasaṅgraha. Colebrooke has devoted a chapter to them in his Memoirs on the Philosophy of the Hindus, Miscellaneous Essays, vol. i. p. 437, ed. Cowell.

[2] Çaṅkara ad Vêdânta Sûtra, ii. 2, 42–45, p. 600, ed. of the Biblioth. Indica.

[3] Bhakti Sûtras, 31, ed. of Biblioth. Indica.

[4] Were it only from the way in which the name *Vaishṇava* is employed in it.

[5] Bhâgavata signifies worshipper of Bhagavat, the Most High. As for Pâñcarâtra, which the books of the sect explain metaphorically by "possessor of the Pañcarâtra, of the fourfold knowledge," the origin of it is involved in obscurity. Pañcarâtra signifies the space of five nights, and there are Vedic ceremonies of this name; on the other hand, the Nârada Pañcarâtra is divided into five books, entitled râtras or nights.

[6] Mahâbhârata, xii. 12702 *seq.*

seventh century, the poet Bâṇa speaks of them as of two distinct sects.[1] In the inscriptions the Bhâgavatas are frequently mentioned, in the provinces of the Ganges from the second century, on the Coromandel coast in the fourth, and in Gujarât in the fifth and sixth.[2] But it is by no means certain that in these different texts the same words always denote the same things; it is even probable that in the moumental inscriptions the term Bhâgavata simply means worshipper of Vishṇu.[3]

In the twelfth century this qualified idealism was successfully revived by Râmânuja, a Brahman, and a native of the neighbourhood of Madras,[4] who gave a systematic exposition of it in his commentary on the Vedânta Sûtras.[5] He argued against the absolute Advaita of Çañkara, maintained the separate but finite reality of individual beings, and rejected the theory of the Mâyâ. His followers, called Râmânujas, after his name, worship Râma as the representative of the Supreme Being; they are divided into several branches, and are very numerous, particularly in the South. In the fourteenth century Râmânanda, one of the chiefs of the sect, went to settle at Oude and at Benares. From him the numerous subdivisions of Râmânandis are lineally descended, who differ from the Râmânujas only in their practices, are very widely scattered, and have great influence in Northern India. The celebrated

[1] In his Harshacarita as quoted by Hall, Vâsavadattâ, pref., p. 53. The Çankaravijaya distinguishes them similarly, ch. vi. and viii., ed. of the Biblioth. Indica. In the Varâha Purâṇa, on the other hand, the Pañcarâtra is identified with the doctrine of the Bhâgavatas. Aufrecht, Oxford Catalogue, p. 58.

[2] Inscriptions of the Guptas at Behâr and at Bhitari, in A. Cunningham's Archæological Survey, vol. i. pl. xvii. and xxx. Inscriptions of the Pallavas of Vengi in Ind. Antiq., v. 51, 176. Inscriptions of Valabhî, *passim*.

[3] This is the sense which it has, for example, in Varâha Mihira, Bṛihat Saṃhita, lx. 19, p. 328, ed. Kern.

[4] For the historical sects, we refer the reader once for all to H. H. Wilson's Sketch of the Religious Sects of the Hindus, published in the Asiatic Researches, vols. xvi. and xvii., 1828–32, and reproduced in the first volume of the Select Works of this celebrated Indian scholar.

[5] A short exposition of the Vedânta, by the same author, has been recently published in Calcutta, The Vedântatattvasâra of Râmânuja, 1878.

poet Tulasîdâsa, the author of the Hindî Râmâyaṇa, in the sixteenth century, was one of them. Râmânanda exercised indirectly a great influence over the majority of the modern Vishnuite sects of Hindustan and Bengal, those of Caitanya, Kabîr, Nânak, and a host of others of minor importance. Râmânuja had broken with the prejudices of caste, but he had kept to the Sanskrit as the sacred language, and he attached a great weight to the practices of religion and the prescriptions of legal purity. Râmânanda departed still more from orthodox usage; he adopted the vulgar dialects of the country, and taught the vanity of merely external observances. Among his principal disciples there figure basketmakers, weavers, barbers, water-carriers, and curriers.

At nearly the same period as Râmânuja, another man of the South, Anandatîrtha, born at Kalyâṇa, on the Malabar coast, pushed still farther than he did the reaction against the idealism of the school of Çaṅkara. He taught that matter, the souls of individuals and God, that is to say Kṛishṇa-Vishṇu, are so many irreducible and eternally distinct essences. This was to make a step nearer the fundamental principle of the Sâṅkhya deism (and yet Anandatîrtha was a Vedântin, and commented on the Brahma Sûtras!), that is to say, to a system which had not in the main the predilections of Vishnuism. But even within the circle of the Vaishṇava theology that was not a novel doctrine. In fact, if the dualistic conception is not a dominant one in any of the important Vishnuite works which have reached us, they are nevertheless all, from the Bhagavad-Gîtâ onwards, so profoundly penetrated with ideas that depend on it, that, in spite of the close affinity of the theory of the Avâtaras with Vedantic ideas, we cannot doubt that there existed early a Vishnuism with a Sâṅkhya metaphysics. The followers of Anandatîrtha belong almost exclusively to the extreme South, where they are very numerous. The members of the congregation strictly speaking, the Mâdhvas, so called from a surname of their master, are all Brahmans, for, in opposition to Râmânuja, Anandatîrtha was a strict observer of the distinctions of caste; but the doctrine called the doctrine of the Dvaita or duality is widely spread among the masses, and the popular songs of the Dâsas, many of whom are of low caste, extol it with a sectarian fervour bordering on fanaticism.[1]

That we may not be obliged to return again and again to the same topics farther on, we shall here leave for a little the subject of Vishnuism, and finish off at once with what we have to say concerning the sectarian metaphysic by a *résumé* of the speculative doctrines of Çivaism. The Çivaite religions appear to be more ancient than those of Vishṇu, or at least to have been adopted at an earlier date by the Brahmans. We have already seen that they are the only ones which have left any trace in the Veda, and that, for its part, the epic poetry, which in its existing redaction is Vishnuite in the main, equally presupposes that the cultus of Mahâdeva had to some extent previously prevailed. The first Hindu representations of a character unmistakably religious which we find on coins (of the Indo-Scythian kings, about the beginning of the Christian era)[2] are Çivaite figures alternating with Buddhist symbols. Çivaism, in short, seems to have remained long a sort of professional religion of the Brahmans and men of letters.[3] The most ancient dramatic literature that has reached us is under Çivaite patronage.[4] It is the same with the works of romance.[5] It is likewise to

[1] See F. Kittel, On the Karṇâṭaka Vaishṇava Dâsas, in the Ind. Antiq., ii. 307.

[2] See R. Rochette, Notice sur quelques Médailles de Rois de la Bactriane et de l'Inde, in Journ. des Savants, 1834, fig. 7, p. 389. By the same author, Supplement to the preceding Notice, ibid., 1835, pl. ii. figs. 22, 23, 24. Lassen, Ind. Alterthumsk., t. ii. p. 808 *seq.*, 2d ed.

[3] Even still the proportion of Brahmans among the Çivaites is very great; almost all those in Bengal and Orissa, for instance, belong to the Brahmanical caste.

[4] The dramas of Kâlidâsa, the Mṛicchakaṭikâ, the Mâlatî-Mâdhava of Bhavabhûti. See also Malavikâgnimitra, str. 6.

[5] The ancient Bṛihatkathâ, the original source, now lost, of the most of the collections of tales, began with a dialogue between Çiva and Pârvatî.

Çiva that legend ascribes the origin of grammar,[1] and Gaṇêça, whom we meet with early as the god of arts and letters, is a figure of the Çivaite pantheon. And yet of Çivaism we possess no ancient doctrinal exposition which for beauty of form can be compared, for instance, with the Bhagavad Gîtâ. It early lost its hold over religious epic poetry. Among the Purâṇas, those which properly belong to it are the most spiritless of the collection; they are compilations in which legendary narrative is the leading element, or they interest themselves by preference in rites and observances, and then, like the Tantras, which they much resemble, affect a very special, almost an esoteric character. It appears to have inspired no work of any brilliancy, such as the Bhâgavata Purâṇa, and, with the exception of certain hymns, mostly modern, and some pieces which have really become popular, such as the *Devîmâhhâtmya*,[2] it seems, in its literature anyhow, to have been capable of nothing between the productions of a refined fantastic art and the technical treatise. Of writings of this last kind we as yet know only a small number, of by no means ancient date, through translations from the Tamîl originals.[3] Hence for our knowledge of most

[1] Pâṇini received from Çiva the revelation of his grammar. Kathâsaritsâgara, i. 4 See the same legend, according to the Bṛihatkathâ of Kshemendra, in the Ind. Antiq., i. 304 (Bühler). The fourteen first Sûtras of Pâṇini, which supply the basis of part of its terminology, are quite specially regarded as revealed, and are for that reason called *Çivasûtras.* Another tradition, which ascribes the oldest grammar to Indra, is traceable to myths of the Veda. Taitt. Saṃh., vi. 4, 7, 3; i. 6, 10, 6.

[2] It forms the lxxxi.–xciii. chaps. of the Mârkaṇḍêya Purâṇa, pp. 424–485, ed. of the Biblioth. Indica. L. Poley has given an edition of it, with a Latin translation, 1831. A French translation by E. Burnouf appeared in 1824, in the work of his father, L. Burnouf: Examen du Système Perfectionné de Conjugaison grecque de Thiersch. The Dêvimâhâtmya is the principal sacred text of the worshippers of Durgâ in Northern India.

[3] Th. Foulkes, The Siva-prakasha-pattalai, or The Elements of the Saiva Philosophy, translated from the Tamil, Madras, 1863. By the same author, Catechism of the Saiva Religion, ibid., 1863. Three Çivaite treatises translated from the Tamîl by H. R. Hoisington in the Journ. of the American Oriental Society, vol. iv. Colebrooke has treated of the Mâhêçvaras and the Pâçupatas in his Memoirs on the Philosophy of the Hindus, Miscellaneous Essays, vol. i. p. 430, ed. Cowell.

of the doctrines of Çivaism, we are dependent on documents at secondhand, particularly on the exposition of them which, in the fourteenth century, Sâyaṇa has left us in his Sarvadarçana-sañgraha,[1] and on information collected by H. H. Wilson in his "Sketch of the Religions of the Hindu Sects." Of the testimonies collected in this way, not one, we may be sure, is contemporary with the Pâçupatas (worshippers of Paçupati) of the Mahâbhârata, nor even with the Mâhêçvaras (worshippers of Mahêçvara, the great Lord), which are mentioned in the inscriptions of the fifth century.[2] It is nevertheless probable that they have, under the head of doctrines peculiar to the Pâçupatas and the Mâhêçvaras, preserved for us the old speculations of Çivaism, and that, long before the times of Çaṅkara and Gauḍapâda, who preceded Çaṅkara by two or three generations (the two polemics to whom we owe the first precise, though extremely brief, intimations of the metaphysical systems of the Çaivas),[3] Çivaism had in the main adopted the formulæ of the deistic Sâṅkhya. As in this last system, the soul is clearly distinguished from matter on the one hand, and from God on the other. Matter, the prakṛiti, is eternal; it is the pregnant but blind medium in which the Mâyâ and the different modes of the divine energy work, and in connection with which the soul undergoes the consequences of its acts. United to matter the soul is separated from God; it is a prey to error and sin, and it falls under the law of death and expiation. It is a *paçu*, an animal held back by a chain, by matter namely, which hinders it from returning to its *pati*, or master (for that is the metaphorical meaning, which we now meet with in the old name of Paçupati, "the master of flocks"); and it is to break this bond that all the efforts of the faithful must be directed. God, that is to say Çiva, is

1 Chap. vi.-ix.

2 Inscriptions of Valabhî, *passim*.

3 Çlokas of Gauḍapâda, ii. 26, printed along with the Mâṇḍûkya Upanishad, p. 427, ed. of the Bibl. Ind.; Çaṅkara ad Vêdânta Sûtras, ii. 2, 1–10, p. 497 *seq.*, and ii. 2, 37–41, p. 591 *seq.*, ed. of the Bibl. Ind.

pure spirit, although to render himself perceptible and conceivable he deigns to assume a body, composed "not of matter, but of force." He is the efficient cause of all things; the absolute cause, according to some, determining everything without himself being determined by anything; the omnipotent cause, according to others, but who leaves to the soul a certain freedom of action with reference to its own destiny. The problem of liberty, merit, and grace, which we encounter among the Vaishṇavas also, thus received among these sects a twofold solution: the Pâçupatas adhering to predestination; others, the followers of the Çaivadarçana, properly speaking, leaving to man the initiative in his salvation. Both admitted that there were inferior manifestations of the deity, and both in particular distinguished clearly between Çiva and the different modes of his energy, of his Çakti, by which he produces, preserves, and destroys the world. This is the instrumental cause, as the prakṛiti is the material cause, and as he himself is the efficient cause. It is at once his Mâyâ and his free grace, and is personified in his wife, Devî or Mahâdevî, "the great goddess," with a thousand names and a thousand forms.[1]

The personification of the Çakti is not peculiar to Çivaism. Each god has his own, and Laksmî by the side of Vishṇu, and Sarasvatî by the side of Brahmâ, play the same part as Devî by the side of Çiva.[2] In the Râmatâpanîya-Upanishad, Sîtâ is the Çakti of Râma; she forms with him an inseparable pair, a single being with, as it were, a double face; and the union of Kṛishṇa and his favourite mistress Râdhâ is at times conceived of in a quite similar way (as, for instance, in the Nârada-Pañcarâtra), though the erotic mysticism, which figures to such an extent in these representations, has, in the cultus of Kṛishṇa, taken in general a different course. But it is in Çivaism that these ideas have found a soil most favourable for

[1] Sarvadarçanasaṅgraha, ch. vi., vii.

[2] There is sometimes mention of a Triçakti, which is the exact counterpart of the male trinity. Varâha Purâṇa in Aufrecht's Oxford Catalogue, p. 59.

their expansion, and that they have been distorted into the most monstrous developments. As many as an entire half of the Çivaite religions are, in fact, characterised by the cultus of an androgynous or female divinity. The Çakti, such as she appears in these systems of worship, is no longer derived from the metaphysics which we have just sketched. It has its roots far away in those ideas, as old as India itself, of a sexual dualism, placed at the beginning of things (in a Brâhmaṇa of the Yajur-Veda, for instance, Prajâpati is androgynous), or of a common womb in which beings are formed, which is also their common tomb. It proceeds directly from the prakṛiti of the pure Sâṅkhya, from eternally fertile Nature, whence issue both the sensible forms and the intellectual faculties, and before which the mind, or the male element, acts a part that is featureless in character and barren of result. It is difficult to come to any precise conclusion in regard to the period when these ideas were translated into religious beliefs. Evidences of any antiquity are altogether wanting; in the epic, Çiva does not yet appear in his hermaphrodite form, and we must hesitate to regard him as the *ΑΡΔΟΧΡΟ* of the Indo-Scythian coins.[1] As for the supremacy assigned to the female divinity, that is only affirmed in certain Purâṇas and in the literature of the Tantras. But perhaps there are here special reasons why we should not attach too much weight to the negative argument. These cultuses appear, in fact, to

[1] Lassen, Ind. Alterthumsk., ii. 826 *seq.* See a cast of these coins represented in R. Rochette, Journal des Savants, 1834, p. 392, fig. x. On the other hand, it is properly the androgynous Çiva we must conclude we have got in this statue, which was from ten to twelve cubits high, composed of an unknown substance, the right side of a male and the left of a female, the arms extended like a cross, and the body covered over with representations of the sun, the moon, angels, and all conceivable beings, which the Brahmans worshipped in a large cave on a very high mountain, and which certain Indian envoys on an embassy to Antoninus described to Bardisanes in Stobæus, Eclog. Physic., i. 56. The description perfectly accords with the material pantheism that characterises this branch of the Çivaite religion. An androgynous Çiva (ardhanârîça), appears in the bas-reliefs of Bâḍâmi, Ind. Antiq., vol. vi. p. 359. The Matsya Purâṇa treats of the images of him, Aufrecht's Catalogue, p. 42. See also Mâlavikâgnimitra, str. 1 and 4.

have become early complicated with ritual observances either of a horrible or an obscene nature, which must have led to their being relegated to a special literature of a more or less occult character. Besides, the collections of tales based on the Bṛihatkathâ in which the cultus of the sanguinary goddesses plays such an important part, have an origin which goes much farther back, as far as the fourth or perhaps the third century of our era; and, on the other hand, the obscenities of the Çivaite Tantras have deeply infected the Buddhist Tantras of Nepâl (among others, the *Tathâgata Guhyaka,* which is one of their nine canonical books), and, through them, the Tibetan translations, the majority of which are of a date prior to the ninth century. This infiltration must have gone on but slowly; and as the fact of it implies the necessarily prior development of Hindu doctrines and practices, we may refer these last to the commencement of the middle age. But be that as it may, the cultus of the Çaktis, as it is formulated in certain Upanishads, in several Purâṇas, and especially in the Tantras, must not be confounded with the customary homage rendered by all the sects to the wives of the gods. It forms a religion by itself, that of the *Çâktas,* which again is subdivided into several branches, having their special systems of doctrine and forms of initiation, and in the heart of which there arose a quite distinctive mythology. At the summit and source of all beings is Mahâdevî, in whose character the idea of the Mâyâ and that of the prakṛiti are blended. Below her in rank are arrayed her emanations, the Çaktis of Vishṇu, of Brahmâ, of Skanda, &c. (an order which is naturally altered in favour of Laksmî or of Râhhâ in the small number of writings belonging to the class of Tantras which Vishnuism has produced), and a whole hierarchy, highly complex, and as variable as complex, of female powers, such as the *Mahâmâtṛis,* "the Great Mothers," personifications of the productive and nourishing powers of Nature;[1] the *Yoginîs*, "the Sorceresses," whose interference is always violent and capricious; the *Nayikâs*, the *Ḍâkinîs*, the *Çâkinîs*, and many other classes besides, without consistently definite powers, but almost all malignant, and whose favour is secured only at the expense of the most revolting observances.[2] All this in combination with the male divinities goes to form the most outrageous group of divinities which man has ever conceived. Herself inconceivable in her supreme essence, the Mahâmâyâ, "the Great Illusion," is worshipped under a thousand designations, and invested in an infinite variety of forms. But at the same time, the distinction between these forms is the same as that between different beings, and each of them has its own special circle of devotees. These forms correspond, for most part, to one of the aspects of her twofold nature, *black* or *white*, benevolent or cruel; and they constitute in this way two series of manifestations of the infinite Energy, as it were two series of supreme goddesses, one series presiding more specially over the creative energies of life, the other representing rather

[1] The worship of the mothers, great mothers, or world-mothers (Mâtaraḥ, Mahâmâtaraḥ, Lokamâtaraḥ) has extended far beyond Çâktism, and even Çivaism properly so called. The idea from which it starts is obvious: it is that of the female principle worshipped in its diverse manifestations; but its history is obscure, because each religious scheme has appropriated it in a fashion in keeping with its peculiar theology. A. Weber (Zwei Vedische Texte über Omina und Portenta, p. 349 *seq.*) has attempted to trace the origin of them to the Veda, where we find, in fact, a cultus very similar in that of the Tisro Devîḥ, "the three goddesses." In the Mahâbhârata (iii. 14467 *seq.*) they are the mothers of Skanda, the god of war, and in this connection they appear frequently in the inscriptions of the middle age; for example, in the inscriptions of the Calukyas and the Kadambas of the Dekhan. Varâha Mihira mentions their images (Bṛihat Saṃhitâ, lviii. 56, ed. Kern). Usually 7 or 8, they are elsewhere given at 9, 13, 16 (see the different enumerations in the Dictionary of St. Petersburg, *s. v.* Mâtar). The Pañcadaṇḍachattraprabandha (p. 24, ed. Weber) mentions 64 of them. In Gujarât they worship 120 (Ind. Antiq., viii. 211). They are always invoked together as a troop or circle (gaṇa, maṇḍala); and even when they are conceived as propitious, there is in them a measure of mystery and awe.

[2] See the 5th act of the Mâlatî-Mâdhava of Bhavabhûti; Kathâsaritsâgara, chap. 18.

those of destruction. To both a twofold cultus is addressed: the confessed public cultus, the *Dakshiṇâcâra*, or "cultus of the right hand," which, except in one particular, namely insistance on animal sacrifice in honour of Durgâ, Kâlî, and other terrible forms of the great goddess, observes essentially the general usages of Hinduism; and the *Vâmâcâra*, "the cultus of the left hand," the observances of which have always been kept more or less secret. Incantations, imprecations, magic, and common sorcery play a prominent part in this last, and many of these strange ceremonies have no other object than the acquisition of the different *siddhis* or supernatural powers. These are practices of very ancient date in India, since they are deeply rooted in the Veda,[1] and a special system of philosophy, the Yoga, is devoted to the explanation of them; but nowhere have they found a soil so congenial as in Çivaism and the cultus of the Çaktis. Neither is there room to doubt that the blood of human victims not unfrequently flowed on the altars of these gloomy goddesses, before the horrible images of Durgâ, Kâlî, Câṇḍikâ, and Câmuṇḍâ. Formal testimonies go to confirm the many allusions to this practice which occur in the tales and dramas.[2] In the sixteenth century the

[1] Rig-Veda, x. 136, 3. The Sâmavidhâna Brâhmaṇa is, in fact, a manual of sorcery. The same may be said of the Kauçika Sûtra of the Artharva-Veda. See the analysis which Shankar Pandurang Pandit gives, according to Sâyaṇa, in the Academy for 5th June 1880. We frequently meet with the same characteristic in the sections of the Taittirîya Yajus that refer to the kâmyeshṭis, or offerings presented for the fulfilment of a definite wish.

[2] For example, Mâlatî-Mâdhava, act 5th; H. H. Wilson, Hindu Theatre, ii. 391, 397; Hitopadeça, iii. Fable viii (History of Vîravara); Kathâsaritsâgara, chap. 10, 18, 20, 22, 36, &c.; Vîracaritra, in the Ind. Stud., xiv. pp. 120, 123; Daçakumâracarita, ucchv. vii. p. 169, ed. H. H. Wilson; Pañcadaṇḍachattraprabandha, p. 25 (ed. Weber, in the Memoirs of the Academy of Berlin for 1877). In default of other victims, the offerer is, at least, his own victim: A. Weber, Die Siṃhâsanadvâtriṃçikâ, in the Ind. Stud., xv. pp. 314, 315, and ibid., xiv. 149; Kathâsaritsâgara, chap. 6, 22, &c. The Kâlikâ Purâṇa (an Upapurâṇa) describes these rites in detail: H. H. Wilson, preface of the Vishṇu Purâṇa, p. xc. ed. Hall. This section of the Kâlikâ Purâṇa is translated in vol. v. of the Asiatic Researches.

Mohammedans found it established in Northern Bengal;[1] in the seventeenth, the Sikhs confess that their great reformer, Guru Govind, prepared himself for his mission by the sacrifice of one of his disciples to Durgâ;[2] in 1824 Bishop Heber met with people who told him they had seen young boys offered in sacrifice at the gates of Calcutta;[3] and almost as late as our own time, the Thugs professed to murder their victims in honour of Kâlî. Perhaps we ought to view these practices as derived, by contact or by heritage, from the bloody rites of the aboriginal tribes. It is beyond question that many *forms* of the great goddess (and we may say the same of Çiva and Vishṇu) are those of ancient local deities adopted by Hinduism. Several, and some of the most inhuman, appear to be native to Central India, and, as regards one of these at least, the very name, Vinhyavâsini, "the inhabitant of Vindhya," implies that she must have held sway over these mountains, where human sacrifice, less than half a century ago, still formed part of the national cultus of the Gonds, the Kols, and the Uraons.[4] In our own days the English police have put an end to these rites, which, however, in the civilised districts of India, have always been more or less exceptional occurrences. This is not the case with those coarsely sensual and obscene observances which form the other side of these secret cults, and the indecent regulations in regard to which the Tantras expound with minuteness. The use of animal food and spirituous liquors, indulged in to excess,

[1] H. Blochmann, Contributions to the Geography and History of Bengal, in Journ. of the As. Soc. of Bengal, vol. xlii. Shahrastâni (twelfth century) mentions the human sacrifices of the Çâktas, but adds that the people commonly repudiate them; translation by Haarbrücker, t. ii. p. 370. See Dabistân, ii. p. 155, translated by Shea and Troyer.

[2] T. Trumpp, The Adi Granth, Introduction, p. xc.

[3] Letter of the 10th January 1824 to Mrs. Douglas, in the Correspondence printed as a sequel to the Narrative of a Journey through the Upper Provinces of India.

[4] W. Hunter, Statistical Account of Bengal, vol. xvi. pp. 291, 313; xvii. 281, 283; xix. 218. For a recent case (1872) among the Tamils of Ceylon, see Ind. Antiq., ii. 125. Similar observances have been practised, to our own days, among the Banjâris and among the Kois of the Telugu country; ibid., viii. 219, 220.

is the rule in these strange ceremonies, in which Çakti is worshipped in the person of a naked woman, and the proceedings terminate with the carnal copulation of the initiated, each couple representing Bhairava and Bhairavî (Çiva and Devî), and becoming thus for the moment identified with them. This is the *Çrîcakra*, "the holy circle," or the *Pûrṇâbhishêka*, "the complete consecration," the essential act, or rather foretaste of salvation, the highest rite of this delirious mysticism. For there is something else than licentiousness in these aberrations. The books which prescribe these practices are, like the rest, filled with lofty speculative and moral reflections, nay, even with ascetic theories; here, as well as elsewhere, there is a profession of horror at sin and a religiosity full of scruples; it is with pious feelings, the thoughts absorbedly engaged in prayer, that the believer is to participate in these mysteries, and it would be to profane them to resort to them for the gratifications of sense. In fact, a Çâkta of the left hand is almost always a hypocrite and a superstitious debauchee; but there can be no doubt that among the authors of these contemptible catechetical books there were more than one who sincerely believed he was performing a work of sanctity. Statistical science has naturally little or nothing to say in regard to such observances. No Hindu with any self-respect will confess that he has any connection with the Vâmâcârins. But they are reputed to be numerous, many adherents who profess to belong to the right hand belonging in secret to the left. They form small fraternities, and admit into their number people of every class, but it it is said that in Bengal especially their ranks are recruited to a great extent from among the Brahmans and the rich classes. It is proper to add, however, that those who make no mystery of their initiation insist that their sect should not be judged according to its books, and it is probable, in fact, that there are degrees of baseness in these proceedings, and that among people of culture and little faith a sort of superstitious Epicureanism has taken the place of the revels of the ancient ritual. The Dakshiṇâcârin Çâktas, or adherents of the right hand, are met with in great numbers all over India. In Hindustan the great mass of the Çivaites are of this class, and in Bengal the entire population takes part in the Durgâpûjâ, the great festival in honour of their goddess, although the stricter Hindus reprobate the indecencies which are perpetrated in public on this occasion, and stigmatise the whole celebration as one that belongs to the observances of the left hand.[1]

Alongside of the Çivaism which we have just been surveying, and which has recourse more or less directly to the Sâṅkhya system, there is another which is inspired with the idealism of the Vedânta, and maintains consequently the essential unity of the world, the soul and God. The most ancient sects that profess it in our day, the *Tridaṇḍins* (literally, "the bearers of the triple baton," metaphorically, "those who exercise a threefold sovereignty, viz., over their words, their thoughts, and their actions," carrying as a symbol of this sovereignty a stick with three knots), and the majority of the *Smârtas* (adherents of the Smṛiti or orthodox tradition), maintain that they are connected with Çaṅkara. The first of these, who are divided into ten tribes, according to the districts of country where they originated, and who, for that reason, are also called *Daçanâmis*, "those with the ten surnames," are ascetics, and have their centre at Benares. The second, who are numerous, especially in the Dekhan, live partly in the world and partly in convents.[2] Many of them are pure Vedântins, and hardly belong to Çivaism. They both admit into their order only Brahmans, and they themselves do not make their direct tradition go farther back than the eighth century. But here again it is proper

[1] The Dabistân (ii. 148–164, translated by Schea and Troyer) contains a curious notice of the Çâktas (seventeenth century). From this period they constituted the majority of the Çivaites in Hindustan.

[2] Their chief guru resides in the convent of Çṛingeri in Mysore. See A. C. Burnell, Vaṃçabrâhmaṇa, pref., p. xii.

to recall the remark already made when speaking of the Vishnuite systems, that in matters of doctrine the historical sects have invented little. Long before the eighth century we, in fact, find in the non-technical literature Çivaism connected with ideas derived from a system of doctrine very different from that of the Sâṅkhya. The Çiva, for instance, who is invoked at the commencement of the drama of "Çakuntalâ," who is at once god, priest, and offering, and whose body is the universe, is a Vedantic idea.[1] These testimonies appear to be forgotten when it is maintained, as is sometimes done, that the whole sectarian Vedantism commences with Çaṅkara.

This branch of the Çivaite theosophy received its final form at Kashmir, between the ninth and eleventh centuries, in the writings of the school of Somânanda and Abhinavagupta.[2] These are the most ancient technical treatises on the subject which have reached us, the most ancient also to which Sâyaṇa refers in the exposition which he has given of the system. This system is pure idealism. God is the only substance, objects are his ideas; and as he is identical with ourselves, these objects are really in us. What we think we see outside of us we see within. The individual *ego* perceives, or rather reperceives in itself, as in a mirror, the ideals of the transcendental *ego,* and cognition is only a recognition. Hence the name of the system, which is that of *Pratyabhijñâ,* or Recognition. Guided by the true method of interior contemplation, and enlightened by the grace which it has merited through its faith in Çiva, the individual soul triumphs over the Mâyâ, from which all diversity proceeds and ends by the consciousness of self in God.[3]

In passing from this system, which we know only in its

[1] See besides the beginning of the Vikramorvaçi. The Çvetâçvatara Up., which is certainly of date prior to Çaṅkara, is a sort of Çivaite Bhagavad Gîtâ. See especially sections iii. and iv.

[2] G. Bühler, who lately recovered at Kashmir a good portion of the writings of this school, has given us valuable information regarding it in the Journ. of the Roy. As. Soc., Bombay, xii. (extra number), p. 77 *seq.*

[3] Saradarçanasaṅgraha, ch. viii.

learned form, to the sect of the *Lingâyits*, which is known to us only as a popular religion, we descend from the heights of the Timæus down to the level of the grossest superstitions. The Lingâyits appear, on the whole, to be connected with Çivaism in its idealistic form, since the *Jangamas*, "the vagrants," who form among them the religious and ascetic order, accept as their principal authority a Çivaite commentary on the Vedânta Sûtras. But it is difficult to extract any creed whatever from the confused mass of legends, which, along with certain particulars in regard to their history, organisation, and cultus, constitute nearly all that we know about them. Their founder, Basava (which is a Dravidian form of the Sanskrit Vṛishabha), who was a Brahman, was born in the west of the Dekhan, in the first half of the twelfth century. He contended at once against the orthodox, the Vishnuites, and the Jainas; he preached Çivaism, the abolition of sacrifice and of the distinctions of caste, and rose by rapid stages to great influence. When the Kaluburigi Bijjala, who ruled at that time as king in the Dekhan, and had become his son-in-law, set himself up against him as the defender of the Jainas, he procured his assassination by the hands of his disciples, but he was obliged to destroy himself in order to escape the vengeance of that prince's successor. His work, however, did not perish along with him; the sect, or rather sects, which owe their origin to Basava, are at the present day dominant in the dominions of the Nizam and Mysore, and are widely spread in the extreme South; while their itinerant monks, the Jangamas, are to be met with in every part of India.[1] Their principal books are writings entitled Purâṇas, in which the biography of the founder is interlarded with a great number of legends

[1] The Jangamas do not always lead a wandering life; like other religious, they live sometimes in community in colleges (maṭhas). The name they go by, which signifies "ambulants," is thus considered as expressing their character of "moveable" or living lingas. See the description of one of these people in an inscription of the thirteenth century, Journ. of the Roy. As. Soc., Bombay, xii. p. 40.

concerning Çiva and his different local manifestations. They have also hymns for popular use, which breathe at times an elevated spirit. Almost the whole of this literature, of which we as yet know but little, is in the Canarese and Tamîl languages. As in the majority of these religions, the religious beliefs appear to be a mixture of Vedantic mysticism, deism, and gross idolatry.[1] They worship Çiva under the form of the *linga*, or phallus, and they always carry about with them a small image of this in copper or silver; whence their name, Lingâyits, or "phallus-wearers." Alongside of them there are other Çivaite sects more ancient, which observe the same custom, but have not broken so openly with the old traditions in regard to caste and ritual. The principal of these appears to be the sect of the *Arâdhyas*, or the "Reverends," who are all Brahmans, and who, though once very numerous, are now on the decline.

Far purer is the form in which Çivaism appears in the Tamîl poetical effusions of the *Sittars* (in Sanskrit *Siddhas*), "perfect ones."[2] We know but little of the sect from which these compositions emanate; at the present day it appears to be extinct; but the hymns themselves have retained their popularity, notwithstanding the peremptory way in which they denounce the most cherished beliefs of the masses. They are compositions, in general, of no great age, going back not more than two or three centuries, although they circulate under the names of the famous saints of antiquity, such as Agastya, the fabled civiliser of the Dekhan, and his not less fabulous disciples. In elevation of style they rival the most perfect compositions which have been left us by Tiruvalluvar, Auveiyâr, and the ancient Tamîl poets. But at the same

[1] The most recent communication in regard to the literature and beliefs of the Lingâyits we owe to F. Kittel: Ueber den Ursprung des Lingakultus, pp. 11 and 27, Ind. Antiq., vol. iv. p. 211; v. 183.

[2] For this sect see Caldwell, A Comparative Grammar of the Dravidian Languages, Introd., pp. 127, 146, 2d ed., and E. Ch. Gover, The Folk-Songs of Southern India, Madras, 1871.

time, in their severe monotheism, their contempt for the Vedas and the Çâstras, their disgust at every idolatrous practice, and especially their repudiation of a doctrine so radical to Hinduism as metempsychosis, they much more clearly betray a foreign influence. Very competent critics[1] think they recognise in them an inspiration from Christianity, and, in fact, the native churches who believe in the remote antiquity of these collections profess the same esteem for them as those of the West did for the Sibyline books. But perhaps they are more imbued with Suffism than with Christian ideas. It is not in general the monotheism of the Christian religion which most strikes the Hindu; and these hymns profess a rigid monotheism, which reminds us rather of the Koran than of the somewhat modified religious beliefs of the Christians of St. Thomas. In regard to alchemy, anyhow, in which the Sittars are zealous adepts, they were disciples of the Arabians, although other Çivaites had preceded them in the pursuit of the philosopher's stone. Already, in his exposition of the different doctrines of the Çaivas, Sâyaṇa thought he ought to dedicate a special chapter to the *Raseçvara-darçana*, or "system of mercury,"[2] a strange amalgamation of Vedantism and alchemy. The object contemplated in this system is the transmutation of the body into an incorruptible substance by means of *rasa-pâna*, *i.e.*, the absorption into it of elixirs compounded principally of mercury and mica, that is to say, of the very essential qualities of Çiva and Gaurî, with whom the subject of the operation is thus at length identified. This species of transubstantiation constitutes the *jîvanmukti*, or state of deliverance commencing with this present life, the sole and indispensable condition of salvation. It is clear that the devotional formulæ of the Vedânta are here only a sort of jargon, under which there lies hid a radically impious doctrine; and it is not less clear that in this doctrine, which had from the fourteenth century

[1] Especially R. Caldwell

[2] Sarvadarçanasaṅgraha, ch. ix.

produced a rather considerable literature, there is an infusion of Mohammedan ideas.[1] Criticism is generally on the lookout for the least traces on Hinduism of Christian influence; but perhaps it does not take sufficiently into account that which Islamism has exercised. We seem to form our estimate of this last only through the results, which were on the whole negative, of the conquest, which was the work in general of unimpressionable and coarse races; we forget the ancient presence, in the Dekhan especially, of the Arabian element. The Arabs of the Khalifat had arrived on these shores in the character of travellers or merchants, and had established commercial relations and intercourse with these parts long before the Afghans, Turks, or Mongols, their coreligionists, came as conquerors.[2] Now, it is precisely in these parts that, from the ninth to the twelfth century, those great religious movements took their rise which are connected with the names of Çaṅkara, Râmânuja, Anandatîrtha, and Basava, out of which the majority of the historical sects came, and to which Hindustan presents nothing analogous till a much later period. It has been remarked that these movements took place in the neighbourhood of old-established Christian communities.[3] But alongside of these there began to appear, from that moment, the disciples of the Koran. To neither of these do we feel inclined to ascribe an influence of any significance on Hindu theology, which appears to us sufficiently accounted for by reference to its own resources; but it is very possible that indirectly, and merely as it were by their presence, they contributed in some degree towards the budding and bursting forth of those great religious reforms which, in the absence of doctrines

[1] Sâyaṇa refers to not fewer than eight names of authors or titles of different works.

[2] See Reinaud, Relation des Voyages faits par les Arabes et les Persans dans l'Inde et à la Chine dans le Neuvième Siècle de l'Ere Chrétienne, 1845. The most ancient of these narratives is of date 841. The Arabs at that time carried on a flourishing trade on the Malabar coast.

[3] A. C. Burnell, On Some Pahlavî Inscriptions in South India, Mangalore, 1873, p. 14.

altogether new, introduced into Hinduism a new organisation and a new spirit, and had all this common characteristic that they developed very quickly under the guidance of an acknowledged head, and rested on a species of authority akin to that of a prophet or an Iman. Now, to effect such a result as this, the Arabian merchants in the first centuries of the Hegira, with the Mohammedan world at their back, were perhaps better qualified than the poor and destitute Churches of the Malabar and Coromandel Coasts.

In connection with the systems which precede, we have nearly exhausted the speculative theology of Çivaism, and we may now glance rapidly at the crowd of more obscure sects or associations into which it is split up.[1] These divisions affect to a very slight degree the lay classes, especially in the North, where Çivaism retains its more ancient form. It has not given rise there to great, organised, and compact popular religions, like that of the Liñgâyits of Basava in the South. If we compare it with Vishnuism, we may even affirm that it has, strictly speaking, produced there no modern sects, and that it there represents rather a unity of local cultuses than a unity of doctrinal beliefs. Hence, the divisions in question are

[1] In reference to the majority of the sects that follow, as well as some of those which precede, a great quantity of information and characteristic anecdote will be found in a work quoted from already more than once, "The Dabistân, or School of Manners," translated from the Persian by D. Shea and A. Troyer, 1843, the second chapter of which (vol. ii. pp. 1–228) is devoted to the religious beliefs of India. The author, whoever he was, of this curious history of religions, one of the most singular books which the East has given us, was a very free-thinking Sufi, who took a curious interest in theosophy, secret systems of doctrine, and refined forms of impiety, and was quite *au courant* with all that was happening in the sectarian world of Hinduism towards the middle of the seventeenth century. He had kept up personal, often intimate, relations with a great number of celebrities belonging to the different contemporary sects, with Vedântins, Yogins, Çâktas, Vairâgins, Jainas, disciples of Kabîr and Nânak, &c. He had read a great deal, and he was, for an Oriental, not deficient in critical ability. No work is better fitted than his to introduce us into the heart of that singular medley of religious and moral elevation and debasement, of heroic piety and barefaced charlatanry, which we meet with in Hindu sectarian life.

composed principally of professional devotees, who have no Church behind them. These, whether in the form of religious orders, more or less regular, or of associations without fixed bond of fellowship, are due to ascetic tendencies, or at least pretensions to asceticism. The most respectable are allied to the Tridaṇḍins and the Jaṅgamas, already spoken of, and profess Vedantism; but, in general, they are mainly distinguished from each other by external observances and signs. They are commonly called *yogins*, that is, "possessors or practisers of the yoga," a term which practically has many shades of meaning, from that of saint to that of sorcerer or charlatan. The most widely scattered, perhaps, of these orders is that of the *Kâṇphâṭas*,[1] "slit ears," who are so called from the operation to which they subject their novices. Like the most of the Yogins, they ignore the distinction of caste. They are met with living separately as mendicants, more frequently collected together in groups as cenobites, in the Northern Dekhan, Gujarât, the Punjâb, the provinces of the Ganges, and Nepâl, in which last case they devote themselves to works of charity and the relief of the poor. Their traditions, which are extremely confused, represent each of these countries as claiming to be the native land of Gorakhnâtha, their founder. But as these traditions agree in representing him as the son or the more or less immediate disciple of Matsyendranâtha, who belongs to Nepalese Buddhism (and is even identified with the Bodhisattva Avalokiteçvaṛa), it is probable that, like the *Jatis* and *Savaras*,[2] they were connected originally with the religion of Çâkyamuni. It is not known exactly at what period Gorakhnâtha lived. As for the other sects or varieties of Çivaite yogins, *Gosains* (there are also Vishnuite Gosains), *Bhartharis*, *Çivâcârins*, *Brahmacârins*, *Haṃsas*, *Paramahaṃsas*, *Akâçamukhins*, *Urdhvabâhus*, *Kâpâlikas*, *Nâgas*, *Bahikathâs*,

[1] See Ind. Antiq., vii. 47, 298.

[2] Sherring, Hindu Tribes, p. 265, connects these two divisions with the Buddhists. The description which the author of the "Dabistân" gives of them (ii. 211) would connect them

Aghoris, &c., &c., they have still less any history.[1] The names, in the special acceptation of them, are seldom ancient. Nevertheless, Hiouen-Thsang, and before him Varâha-Mihira (who lived in the sixth century),[2] show that they had a knowledge of the Kâpâlikas, so called because they wore about their person a death's-head, which they used as a drinking-vessel. But the tradition of these sects is their profession itself, and this is immemorial. From the outset, and more than any other Hindu religion, Çivaism has pandered to ascetic fanaticism. No other has exhibited so many horrible and revolting observances, or has worn with so much ostentation the badge, often singular enough, of devotion.[3] Thus Hiouen-Thsang, who is usually so well informed, seems to have seen of the separate Brahmanical sects only the Çaivas during the fifteen years he devoted to the survey of the different countries of India. In our day cruel mortifications are becoming rare, yet there are still Akâçamukhins and Urdhvabâhus—who pose themselves in immovable attitudes, their faces or their arms raised to heaven, until the sinews shrink and the posture assumed often stiffens into rigidity—as well as Nâgas, Paramahaṃsas, Avadhûtas, and others, who, in spite of English interdicts, expose themselves to the inclemency of the weather in a state of absolute nudity. In all this there is no doubt much sincere fanaticism, but there also enters into it a good deal of hypocrisy and charlatanry. Very frequently mendicity is the only motive for these pretended mortifications; and it is not so much to merit heaven as to extort alms, by exciting terror or disgust, that the Bahikathâs tear their bodies

rather with the Jainas. Jati is the Sanskrit Yati; under Savara, Sevra, Çrivara, as the name is severally spelled, there is perhaps hid Çrâvaka, a designation of the lay Jainas.

[1] For the present state of these sects and fraternities see A. Sherring, Hindu Tribes and Castes as Represented in Benares, 1872, p. 255 *seq*.

[2] St. Julien, Voyages des Pélerins Bouddhistes, t. i. p. 222. Varâha Mihira, Bṛihat Saṃhitâ, lxxxvii. 22, p. 432, ed. Kern.

[3] Varâha Mihira gives Sabhasmadvija, a Brahman sprinkled with ashes, as a generic name of the Çivaites: Bṛihat Saṃhitâ, lx. 19, p. 328, ed. Kern.

with knives and the Aghoris feed on carrion and excrement.[1] Of the Yogins, some are found assembled in *maṭhas* or colleges near the sacred places of Çivaism, especially at Benares; others constitute themselves guardians of some sequestered chapel and live as hermits; but the greater number lead a wandering life. They infest the country in bands, sometimes very numerous, going from one place of pilgrimage to another, and flocking by thousands to the *melâs* or fairs, which are held periodically in the neighbourhood of every celebrated sanctuary. Of these last, many sell charms, practise incantations and exorcisms, tell fortunes, or are jugglers or minstrels. They are at once dreaded and despised—the Çâktas, who are numerous among them, still more so than the others—and they to a great extent reinforce the dangerous classes. And this is not a state of things due solely to modern corruption. From the time of Patañjali (that is, the second century before Christ), when the violence of these fanatical devotees had already passed into a proverb,[2] there is evidence to show that all along the maxim *Omnia sancta sanctis* was extensively in vogue among them.[3] In order to conceive what they might be in the troubled periods of the past, it is enough to refer to accounts which refer to events of no distant date. Even at the end of the last century they formed the nucleus of those hordes which traversed Bengal, sometimes to the number of more than a thousand men, all armed to the teeth, accompanied with elephants and artillery, attacking towns and daring to hold the country in the face of detachments of British soldiery.[4]

At the present time Çiva is probably the god who can

[1] There appears to be no doubt that among the observances of some obscene fanatics we must include acts of cannibalism: Dabistân, ii. 153, 156, 157; Ind. Antiq. viii. 88.

[2] Mahâbhâshya, in Ind. Stud. xiii. 347.

[3] As early as the Mṛicchakaṭikâ, p. 35, l. 5, ed. Stenzler, *gosâvid*, a "religious," is synonymous with *veçyâ*, courtesan. See Muir's Sanskrit Texts, vol. ii. p. 25, 2d ed.

[4] W. Hunter, Statistical Account of Bengal, vol. ii. p. 311; vol. vii. p. 159.

reckon up more sanctuaries than any other. From one end of India to the other, at every step, we meet with his temples and chapels, sometimes mere niches or mounds of earth, where he is worshipped principally under the form of the liṅga. But Çivaism, strictly speaking, is far from being the prevailing religion. Except in Kashmir and Nepâl, where the Hindu element[1] is chiefly composed of Çaivas, and at Benares, which is, as it were, its holy city, it has been losing ground in Hindustan. Every one, no doubt, worships Çiva here, but, with the exception of professional devotees, comparatively few Çivaites are met with, that is to say, people who make Çiva their principal god in the *mantra* of whom they have been specially initiated, and in the faith of whom they hope to work out their salvation. And the number would be still more reduced if we were to cut off the Çâktas from it who pay their vows to Devî rather than to her husband. In all the countries to the north of the Vindhya, several of which rank among the most thickly inhabited of the globe, the majority, wherever local cults of aboriginal derivation do not prevail, belong to Vishnuite religions. In the Dekhan the relative proportions are different, the Çivaites constituting large masses, especially in the South, and the two religions being probably equally balanced. But even there Vishnuism seems to be spreading. Naturally more expansive and more attractive—too attractive even, as we shall see by and by—it is more favourable to community of worship and religious sentiment than Çivaism, whose gloomy mysteries, under their triple ascetic, magic, and orgiastic forms, are better suited to the isolation and twilight atmosphere of small communities. It is, moreover, embellished with a richer body of fable, and it has found its expression in more striking literary works, which, translated into, or rather reproduced in, the principal languages, Aryan as well as Dravidian, have furnished

[1] That is to say, non-Mussulman in the former country, non-Buddhist in the latter.

an inexhaustible quarry for popular poetry. In fine, if it affords less nourishment to superstitious appetites, on the other hand, by the deep glimpses which the doctrine of the Avatâras opens in some degree into the divine nature, it allies itself more readily with Vedantic mysticism, that one of all the systems conceived in India which responds best to its aspirations. If it were legitimate to inquire towards what religious future this people would have advanced, had they been left entirely to themselves and their own resources, we might probably be led to suppose a day when they would have for religion some form of Vishnuism combined with Çivaite superstitions.

All the sects which we have just passed in review, Vaishṇavas and Çaivas, the most honoured as well as the least, aim, or at any rate pretend to aim, at one single object, namely, salvation. They have their prescriptions for the acquisition of temporal wealth, but they profess to despise the possession of it. As a means of obtaining salvation, they all prescribe a cultus more or less encumbered or disencumbered with observances, to which we shall have to refer farther on; but above this cultus, harmonising in this respect with the whole body of ancient theology, they place the *jñâna*, the transcendental science, the knowledge of the mysteries of God.[1] The pious legends, the *purâṇas*, which record the actions and manifestations of the gods, are only the veil that conceals a higher truth which the believer must penetrate. From this point of view the epic fable has been reconstrued in special works, such as the *Adhyâtma Râmâyaṇa*, "the spiritual Râmâyaṇa," in which all the events in the history of Râmâ are resolved into the divine order.[2] Side by side with the abstract doctrine there was thus formed in the majority of the sects an allegorical doctrine, a gnosis or a mystic interpretation of their legend, which

[1] Bhagavad Gîtâ, iv. 40-42; vii. 3.

[2] The Adhyâtma Râmâyaṇa forms part of the Brahmâṇḍa Purâṇa. See the analysis of it given by Aufrecht, Oxford Catalogue, pp. 28, 29.

was regarded as far superior to the simple philosophy. Among the Pâñcarâtras, for instance, Kṛishṇa was the supreme *âtman;* his brother, Balarâma, was the *jîva*, the individual soul; his son, Pradyumna, represented the *manas*, perceptive sense; and Aniruddha, his grandson, the *ahaṃkâra*, self-consciousness. In like manner, the amours of Kṛishṇa and the shepherdesses become, among the Vishnuites, the allegorical expression of the relations of the soul with God. In this the sects only applied a method which may be traced back as far as the Veda, and of which the Buddhists and the Jainas have likewise made extensive use. But where they part company, both with the ancient theosophy and modern orthodoxy, such as it has been formulated by Çaṅkara, and in general from the doctrine common to all the *darçanas*, is when they subordinate this science to a psychical fact of a totally different nature, viz., *bhakti*, *i.e.*, "faith, humble submission, absolute devotion, love for God," without which science is either vain or impossible. It is *bhakti* which enlightens the soul, which alone can render the exercises of meditation and asceticism productive of fruit.[1] Or rather it dispenses with these; for to him who possesses it, all the rest is given over and above.[2] It addresses itself, not to the god of the learned and the philosophers, but to the manifestation of God that is most accessible, most at hand; among the Vishnuites, for instance, not to Vishṇu or to Paramâtman, but to Kṛishṇa, to God made man, who makes answer by his grace (*anugraha, prasâda*), or who has rather made answer beforehand, when, condescending to clothe his ineffable and inconceivable majesty in a sensible form, he thus permitted the humblest to love him, and to give himself to him even before knowing him.[3] That was a new idea. The Veda was familiar with *Çraddhâ*, that is, the trust of a man in his gods; and in some Upanishads (the Kaṭha-Upanishad, Muṇḍaka-Upa-

[1] Bhagavad Gîtâ, xvii. 28. [2] Bhâgavata Purâṇa, xi. 20, 31–34.
[3] Bhagavad Gîtâ, xii. 5–8.

nishad[1]), occurs an old expression implying very clearly the notion of grace. But all antiquity had in the end resolved religion into matter of knowledge, either rational, intuitive, or revealed ; the sects resolved it into matter of feeling. Thus the novelty of this doctrine early led to the hypothesis of a foreign influence, of a plagiarism more or less direct from Christianity.[2] This first hypothesis suggested others. The legend of the Mahâbhârata was recalled to mind, in which it was said that Nârada, and before him other mythical personages, had visited the Çvetadvîpa, or "the White Island," and had there fallen in with a race of perfect men, endowed with pre-eminent faith in the only Bhagavat; and it was surmised that there was here the reminiscence of relations long ago between the Brahmans and Alexandrian Christianity.[3] It was remarked that in the epic this doctrine seemed to be connected more specially with Vishṇuism ; that the *Bhagavad-Gîtâ*, where it is fully expounded, and the *Bhakti-Sûtras*, where it is systematically formulated, belong to the religion of Kṛishṇa, which was, more than any other, a religion of love. Stress was laid on the monotheistic character of this religion, on the analogy which there is between the theory of the Avatâras and that of the Incarnation,[4] on the curious similarities which exist between the legend of Jesus and that of Kṛishṇa, in which occur, with more or fewer points of similarity, the pastoral scenes of the nativity, the adoration of the shepherds and the magi, the flight into Egypt, the massacre of the Innocents, the miracles connected with the Infancy, the Temptation and the Transfiguration, and all that in connection with a god whose very name has a certain affinity in sound with that of Christ. Attention was called to certain ceremonies of

[1] Kaṭha Upanishad, ii. 23 ; Muṇḍaka Upanishad, iii. 2, 3. See *supra*, p. 74

[2] H. H. Wilson, Select Works, vol. i. p. 161, and Vishṇu Purâṇa, preface, p. xiv. ed. Hall.

[3] A. Weber, Ind. Stud., vol, i. p. 400 ; ii. p. 168. See Lassen, Ind. Alterthumsk., ii. 1118, 2d ed.

[4] A. Weber, Ind. Stud., ii. 169, 409.

the later Krishnaism, to its festival of the nativity, to the worship of the infant Kṛishṇa, represented as on the lap or the bosom of his mother in a *gokula* or stable. In this way an imposing array of facts was collected together, tending to prove, first, that the appearance in India of a religion of faith and love was an event of purely Christian origin, and, secondly, that Christianity exercised an influence of greater or less account on the worship and myth of Kṛishṇa.

We think we have faithfully summarised the principal arguments in favour of this theory, which in its scientific form belongs almost entirely to Prof. Weber, and which that scholar has developed from time to time with an erudition and critical power to which it would be impossible to render adequate homage.[1] As it is of such importance, we must ask our readers to bear with us for a little while we explain, as briefly as we can, why the theory does not satisfy us. *Bhakti* appears to us to be the necessary complement of a religion that has reached a certain stage of monotheism. It will be all the more active the less this monotheism happens to be a direct product of speculation, and the more concrete and human the nature of the god may be that is the object of worship. It will appear either as love or as a gloomy enthusiasm, according as the deity worshipped is an object of love or an object of terror. If several kindred religions of this nature happen to exist side by side, it will be full of zeal. This being so, we have only to ask ourselves whether India had to wait until the arrival of Christianity, in order, on the one hand, to acquire monotheistic ideas, and, on the other, to apply these ideas to such popular gods as Çiva and Kṛishṇa? To answer No—which we for our part do not hesitate to do—is to confess that this *bhakti* is explicable as a native fact, which was quite as capable of realising itself in India as

[1] In the most thorough style in his learned memoir, Ueber die Kṛishṇa-janmâshṭamî (Kṛishṇa's Geburts) Fest), Memoirs of the Academy of Berlin, 1867, p. 217 *seq.*

it has done elsewhere in its own time, and independently of all Christian influence, in the religions of Osiris, Adonis, Cybele, and Bacchus. We by no means wish to represent ancient India as a world apart, with no communication with the world beyond; and although the legend of Çvetadvîpa, the Albion of Wilford, Alexandria, or Asia Minor, according to Prof. Weber, appears to us a purely fanciful relation, we admit that it is quite possible that Brahmans long ago visited the Churches of the East. At all events, the Buddhists penetrated into those parts, and might fetch them accounts of them; for there were at that time no impassable barriers between Buddhists and Brahmans. In India itself, moreover, there certainly were Christians, and probably Christian Churches, before the redaction of the Mahâbhârata was quite finished.[1] It is not, therefore, on the possibility of plagiarism, but on the fact itself as asserted, that our objections bear. The dogma of faith is not imported as an ordinary doctrine or a custom is; it does not admit of being detached from one religion and grafted on another at a distance; practically it is blended with the faith itself, and, like it, inseparable from the god that inspires it. Now, Weber does not mean to assert that in Kṛishṇa, in whom there is no trace either of the dogma of redemption or the accounts of the passion, the true source and substance of the Christian faith, India ever paid divine honours to Jesus. He does not seek to represent Krishnaism as a distorted form of Christianity, something similar to what the religion of the Taipings in China is in our day.[2] The Hindu god would never have ceased to be himself; there would only have been ascribed to him, besides the dogma of faith, a certain number of Christian endowments; in other words, they would have appropriated

[1] On the origin of the churches of St. Thomas see Lassen, Ind. Alterthumsk., ii. 1119, 2d. ed., A. C. Burnell and R. Collins in Ind. Antiq., iii. 308; iv. 153, 183, 311; v. 25.

[2] M. F. Lorinser has gone so far into this subject in Die Bhagavad Gitâ übersetzt und erlaütert, 1869. He arrives at the singular conclusion that the author of the Hindu poem was well read in the Gospels and the Christian Fathers.

the soul of Christianity without Christ. In our opinion there is here a certain contradiction; but be that as it may, even in regard to these subordinate plagiarisms, we cannot without reserve accept the conclusions of Weber. The theory of the Avatâras appears to us to be a purely Indian one. It was probably formulated in connection with Kṛishṇa (and in this we perhaps go farther than Weber), but the germ of it occurs in ancient fable. It is in harmony with the vague distinction assumed in India to exist between God and man, and it must, as it were, of itself have developed from the Vedantic idea of the immanence of deity, of which it is in a way only an application to particular cases. We have already indicated elsewhere the analogy that exists between it and the theory of the successive apparitions of Buddha, and this last appears to have been conceived prior to our era, since we find it figuring in the bas-reliefs of Barahout. We cannot stop here to examine one by one the other resemblances that have been traced between these two legends, curious as they certainly are. Several, such as the prodigies connected with the Infancy and the Transfiguration, appear not unnaturally in the biography of one who is preconceived as a man-god. But the rest is of a character so peculiar that we are very much constrained to admit that there is a body of common relations which have contributed form and colouring to both. Only, be it remarked, these relations correspond to the most obviously legendary elements in the life of Christ;[1] that they are to be found more or less elsewhere in other biographies of the gods among the Hindus—for instance, in that of Buddha; that the traditions which refer to Kaṃsa, the Indian Herod, are certainly of a date anterior to our era;[2] that the pastoral scenes connected with the infancy of Kṛishṇa,

[1] The resemblances become particularly striking when we refer to the apocryphal Gospels, especially the Gospel of the Infancy, which was in great repute all over Asia. See E. Renan, L'Eglise Chrétienne, p. 515.

[2] See Bhandarkar, Allusions to Kṛishṇa in Patañjali's Mahâbhâshya, in Ind. Antiq., iii. 14.

and the idea of assigning to him a stable as his cradle, are connected in a thousand ways with the most ancient representations of the Veda. With these manifold coincidences before us, we feel we are in contact with an old mythical foundation, in relation to which the question of direct borrowing becomes a complex one, and respects only insignificant details. Perhaps the most obvious trace of such borrowing is found in certain peculiarities particularised by Weber in reference to the festival of the nativity of Kṛishṇa, especially in the images in which Devakî is represented as suckling her son, and which seem to have been really copied from similar representations in Christian iconography. But even here the myth is an ancient one, and, on the other hand, the idea of celebrating the birth of the divine child, and of associating with the worship of him on that occasion the worship of his mother, must have suggested itself so naturally that the probability of borrowing extends no further than to the representation. Devakî does not occupy a very prominent place in the religion of her son (besides, it is in the Çivaite religion of Skanda that the part of goddess-mother is more especially developed); her nearest relation is the Mâyâ Devî, the mother of Buddha, and there is nothing to justify us in regarding the modest and very occasional acts of homage paid to her as a Hindu version of the worship of the Virgin.

The discussion of the counter-thesis, which has long engrossed almost exclusive attention, that of the profound influence which India has had on the doctrines and religions of the West, is outside the limits of the present work. It is well, however, to observe that here, too, it has become necessary to soften down the hypotheses that were at first adopted. The opinions of the neo-Platonists, the Gnostics, and the Manicheans, the spirit of asceticism and the institutions of monasticism, are no longer represented as proceeding indiscriminately from the banks of the Ganges. In spite of the manifold confessions which the

Grecian world has left us of the curiosity it felt to know the mysteries of the extreme East, it appears to have been rather in quest of matter that would justify and illustrate its own peculiar tendencies. The Church, probably by means of the Buddhists, borrowed from India a small number of legends and external practices, such as the use of the bell at the services and that of the rosary (these two practices being common to the majority of the Hindu religions and sects, and appearing to be, the one of Buddhist origin, the other of Çivaite, perhaps Brahmanic); but it has not been indebted to it either for its speculations on the Logos or the doctrine of the Trinity, nor in general for any one of those doctrines the borrowing of which would be equivalent to a species of conversion. For a stronger reason we incline to think that this must have been the case with India, which, in the matter of religion, has never confessed herself under obligation to the West, and whose professed ignorance in regard to foreign matters, whatever reason there may be to distrust it, cannot be entirely put to the credit of dissimulation. To sum up, we believe that the traces of a Christian influence on the myth of Kṛishṇa are highly problematic; that they do not with any clearness appear till much later in certain peculiarities of worship; and that at any rate this influence has told on points of such secondary importance that the Christian derivation of the doctrine and the sentiment of faith, such as they have developed in the sectarian religions, must be set aside as absolutely improbable.[1]

Bhakti, to which we now return after this long digression, has always for its immediate object the divine being, conceived, or rather represented, under the most

[1] In regard to this whole question of the ancient effects of Christianity on the religion of India, the reader will consult with advantage the highly exhaustive and impartial *résumé* given by Dr. J. Muir in the Introduction to his Metrical Translations from Sanskrit Writers, 1879 (compare Rev. Critique, October 30, 1875, p. 275); and C. P. Tiele, Christus en Kṛishṇa, in the Theolog. Tijdschr., 1877, No. 1, p. 63. On the side of Professor Weber stands F. Nève, Des Elements Etrangers du Mythe et du Culte de Kṛishṇa, 1876.

definite form, and with attributes the most personal. It addresses itself less to Vishṇu than to Kṛishṇa or Râma, less to Çiva than Bhairava, or some other of his manifestations. It has thus proved one of the most efficient causes in breaking up the sects. As early as the Mahâbhârata there are obscure allusions to a false Vâsudeva (Vâsudeva signifying son of Vasudeva, that is to say, Kṛishṇa-Vishṇu), who is called the Vâsudêva of the Puṇḍras, a tribe of Bengal.[1] On the other hand, notwithstanding its spiritualistic leanings, it has developed into idolatrous forms. By reason of its attempts to define the deity it has confounded him sometimes with his image; and just as it has distinguished between different forms of the same divinity, it comes at length to distinguish between different images of the same form. It has predilections for particular localities. In the popular songs, for instance, care is often taken to state exactly, while appending the name of the sanctuary, to what Hari or Hara the *bhakta*, or devotee,[2] regards himself as belonging; and it is difficult to say in this case whether it is the god or his idol that is the object of worship.

Considered at first as a simple fact, which it was enough to affirm without other explanation, it was not long before it was subjected to analysis. Different degrees and different shades were discovered in it. A distinction was drawn between *çânti*, quiet repose, calm and contemplative piety, and *dâsatva*, the slave state, surrender of the whole will to God, and between this last and different degrees of the active sentiment of love, such as *sâkhya*, friendship, *vâtsalya*, filial affection, and *mâdhurya*, ecstatic susceptibility;[3] these last shades being peculiar rather to the Vishnuites, but appearing also among certain peculiarly spiritualistic Çivaite sects, such as the Tamîl Sittars, who say in one of their collections, "The ignorant think that God and love are

[1] Mahâbhârata, i. 6992; ii. 583, 1096, 1270. The Agni Purâṇa (xii. 29) identifies him with King Jarâsandha.

[2] See F. Kittel in Ind. Antiq., ii. 307; iv. 20.

[3] H. H. Wilson, Select Works, vol. i. p. 163.

different; none see that they are one. If all men knew that God and love were one, they would live towards each other in peace, regarding love as God himself."[1] In its highest sense it is synonymous with *yoga*, the mystic union in which the soul feels that "it is in God, and that God is in it."[2] At the same time there reappears, from a new point of view, however, a very old theory, that of the kind of acts which are adapted to develop and nourish it, such as the practice of observances and worship, spiritual exercises, contemplation, an ascetic life, each sect having its own standard for estimating the importance of these acts, some, such as the Râmânujas (Vishnuites) and the Smârtas (Çivaites), attaching a great value to attention to minutiæ in the observances; others, such as the Râmânandis (Vishnuites) and the Liṅgâyits (Çivaites), affecting more or less to despise these; the Vaishṇavas inclining in general to idealism and meditation; the Çaivas devoting themselves more to observances and mortifications. But these acts are only aids to *bhakti*; they do not generate it. It is a primal fact, existing prior to knowledge. "He who has faith," says the Bhagavad Gîtâ, "attains to science."[3] So that at its origin at least it is either an *a priori* act of the will or a gift of God.

In this way the sects were led to elaborate the doctrine of grace, to which, on the other hand, the speculations on the divine omnipotence and omnipresence also led up. We have already seen the opposite interpretations to which this doctrine was subjected in the metaphysics of Çivaism. We meet with the same diversity of view, only still more pronounced, among the adherents of Vishnuism. All the Vaishṇavas ascribe in the main the initiative in grace to God. In incarnating himself the deity anticipates human weakness, and the theory of the Avatâras presupposes that

[1] R. Caldwell, Comparative Grammar of the Dravidian Languages, Introd, p. 147, 2d ed. It is proper to remark, however, that the word which Caldwell renders by "God," *çivam*, it would be perhaps more correct to translate by "salvation."

[2] Bhagavad Gîtâ, ix. 29; Nârada Pañcarâtra, i. 36.

[3] iv. 39.

of exterior operations of grace, or prevenient grace. But on the question of interior operations of grace they are divided, some recognising here only the irresistible and free action of God, others admitting the co-operation of man in the work of salvation. It was especially among the sects that arose out of the reform of Râmânuja that this controversy assumed such importance. Agreeably to Hindu habits of thought, each opinion was formulated in a figurate argument. Those on the one side held by the *argument from the cat;* God, they said, seizes the soul and saves it, just as a cat carries away its little ones far from danger. Those on the other side appealed to the *argument from the monkey;* the soul, they said, seizes hold of God and saves itself by him, just as the young one of the monkey escapes from danger by clinging on to the side of its mother. These questions gave rise to many others: How can God, if he is just and good, resolve to choose? How, if he is all-powerful, can there be an action outside of his? Are faith and grace, when once obtained, capable of being forfeited? From these questions, but for the tinge of local colouring, we could sometimes fancy ourselves transported into the heart of the Western world, and in the midst of controversies between Arminians and Gomarists. But we are very soon brought back into India when we see that this grace is immediately personified in Lakshmî or Râdhâ, and that the very theologians who discuss these positions are often in close affinity with the Çâktas.

The more the doctrine of *bhakti* is developed in this way the more it becomes extravagant. From being the first and indispensable condition of salvation, it by degrees becomes the only one. A single act of faith, a single sincere invocation of the name of God, cancels a whole life of iniquity and crime. Hence the importance attached as early as the Bhagavad Gîtâ [1] to the *last thought,* and the idea of attaining complete possession of this thought by

[1] viii. 5; 6; 13.

an act of suicide, of throwing one's self into the fire after being translated to a state of grace, or drowning one's self in some sacred river. Hence, too, that maxim, which has been fatal to so many mystic sects, that the acts of the true devotee, of the *bhakta*, are indifferent, and that the man who has once experienced the effects of grace, whatever he may do, can sin no longer. From one exaggeration to another, *bhakti* came at length to be sublated. As the result of ascribing the most surprising results to a minimum of intention, they came at length not to require any intention at all. In the Purâṇas it is enough, even in the case of the greatest criminal, when at the point of death, to pronounce by chance some syllables forming one of the names of Vishṇu or Çiva, in order to attain salvation. In the Nârada Pañcarâtra, one of the books which displays most enthusiasm in professing the doctrine of *bhakti*, a Brahman of no great faith, after having unsuspectingly partaken of the remains of some consecrated food and given some of it to his wife, is himself eaten up by a tiger; the wife burns herself on the funeral pile of her husband, and the three participants, the Brahman, his wife, and the tiger, being purified by this unconscious act of communion, go straight to *gôloka*, "the world of the cows," or the supreme heaven of Kṛishṇa.[1]

With these fanatical doctrines there is closely connected another characteristic feature of Hinduism, and the most noteworthy novelty, perhaps, in connection with the historic sects—the deification, namely, of the *guru*, founder, which almost always involves the duty of absolute devotion to the person of the existing *gurus*, who are the heirs of his powers either through blood or consecration. In the Brahmanism of antiquity, homage is paid to the holy men of ancient times, to the inspired founders of the school to which the worshipper belongs, and the most imperative directions are given in regard to the immediate *guru* or spiritual preceptor. The latter is more than a father;

[1] Nârada Pañçarâtra, ii. 69-77.

the pupil owes to him a perfect obedience (*çuçrûshâ*) during the entire term of his novitiate, and a pious regard to the end of his days.[1] But he owes him nothing further, and his apprenticeship once terminated, he expects nothing more from him.[2] In the neo-Brahmanic religions, these relations appear to have continued for long nearly the same; the ancient sects, at least, are all without the founder's name. From the twelfth century, on the contrary, the founder rises to the rank of Buddha or Jina; he becomes what the Prophet or the Imams are for the Moslem, a revealer, a supernatural saviour. He is confounded with the god of whom he is an incarnation. Like him, he is entitled to *bhakti;* and if the sect admits of a traditional hierarchy, his successors share more or less in the same privilege. Râmânuja, Râmânanda, Anandatîrtha, Basava, and many others who established subordinate divisions, or who have been distinguished as saints or poets, were from an early date regarded as Avatâras of the deity, whether Vishṇu or Çiva. Caitanya, Vallabhâcârya, Nânak, and the majority of the reformers of more recent times, were treated as such during their lifetime. The most orthodox Vedântins themselves claim as much in the end for Çaṅkara; and even in our own time, the chief of the Smârtas of Çṛiṅgeri, in Mysore, who is reputed to have succeeded to his *gaddî*, or seat, assumes the title of *jagadguru*, or "*guru* of the world," to which is attached the attribute of infallibility.[3] Thus in certain sects there was instituted a sort of Lamaism, which imparted to them no small consistency and stability. But with others not so well organised or so well favoured by circumstances, the fanatical worship of the *guru* was as much a principle of division as of discipline. Secessions

[1] Açvalây. Gr. S., iii. 4, 4; Apastamba Dh. S., i. 1, 13–17; Manu, ii. 146, 148; Nirukta, ii. 4 (= Manu, ii. 144; Saṃhitopanishadbr., iii.).

[2] Apastamba Dh. S., i. 13, 5; 18–21. The case, however, in which the pupil might prefer to remain all his life with the *guru* is not unprovided for: Gautama, iii. 5; Manu, ii. 243, 244.

[3] A. C. Burnell, Vaṃçabrâhmaṇa, Pref., p. xiii.

began to multiply no longer on questions of doctrine but on questions respecting persons; divine honours were bestowed with extreme facility; and communities, sprung from the same sect, connected with the same founder, but at variance only in regard to the choice of an immediate chief, who was deified in his turn, were as profoundly divided at times as others who worshipped different gods. We shall see by and by to what extremes certain branches of Hinduism were led by this superstition. Here we shall only add that, side by side with these novel applications of *bhakti*, theology retired into the background, and was simplified to a singular degree. Authority, instead of resting, as of old, on a more or less fanciful agreement with immemorial tradition, came now to reside entirely in the word merely of the *guru*. Thus we see the majority of the new sects almost as careful to define their origin as those of former times were to disguise theirs. The sects did not always abjure the ancient sacred literature, and the Vedas, the Purâṇas, the epics, &c., retained in general the halo of sanctity which of old belonged to them. But the books of the sect that emanated directly or indirectly from the *guru* were no longer deduced from them. For want of such writings every kind of sacred code came to be dispensed with, and thus among several sects we see this old feature of the religions of India completely disappearing, that they were, as was the boast, "religions of the book."

Finally, it is chiefly owing to the undue importance assigned to *bhakti* that Vishnuism gradually lost sight of the heroic side of its legends; that it preferred to fall back upon the idyllic episodes in the history of Kṛishṇa and Râma; that it made divine love speak more and more the language of human passion, and that it became at length an erotic religion. This tendency is visible in several Purâṇas; it was expressed with singular effect in the Bhâgavata, which, translated as it is into most of the dialects, Aryan as well as Dravidian, of India, contributed more than any other writing to spread it; and it appeared with still more intensity in the popular adaptations of this work, such as the Hindî *Premsâgar*,[1] the "Ocean of Love," the spirit of which is amply enough indicated by the mere title. The joyful and tender idyll of the groves of Vṛindâvan became a mystic romance of the relations of the soul with God, and a principal source of nourishment to piety. The enthusiasm of faith and the inexhaustible liberality of grace found their symbol in the sensual ardour of the Gopîs, and in the eagerness of the deity to respond to them, and to give himself entirely to all at once. Or else in those same amours to which Kṛishṇa surrenders himself, but which cannot make him forget Râdhâ, the true object of his affections, we have a picture of the wanderings of the soul (for Kṛishṇa is also the universal soul), and the ineffable blessedness which it experiences when, restored to itself and yielding to the invitations of grace, it throws itself into the arms of God. These descriptions, which have never been distinguished for moral purity,[2] soon became licentious. In the lyric drama of the Bengalese poet Jayadeva, in the twelfth century, entitled *Gîtagovinda*,[3] or the "Song of the Shepherd" (*Govinda*, shepherd, is an epithet of Kṛishṇa), which has been often compared with the Song of Songs, and which recalls also certain productions of Sufism, the sensual delirium defies all translation; and we do not know which is more astounding, the lewdness of imagination or the devout frenzy which have inspired these burning stanzas.

This erotic mysticism has, with few exceptions, infected nearly all the branches of Vishnuism, the religions of

[1] It has been edited several times, by E. Eastwick among others, 1851.

[2] See Hauvette-Besnault, Pantchâdhyâyî, ou les Cinq Chapitres sur les Amours de Crichna avec les Gopîs, extrait du Bhâgavata Purâṇa, livre x., in Journal Asiatique, vol. v., 5th ser., 1865.

[3] Often edited, by Lassen among others, "Gitagovinda, Jayadevæ Poetæ Indici Drama Lyricum," with a Latin translation, 1836.

Râma as well as those of Kṛishṇa. But it has manifested itself in a peculiarly intense fashion among two new sects which arose about the same time, at the commencement of the sixteenth century, in Northern India. One of these, which prevails most in the Eastern districts, had for its founder a Brahman of Nadiyâ in Bengal, a poor enthusiastic visionary, known by the surname of Caitanya,[1] who proclaimed himself to be an incarnation of Kṛishṇa, and who is revered as such by his followers. His principal disciples, in particular his own brother Nityânand, and Advaitânand, another Brahman, who appears to have taken a leading part in the formation of the sect, are likewise accepted as having been manifestations of the deity. Their descendants, who occupy the first rank among the *gosains*,[2] doctors, all inherited this sacred character, and continue to the present time the principal centre of authority in the sect. This last, however, professes very little of a dogmatic nature, especially in Bengal, where it draws its recruits indiscriminately from the lowest castes, faithful in this respect to the example of Caitanya, who gathered about himself people of every birth, and even Mussulmans.[3] The *bhakti* of Kṛishṇa, Râdhâ, and Caitanya, and the superstitious respect for the *guru*, which has been carried to the extent of worship, constitute nearly the entire creed of these popular communities. Like all the Vishnuites, they entertain a devout regard for the sanctuary of Jagannâtha in Orissa, and those of Mathurâ, the birthplace of Kṛishṇa, where the principal *gosains* reside. But the essential act of their peculiar worship is the *kîrtan*, "the glorification," which they celebrate in common, and in which, by means of long-drawn litanies and hymns,

[1] One of the terms used to denote the supreme intelligence.

[2] *Gosain*, in Sanskrit *gosvâmin*, "possessor of cows," which, like all the words signifying "shepherd," is also one of Kṛishṇa's names, denotes in general one who professes the life of a religious; it is applied, moreover, in a special sense, as well among Vishnuites as Çivaites, to the members of certain brotherhoods.

[3] The author of the Dabistân (ii. 185, 193) bears testimony in a general way to the tolerant spirit of the sects of the Vishnuite Vairâgins.

mingled with dances, and sometimes followed by a kind of love-feast, they rival each other in the excited worship they pay to the Shepherd of Vṛindâvan. These hymns, or *padas*, in Hindî and in ancient Bengalî, several of which date from a period prior to the time of Caitanya, and which, with certain biographies of the founder, constitute their true literature, are all erotic, and almost all licentious.[1] It is not surprising, therefore, that the moral standard among this sect should be rather low. What is much more surprising is, that it has not sunk still lower into practices absolutely immoral. The higher classes, in Bengal at least, spurn it;[2] in the upper provinces, where it is composed of better elements, it is held in more esteem, and reckons among its adherents individuals of influence and education.

The other sect, founded, like that of Caitanya, in the beginning of the sixteenth century, originated with Vallabhâcârya, a Brahman, who was born in the district of Campâran, on the borders of Nepâl, and was of a family of Southern extraction. After long travels, he took up his residence at Gokula, on the Jumnâ, amidst the very scenes where the infancy of Krishṇa was passed. This sect is therefore commonly called, after the name of its chiefs, the *Gokulastha Gosains*, or the "Saints of Gokula." The forty-eight disciples of Vallabhâcârya disseminated its principles in the different districts of the Peninsula; but its followers are most numerous in Hindostan and the Presidency of Bombay. Without scorning the inferior castes,

[1] J. Beames has given specimens of this literature in Ind. Antiq., i. 215, 323; ii. i. 37. The reader will find others in "The Literature of Bengal, being an Attempt to trace the Progress of the National Mind in its various Aspects, as reflected in the Nation's Literature," by Ar Cy Dae, Calcutta, 1877. The only blemish of this charming little work is that it puts too favourable a construction upon things. Among the works which belong, in a more general way, to the Vishnuite literature of Bengal, the Caitanyacandrodaya, or "the rising of the moon of Caitanya," a glorification in the form of a drama of the founder of the sect, has been edited by Râjendralâla Mitra in the Bibliotheca Indica.

[2] Interesting particulars will be found on the present state of the Caitanyas of Bengal and Orissa in W. Hunter's Statistical Account of Bengal, *passim*, principally in vol. xix. p. 50 *seq.*

its ranks are largely recruited from the well-to-do classes; one-half, for instance, of the rich merchants of Bombay belong to it. Its *gosains*, or doctors, very few of whom live in retreat or celibacy, are themselves often bankers or merchants, and they take advantage of an unsettled mode of life, which leads them from sanctuary to sanctuary, from one end of India to another, to combine the pursuits of business with those of piety. In short, the supreme authorities of the sect, the direct descendants of Vallabhâcârya, who by themselves alone form a numerous tribe (being divided into seven principal branches, each branch sprung from one of the seven grandsons of the founder), are almost all people of influence, even outside the circle of their faithful followers, who live in opulence, and whose right to the pompous title of Mahârâja is conceded without challenge. Vallabhâcârya appears to have been better than an ordinary mystic. He is one of the authorities of the Vedânta, on which he has left several treatises, written in the idealistic spirit of the Advaita; and he gave proof of no small intellectual strength and courage in daring openly to repudiate the theories of asceticism in a country where the most sensual doctrines usually affect the language of renunciation. He taught that to renounce well-being was to insult the deity, and that worship ought to be celebrated with expressions of joy. His adherents to-day are but little taken up with the Vedânta, and Epicureanism is only the least of their faults. To whatever extent they may have gone beyond the lessons of their masters, they are in point of fact one of the most corrupt sects in India. Of the writings of their founder they have preserved little, except his commentary on the Bhâgavata Purâṇa, the tenth book in which, the most erotic of the whole, constitutes, along with the Premsâgar, nearly the whole body of the literature they possess that is intended to edify. Like the Caitanyas, they worship the Shepherd of Vṛindâvan, the lover of Râdhâ, and the Gopîs: and, by a refinement of morbid piety, they represent him with the features of a child, as *Bâla Gopâl, Bâla Lâl,* "the Little Shepherd," "the Little Darling." They surround his images with a worship which, in public as well as private, is attentive to external punctilios, and to which women especially address themselves with enthusiastic fervour. Like the Vaishṇavas of Bengal, they seek opportunities of exciting their enthusiasm in common, but they do this in a manner still more questionable; and their *râsmaṇḍalis*, which they celebrate among themselves, in imitation of the gambols of Kṛishṇa and the Gopîs, display extreme licentiousness. No sect has carried the idolatrous worship of the *guru* so far. All the descendants of Vallabhâcârya, whether personally estimable or not, are worshipped as incarnations of Kṛishṇa. The saliva which they eject while chewing the betel-nut, the water which they have used to wash their feet, are greedily swallowed by the faithful.[1] These last owe to them the triple *samarpaṇa*, the threefold surrender of *tan, man, dhan*, body, mind, and fortune; and for the women of the sect it is the greatest of blessings to be distinguished by them and to serve their pleasure. A score of years ago the single Presidency of Bombay could reckon up about seventy of these men-gods, and a *procès célèbre* before the High Court in 1861 supplied evidence to show that they are not slack in asserting their prerogatives.[2]

Like all the branches of Hinduism, these sects are in their turn subdivided into smaller. Even among that of the Vallabhâcâryas, which is one of the most compact, there are groups which are not in communion with the rest of the community. Of the dissentients, some are connected with a movement for reform, while others even go beyond the principal sect in extravagance. Such,

[1] These practices, which recall those of Tibetan Lamaism, are also met with among other sects: Dabistân, ii. 112; Ind. Antiq., viii. 292.

[2] The pleadings in this case, with a history of the sect prefixed, are recorded in the anonymous work, History of the Sect of Mahârâjas or Vallabhâchâryas in Western India, 1865.

among the Caitanyas, are the *Kartâbhâjs*, "the faithful ones of the Creator," who originated at the close of the last century, and who recognise no other god than the *guru*.[1] Such, moreover, are the *Râdhâvallabhîs*, who date from the end of the sixteenth century, and worship Kṛishṇa, so far as he is the lover of Râdhâ; and the *Sakhîbhâvas*, "those who identify themselves with the Friend" (fem.), that is to say, with Râdhâ, who have adopted the costume, manners, and occupations of women.[2] These two last sects are in reality Vishnuite Çâktas, among whom we must also rank a great many individuals, and even entire communities, of the Caitanyas, the Vallabhâcâryas, and the Râmânandis. Like the Çivaite Çâktas, they have observances of the *left hand*, which they keep secret. They have special Tantras, of which little is yet known; the *Brahmavaivarta Purâṇa*, which is better known, belongs radically to the same literature.[3]

It is not difficult to understand the mischief which these impure beliefs must have at length produced. It would be to display great ignorance, however, of the immense resources of the religious sentiment to presume that the effect of these must have been necessarily and universally demoralising. The common people have a certain safeguard in the very grossness of their superstition; and among the higher ranks there are many souls that are at once mystically inclined and pure-hearted who know how to extract the honey of pure love from this strange mixture of obscenities. That is a touching legend, for instance, of that young queen of Udayapura, a contemporary of Akbar (in the end of the sixteenth century), Mîrâ Bâî, who renounced her throne and her husband rather than abjure Kṛishṇa, and who, when close pressed by her persecutors, went and threw herself at the feet of the image

[1] On this sect see Hunter, Statistical Account of Bengal, i. 73; ii. 53.

[2] They appear to have been numerous in the seventeenth century: Dabistân, ii. pp. 182, 185.

[3] See particularly the analysis of the fourth section, the Kṛishṇakhaṇḍa, in Aufrecht's Catalogue, pp. 26–27.

of her god, exclaiming, "I have abandoned my love, my wealth, my kingdom, my husband. Mîrâ, thy servant, comes to thee, her refuge; oh, take her wholly to thyself! If thou knowest me to be free from every stain, accept me. Except thee, no other will have compassion on me; pity me, therefore. Lord of Mîrâ, her well beloved, accept her, and grant that she be no more parted from thee for ever!" Upon this the image opened, and Mîrâ Bâî disappeared in its sides.[1] The worship of her, associated with that of her god, gave rise to a new sect, that probably sprang originally from the Vallabhâcâryas, and which subsists still under her name. All these religions, besides, reckon up their severe moralists, who, without breaking with their sect, more or less repudiate its doctrines and practices, whether, retired from the world, they lead the devotee life of the *Vairâgins* ("free from passions," the most common designation of the Vishnuite Sannyâsins), or whether, along with their family, at times with some neighbours, they form little groups in which a profession is made of a more enlightened piety and Puritan tendencies. Whenever this circle goes on enlarging, it gradually expands into an independent community. In this way, for instance, arose among the Caitanyas the *Spashṭhadâyakas*, who recognise no *guru*, and live in convents, men and women together, under the same roof, in the practice of celibacy and chastity. So also among the Vallabhâcâryas the *Carandâsîs* arose, being founded towards the middle of the last century by a merchant of Delhi, Caraṇ Dâs, and his sister Sahaji Bâî; as well as among the Râmânandis, a whole swarm of small sects, of which a pretty considerable number exists still. All these communities are less distinguished for novelty in dogma than for a certain tendency to pietism and austerity of life.

[1] H. H. Wilson, Select Works, vol. i. p. 138.

HINDUISM.

III. REFORMING SECTS.

Kabîr-Panthis and other sects sprung from the reforming movement of Kabîr.—Mussulman influence.—The Sikhs: Nânak and his successors the Gurus.—Guru Arjun and the Adigranth.—Guru Govind and the Holy War.—The Sikh state.—End of Sikh independence: their cultus and principal divisions.—New sects still forming in India.

ALONGSIDE of these somewhat timid protestations, others of a bolder and more uncompromising type were being constantly put forth, one of which, at least, proved highly successful, and all of which, even those which had few direct adherents, exercised a wholesome influence in the midst of the confusion. Combined with what of good remained from the old traditions of the country, these acted on Hinduism as a sort of leaven, which prevented it from decaying by stagnation and corrupting altogether. The most perfect representative, perhaps, of this reforming movement was Kabîr, or, as his disciples, who revere in him an incarnation of the deity, also surname him, Jñânin, "the One who has Knowledge, the Seer." So little is known of a positive kind in regard to this remarkable man, that some have gone so far as to doubt his existence.[1] The most probable hypothesis is that he was born at Benares, and was of the weaver caste; that he was a Vairâgin of the sect of Râmânanda perhaps, as tradition surmises, an immediate disciple of that master, and that he taught at the beginning of the fifteenth century (the legend making him live three hundred years, from 1149 to 1449).

[1] H. H. Wilson, Select Works, vol. i. p. 69.

Kabîr has left no writings, but his sect possesses pretty numerous collections in Hindi, the composition of which is, with more or less reason, ascribed to his first disciples, in which are preserved a great number of the *sayings* of the master, forming at times pieces to some extent in verse, as well as dialogues, reproducing controversies, which are in part certainly imaginary, and in which he is the chief interlocutor. In these teachings of his, Kabîr sets himself against the whole body of Hindu superstitions. He rejects and ridicules the Çâstras and the Purâṇas; he severely chastises the arrogance and hypocrisy of the Brahmans; he rejects every malevolent distinction of caste, religion, and sect. All who love God and do good are brothers, be they Hindus or Mussulmans. Idolatry, and everything which approaches to it or may suggest it, is severely condemned; the temple ought to be only a house of prayer. He tolerates among his disciples neither practices that are too demonstrative, nor singularities of costume, nor any of those external marks which are the distinctive badges of the Hindu sects, and which serve only to divide men. Yet, not to scandalise a neighbour, he enjoins on them conformity to usage in indifferent matters. He recommends renunciation and a contemplative life; but he demands, above all, moral purity, and does not restrict it to one particular kind of life. All authority in the matter of faith and morals belongs to the *guru;* yet obedience to his commands must not be blind obedience, and a reservation is expressly made on behalf of the rights of conscience of the believer.

Of these features, taken separately, there are not many which we do not meet with again more or less elsewhere in the past history of the sectarian religions; but the whole is new, and singularly recalls the quietism of the Moslem. This resemblance has been recognised in India itself; the Mohammedans claim Kabîr as one of themselves, and among the Hindus there is a widespread tradition which represents him as a converted Mussulman. One thing is certain, that Kabîr was much occupied with Islam. His aim obviously was to found a unitary religion, which would unite in the same faith the Hindus and the followers of the Prophet, and with that view he assailed the intolerance of the Koran and the fanaticism of the Mollahs with no less vigour than the prejudices of his compatriots. We cannot doubt that the spectacle of Islam, with its triumphant monotheism, its severely spiritualistic worship, its large fraternity, and its morality practically so incontestably superior to Hinduism, left a very deep impression on his mind. At the same time, this impression appears to have been only quite general. Kabîr was indifferently acquainted with the Mussulman theology; his god is neither that of the Koran nor even that of Sufism, but that of the Vedânta. The mantra of initiation with which he receives his disciples is in the name of Râma, and, notwithstanding the very explicit profession which he makes of monotheism, he seems to have himself admitted—anyhow those who believed in him afterwards admitted—the majority of the personifications of Hinduism. The members of this sect, the *Kabîr-panthis*, "those who follow the path of Kabîr," form at present twelve principal branches, which have remained in communion with one another in spite of sundry differences in regard to both doctrine and practice. Their centre is at Benares, but we meet with them throughout the whole Presidency of Bengal, in Gujarât, in Central India, and as far as the Dekhan. Their number, difficult to estimate because of the pains they take to conform to the customs in the midst of which they live, appears to be pretty considerable. At the end of the last century, their religious order by itself alone contributed, it is said, 35,000 of those who took part in a *melâ* held at Benares, and they are still more influential than numerous. Kabîr himself is revered as a saint by the majority of the Vishnuites; his authority is directly recognised by many reforming sects, and his influence is visible in all of them.

It is thus that the *Dâdû-panthis,* founded at the end of the sixteenth century by a bleacher of the name of Dâdû, and who are numerous among the Rajputs of Ajmeer and Jaypore; the *Bâbâ-lâlîs,* or followers of Bâbâ Lâl, a Rajput of Mâlva, who counted among his adherents the noble and ill-fated brother of Aurangzeb, Dâra Shakôh (in the middle of the seventeenth century); the *Sâdhus,* "the pure ones," very numerous in the neighbourhood of Delhi, and whose founder, Bîrbhân, lived in the second half of the seventeenth century; the *Satnâmis,* "the worshippers of the true name,"[1] who date from the middle of the following century, and are connected with Jîvan Dâs,[2] a man of the military caste, a native of Oude—are all in a way branches sprung from the sect of Kabîr. The *Prân-nâthîs,* or followers of Prân Nâtha, a Kshatriya of Bândelkhând (end of the seventeenth century), who admit indiscriminately Hindus and Mussulmans, interfering with the peculiar beliefs and practices of neither, and exacting no other confession than that of faith in one God;[3] the *Çiva-nârâyaṇis,* founded in the first half of the eighteenth century by Çiva Nârâyaṇa, a Rajput of Ghazipore, who recognise no *gurus* and also profess deism, and many more besides adhere to the same movement. Less direct, but no less evident, is the influence of the same doctrines in the work of Svâmin Nârâyaṇa, who, in the first quarter of the present century, raised his voice in Gujarât against

[1] There has been a sort of revival in this sect lately under the influence of a certain Ghâsi Dâs, who died in 1850, and who had gathered about nearly half a million of followers. Max Müller, Chips from a German Workshop, vol. iv. p. 329.

[2] The full name is Jagjîvan Dâs, "the servant of (him who is) the life of the universe." A very interesting notice of this reformer, his works, his chief disciples, and the present condition of the sect, the level of which appears to have sunk considerably lower, has been recently reproduced in the Indian Antiq., viii. 289 *seq.* The *gaddi,* or seat of the founder, is at the present time still occupied by one of his lineal descendants. The sect buries its dead instead of burning them.

[3] See P. S. Growse, The Sect of the Prân-nâthis, in the Journal of the Asiatic Society of Bengal, vol. xlviii. p. 171 *seq.*

the idolatry and superstitions of his fellow-countrymen, and in particular the impure religious beliefs of the Vallabhâcârya *gosains*. He preached a severe morality, the love of one's neighbour without distinction of caste, and the unity of God; adding that this God, who had incarnated himself of old in Krishṇa, and whose name Vallabhâcârya had unjustly assumed, had condescended to reappear again here below in his own person. Bishop Heber, who met him in the spring of 1825, has left us a curious account of the interview, which might well deserve to be reproduced here *in extenso*.[1] Nothing is better fitted than this account to give us an idea of the indescribable mixture of elevated views and gross superstitions which coalesce together at all stages of Hinduism, and it enables us to touch, so to speak, with the finger all the reservations we must make when we begin to speak of the monotheism of the Hindus. Svâmin Nârâyana, who appeared at this interview at the head of two hundred horsemen, armed to the teeth, then exercised authority, as absolute master, over more than 50,000 believers. At present the sect numbers about 200,000, and, according to a law which regulates all these communities, it is beginning to split up into two groups.

But the most remarkable of the numerous sects connected more or less directly with Kabîr is that of the Sikhs, the "disciples," which alone of all the branches of Hinduism took shape in the end as a national religion, or rather, we should say, gave birth to a nation.[2] The founder of their faith, Nânak, was born in 1469 in the

[1] Narrative of a Journey through the Upper Provinces of India, chap. xxv.

[2] For the general history of the Sikhs consult J. Malcolm, Sketch of the Sikhs, in Asiatic Researches, vol. xi.; H. T. Prinsep, Origin of the Sikh Power in the Punjâb, and the Political Life of the Maharajah Runjeet Singh, Calcutta, 1834, translated into French by X. Raymond, 1836: W. L. MacGregor, History of the Sikhs, 2 vols., 1846; J. D. Cunningham, A History of the Sikhs, 1849. For their religious history see H. H. Wilson, Account of the Civil and Religious Institutions of the Sikhs, in Journ. of the Roy. As. Soc., vol. ix. (1848), reproduced in Select Works, ii. 121, &c.; E. Trumpp, Nânak, der Stifter der Sikhreligion, in the Memoirs of the Academy of Munich, 1876, and especially the Introductory Essays at the beginning of the same author's translation of the Adi-Granth, 1877.

Punjâb, a short way from Lahore, in the commercial caste of the Khatris. For a while he led a wandering life, and it was probably in the course of these travels that he entered into relations with the disciples of Kabîr. Like this last, he constituted himself the apostle of a unitary religion grounded on monotheism and moral purity. "There are neither Hindus nor Mussulmans" was, it is said, the thesis of one of his first sermons, and, like Kabîr, he continues to be held in repute for his sanctity among the Sufis, the Fakirs, and in general the moderately orthodox Mussulmans. But, like him, and others besides, he was a Hindu at bottom; he rejected the Vedas, the Çâstras, the Purâṇas, as well as the Koran; but he retained the majority of the *saṃskâras*, or private ceremonies, which were abolished only a long while after, and he even did not break in an absolute way with caste, which he tolerated as a civil institution, and of which the sect, in spite of attempts afterwards made in the direction of its complete abolition, has always preserved some traces. It has never ceased, for instance, to testify considerable respect for the Brahmans; and almost all the *gurus* are said to have maintained some of them about their person in the character of domestic priests. Moreover, since the publication of the *Granth*, the Bible of the Sikhs,[1] there cannot, in a dogmatic reference, be any longer much question of the profound influence of Islam on the thinking of the founders of this religion. From first to last, both as regards the form and the foundation of its ideas, this book breathes the mystic pantheism of the Vedânta, reinforced by the doctrines of *bhakti*, of grace, and of absolute devotion to the *guru*. It is specially distinguished from the sectarian literature in general by the importance which it attaches to moral precepts, by the simplicity and spiritualistic character of a worship stripped of every vestige of idolatry, and especially by its moderation in regard to mythology, although

[1] The Adi-Granth, or the Holy Scriptures of the Sikhs, translated from the original Gurmukhî, with Introductory Essays, by Dr. E. Trumpp, 1877. Published by order of the English Government.

we find in it a considerable number of the personifications of Hinduism, and even detect at times in it a sort of return to the Hindu divinities. But it would be difficult to eliminate from all this what is due to Mussulman influence. Practically, it is true, the Sikhs came in the end to worship a personal God, and their religion may be defined a deism more or less tinctured with superstition. But that was a modification which it must necessarily undergo, pantheism, which may indeed become the faith of a limited circle of mystics, being inconceivable as the positive belief of a large community. On the other hand, there is no question that contact with the Mussulmans, which has nowhere been more intimate than in these border countries, has had a powerful effect upon the minds and manners of the Sikhs. It is from the followers of the Prophet that they have especially borrowed their military fanaticism and the dogma of the holy war, a notion which is in no respect a Hindu one, but which under the same influence has developed in like manner among other populations of India; for instance, among the Marhattas and certain Rajput tribes. The *Adi-Granth*, "the fundamental book," was compiled by the fifth successor of Nânak, Guru Arjun (1584–1606). He collected in it the poetical pieces left by the founder and the three *gurus* who came after him, and he added to these his own compositions, as well as a great number of sentences and fragments by Râmânanda, Kabîr, the Marhatta poet Nâmdêv, and other sacred personages. Some more additions were made to it by Govind (1675–1708), the tenth and last *guru*, who composed besides a second Granth, entitled "The Granth of the Tenth Reign." These two books, both voluminous, are drawn up in an antiquated form of Punjâbi, called *Gurmukhî*, "that which comes from the mouth of the *guru*." These, along with biographies of the *gurus*[1] and the saints,

[1] These biographies have been in part translated by E. Trumpp in his Introductory Essays at the beginning of his translation of the Adi-Granth.

and a certain number of directions in regard to ritual and discipline, constitute the sacred literature of the sect.

For nearly a century the Sikhs appear to have remained a purely religious community of inoffensive Puritans. As Nânak, though he did not make it the subject of a formal prohibition, had dissuaded his disciples from renouncing active life, the sect, with few exceptions, was composed of industrious heads of families, who were husbandmen or merchants. As infanticide, too, one of the gloomy practices of Hinduism, and much practised among the tribes of the West, Jâts and Rajputs, was among them strictly interdicted, and as its ranks were recruited indifferently from all sections of the population, Mussulman as well as Hindu, it was not long in waxing numerous under the authority of its *gurus*. This authority was absolute. The *guru* is the *mediator* and *saviour;* he is infallible; the believer owes to him a blind obedience, and his rivals, the abettors of heresy, were in the end devoted to the flames, they and their families. Although Nânak speaks in many passages with modesty respecting himself, we cannot doubt that he believed he had a divine mission, which, translated into the Hindu language, amounts to saying that he was an incarnation of Hari, a name for Kṛishṇa-Vishṇu, the most usual designation in the Granth of the supreme being. For himself and his disciples, he was identical with God, and all his successors were, like him, manifestations of the deity. As far as the fifth *guru*, the supreme authority was transmitted by means of consecration, at the hands of the dying titulary, to the worthiest of his disciples.[1] Guru Arjun, the compiler of the Granth, made it hereditary. He was the first to surround himself with the paraphernalia of royalty, and he took advantage of his power to play a political part. He *prayed* for Khusrô,[2] the rebel son of the emperor,

[1] Nânak himself set this example in nominating Angad in preference to his two sons, whose descendants, the *Nânakpotras*, are to this day held in great respect by the Sikhs.

[2] Dabistân, vol. ii. p. 272. The author had had personal relations with the eighth *guru*, Hari Govind.

Jahângir, and perished the same year at Lahore, in the prisons of the Padishah (1606). From this moment the community of the Sikhs rapidly changed into a military theocracy, to which the fierce population of the Jâts supplied a fanatical soldiery. Under the reign of the bigoted Aurangzeb the struggle with the imperial power was resumed, never more to terminate. Teg Bahâdur, the ninth *guru*, was beheaded at Delhi (1675). His son, Govind Singh, whose pontificate was only a long succession of battles, completed the transformation of the sect, or, as it was henceforth called, after a name borrowed from the Arabic, the Khâlsâ, "the property, the portion (of God)." He surrounded it with a body of regulations, under which it became a people by itself, devoted to triumph or extermination.[1] All social inequality was abolished in the heart of the Khâlsâ, every member of which received the aristocratic surname of Singh (in Sanskrit *siṃha*, lion). Costume was regulated in a uniform fashion. With the exception of the religious respect paid to cows, all that recalled the usages, practices, and ceremonies of Hinduism was rigorously proscribed, although Govind himself personally took a part in some of the worst Hindu superstitions, to the extent of sacrificing one of his followers to Durgâ. No connection was to be henceforth tolerated with the unbeliever, with him who had not been admitted as a member of the Khâlsâ by five of the initiated drinking along with him the sherbet of the Pahul. A Sikh was not even to return the salutation of a Hindu. As for the Mussulman, he was bound to put him to death without mercy in whatever place he happened to meet with him. From the moment of initiation he was a soldier. The holy war became his permanent occupation; he was always to go armed, or at least, as a sign of his vocation, to wear on his person some steel,

[1] For the reforms effected by Govind Singh, see Sakhee Book, or the Description of Gooroo Govind Singh's Religion and Doctrines, translated from Gurmukhî into Hindi, and afterwards into English by Sirdar Attar Singh, chief of Bhadour, Benares, 1873.

which became a sort of charm. The deity himself received the name of *Sarba Lohantî*, "all of iron," and by this means certain observances of fetishism crept into this iconoclastic religion. The Sikh soldier addresses his prayer to his sword; the book of the Granth, too, became also the object of a sort of worship.

In this unequal struggle against the formidable empire of Aurangzeb, Guru Govind Singh had in the end to succumb. Hunted like deer, after thirty years of fighting, what remained of his faithful ones were dispersed among the mountains; he himself accepted a post of command in the imperial armies, and fell at last by the hand of an Afghan assassin near Nander, in the territories of the Nizam (1708).[1] The Sikhs had not all adopted his reforms, and he appears to have clearly foreseen that, at the stage which the sect had reached, the personal influence of the *guru* would henceforth be a source of schism rather than of union. When pressed on his deathbed to appoint his successor, he declared that the dignity was abolished, and that the Granth would for the future be the *guru* of the Sikhs.

After his decease the direction of the Khâlsâ in the Punjâb passed into the hands of an ascetic of the name of Bandâ. Thrice under the command of this ferocious chief, the Sikhs issued forth from their retreats in Sirhind, and each of these irruptions was accompanied with massacres such as even India itself has rarely seen the like. Soon after the last of these, they were nearly annihilated by the generals of the Emperor Farokshîr. Bandâ himself was captured and sent to Delhi. After being present for seven consecutive days at the torture of 740 of his companions, not one of whom even winced, and after seeing his son butchered under his very eyes, and his heart taken out by the executioner and thrown in his face, he himself had his life tortured out of him, his flesh being torn with red-hot pincers, while his lips praised God for having chosen him

[1] M. Elphinstone, History of India, vol. ii. p. 564.

to be the executor of his vengeance on the race of the wicked (1716).[1] With the horrors of this merciless war the Sikhs had mixed up internal dissensions. Like Guru Govind, Bandâ had introduced novelties, not into their dogma, but into their usages. He had interfered with the costumes, and to the prohibition of tobacco he had added that of spirituous liquors and animal food (the Sikhs having abstained only from the flesh of the cow). This was a return to the maxims of Hindu devotion. In his fanatical community, in whose eyes the most insignificant matters assumed outrageous proportions, he had met with an infuriated resistance, and blood had flowed like water in the Khâlsâ. As, however, he had only been a chief, and not a divine authority in the manner of the *gurus*, his innovations were abolished easily after his death. From this moment the direction of the sect passed into the hands of a military corporation of zealots, the *Akâlîs*, "the Faithful of the Eternal," instituted, they say, by Guru Govind, who constituted themselves the savage defenders of orthodoxy. When the dissolution of the Mogul empire permitted the Sikhs to regain a footing on the plain, the Akâlîs set themselves up as the guardians of the sanctuary of Amṛitsar, where the original copy of the Granth of Guru Arjun was kept preserved. On great occasions they summoned together here the *Gurmatâ*, "the Council of the Guru," the general assembly of the Sikh chiefs, in which the supreme temporal and spiritual authority of the nation was vested, and which, though it did not ensure a perfectly stable unity to this singular mixture of theocratic oligarchy and military federation, kept up in it, however, a sufficient coherence, and prevented the occurrence of new divisions in the bosom of the Khâlsâ.

Here ends the religious history of the Sikhs; what follows is entirely political. Forty years after the last disaster that befell them, they had recovered to their

[1] M. Elphinstone, History of India, vol. ii. p. 575.

federation the greater part of the Jât Sirdars. In 1764, after the final retreat of the Afghans, they took possession of Lahore, and became the undisputed masters of the Punjâb; they could at that time muster 70,000 cavalry.[1] Ranjit Singh (1797–1839) succeeded in imposing on them the monarchical form of government; but their turbulent fanaticism, which the "Lion of the Punjâb" had been able to hold in check, re-awoke under his feeble successors. Twice over they came, and were shattered to fragments under the charge of British bayonets. At length, in the spring of 1848, the Punjâb was annexed to the possessions of the Company, and the army of the Khâlsâ ceased to exist. At present, the Sikhs, although composed of different ethnic elements, form a race with as marked features as any other in the Peninsula. They have preserved their ancient talent for war, and they supply a contingent of picked men to the Anglo-Indian army. But their fanaticism has gone to sleep. They are outside Hinduism, properly so called, although some of their subdivisions tend to return to it. To the number of 1,200,000 they form a compact population confined to the Punjâb, but they are met with scattered about in small groups all over Hindustan and in some parts of the Dekhan. In a religious point of view they have continued a pretty compact body, although there have arisen among them orders which have taken the form of distinct communities. Such, besides the Akâlîs, already mentioned, and who have no longer the influence they had, are the *Udâsîs*, "the Renunciants," who reject the Granth of Guru Govind, and end their days in a life of asceticism and celibacy; the *Nânakpotras*, the descendants of Nânak, who form a section of the Udâsîs; the *Divânê sâdhs*, "the mad saints," some of whom also practise celibacy, and who, like the preceding, recognise only the Adi-Granth; the *Suthrês*, "the pure ones," and the *Nirmalê sâdhûs*, "the pure saints." These last live together as cenobites; they are mostly men of letters, and

[1] H. T. Prinsep, Origin of the Sikh Power in the Punjâb, p. 29.

incline to an alliance with Hinduism, of which they have adopted many of the practices. As for the Suthrês, they are vagrants, addicted to every vice, despicable and despised, and distinguished in no respect from the worst classes of fakirs and yogins. The worship of the Sikhs is simple and pure. With the exception of Amṛitsar, which is the religious centre of the nation, and a few sanctuaries in places consecrated by the life or the death of gurus and martyrs, they have no holy places. Their temples are houses of prayer. Here they recite pieces and sing hymns extracted from the Granth; and the congregation separates after each believer has received a piece of the *karâh prasâd*, "the effectual offering," a kind of pastry ware consecrated in the name of the *guru*. As tolerant as they were formerly fanatical, they do not object to admit to their religious services strangers, whom they allow even to participate in their communion. It is true that under this tolerance there lies concealed no little lukewarmness, and that, in the opinion of the best judge in this matter, Dr. Trumpp, the translator of the Adi-Granth, "Sikhism" is a religion which is on the wane.[1]

We have cut short this review of the Hindu sects, although the movement we have tried to trace is far from exhausted. Hari has not ceased to come down to the earth, and even at the present time among the people, especially in the country districts, new religious bodies are in process of formation here and there around new incarnations. These manifestations, which are always springing up anew, and to which, moreover, the upper classes and the Brahmans have for long remained indifferent, are interesting to study, because they bear testimony to the unquenchable thirst after a revelation with which this people is possessed more than any other race in Asia. But the description would teach nothing new in regard to Hinduism. Even among the sects of the past we have selected only those which have appeared to us to contri-

[1] Adi-Granth, Introduction, p. cxviii.

bute best towards the exposition of the essential doctrines, or such as have supplied us with some feature in characterisation of one of the phases of this singular religious whole. Important communities have in this way been passed over in silence; there has been no mention, for instance, either of the *Nimbârkas*, one of the most ancient surviving branches of Vishnuism, which claim to be related to the astronomer Bhâskara (born 1114),[1] or of the *Vishṇubhaktas* of the Dekhan, who worship Vishṇu under the names of Pâṇḍuraṅga and Viṭhṭhala, and who are very numerous among the Vaishṇavas of the Mahratta countries.[2] To have mentioned these sects, as well as many others, would have been, within the limits possible to this treatise, only to have added names to names, a very useless proceeding after all, when the discussion respects a country like India, where the religious varieties reckon by thousands. Besides, certain additions, absolutely indispensable, will be more in place in the investigation which we have still to make into the worship, and, in some measure, into the externals of Hinduism, a subject which we have till now touched on only incidentally, and of which it is of some consequence, however, to take a rapid and general survey.

[1] H. H. Wilson, Select Works, i. 150.

[2] Lassen, Ind. Alterthumsk., iv. 589. The celebrated Marhatta poet Tukârâma was a zealous devotee of this god, whose principal sanctuary is at Pandharpur; see Ind. Antiq., ii. 272.

HINDUISM.

IV. WORSHIP.

Diversity of the Hindu systems of worship.—These independent of one another.—Manifold divinities to which they address their worship.—Worship of the stars; that of Gaṇeça.—Worship of the sun: Iranian influences.—The Neo-Brahmanic religions essentially idolatrous: origin and development of the worship of images.—Sacred symbols: the liṇga and the yoni: the Çâlagrâma and the Tulasî.—Sacred plants and trees.—Sacred animals: the cow, the bull, and the monkey: the worship of the serpent.—Private religious observances: the Acâra and its varieties.—Mystic formulæ and litanies.—Forms of public worship: the Grâmadevatâs.—Worship and service in the temples.—Offerings and victims.—Communion.—Festivals and Melâs.—Pilgrimages: the Ganges and other sacred rivers.—Benares.—Religious suicide.—Mathurâ, Gayâ, Jagannatha, Somnâth, &c.—Statistics of pilgrimages: their importance in preserving a certain unity in Hinduism.—Limits of Hinduism: excommunicated castes.—The aborigines, Dravidians, and others, and their religions.—A retrospective glance.—Religious future of India: Hinduism falls in pieces, and seems to have no successor.—Negative results of the Mussulman conquests and Christian missions.—The Brahma-Samâj.

THOUGH it is hardly necessary to say so, there is a still greater diversity in India between the forms of worship than there is between the systems of doctrine. Not only has each figure in the pantheon his own, but usually he has several, as many sometimes as the names he has and the number of his principal sanctuaries. This pantheon itself is formed of heterogeneous elements, in which all the religious systems which have arisen in the course of ages have left their several contributions. Alongside of the great sectarian divinities and their personal surroundings, their wives, fathers, mothers, sons, brothers, and servants, we meet with the ancient gods of Brahmanism, Agni, Indra, Varuṇa, &c., powers that have fallen mostly into decay, but which survive in what remains of the ancient ritual, especially in the domestic ceremonies. The heroes of the epic legend, such as Hanuman, the monkey associated with Râma, or the five sons of Pâṇḍu and their common spouse Draupadî, whose worship is highly popular throughout the Peninsula,[1] are found here again associated with impersonations of a very different origin, such as the Gaṅgâ (the Ganges), the Sun, Moon, and Planets.[2] Each several district, especially in the Dravidian South, has besides its own local deities, which have been identified in the main with the general types of Hinduism, but rarely to the extent of being absolutely confounded with them. Finally, the *personnel* literally baffles calculation, when we add to it, as we must, a crowd of powers without names, of subordinate rank in the literature, but which at times play a prominent part in the prepossessions of the people, such as the Bhûtas or demons, the Vetâlas or vampires, the Piçâcas and other mischievous goblins, the Pretas or ghosts, the Yakshas

[1] In the single district of South Arkot, which surrounds Pondicherry, there are not less than 500 temples dedicated to the Pâṇḍavas; Ind. Antiq., vii. 127.

[2] For the Ganges and the Sun see *infra*. The Moon, Candra, early likened to Soma, was, from the time of the Brâhmaṇas, the centre of numerous legends, and the object of divine honours. The Çaṅkaravijaya, ch. xliv., and the Mussulman writers (Ketâb-al-fihrist, in Reinaud's Mémoire sur l'Inde, p. 293, and Shahrastâni, t. ii. p. 367, translated by Haarbrücker), speak of a sect of Moon-worshippers. The Planets, Graha, are rarely referred to with any certainty in the ancient literature. They were, however, not quite unknown, as is for most part alleged, since they are invoked, Atharva-V., xix. 9, 7, and 10. Mention is made of them besides in the verses of the *khila*, inserted under the name of Râtrisûkta after Rig-Veda, x. 127; in the Maitrî Up., vi. 16; in Manu, i. 24; vii. 121, &c. They figure, along with the sun and the moon, and doubtless with a religious signification, on the coins of the Satrap kings. Lassen, Ind. Alterthumsk., ii. 918 and 1134, 2d ed. The cultus of these stars is prescribed at length by Yajñavalkya, i. 294–307. Compare Bṛihat Parâçara Saṃhitâ, ix., in Dharmaçâstrasaṅgraha, ii. 250 *seq.* Varâha Mihira, Yogoyâtrâ, vi. 2–18, in Ind. Stud., xiv. 326 *seq.*, describes their images; and a sect of planet-worshippers is mentioned in ch. xlv. of the Çaṅkaravijaya. It is impossible at present to say to what extent the Hindus had an independent planetary astrology. What we know of it is derived from the Greeks, as the

or gnomes, the Vidyâdharas or sylphs, the Râkshasas or ogres, the Nâgas, a species of *genii*, half men, half serpent, and the endless number of local deities.[1] There is no mountain, river, rock, cave, tree of any note, which has not its *genius loci*; no village especially which has not its *grâma devatâ*, which, even where it is one of the figures of the great pantheon, nevertheless appears to the popular conscience distinct from the same divinity as worshipped elsewhere.

Almost all these forms of worship are more or less independent of one another. There are indeed allied gods, but these alliances are far from being stable. At any rate, there are no longer, in the modern religious ritual, observances to be compared with the grand Vedic ceremonials, where all the powers of heaven and earth participated in common in a prescribed series of acts of homage. What of this nature still remains is either a relic or an imitation of ancient Brahmanism. These forms of worship are independent in still another sense. Speculation, which at times asserted itself so freely in regard to the doctrines, had much less hold on the practices. On this side it came into collision, and that not among the masses only, with an array of habits and beliefs before which sectarian enthusiasm itself has almost always in the long-run recoiled exhausted. The idea even, so universally accepted, that all things depend in the end on an Içvara, a sovereign lord, has been transfused very imperfectly into the worship. Here the gods are small or great according to the nature and extent of their functions; within the limit of these functions they are not mere lieutenants. Hence, among the many ways that offer of securing the favour of Heaven, every Hindu has his own predilections; but, unless it be from superior education or connection with a rigid sect, he is indifferent to none of those which

name Horâ implies, by which it is designated. Stellar astrology, however much its origin is still matter of debate, is of ancient date among them, and ever since the Vedic epoch certain groups of stars, particularly the Nakshatras, have been objects of worship. See *supra*, pp. 23 and 41.

[1] See a curious invocation of these many-formed beings in Varâha Mihira, Yogoyâtrâ, vi. 20–29, in Ind. Stud., xiv. 329. See also *supra*.

are within his reach. In spite of all her high aspirations, we must say then that, taken in the mass, India has in practice remained polytheistic;[1] and it is easy to understand that it has necessarily taken the Mussulmans, and after them the Europeans, some time to see that beyond all the motley colouring of these religions there existed among these *gentiles* a confessed theology and speculations worthy of account in the history of the human spirit.[2]

Although there are still here and there populations in a backward state (and we are speaking here only of Hindu populations, or those who have more or less adopted Hindu manners), whose whole religion consists in conforming to custom, and worshipping the fetish of the village, this polytheism has at the present time hardly any other centre than Çiva or Vishṇu. But the preeminence of these two divinities has not always been so universally recognised, and in the past other forms of worship have contended with theirs for the first rank. Our knowledge of the most of these last religions is very limited. They have left no literature, and, except their preference for a particular god, we know nothing of their theology. We do not even know whether they ever had a body of doctrines which was peculiar to them, whether they in the end took shape as real sects, or whether we ought not rather to regard them simply either as popular superstitions, or more or less prevalent devotions, retaining always something, however, of a personal element. This is certainly the case with the majority of those which the pseudonymous author of the Çaṅkaravijaya passes in review when they are not mere creations of his fancy.

[1] Gauḍapâda, who lived probably at the end of the seventh century, mentions besides a dogmatic polytheism in his çlokas on the Mâṇḍûkya Upanishad (ii. 21, 424, ed. of the Bibl. Ind.). He meant doubtless to describe the ancient Mîmânsistes, who accepted no Îçvara.

[2] "It has now come to light that the generally received opinion of the Hindus being polytheists has no foundation in truth; for although their tenets admit positions that are difficult to be defended, yet that they are worshippers of God, and only one God, are incontrovertible points." Ayeen Akbari, translated by Gladwin, vol. iii. pp. iv., v., Calcutta, 1876.

There is not the slightest evidence, for instance, that communities were ever formed under the names of Agni, Indra, Yama, Varuṇa, Kuvera (Plutus), Manmatha (Cupid), the Gandharva Viçvâvasu,[1] &c. Regarding Vâc or Sarasvatî,[2] the wife of Brahmâ and the goddess of eloquence, we know that she was the patroness of Kashmir; but Kashmir was, nevertheless, Çivaite. The religions of Garuḍa, the bird of the sun, of Çesha, the king of the serpents, of the Bhûtas, or demons,[3] have never been able to be more than popular beliefs, such as we may still see among many tribes. That of Hiraṇyagarbha or Brahmâ[4] was the fruit, on the contrary, of learned tradition. It is probable that, though it was never far spread, it was more so formerly than now, when it is professed only by Brahmans specially scrupulous on the point of orthodoxy. Besides, there are still here and there *Gâṇapatyas,* who keep up a quite special devotion for Gaṇapati or Gaṇeça, "the chief of the troops (which attend on Çiva)," the god with the elephant's head, who clears away obstructions and inspires prudent resolutions, whom every Hindu, however, invokes before undertaking anything, and who, in his character of patron of letters and arts, is mentioned at the beginning of almost all books. The Çaṅkaravijaya distinguishes as many as six subdivisions of the Gâṇapatyas, who must have each worshipped a particular form of the god.[5] But the most powerful of all these religions, the only one which has really been able to rival those of Vishṇu and Çiva, the only one withal concerning which we have numerous

[1] Çaṅkaravijaya, ch. xii., xxxiii., xxxiv., xxxv., xxxii., xxxi. l., ed. of the Bibl. Ind. For Yama see Mudrârâkshasa, act i., where Nipuṇaka enters.

[2] Çaṅkaravijaya, ch. xxi.

[3] Çaṅkaravijaya, ch. xlviii., li.

[4] Çaṅkaravijaya, ch. xi.

[5] Çaṅkaravijaya, ch. xv.–xviii. Yâjñavalkya, i. 289–293, attaches a quite special importance to the worship of Gaṇeça. It figures prominently in several Purâṇas; for example, in the Brahmavaivarta and the Bhavishya. Besides an Upapurâṇa, the Gaṇeça-Purâṇa is specially consecrated to it. See the analysis in Aufrecht's Oxford Catalogue, pp. 78, 79. Compare Bṛihat Parâçara Saṃhitâ in the Dharmaçâstrasaṅgraha, ii. 247 *seq.*

and positive testimonies, is that of the Sun. Ever since Vedic times the Sun has not ceased to figure prominently in the pantheon, as well as in the poetic and religious literature of India. A great part of the Bhavishya Purâṇa is specially consecrated to him.[1] Traces of his worship are found on the coins of the satrap kings who ruled over Gujarât towards the Christian era,[2] as well as on those of the Indo-Scythian princes.[3] At a later date, in the same region, one at least of the kings of Valabhî is designated in the inscriptions *Adityabhakta*, worshipper of the Sun.[4] A little more towards the north, at Multân, in the Punjâb, a temple was erected to this god, the most celebrated in India, the splendours of which have been described by Hiouen-Thsang and the Mussulman writers,[5] and which was finally destroyed only under Aurangzeb. There were other sanctuaries at Gwalior in Râjastan,[6] in Kashmir,[7] and in Orissa.[8] Perhaps Iranian influences had something to do with the organisation of this worship during the middle age;[9] at any rate, a great

[1] See the extracts from this Purâṇa in Aufrecht's Oxford Catalogue, p. 31 *seq.*

[2] Lassen, Ind. Alterthumsk., ii. 919, 2d ed.

[3] Lassen, *op. cit.*, ii. 832, under the Iranian name of MIIPO and the Greek name of ΉΛΙΟΣ.

[4] Inscriptions of Dharasena II., in Journal of the As. Soc. of Bengal, vol. iv. p. 482, and Ind. Antiq., vi. 11, vii. 69, 71, viii. 302.

[5] St. Julien, Voyages des Pélerins Bouddhistes, t. iii. p. 173. Hiouen-Thsang declares that the temple and the cultus are very ancient. For the Mussulman testimonies see A. Cunningham, Archæological Survey, vol. v. p. 115.

[6] Inscript. of Gwalior, in Journ. of the As. Soc. of Bengal, vol. xxx. p. 275; the text adjusted in H. Kern, Over eenige Tijdstippen der Indische Geschiedenis, Memoirs of the Academy of Amsterdam, 1873.

[7] Râjataraṅgiṇî, iv. 187.

[8] Hunter, Statistical Account of Bengal, vol. xix. p. 85. Among the kings of Canoje we know of three at least (from the seventh to the tenth century) that were Adityabhaktas: Bâṇa in Hall, Preface to the Vâsavadattâ, p. 51, and the inscription of Udayapura in Hall, Vestiges of Three Royal Lines of Kanyakubjâ, Journ. of the As. Soc. of Bengal, vol. xxxi.

[9] See Reinaud, Mémoire Géographique, Historique et Scientifique sur l'Inde, pp. 102, 122; as well as the note by H. H. Wilson, ibid., p. 391 *seq.* Varâha Mihira, Bṛihat Saṃhitâ, lx. 19, p. 328, ed. Kern, says that the priests of the Sun are called Magas; and the Bhavishya Purâṇa relates the legend of these Maga-Brahmans, their arrival from Çakadvîpa (here the country of the Çakas or Indo-Scythians, Iran?), with a ritual, certain peculiarities of which recall that of the Parsees. This question has been recently taken up

array of Indian proper names would by itself show how much this cultus was in vogue throughout India.[1] In fine, the Sun has always been in a way the professional and family god of astronomers and astrologers, who rarely fail to invoke him at the commencement of their writings. In our day there are no Adityabhaktas or *Sauras* except in the South, and even there they are far from numerous. But the Sun has not ceased to fill a large space in the prayers of the Hindus. Very few Brahmans especially commence their daily duties without saluting him with the old salutation, now scarcely understood, of the *Sâvitrî*, and in the imagination of these people he has remained, as it were, the very symbol of the deity. When Bishop Heber interrogated Svâmin Nârâyaṇa regarding the character of his god, the latter made reply by producing an image of the sun.[2] Temples are no longer built to him, but idols are still consecrated to him, and he takes his place as an allied god in many of the sanctuaries of Vishnuism, which has besides never ceased to be itself in many respects a solar religion.

again by Professor Weber, at the point at which Wilson had left it, in relation to a little writing bearing upon the same subject, the Magavyakti, published by him in the Proceedings of the Academy of Berlin for June and October 1879. After discussing all the traces still discoverable of the relations that may have existed anciently between Iran and India, he arrives at the very plausible conclusion that the testimony of Varâha Mihira refers to Mithriac colonies, which probably came from Persia at the time of the Indo-Scythian kings, and whose chiefs, the Magas, had been admitted into the Brahmanic caste; that at a later period, somewhere about the seventh or eighth century, the memorials of this first settlement were mixed up with records in regard to the advent in Gujarât of bodies of fugitive Parsees, and that the legend of the Bhavishya Purâṇa was the result of this confusion. See further Ueber zwei Parteischriften zu Gunsten der Maga, resp. Çâkadvîpîya Brâhmaṇa, ibid., January 1880, by the same scholar.

[1] A distinctive feature of this cultus, from the times of the Rig-Veda (viii. 91, legend of Apâla) to the Mussulman accounts (Ketâb-al-fihrist, in Reinaud's Mémoire sur l'Inde, p. 292), was its efficacy in accomplishing the cure of maladies, particularly leprosy. It was to obtain deliverance from leprosy that Çâmba, the son of Kṛishṇa, founded the temple of Multân (Bhavishya Purâṇa, in Aufrecht's Oxford Catalogue, p. 31), and that the poet Mayûra is said to have composed, in honour of the Sun, the Sûryaçataka: Hall, Vâsavadattâ, Pref., p. 8, 49; Ind. Antiq., i. 114.

[2] Narrative of a Journey, &c., ch. xxv.

A polytheistic system, even when it has reached an advanced stage of anthropomorphism, may, if it preserves the unity of its rites, like that of the Veda and the Avesta, dispense for long with images. But it can do so no longer when this unity begins to break up, and when to plurality of gods is added plurality in the forms of worship. Thus the Neo-Brahmanic religions became at an early age idolatrous. In the most recent writings of Vedic literature, in the Sûtras, and even in a piece, of no ancient date, it is true, from a Brâhmaṇa,[1] express mention is made of temples and images of the gods, which can only refer to these religions, for neither the one nor the other is ever spoken of in the directions which these writings contain with reference to their proper worship, which is just the old Brahmanical worship. There are also allusions to figured representations in Pâṇini, which is usually assigned to the fourth century before Christ; and Patañjali, which belongs to the second, and has preserved to us on this subject some curious notices, makes express mention of the idols of Çiva, Skanda, Viçâkha (a form of Skanda), Kâçyapa (probably a solar god).[2] These images were in general small sized, as is evident, since the names of them were formed by the help of a diminutive suffix, and since, according to a gloss of rather modern date, it is true, their owners took them about at times from house to house, and offered them for a consideration to the homage of the faithful.[3] Those who plied this trade were called *Devalas*,

[1] The Adbhutabrâhmaṇa, published by A. Weber in Zwei Vedische Texte über Omina und Portenta. For other Vedic passages where there is mention of idols, see ibid., p. 337. To these add Gautama, ix. 12, 66; Apastamba, i. 30, 20; 22.

[2] A. Weber, Ind. Stud., xiii. 344. With the gloss on Pâṇini, i. 2, 49, and the passage from the Mahâbhârata, pointed out ibid., p. 346, compare the erection of the "five Indras," of which there is mention in the inscription on the pillar of Kahaon, Journal of the As. Soc. of Bengal, vol. vii.; and A. Cunningham, Archæological Survey, vol. i. p. 94, pl. xxx.

[3] Goldstücker, Pâṇini, his Place in Sanskrit Literature, p. 229. We think involuntarily of Ṛig-Veda, iv. 24, 10. For the age of Kaiyaṭa, the author of the gloss, see Kielhorn, Kâtyâyana and Patañjali, p. 12; and Bühler in Journ. of the Roy. As. Soc., Bombay, vol. xii., extra number, p. 71.

Devalakas, and, like all those who subsisted by these popular systems of worship, they were exposed to the official disdain of the Brahmans.[1] The first temples, moreover, were simply places consecrated by the presence at the fixed spot of an idol, at most erections of the most primitive construction, such as we find still everywhere in the country. In the first rank of these the Sûtras of Gautama mention the cross-roads;[2] and smallness of dimension has always continued one of the distinctive features of the Hindu temple. It has increased by additions from without, but in the interior suffered little change. Even at a later date, when the religious edifices came to cover an enormous extent of ground, and sometimes to form whole towns, the sanctuary, properly speaking, remained what it was at first, a narrow and dingy cell, a *devatâyatana*, the home of a god. This is not the place to classify or describe the countless images which by degrees composed the figured pantheon of India, from the shapeless stone, smeared with vermilion, erected at the entrance of villages, to the idol fashioned of massive gold and covered all over with precious stones, which is sheltered, or rather was sheltered,[3] in the centre of the pagodas. There is no one who does not remember some of these figures, often colossal, sometimes indecent, always monstrous, of divinities with many heads, arms, legs, and manifold symbolic shapes, such as dwell in the shade of the great sanctuaries, and inhabit their porches and precincts, raised at times to the summit of their high pyramids, productions of a fantastic art, which

[1] Gautama, xv. 16; xx. 1; Manu, iii. 151, 152, 180; iv. 205.

[2] ix. 66.

[3] From the days of Mahmoud the Ghaznévide, who plundered Nagarkot, Thanessar, Mathurâ, and Somnâth (1008–24), the Mussulmans have been terrible destroyers of idols in India. Kutb-Uddin, the conqueror of Delhi (1191), built his great mosque on the site and with the materials of twenty-seven pagan temples. A. Cunningham, Archæological Survey, vol. i. p. 175. Long before the conquest, the avarice of the Mussulmans had been excited by the wildest descriptions of the riches collected in the sanctuaries of India. See, for example, those of the Ketab-al-fihrist (tenth century, according to documents of the ninth), in Reinaud's Mémoire sur l'Inde, p. 289, and the Journ. of the Roy. As. Soc., Bombay, vol. xiv. p. 44.

seems to have aimed at realising all imaginable forms outside the limits of the possible and the beautiful.[1]

Besides images there are also symbols; in the first rank the phallus, that of Çiva. This god is, in fact, imaged in many ways, but his true idols are the *liṅgas.* The origin of the worship of the *liṅga* is hid in obscurity. Creuzer represented it as, next to that of the trinity, the most ancient religious form of India,[2] and it may be in point of fact that, like the popular practices of fetishism, it goes back to the most remote period. But it certainly did not penetrate into the great religions of the Veda, where there are many phallic ideas and rites,[3] but no worship of the phallus. The origin not being referable to the Veda, it has been sought for, without sufficient reason, at one time among the Dravidian races,[4] at another among the Western nations, and even among the Greeks.[5] The most probable supposition is, that the Hindus, once in search of symbols with figures, must have found it out of themselves, which could not have been difficult to a people with whom the names for "male" and "bull" had for long been synonyms

[1] Varâha Mihira (sixth century) has left us curious descriptive lists of images of the gods. One is found in his Yogayâtrâ, vi. 1–18 (ed. Kern, in the Ind. Stud., xiv. 326 *seq.*); it comprehends only the divinities which preside over the eight points of space and the planets, Indra, the Sun, Agni, Venus, Yama, Mars, Nirriti, Râhu (the dark planet which is thought to cause eclipses), Varuṇa, Saturn, Vâyu, the Moon, Kubera, Mercury, Çiva, and Jupiter. The other, of greater extent, and which Reinaud first introduced to us in his Mémoire sur l'Inde, p. 119 (according to the Arabic version of Albirouni), is found in the Bṛihat Saṃhitâ, ch. lviii. 29–58, pp. 317–322, ed. Kern. It comprehends Râma, the Asura Bali, Vishṇu-Kṛishṇa, his brother Baladeva, his wife Lakshmî, his two sons Çâmba and Pradyumna, with their wives, Brahmâ, Skanda, Indra, Çambhu (Çiva) and his wife Pârvatî, Buddha, Jina, the Sun, the Liṅga, the Mothers, Revanta (a son of the Sun), Yama, Varuṇa, Kubera, and Gaṇeça. Similar lists are met with in the Matsya and the Varâha Purâṇa, in Aufrecht's Oxford Catalogue, pp. 42, 60.

[2] Symbolik, t. i. p. 575, 2d ed.

[3] See Muir, Sanskrit Texts, vol. iv. p. 406, 2d ed., vol. v. 384; A. Weber, Indische Literaturgeschichte, p. 322, 2d ed.; and Ind. Stud., i. 183.

[4] Stevenson, On the Ante-Brahmanical Religion of the Hindus, in Journ. of the Roy. As. Soc., vol. viii.; Lassen, Ind. Alterthumsk., t. i. p. 924; t. iv. p. 265.

[5] F. Kittel, Ueber den Ursprung des Lingakultus in Indien, p. 46. The author of this little piece, full of valuable information on the religions of Southern India, has completely refuted the hypothesis of the Dravidian origin of the worship of the *liṅga.*

of "god." Anyhow, we see this worship appear contemporaneously with Çivaism. Already, in the Mahâbhârata, it is the symbol of Mahâdeva, and the Purâṇas make it the subject of the strangest speculations.[1] In the monuments of the worship it has often the female part for support, the *yoni*, which symbolises Devî. There is nothing indecent, however, in the form of these figures. In appearance they are pure symbols, in no respect images, as we meet with elsewhere; in Italo-Grecian antiquity, for instance. The *liṅga* is a cone, the *yoni* a triangular prism,[2] with a depression on the upper surface, into which the *liṅga* is inserted; and of all the representations of the deity which India has imagined, these are perhaps the least offensive to look at. Anyhow, they are the least materialistic; and if the common people make fetishes of them, it is nevertheless true that the choice of these symbols by themselves to the exclusion of every other image was, on the part of certain founders of sects, such as Basava, a sort of protest against idolatry.

What the *liṅga* and the *yoni* are for Çiva and Devî, a petrified ammonite, the *çâlagrâma* (so called from a spot on the banks of the Gaṇḍakî where it is found), and the *tulasî*, a plant of the basil species, are for Vishṇu and Lakshmî. Here, too, we have symbols as regards the form, but in point of fact these objects have become real fetishes. The *çâlagrâma*, for instance, is not merely the symbol of Vishṇu; the god resides and is present in it,[3] as Çiva is in the *liṅga*. They differ, however, from this last, that they do not play such a part in the worship of the temples, and that they continue to belong rather to the circle of

[1] See Muir, Sanskrit Texts, vol. iv. p. 386.

[2] Sometimes the *liṅgas* are covered with daintily carved sculptures and ornaments of precious metals. The number of the principal is usually reckoned at twelve, which are enumerated in the Çiva Purâṇa in Aufrecht's Catalogue, p. 64. Besides these twelve, the Purâṇa enumerates and describes several hundreds belonging to all the countries of India. See also Weber's Catalogue of the Berlin MSS., p. 347.

[3] See Çaṅkara, Commentary on the Chândogya Up., p. 530, ed. of the Bibl. Ind. The Brahmavaivarta Purâṇa treats at length of the tulasî and the çâlagrâma: Aufrecht's Catalogue, p. 24.

private devotion. Çiva, Gaṇeça, Agni, the Sun, the Moon, and other deities besides, have likewise their sacred stones, herbs, and trees. The products of the vegetable kingdom, in particular, have always been the object of a worship, the presence of which, as regards some at least, may be traced all through Indian antiquity as far as the most ancient myths and most ancient usages.[1] The majority of those kinds especially which were used in the Vedic sacrifice still retain something of their sacred character: by a strange chance one alone, the soma, the most sacred of all, has so faded from the memory that it is no longer possible to identify it with accuracy.[2] Alongside of her images representing the gods, India has thus an infinite number of deified objects. It is no uncommon thing to see the soldier pay homage to his arms, the artisan address a prayer to his tools; and so uncertain and confused is the character of all these religions, that, notwithstanding the distinction there is between the highest and the lowest, it is next to impos-

[1] For the myths of the tree see A. Kuhn, Die Herabkunft des Feuers, *passim;* Senart, La Légende du Buddha, Asiatic Journal, 7th series, t. iii. pp. 280, 302, 325, 352, t. vi. p. 100, &c.; J. Darmesteter, Haurvatât et Ameretât, pp. 52, 64, 76. In the Ṛig-Veda (x. 135, 1), it is under a "tree with beautiful foliage" that Yama drinks with the gods and the ancestors (see "the fig-tree under which the gods sit in the third heaven," Atharva-Veda, v. 4, 3; see also *supra*, p. 7). The Chândogya Up. (viii. 5, 3) and the Kaushîtaki Up. (i. 3) have a knowledge of "the fig-tree which distils the soma," and "the tree of life, ilyovṛikshaḥ," of the celestial world. In classic literature these myths are represented by Pârijâta, Kalpadruma (the tree of wishes), and other celestial trees, as well as by the singular trees which are the distinctive symbols of, and give their names to, the different dvîpas or continents of the fantastic cosmography of the Purâṇas. Every Hindu village has in its vicinity some tree venerated as *caitya*, as a sacred object, and the pipala fig-tree is botanically called the *Ficus religiosa*. The Buddhists, for their part, have quite a collection of sacred trees; among others, the different Bodhi trees, of which each Buddha has had his own, and four of which, already specified in the Dîpavaṃsa, xvii. 16–24, 73, are the objects of a special adoration. The worship of trees existed among the Jainas also, A. Weber, Çatruñjaya Mâhâtmya, pp. 18, 19. The reader will find many curious facts, but, at the same time, very daring speculation, in J. Fergusson's splendid work, Tree and Serpent Worship, 2d ed., 1873.

[2] In Southern India alone there are three different plants from which the soma is prepared: Burnell, South Indian Palæography, p. viii., 2d ed., and Classified Index of the Tanjore MSS., i. 72; see Haug in Götting. Gel. Anz., 1875, p. 584, and *supra*, p. 56.

sible to draw the line where the one set ends and the other begins.

Finally, like Egypt long ago, India has its sacred animals. Already in the ancient religion cows are the object of a special worship.[1] It is expressly enjoined to treat them with gentleness, and the Smṛitis require the same respect for them as for the images of the gods.[2] It soon became matter of religious scruple to offer them in sacrifice;[3] to slaughter them for a profane purpose is one of the greatest crimes;[4] to tend them, provide for them, serve them, is reckoned in the first rank of good works and of acts of expiation;[5] to risk one's own life to save theirs atones for a Brahmanicide;[6] contact with them purifies, and, as in the Parsi ritual, their very dung and urine have the power of preventing or cleansing away material and moral defilements.[7] These customs subsist still in some degree in our own day. The Hindus do not scruple indeed to subject their miserable cattle to a labour that is often excessive, but it is rare that they ill-use them. Very few, especially, will consent to feed on their flesh, and the slaughter of a cow excites more horror among many of them than the slaying of a man. The manifold relations which connected these animals with the ancient worship are not better, for most part, it is true, than matter of memory, but others were instituted in the new worship. It is one of the most meritorious acts to dedicate bulls to Çiva, and to multiply around the god the living images of Nandi, his divine steed.[8] Accordingly these animals are

[1] Atharva-Veda, xii. 4, 5.

[2] Taitt. Br., iii. 2, 3, 7; Apastamba Dh. S., i. 30, 20; 22; i. 31; 6–12; Gautama, ix. 12, 23, 24; Manu, iv. 39; Yâjñavalkya, i. 133.

[3] Ṛig-Veda, viii. 101, 15; Pâraskara Gr. S., i. 3, 27, 28; Vâjas. S., xxx. 18. For more singular scruples see Sâyaṇa ad Taitt. S., i. 7, 2, 1, 2.

[4] Apastamba, i. 26, 1; Gautama, xxii. 18; Manu, xi. 108; Yâjñav., iii. 263.

[5] Manu, xi. 110–114.

[6] Manu, xi. 79; Yâjñav., iii. 244.

[7] Açvalây. Gr. S., i. 3, 1; Gobhila Gr. S., i. 1, 9; ii. 9, 2; iii. 7, 3; Manu, iii. 206; v. 105, 121, 124; xi. 78, 109, 202, 212; Yâjñav., i. 186; iii. 315; Ṛigvidhâna, i. 7, 4.

[8] The consecrating and setting at liberty of a bull, *vṛishotsarga*, is borrowed from the ancient ritual: Pâraskara Gr. S., iii. 9; Çâṅkhâyana Gr. S., iii. 11; Vishṇu-Smṛiti, lxxxvi.;

numerous in the neighbourhood of his sanctuaries, where they live in perfect freedom. At Benares especially they obstruct the narrow streets of the Holy City, and nobody thinks of complaining or of interfering with them in any of their whims. These are walking idols, absolutely inviolable; and one would be liable to be put to death on the spot if he offered the least insult to them. What the bulls are to Çiva the monkeys are to Vishṇu. Legions of these animals infest the neighbourhood of his temples, where they are kept up and revered as the representatives of Hanuman, the monkey-god associated with Râma. There are in these, to all appearance, the remains of an ancient popular religion, of much greater antiquity than the epic legend under cover of which they survive. The *Vṛishâkapi*, for instance, the "male monkey" of the Ṛig-Veda,[1] might very well be an ancestor of Hanuman. At all events, we must admit a similar explanation of the sacred character which has from remote antiquity been ascribed to another animal, viz., the serpent.[2] One of the most celebrated transactions of the epic legend is the great sacrifice offered by King Janamejaya for the destruction of the serpents,[3] on which occasion there are said to have been recited the Mahâbhârata and several Purâṇas. In the mythology the serpents are the sons of Kadru, the tawny, a personification of darkness, and their enemy is Garuḍa, the solar bird.[4] They are usually described, particularly under the name of Nâgas, as more or less invested with the human form, and endowed with

Kauçika S., in the Academy for 5th June 1880, p. 424. But the act in this case is not yet specially a Çivaite one.

[1] Rig-Veda, x. 86.

[2] Âtharva-Veda, viii. 8, 15; 10, 29; ix. 2, 22; x. 4; Khila ad Ṛig-Veda, vii. 55; Taitt. Saṃh., i. 5, 4, 1; Chândog. Up., ii. 21, 1; vii. 1, 2; Apastamba Sûtra in Taitt. Saṃh. Commentary, t. i. p. 957, ed. of the Bibl. Ind.; Açvalây. Gr. S., ii. 1, 9–14; iv. 8, 27, 28, and the note of Stenzler, ii. 3, 1. According to Taitt. Saṃh., iii. 1, 1, 1, serpents are the first-born of all creatures. Compare Mahâbh., i. 793–800; Strabo, xv. 1, ch. 28.

[3] Mahâbh., i. 1547–2197.

[4] Taitt. Saṃh., vi. 1, 6, 2; Çatap. Br., iii. 6, 2, 2; Suparṇâdhyâya (a little treatise connected with the Ṛig-Veda, and edited by E. Grube, 1875), *passim*; Mahâbh., i. 1073–1545.

knowledge and strength and beauty. They reside for most part in the depths of the ocean and at the bottom of lakes or large rivers, more frequently still in the subterranean world of Pâtâla, where their capital, Bhogavatî, exposes to the vision a display of the most dazzling riches.[1] They are not always represented as harmful and wicked; they are armed indeed with the most formidable poison; still they possess also the elixir of strength and immortality.[2] Their sovereign chief is at one time Vâsuki,[3] at another Çesha, he who, according to other legends, is the support of the universe and forms the couch of Vishṇu, who appeared among men in the person of Balarâma, and of whom Patañjali, the grammarian, is also reputed to have been an incarnation. In the chronicle of Kashmir they appear as the first inhabitants of the country, at a time when it was all a marsh, and even still they inhabit the waters of the valley, of which they are the protectors.[4] In a great many local legends a Nâga is the *genius loci*. They are honoured amongst the Buddhists, and they hold an equally prominent place in the literature and iconography of the Buddhism of the North as well as the South.[5] The great number of proper names, both of persons and places, into which the word Nâga enters, is a fact that by itself alone proves the extent of their worship. Hiouen Thsang found it very extensively spread in the north-west of India. And even still it is in great favour among the aborigines of the east and centre (the most of the Gond chiefs claiming to be descended from the Nâgavaṃça, the race of the Nâgas), as well as in all the countries of the west and south.[6] These brief indications are enough to show that the serpent religions of India form a complex whole,

[1] Mahâbh., i. 1282; Suparṇâdhy. vii. 2; Râjatarañg, iv. 597; Mahâbh., i. 5018; Bhâgav. Pur., v. 24, 31; Mahâbh., v. 3617 *seq.*

[2] Mahâbh., i. 1500–1505; 5018–5033.

[3] Sâmavidhâna. Br., iii. 3, 5; Bhagavad Gîtâ, x. 28, 29. He has a temple and a celebrated festival in his honour, at Prayâga, Ind. Antiq., ii. 124.

[4] Râjatarañg., i. 25 *seq.*

[5] Senart, Journ. Asiat., 7th series, vi. 136 *seq.*

[6] Ind. Antiq., iv. 5; vii. 41.

and such as is not accounted for by viewing it as a simple worship of deprecation. We can distinguish in it—(1.) the direct adoration of the animal, the most formidable and mysterious of all the enemies of man; (2.) a worship of the deities of the waters, springs, and rivers, symbolised by the waving form of the serpent;[1] (3.) conceptions of the same kind as that of the Vedic Ahi, and connected closely with the great myth of the storm and the struggle of light with darkness.[2] Even in places where serpent-worship, properly speaking, is out of the question, offerings are made to these reptiles, and almost everywhere the people manifest a repugnance to the killing of them, notwithstanding the ravages wrought by their stings.[3]

The observances of a religion like this are naturally as heterogeneous as the objects to which they are addressed. Though little known in the past, in their present state they defy description by their extreme diversity. They vary with the god, with race, with country, with sect, with caste, with profession. They are different for the countryman and the townsman, for the stated resident and the nomad, for the rich and the poor. They change sometimes from village to village, and from family to family. Any attempt at a general description, too, would necessarily end in failure, and we must restrict ourselves to the task of classifying them. We shall therefore, in the first place, single out those which refer to domestic life. Still, as of old, all the acts of this life are accompanied with religious practices, and regulated by *âcâra*,[4] that is, by custom, derived at one time from scripture, at another from simple

[1] Bühler, Ind. Antiq., vi. 270.

[2] Senart, Journ. Asiat., ibid., 153 *seq.*; compare Rev. Critique, 1876, t. ii. p. 35; Ind. Stud., xiv. 149.

[3] In Bengal, according to official numbers given by Hunter, Statistical Account of Bengal, *passim*, on the average four times more people fall victims to serpents than to all the other wild animals together, the tiger included. But the statistics are very imperfect in regard to such accidents, and the proportion in reality is much greater. J. Fayrer, Thanatophidia of India, estimates the number of people who perish annually in India from the sting of serpents at 25,000.

[4] Âcâra is the supreme dharma, Vaçishṭhasaṃhitâ, ch. vi., in Dharmaçâstrasaṅgraha, t. ii. p. 467.

tradition, and the local diversities of which have almost everywhere outlived the influences of sect as well as those of orthodoxy. To outrage *âcâra* openly is for the Hindu to lose his caste, a thing which he dreads more than any other, for however humble it may be, his caste is everything to him, in a country where, outside these barriers, there exists no social life, and where the purely civil law is represented only by the regulations of general administration issued by a foreign authority. To what extent this custom sometimes contradicts orthodox prescription may be gathered from the fact that among the Nairs of Malabar, who are considered, however, as Hindus and of high caste, it sanctions plurality of husbands. This custom exists elsewhere, too, in the Dekhan, and recently traces of it have been observed in the Punjâb,[1] where it had been already remarked by the Greeks,[2] and where its existence in ancient times is also attested by the Mahâbhârata.[3] Higher up, in the hill districts, we find instances among the Rajputs, and even the Brahmans.[4] However, notwithstanding all local differences, these customs, as regards the Brahmans and upper classes at least, are nevertheless obviously grounded on a common basis. The majority of the domestic rites which they prescribe are directly connected with the old Smṛiti, and it is only in it that the use of the old liturgy and the worship of the gods of the Veda[5] have been in part preserved. With the rest of the population tradition has changed more, but we must go down low indeed, we must go

[1] Ind. Antiq., vii. 86.

[2] Lassen's Ind. Alterthumsk., t. ii. p. 454, 2d ed.

[3] J. Muir in Ind. Antiq., vol. vi. pp. 260, 315.

[4] Ind. Antiq., vol. vii. p. 135. In Tibet it is the prevailing custom.

[5] Compare, for example, the nuptial ceremonies in Colebrooke, Miscellaneous Essay, vol. i. p. 217, ed. Cowell, with the ceremonies described according to the Sûtras by E. Haas in Ind. Stud., vol. v. p. 267. We must remark, however, that Colebrooke's description rests, not on the ground of direct observation, but on the examination of documents, the prescriptions in which are more or less become obsolete. Compare besides the Âcâras, ascribed to Çaṅkara, and which are authoritative in Malabar, in Ind. Antiq., vol. iv. p. 255, and what Bühler says of the Kashmir Brahmans in Journ. of the Royal As. Soc., Bombay, vol. xii. (extra number), p. 21.

outside Hinduism, not to find any vestiges of it. No Hindu, for instance, even among the very poorest, even among those who belong to a sect, withdrawn as regards everything else from the religious authority of the Brahmans, will marry, will educate his children, will perform certain funeral rites without calling in the assistance of some member of the priestly caste; and we have seen that even the Sikh *gurus* maintained some of them about their persons in the capacity of domestic chaplains.

To these usages, which go as far back as ancient Brahmanism, we must add the peculiar practices of the sects. There is a private worship of the *liṅga*, of the plant *tulasî*, and the *çâlagrâma ;* and some of the sects of Vishnuism, such as the Vallabhâcâryas, have domestic idols, which they surround with a homely worship copied from that of the temples. As in the ancient religion, there are prayers in connection with the principal acts of the day and the varied occurrences of life; prayers, usually short and simple, at times formulæ of hardly a few syllables, but which those who are fond of refining in their devotions know how to render very complicated. A good part of the ritual of the Tantras has for its object to prescribe the different ways of repeating them, combining them, modifying the effect of them by accompanying them with varied gesticulations; determining the mystical meaning of the letters which compose them, arranging them according to certain diagrams, and thrusting into them, so to speak, by an effort of imagination, new significations and new applications.[1] To these formulæ litanies are added, which are of very great length, and consist in repeating the "thousand names" of Çiva and Vishṇu.[2] To mark one's way through

[1] See Râmatâpaniya Up., ed. A. Weber, p. 300 *seq.*, and the extracts from the Tantras given by Aufrecht, Oxford Catalogue, p. 88 *seq.*

[2] There are similar litanies in honour of Devî, Sûrya, Gaṅgâ, Gaṇeça, &c. A *Vishṇusahasranâman* (the thousand names of Vishṇu) occurs already in Mahâbhârata, xiii. 6936–7078. A long litany of the same kind in honour of Çiva and Devî, the Çivalîlâmṛita (forming part of the Brahmottarakhaṇḍa of the Skanda Purâṇa), in fourteen chapters, is in extensive use, and has been translated into several dialects.

these exercises use is made of beads. Of course, each sect has its fasts, its vows,[1] its penances, its expiations, its rules in regard to purity and impurity. There are *dies fasti* and *dies nefasti*, and the astrologer plies his trade even in the smallest villages. In short, a great importance is attached to certain details of costume, and to the external badges by which these countless communities are distinguished. The most general badge of Hinduism is an heirloom from the ancient religion, the *cûḍâ*, a tuft of hair left growing on the crown of the head of a child, when it is tonsured.[2] Except the ascetics, who shave the head entirely, or who let all the hair grow, whoever does not wear the *cûḍâ* is not considered as a Hindu. Thus the anomalous jumble of beliefs which constitute the national religion is sometimes, by contrast with the faith of the Moslem, the outcastes, and the aborigines, designated as the *sheṇḍîdharma*, the religion of the Sheṇḍi (*sheṇḍi* being the Marhatta name for *cûḍâ*), and more than once the missionaries have agitated the question whether they ought to permit this practice among their flocks.[3] But at the same time each sect and each fraction of a sect has its own peculiar badge; among others, lines and points of different colours traced in divers ways above the root of the nose, "the mark of the beast," as the Rev. J. Wilson somewhere calls them.[4]

The distinction between a worship that is private and one that is public, which is hardly admissible in regard to the ancient ritual, such as it has been transmitted to us, is very appropriate, on the other hand, when applied to the neo-Brahmanic religions. We have already seen that many sects use to assemble together to pray and edify

[1] One of the most widespread of the votive ceremonies, and which has been adopted even by Mussulmans, consists in stepping barefoot over a layer of burning coals: Ind. Antiq., ii. 190; iii. 6; vii. 126.

[2] The *cûḍâkarman*, the tonsure, is one of the *saṃskâras* or consecrations which the ancient ritual prescribes for every member of the Aryan community.

[3] See R. Caldwell in Ind. Antiq., vol. iv. p. 166.

[4] Indian Caste, Bombay, 1877, vol. i. p. 17.

one another in common.[1] Moreover, in the idolatrous cultus, many of the rites are performed collectively, and the sanctuary is for the use of the community. This feature appears even to have attracted attention very early. In the ancient Smṛiti the *grâmayâjaka*, he who performs the service for a village or a community, is pronounced unclean.[2] In order to introduce some little arrangement into these manifold rites, we shall specify just those which, in country districts, have respect to sacred objects of different kinds, principally isolated idols, sometimes the relics of another age and another religion, which continue, under new names, to be worshipped by the common people. It is thus that many figured monuments of Buddhism have now become Hindu fetishes, and that the pillars erected long ago by Açoka, to keep alive the memory of his edicts, are now transformed into *liṅgas*.[3] Naturally these forms of worship, to which we must add those that respect the majority of the *grâmadevatâs*, the guardian divinities or idols of the village, are derived from purely local traditions, and are not subjected to any fixed rule. They have, however, this common double character: first, that they are often attended with the shedding of blood, even when the divinity which the idol is thought to represent admits as a rule of no animal victims,[4] and then that they almost always dispense with the services of the Brahmans. It is only when the place has for one reason or another become a centre of resort to pilgrims that members of the holy caste, sometimes even simple Sannyâsins, come and settle here that they may earn a living by the alms of the faithful.[5]

[1] See also the interesting description of the Vishnuite cultus of Satya Nârâyaṇa in Bengal in Ind. Antiq., iii. 83.

[2] Manu, iv. 205; Gautama, xv. 16.

[3] A. Cunningham, Archæological Survey, i. 67, 74; and Corpus Inscript. Indicarum, pp. 40, 41.

[4] For example, at Baragon, in Behâr, the villagers sacrifice goats to an old statue of Buddha, which has been metamorphosed by them into a figure of Rukmiṇî, the wife of Kṛishṇa, the officially prescribed worship of which has never been bloody. A. Cunningham, Archæological Survey, i. 29. A description of one of these village solemnities will be found in Ind. Antiq., iii. 6.

[5] See, for example, A. Cunningham, Corpus Inscript. Indicarum, p. 24.

Of a character more complex and more pompous than these rites are those which are performed in the temples properly so called. As a general rule, the sacred offices in a Hindu temple are discharged by Brahmans, who are maintained partly from the offerings of the faithful and partly from the revenues of the lands which belong to the temple. To this, however, there are some exceptions. In many of the Çivaite sanctuaries of the Dekhan, specially in all those belonging to the Liṅgâyits (and not, as is supposed, in all the temples of the *liṅga*), the *pûjâris* belong very frequently to other castes.[1] Formerly, it seems, these offices were performed also by women, at least in the cultus of certain forms of Durgâ.[2] These priests, however, are simple attendants; they are, in general, very ignorant. Outside the science of their own ritual, which is at times highly complicated, it is true, and which they transmit from father to son, their knowledge is generally limited to the legends which compose the *Mâhâtmya*, the chronicle of the temple. Neither the spiritual authority in the sect nor what may be called the pastoral functions belong to them, but to the members of the religious order, who sometimes live beside the sanctuary in a *maṭha* or college, and who are themselves not always very learned. Fifty years ago, when H. H. Wilson wrote his Memoir on the sects, one of the principal chiefs of the Vallabhâcâryas had just as much knowledge of letters as to be able to sign his name.[3] In general, the temples are no longer what they once were, centres of intellectual life. They are not frequented, as they were in the middle age, by a brilliant assemblage to listen to the rehearsal of the Mahâbhârata;[4] and even at Benares, the number of these *paṇḍits* is seen daily to diminish, who, squatting under the shade of some porch, pass their lives in

[1] F. Kittel, Ueber den Ursprung des Lingakultus, p. 10 *seq.*

[2] See, for example, the priestess of Câmuṇḍâ in Mâlatî-Mâdhava.

[3] Select Works, i. 136.

[4] See the testimony of Bâṇa, in Ind. Antiq., i. 350, and that of Hemacandra, ibid., iv. 110.

expounding gratuitously the mysteries of the Vedânta and the ancient theology. The worship which is celebrated in these temples is but slightly addressed to the understanding; but according to the evidence of all those who have had occasion to witness it, it has, especially in the great sanctuaries, an impressive effect on the senses and on the imagination. The essential part of it is the service of the idol and of the temple, which is his dwelling.[1] The main daily business is the sweeping of the sanctuary, the keeping up of the lamps, which shed in it a mysterious twilight, the ringing of the bell at every new act of homage, placing of flowers before the god, wakening him up, dressing him, washing him, giving him his food, putting him to bed, watching over him during slumber. These duties devolve upon the Pûjâris, and in the large sanctuaries on a numerous array of menial attendants. Sometimes rich laymen regard it as an honour to discharge these offices; at Purî, for instance, the descendant of the ancient kings of Orissa, the Râja of Khurdhâ, reckons among his special prerogatives the right he enjoys of sweeping the sanctuary of Jagannâtha (the master of the world, Vishṇu). On certain days, the god, mounted on his chariot, changes his residence, and hundreds and thousands of the faithful then contend for the honour of dragging the ponderous vehicle. Female singers and female dancers, the *devadâsîs,* the servants of the god, who have been dedicated to him from infancy, are charged with the duty of amusing him by their representations. Like their sisters, the hierodules of the ancient West, they often join prostitution to their sacred calling.[2]

These ceremonies naturally vary according to the god, the locality, and the importance of the temple. They are not all observed in all the sanctuaries. In those which are dedicated to the *liṅga*, for instance, the worship is comparatively simple, sometimes even severe; while it attains

[1] The installation and the service of the temples are circumstantially described in the Matsya and the Varâha Purâṇa: Aufrecht, Oxford Catalogue, pp. 43, 59.

[2] Meghadûta, str. 36.

the maximum of bewildering intricacy and barefaced indecency in those of Vishṇu and Durgâ. In this worship the faithful, men and women, take part, either individually or collectively, in prayers, in acts of homage and adoration, in ablutions in the sacred pond, which is found beside most of the temples,[1] and, in fine, in gifts and offerings. If these ceremonies are numerous and involved, so that their celebration lasts sometimes over several days, they are performed under the special direction of a priest. Gifts are made to the god or to the priests; these consist of money, articles of value, lands, and jewels (Ranjit Singh, the Mahârâja of the Sikhs, gave his celebrated diamond, the Koh-i-Nor, to Jagannâtha). The offerings are flowers, oil, and perfumes, food of different kinds, and animals, which are set at liberty by consecrating them to the god, or are sacrificed to him as victims. As a general rule, the offerings in the Vishnuite systems of worship are, except in remote country parts, never bloody; to Çiva victims are pretty frequently sacrificed, but not in the temple itself; in the acts of worship, on the contrary, which are addressed to the different forms of Durgâ, immolation is of constant occurrence, and it takes place in the interior of the sanctuary. The food presented to the god, *naivêdya, prasâda*, constitutes a sacrament; the faithful divide it among themselves, and often carry it away to a distance. The *mahâprasâda*, in particular, the prasada by pre-eminence, that which has been dedicated to Jagannâtha, the celebrated idol of Purî, is reputed to be endowed with the most sacred qualities, and has given rise to a singular custom. Between those who partake of it together it creates for a space, which they can fix at will, a stronger bond of connection than ties of blood. During all the time agreed on, they bind themselves to stand by each other to the utmost, even to the extent of

[1] The admirable construction of many of these reservoirs is already matter of astonishment to Albirouni: "Our compatriots," he says, "far from being able to construct similar works, find it hard to describe those which exist." Renaud, Mémoire sur l'Inde, p. 286.

backing up perjury and crime. Thus these alliances, contracted often for a purpose which they dare not confess, form sometimes one of the most serious obstacles to the execution of justice.[1] All the sectarian religions practise this kind of communion, the origin of which goes as far back as the Vedic sacrifice. Among some Çivaites, who think it improper to eat what has been offered to the god, and among sects such as the Sikhs, who offer no food to the deity, the *prasâda* is consecrated in the name of the *guru*.

The majority of the temples belong to sects, and although the Hindu, on the whole, is not exclusive in his acts of adoration, the worship which is celebrated in them is usually only that of a section. There are, however, two classes of occurrences in which these differences disappear, and in which Hinduism manifests more than elsewhere its sense of its own unity; these are the festivals and the pilgrimages. Every locality the least remarkable for its actual importance, or in consequence of memories connected with it, has its festival, its *melâ;* kinds of solemnities which resemble nothing so much as the *pardons* of Bretagne, with their twofold religious and secular character. Though they have always some sanctuary by way of centre, and are in close relation with a definite worship, the neighbouring populations flock to them and take part in them without distinction of sect. It is the same with the great festivals which are not local, and which are graduated to last throughout the length of the Hindu year. Described minutely in several Purâṇas,[2] and regulated in a general way in *traités de comput*, they are marked with care in the almanack for the year.[3] The differences they present from one province to another are

[1] See on this custom Ind. Antiq., vii. 113.

[2] Particularly in the Bhavishya and the Bhavishyottara: Aufrecht's Catalogue, pp. 30–34. The first section or Vratakhaṇḍa of the Caturvargacintâmaṇi of Hemâdri treats of the same subject.

[3] Some of these festivals, those of the first three months of the year, have been described, as regards Bengal, by H. H. Wilson, The Religious Festivals of the Hindus, Select Works, vol. ii. p. 151. An enumeration of the principal will be found in a very ably executed work for popular use by Monier Williams, Hinduism, 1877, p. 181.

often considerable, and some are peculiar to certain districts of country, but where they are kept up they are in more or less general observance. The Hindu calendar is arranged according to districts rather than to sects. Thus the entire population takes part in the rejoicings of Holî, the carnival of India (in March; the carnival is Krishnaite),[1] and to a certain extent they join in the fasts and abstinences in honour of the Mânes, which precede and follow it. The same thing is remarked in connection with the festival of the return of the Sun after the winter solstice (in January), when, as among ourselves, people give presents to each other, and the cattle, as at Rome, are subjected to a sort of lustration. All Bengal goes holiday-making during the ten days of the *Durgâpûjâ* (in September), in which, after interminable processions, intermixed with buffooneries and mimetic representations, the images of the goddess are finally thrown into the water, in presence of an immense concourse of people, and to the sound of whatever instruments of music can be collected together.[2] In Hindustan this solemnity is replaced by another, which is quite as generally observed in honour of Râma and Sîtâ, the story of whom is represented before the eyes of the multitude by a pantomime which lasts several days.[3] Festivals even of a character as decidedly sectarian as the nativity of Kṛishṇa[4] (in August), or the *Çivarâtri* (in February), intended to recall the humiliation inflicted by Çiva under the form of the phallus on Brahma and Vishṇu, are observed alike by the Çaivas and the Vaishṇavas; only the two parties some-

[1] It is only in Southern India that it has retained anything of its ancient character as a festival of spring and love. Wilson, Select Works, ii. 230.

[2] See Pratâpa-Chandra Ghosha: Durgâ-Pûjâ, with notes and illustrations, Calcutta, 1871.

[3] See an animated description of this festival by Bishop Heber, Narrative of a Journey, &c., ch. xiii. The allegation of the Bishop that in former times the children that happened to represent Râma and Sîtâ were poisoned by the Brahmans at the end of the piece, appears to be without foundation.

[4] See A. Weber, Ueber die Kṛishṇajanmâshṭamî. A curious popular hymn in reference to this nativity has been published by G. A. Grierson, Journ. of the As. Soc. of Bengal, vol. xlvi. p. 202.

times put different constructions upon them. Thus the festival of the lamps (in October), when innumerable floating lights are allowed to drift on the currents of the rivers, is celebrated more especially in honour of Devî by some, in honour of Lakshmî by others. There is a numerous class indeed who refrain from these solemnities; but it is composed of rigorists of every communion, who, in the name of religion and morality, condemn the profane and often indecent displays connected with them.

These great festivals and the pilgrimages are naturally closely connected. The latter are generally so arranged as to coincide with the former, and nowhere are the former celebrated with such splendour as in places which are the focus of these pious journeys. Unknown, as far as we are aware, to the Vedic epoch, these pilgrimages occupy from the time of the Mahâbhârata a prominent place in the religious life of India. The *tîrthayâtrâs*, visits to the *tîrthas*, the fords or landing-places of rivers, rendered sacred by the sacrifices of the ṛishis[1] and the presence of the gods, are declared in it to be more meritorious than the most solemn offerings.[2] Manu mentions specially only the Kurukshetra (in the neighbourhood of Delhi) and the Ganges;[3] but the great poem enumerates and describes a considerable number of these sacred places in Hindustan and the Dekhan, and as far as the extreme North, where Hindu devotion had at that date found out the road to the holy lakes of Kailâsa across the snows of the Himalaya.[4] In the Purâṇas appear afterwards in succession the other localities, which have continued famous to our own days, with their sanctuaries and their special rites. Almost all these works contain either a general sketch of the religious

[1] Sacrifices were always offered in the vicinity of a river, for the sake of the ablutions and to obtain the water required by ritual prescription. For these rites stagnant water is inadmissible: Taitt. Saṃh., vi. 4, 2, 2, 3; vi. 1, 1, 2. The confluence of a river was called *prayâga*, *i.e.*, place for sacrifice.

[2] Mahâbhârata, iii. 4059; see Gautama, xix. 14.

[3] Manu, viii. 92.

[4] There are several tîrthayâtrâs in the Mahâbhârata; one of the best developed occupies a great part of book iii. 3090–11450.

geography of India,[1] or complete descriptions, topographical and legendary, of one or other of these localities. These chapters, entitled *Mâhâtmyas*, "Majesties," are real manuals for the pilgrim.[2]

The number of these centres of resort for pilgrims is very considerable. From Lake Mânasa in Tibet to Râmeçvaram over against Ceylon, and from Dvârakâ in the peninsula of Gujarât to the fever-infected dunes of Orissa, where Jagannâtha has his seat, the country is, as it were, covered with a network of privileged sanctuaries. The first place in this sacred geography belongs to the Ganges, which we find already invoked along with other rivers in the Ṛig-Veda, and which, from the Macedonian epoch, was the object of one of the principal cultuses in India.[3] From Gangotrî in the Himalaya, where the sacred river has long before descended from heaven,[4] to the Isle of Sâgar, where it reaches the sea, its course is fringed with holy places. A particular class of Brahmans, the Gaṇgâputras, sons of the Ganges, live by the service of the innumerable *ghaṭs* by which a descent is effected into the river. Its water is sent to a distance, and râjas and private individuals of wealth keep up, at great expense, special services in order that they may be regularly supplied with provisions. It is the dream of every devout Hindu to go some day to cleanse himself from his sins in the "river of the three worlds,"[5] to gain heaven at Badrînâth, where it

[1] See, for example, Agni Purâṇa, ch. cix.–cxvi. t. i. p. 371–ii. p. 14, of the ed. Bibl. Ind.

[2] Such are the Mathurâ Mâh. (Varâha P.), the Gayâ Mâh. (Vâyu and Agni P.), the Kâçi Khaṇḍa, the Utkala Khaṇḍa, the Prabhâsa Khaṇḍa, which all three pass for portions of the Skanda Purâṇa, and describe, the first, Benares (see analysis given by Aufrecht, Oxford Catalogue, p. 69), the second the sanctuaries of Orissa, especially that of Jagannâtha, the third Girnar, Dvârakâ, and Somnâth in the peninsula of Gujarât. The most of these pieces are interpolations. There is besides a great number of Mâhâtmyas, which form works apart. Each sanctuary of any consequence has its own, and in some instances all those of a province have been blended together into compilations, of which some, such as the Kashmir Tîrthasaṅgraha, appear to be of real value in a historico-geographical point of view. See Journ. of the Roy. As. Soc., Bombay, vol. xii. (extra number), p. 58.

[3] Strabo, xv. 1, ch. 69.

[4] This descent is the subject of the beautiful episode of Râmâyaṇa, i. 45. Compare Mahâbhârata, iii. 9933 *seq*.

[5] It is thought to flow in heaven, on earth, and in hell.

separates from the glaciers, at Hurdvâr, where it enters on level ground, at Prayâga,[1] where it receives its sister the Jumnâ, sacred like itself, and whose banks witnessed long ago the gambols of Kṛishṇa, and especially at Benares, the "lotus of the world," the city with 2000 sanctuaries and 500,000 idols, the Jerusalem of all the sects of both ancient and modern India.[2] The number of pilgrims is rarely under 30,000; they flock hither from the most remote provinces, from all countries where the Bânian goes. Buddhists come to it from Nepâl, Tibet, and Burmah.[3] The old, the dying, the sick get carried to it from afar. Happy they who die here, whose funeral pile is kindled on the banks of the "river of the gods," or who, hurrying on their last hour, find their tomb in its purifying waters![4] An almost equal sanctity attaches to other rivers, to the Narmadâ, the Godâvarî and its affluents, the Kâverî (all already mentioned in the Mahâbhârata),[5] the

[1] See the description of Prayâga (*i.e.*, of the confluent *par excellence*) in the 7th century by Hiouen-Thsang, St. Julien, Voyages des Pélerins Bouddhistes, t. ii. p. 276. The place is also called Triveṇî, the triple river, because the Sarasvatî is reputed to flow under the earth, and unite here with the Gaṅgâ and Yamunâ. It has, however, lost somewhat of its sanctity ever since Akbar profaned it by erecting the fortress of Allâhâbâd at the very point of junction of the two rivers.

[2] For Benares see the interesting work of A. Sherring, The Sacred City of the Hindus; an Account of Benares Ancient and Modern, 1868. Albirouni compares it to Mecca: Reinaud, Mémoire sur l'Inde, p. 288. The mystic glorification of Benares forms the subject of several Upanishads, among others the Jâbâla Up. It was at Benares that Buddha commenced the proclamation of his doctrine, that he for the first time made "the wheel of the law to turn." See L. Feer, Journ. Asiat., 1870, t. xv. p. 345 *seq.*

[3] Thither they transport also the ashes of the dead.

[4] Religious suicide, especially suicide by drowning, appears to have been frequent in former times at these tîrthas of the Ganges. On the inscriptions we see kings and ministers preparing to end their days in such places. A certain King Dhâṅga was over a hundred when he went to drown himself at Prayâga. Inscript. in Journ. of the As. Soc. of Bengal, vol. viii. p. 174, and Asiatic Researches, vol. xii. p. 361. Compare Hiouen Thsang, Op. Laud., t. ii. p. 276, and the testimonies of Albirouni and Massoudi in Reinaud's Mémoire sur l'Inde, p. 230, and Fragments Arabes et Persans, p. 103. They were also frequent at other spots on other sacred rivers; see, for example, the suicide of the Câlukya Somêçvara in the Tungabhadrâ, Vikramâṅkacaritr, iv. 59, 60, ed. Bühler. See also Ayeen Akbari, translated by Gladwin, vol. iii. p. 274, ed. of Calcutta, 1786. The practice has not quite disappeared even in our own day. Heber, Narrative of a Journey, &c., ch. xii.

[5] iii. 4094, 8151, 8175–77, 8164. The sanctuaries of the Narmadâ are described in the Revâmâhâtmya, which forms part of the Çiva Purâṇa: Aufrecht, Catalogue, p. 69.

Kṛishṇâ, and especially the Tungabhadrâ, its southern branch, which is called the Gangâ of the south. Like the Ganges and the Jumnâ, they have their holy places, to which there flock every day troops of devotees. Another river, on the other hand, the Karmanâçâ, "the destroyer of pious works," which falls into the Ganges near Chausâ, is accursed, and to be touched by a single drop of its impure water is enough to cancel the accumulated deserts of years.[1]

We shall not attempt here to make a selection, which would in the end amount to a dry enumeration, of the numerous centres of pilgrimage which, from the Himalayas to Cape Comorin, attract the homage of Hindu devotion. An arranged list of the most celebrated will be found in a recent work by Monier Williams, entitled "Hinduism," pp. 177 *seq.*[2] But in order to give an accurate idea

[1] The name, and consequently the superstition, can be traced as far back as the Macedonian epoch: Lassen, Ind. Alterthumsk., t. i. p. 161, 2d ed.

[2] See the very interesting remarks by the same author, especially in connection with the sanctuaries of the Dekhan, in the Annual Report of the Royal Asiatic Society for 1877, p. lxxvii. Abul Fazl, in his Ayeen Akbari (t. iii. p. 254, ed. of Calcutta), gives also a list of the chief resorts for pilgrims, and distinguishes twenty-seven sacred rivers, ten towns or holy districts of the first rank, besides an indefinite number of others of the second, third, and fourth. For Mathurâ and the sacred places which surround it, the Bethlehem and Nazareth of Krishnaism, see F. S. Growse, Sketches of Mathurâ, in Ind. Antiq., i. 65, and Mathurâ Notes, in the Journal of the Asiatic Society of Bengal, vol. xlvii. p. 97 *seq.*; for Gayâ, which owes perhaps its first celebrity to Buddhism (it is near Gayâ that the Bodhi tree is, at the foot of which Çâkyamuni attained the state of Buddha), see Monier Williams, Çrâddha Ceremonies at Gayâ, in Ind. Antiq., v. 209; A. Cunningham, Archæological Survey, iii. 107; W. Hunter, Statistical Account of Bengal, vol. xii. p. 44; and the richly illustrated work of Râjendralâla Mitra, Buddha Gayâ, the Hermitage of Sakya Muni, 1879. Gayâ is still to-day, as in the sixth century at the time of Varâha Mihira (Yogayâtrâ, iv. 47, in Ind. Studien, xiv. 318), a place of resort for mourners, and about 100,000 pilgrims come here annually to pray for their dead. Buddhists also frequent it. Abundant information, from a topographical and archæological point of view, will be found on the sanctuaries of Hindustan in the Reports of the Archæological Survey of India of General A. Cunningham; on those of Western India in the Reports of the Archæological Survey of Western India by J. Burgess; on those of India in general in J. Fergusson's History of Indian and Eastern Architecture, 1876. The reader will consult with interest, particularly on account of the beautiful execution of the engravings, the publications of MM. Rear-Admiral Paris, G. Lejean, A. Grandidier, and L. Rousselet, that appeared in the Tour du Monde, t. xvi., xviii.-xx., xxii.-xxvii.

of the importance attached to the worship connected with places of pilgrimage, we shall give some figures relative to the best frequented perhaps of all these holy places next Benares; we refer to the celebrated sanctuary of Vishṇu-Jagannâtha at Purî in Orissa.[1]

Jagannâth is not, like Benares, a large town full of temples; it is a temple surrounded by others, and which has given rise to a town. The net annual revenue of the real estate constituting the domain of the god is about £31,000, to which must be added the gifts of the faithful, amounting to a sum impossible to determine with accuracy. It has been estimated at £70,000, a figure probably too high, though the Mussulman Government, it is said, formerly drew as much as £100,000 a year from the farming of the taxes levied on the pilgrims. Now, since 1840, the English Government has collected no tax; and, on the other hand, we may reckon that every rupee brought to Jagannâth remains there. Mr. Hunter, author of a learned work on Orissa, and Director-General of the Statistics of British India, estimates on the average about £37,000 as the annual amount of these gifts, say altogether a total revenue of £68,000 at the lowest, and that in a country where the day's wages of a land-worker are 2½d., and those of an artisan 6d. The *personnel* of the temple is divided into thirty-six orders and ninety-seven classes, such as officiating priests of different sorts, having each his special functions; besides bakers, cooks, guards, musicians, female dancers, female singers, torch-bearers, grooms, and elephant-keepers, artisans of different crafts, &c. To these immediate attendants on the god we must add the religious of the *maṭhas*, who depend on the sanctuary, their domestics, and their under-tenants, and, in fine, a

[1] These figures are taken from the note on Jagannâth in vol. xix. of the Statistical Account of Bengal by W. Hunter, a note which is abridged from the description given by the same author in his "Orissa, or the Vicissitudes of an Indian Province under Native and British Rule," vol. i. ch. iii., iv. For this sanctuary and others of the same province consult also the splendid publication of Râjendralâla Mitra, The Antiquities of Orissa, Calcutta, 1879–80.

great number of agents, about 3000, whom the vestry-board of the temple sends into all the provinces of India to beat up for pilgrims—an organisation which is met with elsewhere as well as Purî, and which is not of yesterday, but which has been rendered much more perfect, since the railroads are now at the service of Jagannâth. In all, the *personnel*, which, directly or indirectly, is maintained by the sanctuary, is estimated at 20,000 men, women, and children. In the most favourable years the number of the pilgrims, or rather the pilgrimesses, for five-sixths at least of the number are women, amounts to 300,000. In the worst years it never falls below 50,000. At the *Ratha-yâtrâ*, "the going forth of the car," the principal of the twenty-four great festivals, between which the religious year of Jagannâth is divided, it is generally reckoned that from 90,000 to 140,000 are present at once. It is not difficult to conceive what must be the condition as regards health of these multitudes ,already exhausted by a long journey. Ninety-five in the hundred come on foot, sometimes from the extremities of India, dragging with them sick relatives and children, or with vessels full of water from the Ganges, walking by day and encamping by night, in the rainy season too (for the rain falls in June or July), at a time when oppressive heats are rendered more treacherous by the moisture and sudden changes in temperature. Arrived at their destination, at this "gate of heaven," they find matters if possible worse. It is the exact time of the year when putrid fevers and cholera, endemic in this desolate region, are in their full force. Ill-fed,[1] packed close together, deprived of all shelter,[2] excited incessantly, even to ecstasy, by the pomp of the worship, crammed together several times a day in fetid tanks, they

[1] Food, consisting of boiled rice, is supplied at a low price by the kitchens of the temple. But as it has been consecrated to the god, none of it must be lost. What is left is kept from day to day, and is therefore often eaten in an advanced state of fermentation.

[2] The town of Purî (23,000 inhabitants) has only 5000 houses or huts for the pilgrims.

spend here one or two weeks, sometimes more fatal to life than a great battle. Then, when their last coin is gone, they resume, as they best can, their road homewards, not unfrequently carrying contagion along with them, and, like the caravans from Mecca, strewing the roads with their dead. According to the English doctors, the poor pilgrims leave an eighth, sometimes a fifth, of their people behind them. Mr. Hunter thinks we must accept a lower figure; but even under the most favourable circumstances, when no epidemic supervenes, and we make allowance for the normal chances of mortality, he is of opinion that the number of victims due to the pilgrimage to Jagannâth cannot be reckoned at less than 10,000 a year.[1]

And what takes place at Purî is repeated on a proportionate scale in a hundred other places. Mathurâ and Vṛindâvan, Gayâ in Behar, Gokarṇa on the Malabar Coast, the large pagodas in the Presidency of Madras, such as Conjevaram and Tricinâpalli, Râmeçvaram, especially, in the Gulf of Manaar, which is, as it were, the Benares of the South, see flocking to them at certain periods crowds nearly as numerous.[2] It is when face to face with these eager crowds that we feel what a *vis inertiæ* there still is in these decadent religions. Anyhow it would be impossible to over-estimate the effect of these pilgrimages on the religious temper of the nation, and it is no exaggeration to regard what goes on here as the vital function, so to speak, of Hinduism. The Hindu is all his days isolated

[1] See also what the historians of Mahmoud of Ghazna, Mirkhond, and Ferishta (writing, it is true, the first in the fifteenth, the second at the commencement of the seventeenth century), relate of the splendours which were displayed in the eleventh century, and at the opposite extremity of India, in the peninsula of Gujarât, in connection with the Çivaite sanctuary of Somnâth. From 200,000 to 300,000 pilgrims at the great festivals, 2000 Brahmans, 300 barbers, 300 musicians, 500 dancing girls, and no end of servants were attached to the sanctuary, which possessed the revenues from 2000 villages (10,000 according to Mirkhond). Every day water was brought to it from the Ganges for the ablutions of the liṅga. Mahmoud is said to have carried away the value of more than 20,000,000 dirhems of gold: Elphinstone, History of India, vol. i. p. 550; Journ. of the Roy. As. Soc. of Bombay, xiv. 42.

[2] At Pandharpour, in the Marhatta Dekhan, some days the pilgrims amount to 150,000: Ind. Antiq., ii. 272.

within his own sect, and does not rise above a mere mechanical devotion; but on these great occasions he experiences an excitement which lasts for years, and he finds himself the member of an immense community. Here the ranks of Vishnuism and of Çivaism blend together. At Benares, for instance, the pilgrim not only visits the sanctuaries connected with his own peculiar faith, but the holy places in general. At Jagannâth each particular sect is represented, and each divinity has his chapel, his idol, and his rites. Durgâ herself has her altar here, where, in spite of the rule which prescribes that no living creature shall be allowed to die within the sacred precincts, even victims are sacrificed to her honour. Each of these great pilgrimages, therefore, is a sort of *colluvio religionum.* Elsewhere Hinduism is breaking up and crumbling to pieces; here it gains new vitality and recovers the sense of its unity.

What are the limits of this unity? Under what conditions and at what stage in the social scale does one cease to be a Hindu? To this question there is no satisfactory reply. The ancient religion excluded the Çûdra; it was forbidden to reveal to him the Veda and to offer sacrifice on his behalf. The Neo-Brahmanic religions indulge in none of these peremptory interdictions. For the most part, they profess to take in hand the cause of the disinherited. The Mahâbhârata and the Purâṇas must have been composed expressly for the benefit of women and Çûdras, those excluded from the Veda.[1] There is no express and regular prescription which absolutely debars from the cultus such classes of the population, and to the numerous tirades directed against the impure classes which the literature of the different epochs contains we might easily oppose an almost equal number of professions of equality. Finally, we have seen that the majority of the sects have gone a great way in their protestations against distinctions of caste, and that some even went the length of declaring

[1] Bhâgavata Purâṇa, i. 4, 25.

them formally abolished. In point of fact, however, they have multiplied them, each sect uniformly giving birth in no very long time to a certain number of new castes. The population of India has come in this way to be broken up into thousands of sections, which do not intermarry, do not eat together, do not accept from one another particular articles and particular kinds of food, and leave no room for the mutual exercise of anything akin to charity. The Brahmans by themselves alone form several hundreds of classes, separated at times by barriers the most rigorous, and this exclusive spirit has deeply infected even the Mussulmans and the native Christians.[1] But outside or beneath the circle of these castes there is a certain number whom this circle, for one reason or another, rejects with a detestation so emphatic that religious communion, even of the simplest sort, becomes almost always impossible. There is no general test which enables us to distinguish those castaway classes, for which Europe long ago adopted the common designation of parias; and the exclusion with which they are smitten is in each separate province an affair of tradition and local custom. Several sects, such as the Liṅgâyits of the Dekhan, the Çâktas, the Çaitanyas of Bengal, proselytised at first indiscriminately among all and sundry. In former times, as appears, the sanctuary at Purî also was open to the most despised classes.[2] But in almost every case prejudice has in the long-run prevailed. At the present time there are fifteen castes, and these do not include Christians and Mussulmans, which are excluded from the sacred precincts

[1] Caste distinctions have been introduced among the Mussulmans of the Dekhan, Gujarât, and several districts of Bengal: Ind. Antiq., iii. 190, v. 171, 354; Hunter's Statistical Account of Bengal, ix. 289, xi. 52, 255, &c.

For the Christians, those of the ancient communities as well as those connected with the missions, see in the correspondence of Bishop Heber the letter of the 21st March 1826 to Williams Wynn. Compare Zeitsch. der Morgenl. Gesellsch., xxxiii. 579, 585.

[2] As a rule all distinction of caste ceases within the borders of the Purushottamakshetra. Compare Mahâbhârata, iii. 8026, in which all castes become Brahmans whenever they have crossed the Gomatî on a visit to the hermitage of Vaçishṭha.

of Jagannâth, while two others, the washermen and the potters, may enter, but not farther than the first court.[1]

Like the ancient religion, Hinduism, then, has its excommunicated races; but alongside of those who are thus repudiated by it there are some which repudiate it in their turn—we mean the tribes in a more or less wild state, which represent, the majority of them at least, the first tenants of the soil before the arrival of the Aryans. In Hindustan and the north of the Dekhan the great body of these tribes has become indistinguishably blended with the victorious race. In the South they have also adopted the Aryan culture and religion, preserving, however, their languages, which are different forms of the Dravidian, radically distinct from the Sanskrit. It is a question which is not yet ripe for solution, how far they in turn have been able to infect their conquerors with their own ideas and customs. It is probable, however, that some at least of the goddesses of the Hindu religions which sanction the sacrifice of blood are of Dravidian origin. But this is an assimilation which has not taken place everywhere. All along the northern and eastern frontier, in the centre among the Vindhya mountains, and over the least hospitable portions of the tableland of the Dekhan; farther to the south, in the recesses of the Ghaṭs, and in the Nilgherries, we meet with tribes connected, those of the north and centre with Tibetan or trans-gangetic races, and those of the centre and south with the Dravidian races, who have remained more or less pure, and have preserved their national customs and religions. We shall not enter into the examination of those religions. Like the tribes which profess them, they have no history, and their classification ethnographically is far from complete and settled. The most interesting and best known are those of the aborigines of the Dravidian race. They have as their common character the adoration of divinities connected with the elementary

[1] Hunter, Statistical Account of Bengal, vol. xix. p. 62.

powers and the earth, mostly female and malignant, the worship of ghosts and other mischievous spirits, which they seek to appease by bloody sacrifices and orgiastic ceremonies, which recall the Shamanism of the tribes of Northern Asia.[1] The priest or the sorcerer, the devil-dancer of the English, abandons himself to a frantic dance until he falls down in convulsions. He is then possessed, and the incoherent expressions which he lets drop express the will of the spirit whose wrath it is sought to disarm. Many of these practices have left traces among all the Dravidian populations, even among those that are most thoroughly assimilated. Hinduism, however, makes steady progress among these tribes: the modes, the forms of worship, the deities of the plain rapidly encroach on their mountains. But those who have kept apart without commingling return, for most part, to the Hindu, especially the Brahman, aversion for aversion, contempt for contempt. During the famine of 1874, for instance, some Santâls preferred to die of hunger at the door of the charity-food dispensaries rather than accept food at the hands of the Brahmans.[2]

Now that we find ourselves at the end of our long task, must we sum up all in a final judgment? All that precedes already is little more than a long summing up, and our greatest fear is that we have not succeeded in giving a sufficiently comprehensive idea of the complex, manifold, and outrageously confused character of these religions. Perhaps before there were any Homeric poems they had already gone beyond Parmenides, and at the present time, after centuries of intercourse with the Western world, they display to view, even in the most enlightened centres, a fetishism that is matchable only among the negroes

[1] On these religions, their divinities and practices, see F. Kittel, Ind. Antiq., ii. 168, and Ursprung des Lingakultus, p. 44, and R. Caldwell, Comparative Grammar of the Dravidian Family of Languages, p. 579 *seq.*, 2d ed.

[2] Hunter, Statistical Account of Bengal, vol. xiv. p. 313. Among the Holiyars of the Dekhan, in certain customs we remark a trace of the same hostile feeling.

of Guinea. Is their history that of a long process of decay, and have they, as some incline to believe, since the Veda been only gathering around them thicker darkness? or must we admit a real progress in this long succession of efforts? For the thirty centuries, at least, through which we can trace them, we find them constantly changing and constantly repeating themselves; so much so, that we seek in vain for notions of which we can without reservation affirm at any given moment that they are new or fallen into oblivion. No other among the Indo-European peoples had so early as this an idea of an absolute law universally binding, and yet we would like to know to what degree in practice it ever had a legislation. In how many cases can we say, Here is what India believes or does not believe, here is what it approves or what it condemns? Long before our era it contended theoretically against caste, and confessed the vanity of it,[1] yet it retains it all the same to this day; nay, more than that, it has carried it to excess, and brought it to an issue at once so odious and so chimerical that it is impossible to know how to account for it. And what contradictions there are if we examine the *morale* of these religions! Not only have they given birth to Buddhism, and produced, to their own credit, a code of precepts which is not inferior to any other, but in the poetry which they have inspired there is at times a delicacy and a bloom of moral sentiment which the Western world has never seen outside of Christianity. Nowhere else, perhaps, do we meet with an equal wealth of fine sentences. One of the men who have done most to promote an acquaintance with the Hindu religions, Dr. John Muir, has collected a certain number of these maxims and thoughts in an exquisite anthology,[2] which must have gained many friends to

[1] Bhagavad Gîta, v. 18.

[2] Religious and Moral Sentiments from Sanskrit Writers, 1875. The author has just included this first selection in a larger work: Metrical Translations from Sanskrit Writers, with an Introduction, Prose Versions, and Parallel Passages from Classical Authors (vol. viii. of Trübner's Oriental Series), 1879.

India. And yet what an absence of every moral element in the majority of these cultuses! What gloomy sides there are to these practices and these doctrines! The astonishing preservation of Hinduism is by itself alone a problem. It is certain that for a long while back the Hindu people have been better than their religions, and that these, on many sides, threaten to fall in pieces. They continue to subsist, however, and neither the gospel nor the Koran has till now seriously laid hold of them. Several centuries of Mussulman domination have hardly touched them. They have reacted at least as much on Islam as Islam has acted on them;[1] and it would seem at the present time that, in certain provinces at least, they are making it recoil.[2] As for Christianity, at this very time, when it has the command of unparalleled resources and everything in its favour to raise it to pre-eminence and lend it prestige, the success that accompanies its efforts is the smallest conceivable. The operations of the Catholic Propaganda, which are more remarkable for the wonderful solidity of their groundwork than their extent, have long since come to a standstill, and up to the present time those of the Protestant missions have perhaps been still less successful. Notwithstanding the great number of eminent men, some of them of quite singular merit, which they reckon in their bosom, none of the English, American, or German Protestant missions, which are labouring at the present time in India (except, however, those whose operations are among the aborigines, especially among those of Chota Nâgpore and the Central Provinces), have reason to feel satisfied with the results.

[1] See Garcin de Tassy, Mémoire sur les Particularités de la Religion Musulmane dans l'Inde, 2d ed., 1869; Colebrooke, On the Peculiar Tenet of Certain Muhammadan Sects, in Miscellaneous Essays, vol. ii. p. 202; Hunter, Statistical Account of Bengal, vol. ix. p. 289, and *passim*. This influence has been especially powerful in the West, where it has produced really mixed sects, such as that of the Sangârs and the Khojâs of Gujarât and Sindh: Ind. Antiq., v. 171, 173.

[2] In Bengal, except in the district of Gayâ, the Mussulmans are either stationary or on the decline: Hunter, *op. laud.*, *passim.*

Not one has till now succeeded in founding anything which can be compared with the work of the unknown apostles who, in the first centuries, established Churches called after St. Thomas, or even with that of St. Francis Xavier and the first Jesuit missionaries. This is due, perhaps, to the circumstance that the Protestant missionary comes and settles down, surrounded by a family with whom he lives in citizen comfort, while the native is impressible only by display or by asceticism. But it is especially due to this, that he reasons so much. Now, controversy, on which the Hindu dotes, and in which he excels, has no hold on his religion, which has, so to speak, no definite dogmas. Arguments sink into this soft mass, and are lost, like a blow with a sword in one of those inferior organisms which have no fixed centre of vitality. The missionary is loved and respected, the moral truth of his teaching is approved of and admired, and it cannot be questioned that in this respect alone his presence has been productive of much good; but there are no conversions. It is, then, more than doubtful whether Hinduism must, in even a distant future, give way to another religion; and yet it is visibly collapsing and deteriorating. At this very moment it is very near becoming little better than a form of paganism, in the etymological sense of the word. Science, industry, administration, police, sanitary regulation, all the conquests and all the exigencies of modern life, are calmly waging against it a war with far greater results than the work of missions. Will it find it has within itself resources enough to adjust itself to the new conditions which are pressing upon it with increasing rapidity? The experience of the past is calculated to inspire in this respect almost as many fears as hopes. The whole history of Hinduism is, in fact, that of a perpetual reform, and it is impossible not to be struck with the persistency in the effort. But, at the same time, we are obliged to confess how ephemeral and how liable to be corrupted each of these endeavours has till now proved to be. Will this be the case with that which is going on in our own time, and, so to speak, under our own eyes, the effort after a deistic reform maintained by the *Brahma Samâj* (Church of God)? We have intentionally said nothing till now of this movement, which takes its rise from the direct and avowed influence of Europe, although from the first it has been conducted from an exclusively Hindu point of view and by Hindus.[1] The founder of the movement, in the first years of this century, was the Brahman Ram Mohun Roy (who was born at Burdwan in 1772, in Lower Bengal, and died at Bristol, in England, in 1833), one of the noblest figures offered to view in the religious history of any people, but who was, in fact, better conversant with Christian theology (having with this object, besides English, acquired Latin, Greek, and Hebrew) than with the Vedas, although he knew of them all that it was possible to know then. He believed that these old books, in particular the Upanishads, rightly interpreted, contained pure deism, and he endeavoured to persuade his fellow-countrymen to renounce idolatry by appeals to tradition. With this aim he translated and published a certain number of these texts, and expounded his views on reform at the same time in original treatises. Becoming soon an object of attack, at once on the part of his own people and that of certain missionaries, he replied to them in writings in which the science of the theologian is found in alliance with a power of thinking of rare elevation, and some of which continue to this day models of controversial literature.[2] The Brahma Samâj, it thus appears, had recourse from the first to the methods of propagandism in

[1] The Brahma Samâj has already produced a considerable literature. References to this subject, as well as a general estimate of the movement, will be found in Max Müller's Chips from a German Workshop, vol. iv. pp. 271–275, 283–290. See also the Revues Annuelles, which Prof. Garcin de Tassy published from 1850 till the year he died, 1878, and which are devoted to the examination of everything affecting in any degree the Hindustani language or literature. These Revues form the most accurate and perfect record of the intellectual progress of Northern India during the last thirty years.

[2] See in particular his treatise, The Precepts of Jesus, the Guide to

use in Europe, and it has remained faithful to these since. In its aim it is a Hindu sect; in its organisation, in its means, and all its modes of action, it is an association analogous to that of theological parties among ourselves. It has its places of meeting and prayer, its committees, its schools, its conferences, its journals, and its reviews. The revealed authority which the founder had thought, in the beginning at least, he ought to claim for the Veda has been gradually given up, especially since a kindred association, the *Dharma Samâj* (the Church of the Law), was founded for the defence of the old orthodoxy. For over a dozen years now the sect has been split into a conservative party, the *Adi* (*i.e.*, ancient) *Brahma Samâj*, and an advanced party, which was formed under the direction of Keshub Chunder Sen, the *Brahma Samâj of India*, the former more respectful to the old usages, the other driving at a more radical reform. In this work there is an immense deal of what is right in itself, devout in sentiment, and great and even noble in aspiration. It is impossible sufficiently to honour these truly worthy men, who labour with so much zeal to raise the intellectual, the religious, and moral level of their fellow-countrymen; and the good which they do is unquestionable. But it is more than sixty years since the *Brahma Samâj* was founded; and how many adherents can it reckon up? In Bengal, its cradle, among a population of 67,000,000, some thousands, all in the large towns; in the country districts (and India is an essentially rural country), it is hardly known. Doubtless it is not exposed, like the other sects, to the risk of sinking into corruption or falling back under the yoke of superstition. But will it grow up quick enough to become their heir? And when will it ever be strong enough to exercise an influence with effect on 200,000,000 of men? There are, then, in the existing

Peace and Happiness, as also his First, Second, and Final Appeal to the Christian Public in reply to the Observations of Dr. Marshman several times reprinted.

circumstances in which Hinduism is placed, the elements of a formidable problem, a problem which is being proposed, at the same time, it is true, all over Asia, but nowhere with more directness than here. The material civilisation, in the hands of a sprinkling of strangers, who are dreaded for their power, sometimes honoured for their moral superiority, but in nowise loved, is overrunning it with the rapidity of steam and electricity, while the moral civilisation stands absolutely still. For the last dozen years especially the Colonial Government has done much for the multiplication of schools of every grade. But India is a poor country, its revenue is deficient, and the resources of the state are insignificant in the presence of the enormous wants there are to satisfy. The Government is obliged, besides, to take its first steps with caution, so as not to rouse, in these easily excitable masses, feelings of distrust, which it would afterwards find it difficult to allay. But suppose India possesses a system of school instruction as effective as heart could wish, it will be impossible on that account to suppress a question which is pressing for answer, and to which we see no reply: What will the faith of India be on the day when her old religions, condemned to die but determined to live, shall have finally given way?

INDEX.

THE END.